CW01460786

Birkhäuser Architectural Guide
Switzerland

Birkhäuser Architectural Guides
20th Century

Previously published
Germany
Japan

Forthcoming
Spain
Netherlands, Belgium, Luxemburg
Scandinavia
USA

Birkhäuser Architectural Guide Switzerland

20th Century

Mercedes Daguerre

With a Critical Essay by
Roman Hollenstein

Birkhäuser
Basel · Berlin · Boston

Originally published in 1995 under the title „Guida all'architettura del Novecento Svizzera" by Electa, Milano.

Series editor: Sergio Polano
Copy editor: Fiorella Bulegato
Photographic Documentation: Carlos Heras

Translation into English:
David Kerr
and
Michael Robinson (Text by Roman Hollenstein)
Gerd H. Söffker
Philip Thrift

To Carlos

Acknowledgments of the author:
I am indebted to all the friends who followed or offered me hospitality in my Swiss peregrinations; a special thanks to Sergio Polano, for his advice, and to Thomas Hegi and Alfredo Mumenthaler for their invaluable collaboration.

A CIP catalogue record for this book is available from the Library of Congress, Washington D.C., USA

Deutsche Bibliothek Cataloging-in-Publication Data
Daguerre, Mercedes:
Birkhäuser architectural guide Switzerland - 20th century / Mercedes Daguerre. With a critical essay by Roman Hollenstein. – Basel ; Berlin ; Boston : Birkhäuser, 1997
(Birkhäuser architectural guides 20th century)
Dt. Ausg. u.d.T.: Daguerre, Mercedes: Birkhäuser Architekturführer Schweiz - 20. Jahrhundert
ISBN 3-7643-5713-4 (Basel...)
ISBN 0-8176-5713-4 (Boston)

Printed on acid-free paper produced from chlorine-free pulp. TCF ∞
Cover design: Ott + Stein, Berlin
This book is also available in a German language edition (ISBN 3-7643-5712-6)
Printed in Italy
ISBN 3-7643-5713-4
ISBN 0-8176-5713-4

9 8 7 6 5 4 3 2 1

Contents

Using the Guide

This guide to twentieth-century architecture in Switzerland surveys around 550 works in 450 entries, carefully selected from over 1,000 works considered. As well as being a specialized source of information and knowledge, the guide is intended as a travel companion for any visitors to Switzerland with an interest in architecture.
The difficult task of selecting the works to be included was carried out with the aim of illustrating examples of twentieth-century architecture in Switzerland without, however, attempting a comprehensive survey. The choice of works was based on long research into mainstream historiography, local studies and recent contributions to urban history as well as the various guides to the Swiss architectural heritage. Given that the guide is intended as a reference book, the entries have been conceived as self-contained descriptions and no attempt has been made at comparative or thematic studies.
Despite the inevitable implicit value-judgments in providing descriptions, the general approach has been to highlight all architectural trends without any particular bias. In selecting the works we sought to strike a balance between various aspects, such as the importance of buildings in the main cities and small towns, between central and peripheral cantons, built-up and rural areas, etc. A number of puzzling absences may be explained by the fact that examples of buildings which have been remodeled or drastically altered have been omitted. Disinterest and neglect are endangering the very survival of important parts of the architectural heritage, especially as regards buildings from the first half of the century. This is an alarming state of affairs requiring urgent action.

We ask readers to make allowance for any mistakes or inaccuracies. We may even have missed out some important works, despite the care taken over the complicated task of drafting a guide to cover the great variety of twentieth-century Swiss architecture.
Our ideal itinerary begins in the canton of Zurich before crossing the Confederation, from north to south, and from west to east, ending in Ticino. The itinerary also includes the Principality of Liechtenstein, traditionally associated with Switzerland through its history and culture.
Our journey across the country enables us to highlight the diversity of formal language in Swiss architecture and its various registers. At the same time we have focused on examples of Functionalism, which has very strong roots in the German-speaking world and played a key role in the development of central European culture between the wars. Regionalist and centripetal tendencies intent on stressing their independence are also given due weight.
Over the last decade, Swiss architecture has been at the center of international discourse mainly thanks to the considerable contribution of Ticino architecture, as well as the work of a new generation of architects in German- and French-speaking areas and Graubünden. These latest developments have been presented in a pluralistic, unbiased approach with the focus on quality in order to convey the objective wealth and diversity of contemporary Swiss architecture.
The guide is divided into sections organized according to the cantons and half-cantons in the German-, French-, and Italian-speaking areas. The entries in each Canton section are arranged following the alphabetical order of the towns and localities. This applies also to those towns and localities which have become part of the agglomerations of big cities, which extend beyond the city districts. Buildings in the same town

are ordered chronologically. In those cases when there are several buildings with the same date, other criteria reflecting aspects of interest are followed. There are some exceptions to this general order: at times several works by the same architect(s) may be grouped in a single entry or in subsequent entries to cater to anyone interested in exploring the work of one studio in greater depth.

Each entry consists of a heading, description and relevant literature.

The heading is made up of the following information:

Locality
Building
Address
Date
Architect(s)
Collaborators (where appropriate)

The description consists of a brief comment on the work and/or architect plus any further interesting information. At times other works by the same architect(s) or other buildings worth visiting in the neighborhood are also included, complete with address and date.

Each entry ends with relevant literature on the work, including recent and contemporary texts. Each entry is also accompanied by a recent photograph; in a few cases period photographs have been chosen, while there are also numerous additional diagrams and drawings.

An index of architects (p. 409) provides an alphabetical list of all the buildings by a given architect included in the guide.

Foreword to the English Edition

Compared to the Italian original, the English edition of this guide has been revised and expanded. The book has been updated and complemented by an overview of "Swiss Architecture Today" by Dr Roman Hollenstein (p. 380), who describes developments since the mid 1990s. Additional material has also been included in many project and building descriptions by Dr Haila Ochs and Dr Annette Ciré. Valuable advice came from Ulrike Jauslin-Simon.

When buildings are featured in recent widely-available standard works, these sources are also mentioned in the literature for individual entries. The essential reference work for English-speaking readers interested in furthering their knowledge of twentieth-century Swiss architecture is the *Guide to Swiss Architecture* (3 vols.) edited by Willi E. Christen, while Peter Disch's works on the architecture of German-speaking Switzerland and Ticino are also particularly valuable. Bibliographical detail concerning these and other works may be found in the selected bibliography (p. 407). Monographs on individual architects have not been included in the bibliography, since they tend to be short-lived and constantly updated by readily available publications. This also applies to local guides to individual cities, cantons and regions.

The publishers would welcome any comments concerning mistakes or omissions.

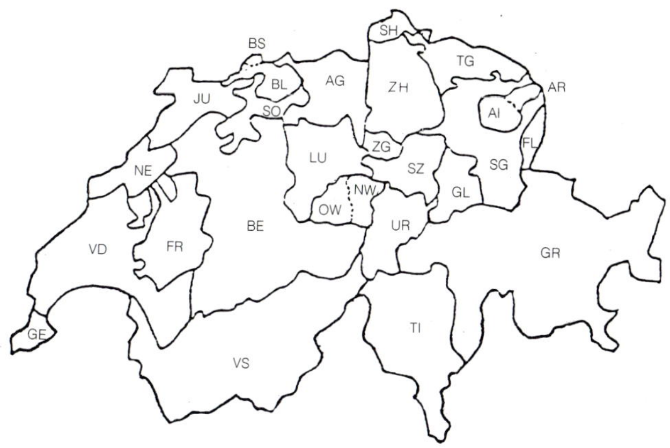

Aargau (AG)
Appenzell: Ausserrhoden, Innerrhoden (AR, AI)
Basel: Basel-Stadt, Basel-Land (BS, BL)
Berne (BE)
Fribourg (FR)
Geneva (GE)
Glarus (GL)
Graubünden (GR)
Jura (JU)
Lucerne (LU)
Neuchâtel (NE)
Sankt Gallen (SG)
Schaffhausen (SH)
Schwyz (SZ)
Solothurn (SO)
Thurgau (TG)
Ticino (TI)
Unterwalden: Obwalden, Nidwalden (OW, NW)
Uri (UR)
Valais (VS)
Vaud (VD)
Zug (ZG)
Zurich (ZH)

Principality of Liechtenstein (FL)

Zurich

Dietlikon
Casa Maria Workers' Accommodation
Aufwiesenstrasse 22
1982–83
Livio Vacchini with Mario Piatti with M. Vanetti, C. Bodmer, and M. Tognola

Situated in the Dietlikon industrial periphery of Zurich, this single-block, inward-oriented complex contains accommodation for workers. Each of its floors has four nuclei of lodgings, whereas the services are centralized. This original approach to the theme of courtyard housing involves cutting two side courts out of the cubic volume. Facing onto the two courts, the ground floor porticoes serve as common spaces. With a load-bearing structure in exposed silicon-limestone bricks and concrete slabs, the building has a uniform facade due to the materials and the regular rhythm of the square windows, flush with the outside edge of the cladding.

Archithese, 3, 1983; Rivista Tecnica, 10, 1983; 7–8, 1988; Lotus international, 44, 1984; a + u, architecture and urbanism, 176, 1985; Parametro, 141, 1985.

Erlenbach
House
Kappelistrasse 20
1932
Ernst F. Burckhardt

This single-family residence on a steeply sloping site has an entrance area at street level, while the living rooms open up towards the wood below. The wooden prism of the upper floor rests on a base faced in plaster, while an additional body creates a portico overlooking the garden.
Among other noteworthy works designed by Burckhardt is the Pestalozzi shop and house (Seestrasse 323) built in Zurich in 1930.

Neues Bauen in der Schweiz, Führer zur Architektur der 20er und 30er Jahre, Blauen 1985.

Fällanden
Im Rohrbuck Youth Hostel
Maurstrasse 33
1937
Emil Roth

At a right angle with a road and a lake shore, this light wooden pavilion overlooks a green area to the south. Still used as a youth hostel, the building's main features are functionality, careful detailing, and simple fast assembling. It is one of the best examples of Swiss Neues Bauen in the 1930s along with the Schlehstud House, built by Hans Fischli at Meilen in 1933 (Schumbelstrasse, see p. 20), and the Mühlehalde Tea Room, designed by Carl Hubacher and Rudolf Steiger at Witikon, Zurich (Trichtenhausenfussweg) in 1934.

Schweizerische Bauzeitung, 112, 1938; Werk, 1, 1943; Max Bill et al., Moderne Schweizer Architektur 1925–1945, Basel 1947; Domus, 752, 1993; Guide to Swiss Architecture 1920–1990, vol. 1, 511, p. 117.

Casa Maria
Workers'
Accommodation

House
Kappelistrasse

Im Rohrbuck Youth
Hostel

Horgen
Feller Factory
Bergstrasse 70
1952–57
Hans Fischli

The main emphasis in this factory for electrical appliances is on formal aspects. The enormous work-space is covered by shed-style roofing, while the prism-shaped window bays round the perimeter make the shell almost transparent. The cleverly controlled handling of light emerges as the principal design interest in the building.

Bauen und Wohnen, 3, 1953; Werk, 6, 1953; H. and T. Maurer and R. Lohse (eds), Neue Industriebauten, Ravensburg 1954; W. Rotzler, Der Mensch und das Licht, Zurich 1960; Guide to Swiss Architecture 1920–1990, vol. 1, 515, p. 119.

Kilchberg
Dunkel House
Lärchenweg 5
1932–33
William Dunkel

Dunkel designed his own house on a slope to the north of the Neubühl quarter. The building is a parallelepiped modified by rotating the open body with the living-room and terrace towards the garden. The clever use of sliding doors and windows has eliminated all barriers between interior and exterior. Various devices used to control the sunlight (such as slightly tinted yellow glass) and a rational use of central heating transform the space into a virtual conservatory.

Another interesting building by Dunkel is the Holbeinplatz housing in Basel (1939).

Feller Factory

Dunkel House

Schweizerische Bauzeitung, 113, 1939; Bax Bill et al., Moderne Schweizer Architektur 1925–1945, Basel 1947; R. Winkler, Das Haus des Architekten, Zurich 1955; Guide to Swiss Architecture 1920–1990, vol. 1, 516, p. 119.

Küsnacht-Itschnach
Rebhaus
Zumikerstrasse 20
1929
Sunnebüel House
Itschnacherstich 1
1929–30
Mendel House
Itschnacherstich 3
1931
Lux Guyer

Lux Guyer was the first independent professional female Swiss architect. In these country houses built at a Küsnacht she was influenced by new developments in English domestic architecture as she tackled themes previously explored by Muthesius in his search for a "clear, light, simple style". There are a number of typical elements from the early twentieth-century innovative discourse on housing, although today critics tend more to see these works as reflecting a "feminine sensibility".

See also Guyer's Villa Im Düggel, Im Düggel 3, built at Küsnacht in 1929–31.

Schweizerische Bauzeitung, 10, 1931; Werk, 12, 1936; Werk, Bauen und Wohnen, 11, 1983; Guide to Swiss Architecture 1920–1990, vol. 1, 519, p. 121.

Rebhaus

Sunnebüel House

Mendel House

Küsnacht
Heslibach Housing
Gartenstrasse 6–16/
Untere Heslibachstrasse 63–63a–65
1931–51
Ernst and Elsa Burckhardt

The architects brought their twenty-years design experience to bear on this project as they combined various residential typologies (terraced housing, corridor-apartments, independent single-family units and studios) in a socially mixed complex. The scheme is organized following the right angles of the urban layout, while the various dwelling blocks are arranged round a central green area.

Max Bill et al., Moderne Schweizer Architektur 1925–1945, Basel 1947; Bauen und Wohnen, 2, 1953; Werk, 1, 1953; R. Winkler, Das Haus des Architekten, Zurich 1955; Guide to Swiss Architecture 1920–1990, vol. 1, 520, p. 122.

Küsnacht-Goldbach
Streiff House
Zürichstrasse 21
1929–30
Otto Zollinger

The most striking external features of the house are the sweeping curved balconies, while inside a circular dining-room gives directly onto the garden by means of sliding curved windows. Built in reinforced concrete, originally painted black (now white), the house rests on a base clad in red clinker tiles.

Innendekoration 3/1932; Werk-archithese 23–24/1978; Domus, 752, 1993; Guide to Swiss Architecture 1920–1990, vol. 1, 522, p. 123.

Küsnacht-Goldbach
Koellreuter House
Goldbachstrasse 64
1931–32
Max Ernst Haefeli

One of the finest examples of twentieth-century architecture in the Zurich environs, this house is adapted to the sloping ground by means of an L-shaped plan, oriented to south-east and open towards the garden. The recent addition of an external insulation cover has altered the original proportions.

In the same period Haefeli also designed the Baumann House, Goldbachstrasse 72, while in 1930 he had built the Ernst House, Mönchhofstrasse, at Kilchberg.

Werk, 1935, 1; 6–7, 1941; A. Roth, Die Neue Architektur, Zurich 1940; Moderne Schweizer Architektur 1925–1945, Basel 1947; Archithese, 2, 1980; Guide to Swiss Architecture 1920–1990, vol. 1, 523, p. 124.

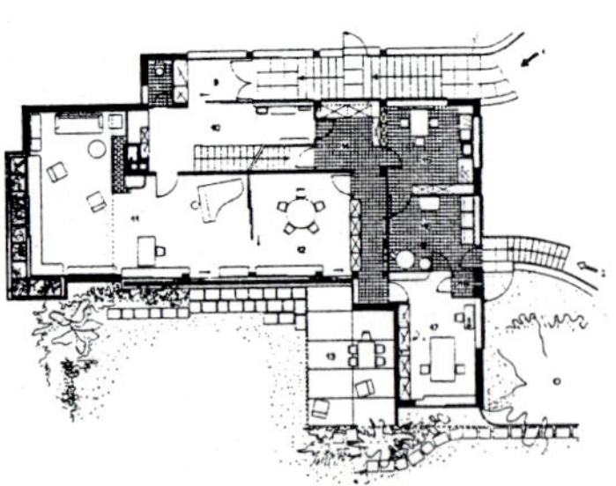

Koellreuter House, plan

Heslibach Housing

Streiff House

Koellreuter House

Langnau am Albis
Studio-House
Oberrenggstrasse 4
1985–87
Marianne Burkhalter and Christian Sumi

This house highlights the plastic potential of wood. The architects drew on the example of wooden constructions from the inter-war period, experimenting with prefabrication and minimal dwellings through the use of more rational building techniques and careful detailing. The two volumes reflect different functions: the set-back body contains the bedrooms, while the front volume is the day area and studio.

Similar criteria were followed in the design for a small house at Eglisau, Hinterer Stadtberg (1984–85), and the Forstwerkhof on the Ramsbergstrasse in Turbenthal (1991–92).

Casabella, 549, 1988; Rivista Tecnica, 1–2, 1988; Werk, Bauen und Wohnen, 9, 1989; P. Disch (ed), L'architettura recente nella Svizzera tedesca, Lugano 1991; Frammenti, interfacce, intervalli: paradigmi della frammentazione nell'arte svizzera, Genoa 1992; Lotus international, 73, 1992; Guide to Swiss Architecture 1920–1990, vol. 1, 524, p. 124.

Meilen
Schlehstud Studio-House
Schumbelstrasse, Hohenegg
1932–33
Hans Fischli

Designed to accommodate three apartments, as well as the architect's atelier (Fischli is also a painter and sculptor), this house is a gem of twentieth-century Swiss architecture. The almost entirely wooden structure has an external entrance stair which becomes a formal feature on the facade facing the path. By harmoniously inserting the building in the context and skillfully handling the composition, Fischli created a dynamic play of vistas, while the mophology shows a rich variety both inside and outside.

Among Fischli's other notable works is the Villa Guggenbühl, Herrliberg (1961–62).

C.A. Schmidt (ed), Schweizer Holzbau, Zurich-Leipzig 1936; Schweizerische Bauzeitung, 108, 1936; Werk, 10, 1936; Max Bill et al., Moderne Schweizer

Studio-House at Langau am Albis

Architektur 1925–1945, Basel 1947; Lotus international, 73, 1992; Guide to Swiss Architecture 1920–1990, vol. 1, 525, p. 125.

Meilen
Indoor Swimming-Pool
Toggwilerstrasse 38
1974–78
Ernst Gisel

Making the most of a splendid panoramic site, this indoor pool is part of an overall project for a school and sports center. Deliberate relations with the landscape are carefully established by the monopitch roof, glazing, and use of natural materials.
Bauen und Wohnen, 2, 1975; a+u, architecture and urbanism, 8, 1977; Rivista Tecnica, 1, 1982; Werk, Bauen und Wohnen, 7, 1982.

Studio-House at Meilen

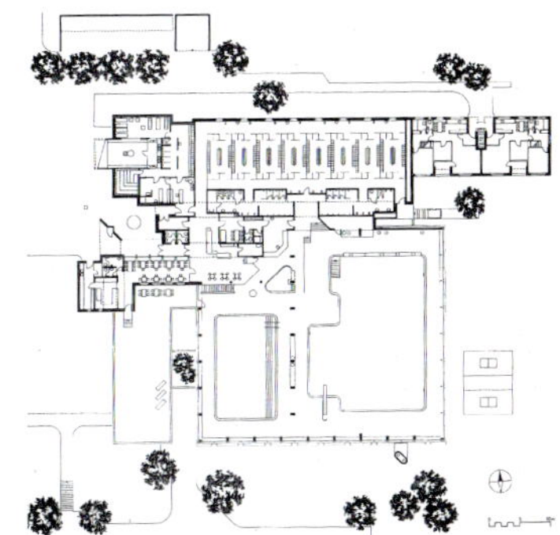

Indoor Swimming-Pool, floor plan and view

Meilen
Fire Station
Bruechstrasse 7
1984–90
Theo Hotz with Heinz Moser
with D. Boermann and P. Kaufmann
Facing onto a main road, the building fully exploits the steeply sloping site for the arrangement of the various spaces. To the rear, a series of services is connected to the street above by skylights. The principal facade with the fire engine showroom is characterized by the curving entrance volume and a projecting metal canopy. Hotz's typical touch of detailing with technical solutions is also found in the Mönchaltorf Crafts and Industrial Center, Isenrietstrasse 21 (1983–85), while in the Wetzikon-Robenhausen Housing, Buchgrindelstrasse 4 (1979–85), he proposed an original building type.
P. Disch (ed), L'architettura recente nella Svizzera tedesca, Lugano 1991.

Schlieren
Mülligen Postal Center
Zürcherstrasse 161
1981–85
Theo Hotz
with R. Blaser, B. Casagrande, H. Moser, R. Steinemann, H. Speli, and H. Suter
Developed after a 1970 competition, the postal center is divided into two sectors: the main work area arranged horizontally and a service tower. Designed along modular lines with prefabricated elements, the complex has a decidedly high-tech style.

Meilen Fire Station

Mülligen Postal Center

Holtz has also designed a railway engine depot in Mülligen (1982–84).
Werk, 11, 1987; P. Disch (ed), L'architettura recente nella Svizzera tedesca, Lugano 1991; Guide to Swiss Architecture 1920–1990, vol. 1, 532, p. 129.

Wädenswil
Siedlung Gwad
Im Gwad 15–65
1943–44
Hans Fischli and Oskar Stock
This scheme was a significant attempt to optimize low-cost subsidized housing. Built in less than five months, it consists of twenty-eight dwellings arranged on a series of stepped terraces on a northeast-oriented slope. Each individual unit (originally clad in wood, now faced in Eternit) occupies one level.
Werk, 7, 1943; 9, 1945; Max Bill et al., Moderne Schweizer Architektur 1925–1945, Basel 1947; G. E. Kidder Smith, Switzerland Builds, New York-Stockholm 1950; H. Volkart, Schweizer Architektur, Ravensburg 1951; J. Maurizio, Der Siedlungsbau in der Schweiz 1940–1950, Erlenbach 1952; Bauen und Wohnen, 12, 1972; Archithese, 5, 1985; 6, 1989; Guide to Swiss Architecture 1920–1990, vol. 1, 536, p. 131.

Siedlung Gwad, view, section and floor plan

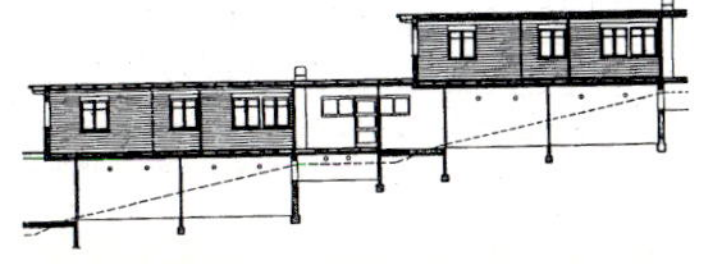

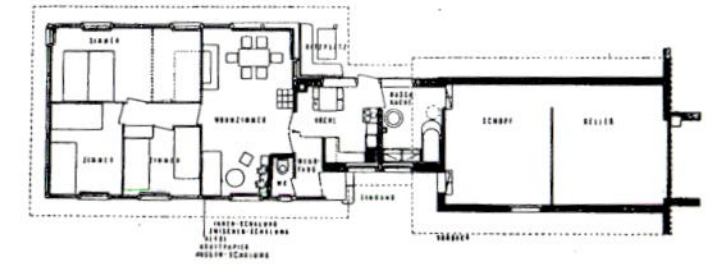

Winterthur

Sulzer Engineering Works

Zürcherstrasse 9

Production Sheds

1834, 1931

Sulzer Construction Department

Thermal Power Plant (former Foundry Plant)

1954–57

Suter & Suter

School of Architecture (former Boiler-Manufacturing Plant)

Tössfeldstrasse 11

1924–25, 1991

Hermann Eppler and Stephan Mäder, Sulzer Construction office, Dept. IBB

The Sulzer engineering works for the manufacture of machines and locomotives is one of the largest nineteenth-century Swiss urban industrial settlements. Having developed gradually, the complex comprehensively illustrates the evolution of modern construction methods: for example, from the nineteenth-century wooden window frames to completely glazed metal structures used from 1909 onwards to meet functional requirements. Suter & Suter's Thermal Power Station of the 1950s reveals a further technological advance, while the decision to convert the former boiler-manufacturing plant into a provisional home for the school of architecture was an appropriate move in a policy to shift production activities into peripheral areas with scope for expansion. In 1992 Jean Nouvel won the competition for a redevelopment project for the old Production Sheds.

Bauen und Wohnen, 1, 1954; Werk, 7, 1954; 10, 1990; Hochparterre, 8–9, 1990; Werk, Bauen und Wohnen, 6, 1992; Guide to Swiss Architecture 1920–1990, vol. 1, 602, p. 142 f.

Winterthur

Art Museum and Municipal Library

Museumstrasse 52

1913–16

Robert Rittmeyer and Walter Furrer

Extension 1996

Annette Gigon and Mike Guyer

Volkart Building

St Georgenplatz 2

1927–28

Robert Rittmeyer and Walter Furrer

Among the many buildings designed by Rittmeyer and Furrer in Winterthur in the first few decades of this century are this stately museum and library complex and the Volkart Building (originally the headquarters for a major European import-export company). The official public image of the Volkart Building is conveyed by the strength of the volumes and the adoption of an essential formal language, albeit with an occasional concession to Art Nouveau elements.

Other interesting works by these two architects are the Rothaus, Marktgasse 37 (1907–32), and a School and Administrative Center, Merkurstrasse 23 (1912).

Schweizerische Bauzeitung, 193, 1929; Werk, 11, 1930; Archithese, 6, 1983; 1, 1993; Guide to Swiss Architecture 1920–1990, vol. 1, 604, p. 145.

Sulzer Engineering Works:

School of Architecture

Thermal Power Plant

Production Sheds

Art Museum and Muncipal Library

Volkart Building

Winterthur
Siedlung Unterer Deutweg
Weberstrasse 12–42
1923–25
Hans Bernoulli and Adolf Kellermüller
Siedlung Selbsthilfe
Schwimmbadweg/Eigenheimweg/
Oberer Deutweg
1925–29
Franz Scheibler and Adolf Kellermüller
Siedlung Stadtrain
Frauenfelderstrasse/
Thalwiesenstrasse
1928–43
Adolf Kellermüller and Hans Hofmann

In the public housing developments of the 1920s, terraced houses with individual gardens were generally preferred to multi-unit blocks. Hans Bernoulli – one of the most authoritative advocates of the garden city – was also fond of this form of development. He adopted this concept for the Unterer Deutweg Estate and for the Eichliacker Estate (Klosterstrasse/Strittackerstrasse/Bütziackerstrasse), where he had also collaborated with Kellermüller in 1924. Single-story terraced houses with habitable basements and attics, and gardens to front and rear, are complemented by public open spaces.

In the Selbsthilfe (self-help) Estate, the standardization of these small houses and the rationalization of the building work was further enhanced by the "do-

Siedlungen:
Unterer Deutweg,
Selbsthilfe,
and Stadtrain

it-yourself" efforts of the future tenants right from the planning stage in order to reduce the costs of construction. The Stadtrain Estate comprises 377 apartments in the form of single and multi-occupancy units. To reduce the cost of this development, a back-to-back layout was employed, with each road serving two terraces and all houses set back from the road by means of their gardens.

Werk, 15, 1928; 5, 1933; Archithese, 6, 1983; I. Noseda and M. Steinmann, Zeitzeichen, Schweizer Baukultur im 19. und 20. Jh., Zurich 1988; H.P. Bärtschi, Die Siedlungsstadt Winterthur, Schweizerischer Kunstführer, Berne 1989; Guide to Swiss Architecture 1920–1990, vol. 1, 601, p. 144; 605, p. 146.

Winterthur

Cantonal School

Rychenbergstrasse 140

1926–28; 1960–63

Otto and Werner Pfister;

Erik Lanter

The imposing school built by the Pfister brothers in the 1920s with all the functions in a single block is contrasted by Lanter's 1960s additions in a free arrangement, responsive to the topography of the site and new pedagogical requirements.

Schweizerische Bauzeitung, 80, 1922; 52, 1965; Werk, 11, 1928; 9, 1965; Detail, 2, 1964; Guide to Swiss Architecture 1920–1990, vol. 1, 604, p. 145.

Cantonal School, front view and the 1960–63 additions

Winterthur

Siedlung Leimenegg

Leimeneggstrasse 27–35, 43–45
1930–32
Hermann Siegrist

Designed as middle-class housing, the Leimenegg estate is arguably Siegrist's finest work. It consists of a row of five single units plus a two-unit house. The complex reflects many of the ideas informing the architect's research interests which are wholly in line with the postulates of Neues Bauen: solid exposed reinforced concrete shaped by ribbon windows which dematerialize at attic level into roof terraces, highly rational plans, and luminous continuous spaces.

Schweizerische Bauzeitung, 101, 1933; Archithese, 6, 1983; Dreissiger Jahre Schweiz – ein Jahrzehnt im Widerspruch, exhibition catalogue, Zurich 1981; H. P. Bärtschi, Die Siedlungsstadt Winterthur, Schweizerischer Kunstführer, Berne 1989; F. Mehlau, A. Rüegg, and R. Tropeano (eds), Schweizer Typenmöbel 1925–1935, Sigfried Giedion und die Wohnbedarf AG, Zurich 1989; Guide to Swiss Architecture 1920–1990, vol. 1, 606, p. 146.

Winterthur

Footbridge over the River Töss near Wulfingen

Schlosstalstrasse
1933
Robert Maillart with W. Pfeiffer

This light, slender structure with its minimal dimensions – the web of the

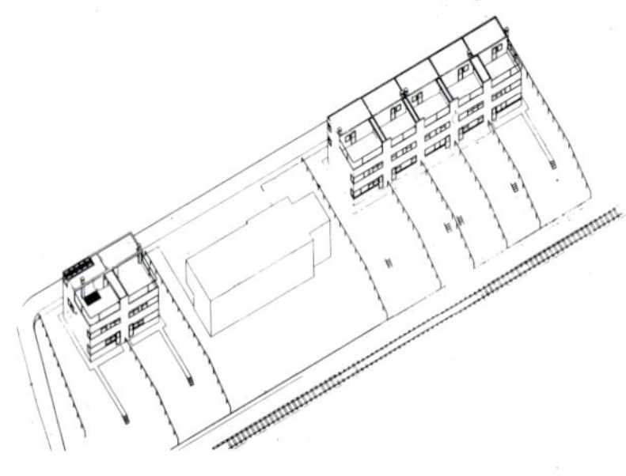

Siedlung Leimenegg

main concrete beam is a mere 140 millimeters thick but spans 38 meters – is undoubtedly one of Maillart's most elegant works.
Max Bill et al., Moderne Schweizer Architektur 1925–1945, Basel 1947; D. P. Billington, Robert Maillart and the Art of Reinforced Concrete, Zurich and Munich 1990; Guide to Swiss Architecture 1920–1990, vol. 1, 608, p. 147.

Winterthur
Lindberg School
Bäumlistrasse 39
1934–36, 1947
Hans Hohloch
The Lindberg school was the first public building in Winterthur which attempted to do justice to the demands of modern architecture. The linear articulation of the structure reflects the topography of the south-facing slope of the site. The incidence of daylight determines the room layout and the terrace can be used as an open-air classroom. The clear arrangement of the façades and technical details like the design of the casement windows are unmistakable signs of the modern style. The extension to the south-west was added in 1947.
Max Bill et al., Moderne Schweizer Architektur 1925–1945, Basel 1947; Archithese, 6, 1983; Guide to Swiss Architecture 1920–1990, vol. 1, 607, p. 147.

Lindberg School

Footbridge over the River Töss

Winterthur
Grüzefeld Housing
Hulfteggstrasse/Strahleggweg
1961–67
Claude Paillard and Peter Leemann with E. Schmid and H. Böhringer
Having designed the In der Au Estate at Opfikonstrasse in the Schwamendingen district of Zurich at the start of the 1950s, the architects once more explored the theme of publicly assisted housing in this complex of 370 apartments. Based on the repetition of an identical module, the project comprises a staggered sequence of buildings ranging from two to twelve stories constructed using prefabricated concrete elements. In expressing the shapes of the large blocks as a dynamic housing landscape and emphasizing the plastic form of the facades, the architecture tries to get to grips with the problems inherent in such a high-rise housing estate.
The architects experimented further with the theme of high-density housing in two other projects in Zurich: the Heuried Estate, Talwiesenstrasse (1969–74) and the Hirzenbach Estate, Altwiesenstrasse (1971–84).
Werk, 10, 1968; J. Bachmann and S. von Moos, New Directions in Swiss Architecture, New York 1969; H.P. Bärtschi, Die Siedlungsstadt Winterthur, Schweizerischer Kunstführer, Berne 1989; Guide to Swiss Architecture 1920–1990, vol. 1, 611, p. 149.

Zollikerberg
Rietholz Housing
Rietholzstrasse 56/Im Ahorn 2
1962
Hans and Annemarie Hubacher, and Peter Issler
Situated in the periphery of Zollikerberg, this housing scheme consists of 300 apartments distributed in several three- to five-story blocks. The scheme is the outcome of the attempt to reconcile various dwelling types and elaborate constructional solutions with a prefabricated modular system.
Werk, 8, 1963; A. Altherr, New Swiss Architecture, Teufen 1965; Guide to Swiss Architecture 1920–1990, vol. 1, 545, p. 136.

Zumikon
Three Houses
Rebhusstrasse 23–25–27
1954–56
Oskar Burri
Arranged in parallel on sloping ground, the three blocks of dwellings were designed following a model of rural life, expressed through the building techniques and traditional materials. The studio-house for a sculptor and the two single-family units (one is Burri's own residence) have a straightforward plan with a double-height living room and a balcony looking out towards the countryside.
Werk, 3, 1956; Schweizer Ingenieur und Architekt, 104, 1986; A. Hablützel and V. Huber, Architecture d'intérieur en Suisse 1942–1992, Sulgen 1993; Guide to Swiss Architecture 1920–1990, vol. 1, 546, p. 135.

Grüzefeld Housing, view and plan

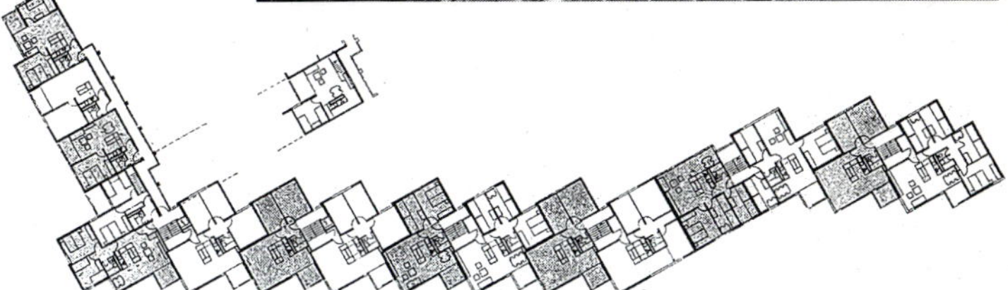

Rietholz Housing

Three Houses

Zumikon
Gisel House
Wengi 6
1965–67
Ernst Gisel

Situated on one of the Zumikon hills, the architect's own house has elaborately arranged volumes. The closed road-side front is in exposed concrete, while the rest of the house is organized round a courtyard, creating a strong presence in the landscape.

Gisel also designed two other studio-houses in Zumikon: Küsnachterstrasse 41–45 (1953) and Langwiesstrasse 13 (1982); also worth noting is the more recent two-unit housing at Erlenbach, Rietstrasse 7–13 (1988–91).

Bauwelt, 48, 1968; a + u, architecture and arbanism, 8, 1977; Werk, Bauen und Wohnen, 5 and 7, 1982.

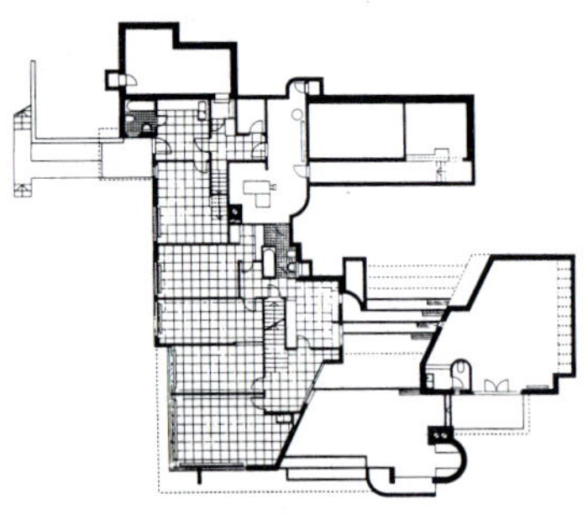

Gisel House, view and floor plan

Bill Studio-House

Zumikon
House and Studio for Max Bill
Rebhusstrasse 50
1967–68
Max Bill

In contrast to his first house, which he had built with modest means in the Höngg district of Zurich in 1932–33, at the height of his success as painter, sculptor and architect, Max Bill was in a position to design a house and studio to suit his own personal requirements. When viewed from the road, his design reveals nothing of its size and composition. The structure opens up like a series of steps leading down the south-facing slope of the 2.5 hectare site – a stack of cubes set into the landscape. Great thought has been given to the transitions between the rooms internally and to the link between interior and exterior; wide staircases and large expanses of glass help to integrate the landscaped garden. A large living room (100 square meters) forms the focal point of the house. A two-story studio and other work rooms are situated on the north-east side of the building. Despite its size, Max Bill did not intend to create a prestige object but wished to apply his principles of abstraction, geometrical form, functionalism, economy and a coherent building logic.

Eva Bechstein, Die Häuser von Max Bill in Zürich-Höngg und Zumikon, in: E. Hüttinger (ed), Künstlerhäuser, Zürich 1986; Max Bill, exhibition catalogue Schirn Kunsthalle Frankfurt/M., 1987; Faces 15/1990.

Zurich

Art Gallery

Heimplatz 1

1904–10, 1944–58, 1969–75

Karl Moser, Hans and Kurt Pfister, Erwin Müller

The austere original building was conceived by Karl Moser as a "temple to art" and erected in 1907–10 (design competition 1902–04). It remained completely faithful to nineteenth-century traditions. In the exterior design of the two parts of the building housing the collection and the exhibition, Moser uses toned-down classical forms but also includes restrained influences from Art Nouveau, as in the work of Peter Behrens and the Vienna Sezession Group. It was not until 1924–26 that Moser's simple design for an extension was realized. The exhibition wing on the north-west side by the Pfister brothers was built in 1954–58 (design competition 1944). The gallery was enlarged again in 1969–75 by the addition of a new wing on the south-east side designed by Erwin Müller.

Schweizerische Bauzeitung, 41 and 42, 1903; 49, 1907; 53 and 54, 1909; 55 and 56, 1910; 89, 1927; Deutsche Kunst und Dekoration, 27, 1910–11; Schweizer Baublatt, 63, 1942; U. Jehle Schulte-Strathaus, Das Zürcher Kunsthaus, ein Museumsbau von Karl Moser, Basel 1982; Werk, Bauen und Wohnen, 5, 1983; Guide to Swiss Architecture 1920–1990, vol 1, 749, p. 194.

Art Gallery

Zurich

Brann Department Store

Bahnhofstrasse 75/
Lintheschergasse 2
1910–11, 1928–29

Münzhof Building

Bahnhofstrasse 45
1914–17

Otto Pfleghard and Max Haefeli

Pfleghard and Haefeli was one of the most celebrated architectural practices in early twentieth-century Zurich, involved in a considerable number of projects and buildings for the city. In 1910–11 they designed a new building for the Brann company, whose department store had been located in the Bahnhofstrasse since 1899. This three-story corner building with its steep roof and conspicuous dormer windows was renovated in 1928–29 by Otto Pfleghard. The stylized pillars on the facade drawn from the Neo-Gothic school remained intact, but two further storys were added and the interior completely redesigned with an elegant inner court and five-flight main staircase.

Pfleghard and Haefeli were also responsible for the Münzhof Building, the headquarters of the *Union Bank of Switzerland (UBS)*, also situated in the Bahnhofstrasse. The monumental neoclassicism of the sandstone facade, with its six doric three-quarter columns which extend over three stories and denote the entrance area, complies with the needs of the owners for an impressive, prominent structure. The column, representing stability and tradition, is an almost obligatory element for the facade of a bank.

Next door (Bahnhofstrasse/Pelikanstrasse) is Max Bill's Pavilion Sculpture dating from 1979–83, which was a gift by the *Union Bank* to the City of Zurich.

Schweizerische Bauzeitung, 69, 1917; 74, 1919; 99, 1932; 25 Jahre Bauen, Zurich 1928; Werk, 46, 1968; W. Baumann, Zürich-Bahnhofstrasse, Zurich 1972; E. Leisi, Zürcher Fassaden: 60 Kommentierte Porträts, Zurich 1987.

Zurich

Fluntern Church

Gellertstrasse
1913–20

Karl Moser (Curjel & Moser)

Karl Moser's works include a number of religious buildings designed in the early decades of this century. After the Church of St Anthony, Neptunstrasse 68, built in 1905–08 to a basilica plan with a Neo-Romantic facade, striking masonry and decorative details with more than a hint of pure Art Nouveau, he designed the Fluntern Church in 1913–15. Although the church built in 1918–20 departs from the competition design, the imposing bell-tower and entrance portico, the plinth and stairway further emphasize its privileged position among the wealthy villas on a hill overlooking the city.

Another interesting work in Zurich by Curjel & Moser is the nearby Villa Müller at Kantstrasse 12–14 (1918).

Schweizerische Bauzeitung, 52, 1908; 62, 1913; 64, 1914; 66, 1915; 76, 1920; Heimatschutz, 156, 1917; E. Fehr, Die neue Kirche Fluntern, Zurich 1922; Werk-Archithese 65/1978; Wilfried Rössling, Curjel & Moser, Karlsruhe 1986.

Brann Department Store

Münzhof Building

Max Bill, *Pavilion Sculpture*

Fluntern Church, view and elevation (early design phase)

Zurich

Bergheim Housing

Witikonerstrasse

1908–09

Im Kapf Garden City

Kapfstrasse/Witikonerstrasse 93–97

1910–11

Otto and Werner Pfister

The masterplan for the quarter consisting of the Bergheim Housing (initially constructed to the south of Witikonerstrasse) and the Im Kapf scheme (added only two years later) reveal the Pfister brothers interest in the theme of the garden city. The Bergheim dwellings are variations on the semi-detached house, while in the Im Kapf scheme the typology is repeated so as to form a row along the road with gardens behind.

The same architects designed the School at Limmatstrasse 80–90 (1908–10).

Bergheim Housing, view and, top, elevation

Im Kapf Garden City, elevation of a unit and view

Schweizerische Baukunst, 55, 1910; Schweizerische Bauzeitung, 9, 1910; Archithese, 1, 1993.

Zurich

University of Zurich

Künstlergasse 16

1907–14, 1976–91

Karl Moser, Robert Curjel, and Robert Maillart

Ernst Gisel

1911–14 saw the building of a major Zurich urban landmark: the university. Curjel & Moser's competition-winning design of 1907 produced a structure which, together with the adjacent Federal Technical University (ETH) by Gottfried Semper (1859–64), rises up as an unmistakable element in the city skyline. A central tower links two groups of four wings organized around two courtyards. The strict Neo-Baroque architecture exhibits interesting constructional details in its interior: in particular the flat-slab reinforced concrete floors designed by the engineer Robert Maillart are a rarity. In 1976–91, in the course of extending and refurbishing the university, Ernst Gisel incorporated an auditorium supported on four reinforced concrete columns in the courtyard of the second college building. This addition extends over five stories and is distinct from the original structure. Daylight is able to penetrate down to the ground floor along the peripheral walls of the courtyard.

Werk, 4, 1914; Schweizerischer Kunstführer, Basel 1980; Abitare, 206, 1982; Parametro, 140, 1985; P. Disch (ed), L'architettura recente nella Svizzera tedesca, Lugano 1991; I. Noseda, Bauen an Zürich, Zurich 1992; Domus, 752, 1993; A. Hablützel and V. Huber, Architecture d'intérieur en Suisse 1942–1992, Sulgen 1993.

University of Zurich

Zurich
Peterhof Building
Bahnhofstrasse 30–32/Paradeplatz
1912–14
St Annahof Building
Bahnhofstrasse 57
1912–14
National Bank
Börsenstrasse 15–17/Fraumünsterstrasse
1919–22
Otto and Werner Pfister

Significant examples of research into buildings types to accommodate the new functions of large department stores, both the Peterhof and the St Annahof buildings have central skylight-covered atriums as the organizing elements in the plan, while their facades have a representative function in keeping with the urban hierarchy of Bahnhofstrasse. The design for the nearby National Bank continues the nineteenth-century tradition of drawing on the model of the fifteenth-century Florentine *palazzo*. Its severe forms make a sharp contrast with the adjacent buildings.
Also of interest in this area are the Tram Waiting-Rooms in Paradeplatz (1928) and Bellevueplatz (1937–38), designed by Hermann Herter.

Peterhof Building

St Annahof Building

Schweizerische Bauzeitung, 50, 1907; W. Baumann, Zürich Bahnhofstrasse, Zurich 1972; H. Rebsamen, Bauplastik in Zürich 1890–1990, Zurich 1989; Archithese, 1, 1993.

Zurich
Enge Station
Tessinerplatz 10–12
1923–26
Otto and Werner Pfister

In 1923 four architectural practices in Zurich were invited by the SBB (Swiss Railways) to submit designs for a new station at Enge. The winning design, which was built in 1924–25, was that of the Pfister brothers. The station building itself with its central ticket hall included waiting rooms and railway facilities in the southern section, while the northern wing accommodated offices, a glass-covered shopping arcade and a post office. Outside, a great semicircular portico in grey granite overlooks the station forecourt on the Seestrasse. With the exception of the station clock borne by two cast-iron figures above the main entrance (Carl Fischer, 1927), the facade refrains from any form of embellishment.

Schweizerische Bauzeitung, 89, 1927; Werk, 3, 1927; W. Stutz, Bahnhöfe der Schweiz, Zurich 1976; H. Rebsamen, Bauplastik in Zürich 1890–1990, Zurich 1989.

National Bank

Enge Station

Zurich
Siedlung Oberstrass
Winterthurerstrasse/
Langmauerstrasse/Zanggerweg/
Scheuchzerstrasse
1923–27
Otto Gschwind
Werk, 5, 1929; Kommunaler und genossenschaftlicher Wohnungsbau in Zürich, Zurich 1990; Guide to Swiss Architecture 1920–1990, vol. 1, 701, p. 162f.

Siedlung Hardturmstrasse
Hardturmstrasse 200–394
1924–29
Hans Bernoulli
Werk, 12, 1924; Archithese, 6, 1981; Parametro, 140, 1985; Domus, 752, 1993; Guide to Swiss Architecture 1920–1990, vol. 1, 701, p. 162f.

Siedlung Erismannhof
Seebahnstrasse/Hohlstrasse/
Ehrismannstrasse/Stauffacherstrasse
1926–28
Kündig & Oetiker
Werk, 5, 1929; 13, 1975; Schweizerische Bauzeitung, 96, 1930; R. Schilling, Architektur in Zürich 1980–90, eine Auswahl von 100 Objekten, Zurich 1990; Guide to Swiss Architecture 1920–1990, vol. 1, 701, p. 162f.

In the 1920s many housing estates were built thanks to the support of the Zurich City Council for social housing programs to meet the serious shortages following the First World War. Respecting traditional formal features, systematic experiments were made with various layouts and types: semi-open arrangements in Oberstrass, blocks round a central courtyard in Erismannhof, and single-family terraced houses in Hardturmstrasse. The housing promoted and designed by

Bernoulli drew on the English model and put into practice the social ideal of the small single-family unit in rows of semi-detached houses forming a kind of cul-de-sac which became the entrance courtyard. Back-to-back gardens behind the houses provided spacious green areas.
Another interesting nearby estate is the Lettenhof Housing at Wasserwerkstrasse 106–108/Imfeldsteig 2-4-6 (1926–27), designed by Lux Guyer.

Zurich
Cantonal Offices
Walcheplatz
1933–35
Otto and Werner Pfister
Recently carefully restorated, this building was constructed in the area of the former abattoir in the 1930s as part of a larger urban redevelopment scheme (the 1927 competition was won *ex aequo* by the Pfister brothers and Hermann Herter). The three prismatic volumes – two horizontal and one vertical – are arranged into a profile highlighting the transition in the landscape from the Limmat Valley to the hills. The essential style of the concrete facade and the regular rhythm of the apertures create an image in keeping with the building's function.
Among other notable works by the same architects are: the Sanitas Building at Limmatstrasse/Kornhausbrücke/Sihlquai (1930); the Nursing School at Klosbachstrasse 112–116 (1934–36); and the Rentenanstalt Insurance Offices at General Guisan-Quai 40 (1937–39).
Schweizerische Bauzeitung, 100, 1932; Werk, 11, 1935; Domus, 752, 1993; Guide to Swiss Architecture 1920–1990, vol. 1, 722, p. 176.

Cantonal Offices

Opposite page:

Siedlung Oberstrass

Siedlung Hardturmstrasse

Siedlung Erismannhof

Zurich
Rotach Prototype Housing
Wasserwerkstrasse 27–31
1927–28
Max Ernst Haefeli
Restoration
1988
Ruggero Tropeano, Cristina Pfister, and Christian Stamm

Designed for a 1927 competition organized by Alfred Altherr for ten young Zurich architects, this complex was presented at the exhibition *The New House II*, held at the Zurich Museum of Arts and Crafts in 1928 with the aim of encouraging new ways of thinking about middle-class housing. The design, which included the interiors (the furniture was also by Haefeli), introduced the latest technological innovations (central heating, gas and electric cookers, and boilers). The Rotach building cooperative then gave the architect the chance to implement the design. Situated on a slope opposite the Platzspitz park, the three staggered volumes, containing two terraced houses and two small dwellings with shared services, open up with balconies and large windows towards the river Limmat. The recent restoration is a particularly interesting operation for the rigorous reconstruction of the historical elements and their context.

S. Giedion, Befreites Wohnen, Zurich-Lipsia 1929; Archithese, 2, 1980; 1, 1988;

Rotach Prototype Housing

E. Blättler (ed), Neue Architektur in Zürich, Heiden 1989; F. Mehlau, A. Rüegg, and R. Tropeano (eds), Schweizer Typenmöbel 1925–1935, Sigfried Giedion und die Wohnbedarf AG, Zurich 1989; Rivista Tecnica, 12, 1992; Domus, 752, 1993; Guide to Swiss Architecture 1920–1990, vol. 1, 704, p. 164.

Zurich

Old Bourse

Bleicherweg 5/Talstrasse 9–25

1928–30

Walter Henauer and Ernst Witschi

The powerful vertical thrust of a large cylinder, containing the stairs and marking out the street corner, counterpoints with the horizontal emphasis of the sleek wings, streamlined by ribbon windows. Inside, the offices are arranged round the large business hall. Recently the Zurich stock exchange was transferred to the New Bourse, Selnaustrasse 32, (1989–92), designed by Suter & Suter.

Schweizerische Bauzeitung, 92, 1928; 101, 1933; Werk, 4, 1931; E. Blättler (ed), Neue Architektur in Zurich, Heiden 1989; H. Rebsamen, Bauplastik in Zürich 1890–1990, Zurich 1989; Guide to Swiss Architecture 1920–1990, vol. 1, 705, p. 164.

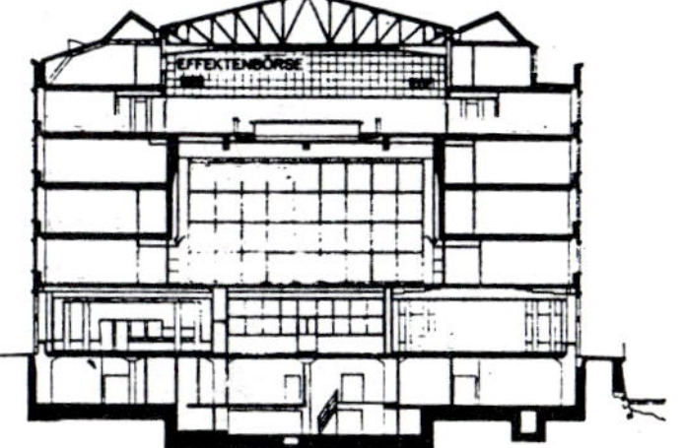

Zurich-Wollishofen

Siedlung Neubühl

Nidelbadstrasse/Ostbühlstrasse/
Westbühlstrasse

1929–32

Carl Hubacher, Max Ernst Haefeli, Werner Max Moser, Rudolf Steiger, Emil Roth,

Paul Artaria and Hans Schmidt

Renovation

1983–86

ARCOOP Ueli Marbach, Arthur Rüegg

Seven Swiss architects, members of the Swiss *Werkbund* and all involved in the Weissenhof Estate at Stuttgart in 1927, founded the Neubühl Cooperative in 1929 with the aim of implementing the new developments in housebuilding in a residential project on the edge of Zurich. An exhibition in 1931 presented the estate to the public as a manifestation of modern architecture in Switzerland. Owing to the high cost of land as well as the high development costs, the apartments built here were never intended for low-income occupants but rather for the middle class, attaching great importance to the attainment of a modern standard of living. The development was built on a hill on the western bank of Lake Zurich: 28 terraces containing a total of 105 single-family houses and 90 apartments in multistory blocks; in total there are nine different types of apartments, varying in size. The rows of buildings are arranged across the slope and perpendicular to the roads, and stepped to follow the line of the ground. This allows all apartments to face south, with an uninterrupted view of lake and mountains. Communal facilities include kindergarten, playground, sports hall, artists' studios, shops and a centralized heating and hot-water supply. In 1983–86 the ar-

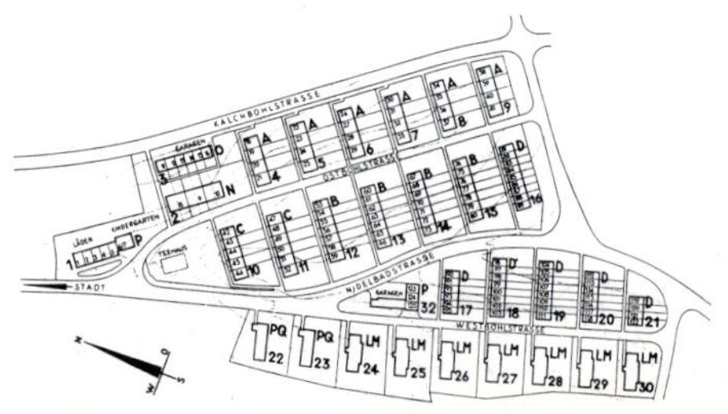

Siedlung Neubühl

chitects Ueli Marbach and Arthur Rüegg carried out admirable refurbishment work in keeping with the listed status of the estate.
U. Marbach and A. Rüegg, Werkbundsiedlung Neubühl in Zürich-Wollishofen 1928–1932, Zurich 1990; Domus, 752, 1993; Guide to Swiss Architecture 1920–1990, vol. 1, 708, p. 168.

Zurich
Eierbrecht House
Wehrenbachhalde 20–22
1930–31
Fleiner House
Forsterstrasse 72
1932–33
Werner Max Moser
The houses of Werner Max Moser are among the best examples of modern architecture in Switzerland built before the Second World War. Eierbrecht House, built on a hill above the city, actually contains two dwellings, one for Adolf Guggenbühl, editor of the *Schweizer Spiegel*, and the other for Moser himself. The southern elevation, facing Lake Zurich, has large windows above a continuous spandrel and projecting balconies supported by light steel framing. Similar elevational treatment can be found at Fleiner House and Villa Hagmann (Hegibachstrasse 131), dating from 1928–31. This notion of the building opening up towards the surrounding landscape, with balconies and large areas of glazing, as well as direct access to the garden from the lower story, is made possible in all three houses by a steel-framed wall, all the other walls being of conventional masonry.
Bauwelt, 25, 1931; Werk, 1, 1932; Baumeister, 2, 1933; Bauen und Wohnen, 11, 1987; Archithese, 2, 1980; Domus, 752, 1993.

Siedlung Neubühl, typical block

Eierbrecht House

Fleiner House

Zurich

Zett House

Badenerstrasse 16–18

1930–32

Carl Hubacher and Rudolf Steiger

The design brief for Zett House was typically metropolitan and multipurpose: shops, offices, a restaurant, underground parking, a cinema in the courtyard and a rooftop terrace with swimming pool. The top story is set back and includes 14 apartments reached via an open walkway. The curved facade follows the line of the road, its expanses of glass providing a sharp contrast to the massive nature of the surrounding commercial buildings. The masterly design includes a number of notable engineering details, such as the opening roof over the cinema. Although some original features are still visible, subsequent refurbishment work and additions have impaired the building's formal purity.

Schweizerische Bauzeitung, 101, 1933; Werk, 1, 1934; 6, 1935; Eva Bechstein, Die Häuser von Max Bill in Zürich-Höngg und Zumikon, in: E. Hüttinger (ed), Künstlerhäuser, Zurich 1986; Max Bill et al., Moderne Schweizer Architektur 1925–1945, Basel 1947; I. Noseda and M. Steinmann, Zeitzeichen, Schweizer Baukultur im 19. und 20. Jh., Zurich 1988; E. Blättler (ed), Neue Architektur in Zürich, Heiden 1989; Domus, 752, 1993.

Zurich

Hotel Rigihof and Post Office

Universitätsstrasse 101

1931–32

Hermann Schneider and Otto Tschumper

Besides the hotel and post office, this elongated complex, with its rounded corners, inset top story and shopping area at ground floor level, also con-

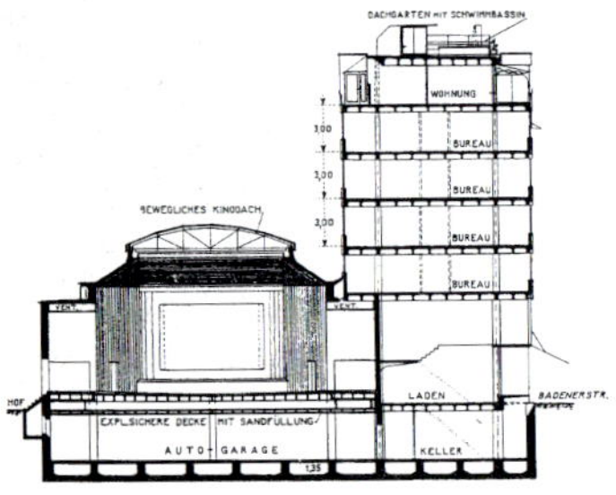

Zett House

tains a number of apartments. The continuous balconies at the rear emphasize the horizontal line of this building, while at the front, accentuation is provided by rows of rectangular windows which follow the line of the rounded corners.
Werk-archithese, 23–24, 1978.

Zurich
Max Bill House and Studio
Limmattalstrasse 383
1932–33
Max Bill and Robert Winkler
The 24-year-old Max Bill built his first house and studio in 1932–33 in Höngg near Zurich. The architecture is determined by the "aesthetic of the functional" postulated by Bill – unequivocal, purposeful forms and the absence of superfluous ornamentation. The two-story structure is accessed from the road on the northern side and opens out towards the south down the slope of the site. The studio window on the entrance side extends over both storeys and is divided up by steel transoms; a rooflight in the shallow-pitch, copper-covered roof provides additional lighting for the studio. The main living area with its open gallery leading to the studio is located on the upper floor. Access to the garden is via a loggia at the lower level.
Max Bill's other notable works in Zurich are the DRS radio studios and offices dating from 1967–68 (Brunnenhofstrasse 30).
Max Bill et al., Moderne Schweizer Architektur 1925–1945, Basel 1947; Bauen und Wohnen, 11, 1957; Um 1930 in Zürich, exhibition catalogue, Zurich 1977; Faces, 15, 1990.

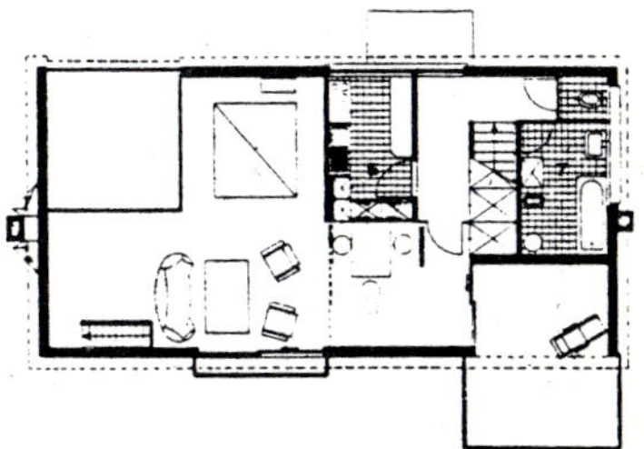

Hotel Rigihof

Bill Studio-House, view and floor plan

Zurich

Sihlhölzli Sports Center and Music Pavilion

Manessestrasse 1

1927–32

Hermann Herter and Robert Maillart

Wollishofen Open-Air Bathing Facilities

Seestrasse 451

1939

Hermann Herter

Indoor Swimming Pool

Sihlstrasse 71

1939–41

Hermann Herter and Robert Maillart

Renovation

1978–80

Frank Bolliger, Heinz Hönger, and Werner Dubach

From 1927 to 1932, a new park was laid out on built-up land on the banks of the River Sihl, including a riverside avenue and sports center. Playing fields and a gymnasium with flat slabs by Robert Maillart, and the elegant music pavilion, the concrete shell roof of which is also by Maillart, promised a generous range of leisure activities.

The public demand for light, air and sunshine was met in 1939 by two further projects by Hermann Herter: Wollishofen open-air bathing facilities and Sihlstrasse indoor swimming pool. The open-air project is screened from the road by the elongated building housing the changing rooms; the concrete roof cantilevers out to form a broad canopy over the spectator terrace and the sweeping line of the stairs down to the grassed areas creates a relaxed, leisurely atmosphere.

In Zurich's first indoor pool, the choice of glass and ceramics as the building materials, as well as the abundance of daylight in the various rooms, emphasize the modern approach.

Other interesting works include Herter's Tram Depot, Elisabethenstrasse 15–43 (1939–49), and the Sihl post office, Kasernenstrasse 95–99, designed by Maillart with Adolf and Heinrich Bräm (1927–30).

Schweizerische Bauzeitung, 101, 1933; 105, 1935; 125, 1945; H. Bärtschi, Industrialisierung, Eisenbahnschlachten und Städtebau, Basel 1983; I. Noseda and M. Steinmann, Zeitzeichen, Schweizer Baukultur im 19. und 20. Jh., Zurich 1988.

Zurich

Applied Arts Museum and School

Ausstellungsstrasse 60

1925–33

Adolf Steger and Karl Egender

Built following competitions in 1925 and 1927, the complex consists of three blocks: the six-story school, the Applied Arts Museum (a basilica-plan building connecting the other two) and the projecting auditorium marking the Ausstellungsstrasse entrance. The outcome of contemporary research into functionality and rational building methods, this work may be seen as a manifesto on how to tackle the theme of the public building.

Um 1930 in Zürich, exhibition catalogue, Zurich 1977; I. Noseda and M. Steinmann, Zeitzeichen, Schweizer Baukultur im 19. und 20. Jh., Zurich 1988; E. Blättler (ed), Neue Architektur in Zürich, Heiden 1989; Domus, 752, 1993; Guide to Swiss Architecture 1920–1990, vol. 1, 714, p. 171.

Silhölzli Sports Center

Wollishofen Open-air Bathing Facilities

Indoor Swimming Pool

Applied Arts Museum and School

Zurich
Volkshaus Limmathaus
Limmatstrasse 118
1930–31
Adolf Steger and Karl Egender
Renovation
1989–90
Felix Schwarz and Frank Gloor

Situated in the Zurich industrial area, this recently renovated building houses a typical social-democratic institution - the *Volkshaus* (People's Palace) - consisting of a common room, meeting facilities for the unions and local-area organizations, rented accommodation (later converted into a hotel), post office, restaurant, and various other services.

Das Volkshaus Limmathaus im Industriequartier, Zurich 1930; Archithese, 3, 1988; Guide to Swiss Architecture 1920–1990, vol. 1, 71, p. 170.

Limmathaus

Zurich-Oerlikon

Sports Center

Wallisellenstrasse 45

1938–39

Karl Egender and Robert Naef with B. Giacometti

The Zurich Sports Center boasts the largest 1930s multipurpose stadium (12,000 capacity) in Europe. The steel structure can only be seen from the inside. The pattern of the facades is set by a glazed frame interrupted by buttresses. The mechanical systems provide great scope for adapting the space to various activities (cycling, ice hockey, concerts, etc.).

Another Zurich work by Egender is the Office and Shopping Center, Talacker 41 (1947–48).

Schweizerische Bauzeitung, 126, 1945; Moderne Schweizer Architektur 1925–1945, Basel 1947; G. E. Kidder Smith, Switzerland Builds, New York-Stockholm 1950; H. Volkart, Schweizer Architektur, Ravensburg 1951; Bauen und Wohnen, 11, 1957; I. Noseda and M. Steinmann, Zeitzeichen, Schweizer Baukultur im 19. und 20. Jh., Zurich 1988; Domus, 752, 1993; Guide to Swiss Architecture 1920–1990, vol. 1, 729, p. 181

Sports Center, view and plan

Office and Shopping Center

Zurich
ETH Power Station and Engineering Laboratory
Sonneggstrasse 3
1930–35
Otto Rudolf Salvisberg
Extra floor added to engineering laboratory, 1947–48
Alfred Roth
Extension to engineering laboratory
Tannenstrasse, 1970
Charles Eduard Geisendorf
ETH Research and Teaching Facilities
Clausiusstrasse
1987–94
Benno Fosco, Jacqueline Fosco-Oppenheim and Klaus Vogt with S. Zopp, H. Remondino, I. Baldinger, P. Monod and M. Bosshard

One of the most important examples of modern architecture in Zurich is the complex designed by Otto Rudolf Salvisberg for the ETH (Federal Technical University) and completed in 1932–33. The large unsupported spans of the bright and airy engineering laboratory with its accessible reinforced concrete and glass roof, and the tower of the heating plant are the statements of engineers in the age of the machine, still making their mark on the city skyline even today.
For the lecture theater building, the windows of the original building (Recordon, 1896) were widened and the facade flattened. Like the new building it was clad with limestone panels so that it is virtually impossible to distinguish the individual elements.

ETH Thermal Power Station and Engineering Laboratory, period photo

ETH Research and Teaching Center, model elevation

The coherently articulated building with its elegant grid-like facade was given an extra story, a light design set back from the line of the main front.
Schweizerische Bauzeitung, 21, 1933; 1 and 2, 1934; Baumeister, 8, 1935; Werk, 8, 1935; Moderne Bauformen, 3, 1936; Werk, Bauen und Wohnen, 5, 1983; Parametro, 140, 1985.

Zurich
ETH-Hönggerberg University Center
Einsteinstrasse
1957–84
Albert Heinrich Steiner, Werner Gehry with A. Stocker
Faculty of Chemistry
1991–
Mario Campi and Franco Pessina
The ETH complex is laid out as an open campus with parks and gardens, also intended for the enjoyment of Zurich's citizens. Hönggerberg's various faculty buildings for teaching and research are distributed over landscaped, traffic-free areas of 46 hectares, originally agricultural and recreational land. The mostly low-rise, cube-shaped buildings permit an intimate dovetailing between developed and undeveloped zones. The design for the faculty of chemistry arranges the various institutes in five wings and includes lecture theaters and smaller, separate units, thereby enabling the teaching and research disciplines to be kept separate but within easy reach of each other.
Schweizerische Bauzeitung, 21, 1968; 18, 1974; Deutsche Bauzeitung, 6, 1976; Werk, 2, 1976; Hochschulbauten Eth-Hönggerberg Zürich, Zurich 1987; K. Feireiss (ed), Mario Campi, Franco Pessina, Berlin 1994.

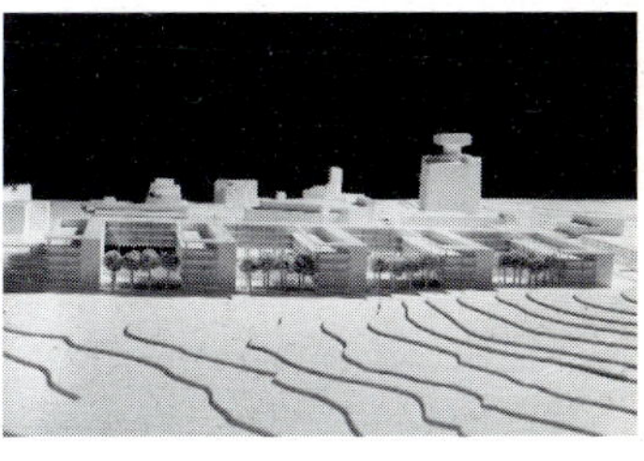

ETH-Hönggerberg University Center, aerial view and model

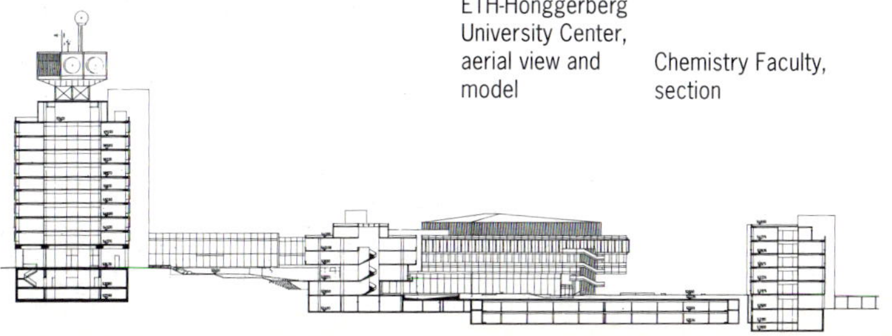

Chemistry Faculty, section

Zurich
Jelmoli Department Store
Seidengasse 1
1931–61
Stadler and Usteri
Otto Pfleghard and Max Haefeli
J.E. Schaudt
J.P. Mongeaud
Roland Rohn

Altered by a series of renovation work and extensions, this "crystal palace" by Stadler and Usteri was built in 1898–99 in the heart of Zurich and illustrates the symbolic and economic changes this building has undergone in order to meet a constantly changing situation. The building's present form is influenced by alterations carried out during the 1930s, the extension designed by Pfleghard & Haefeli together with the department store specialist J.E. Schaudt from Berlin, and the tower at the corner of Steinmühleplatz designed by the Paris architect J.P. Mongeaud. After the war the Uraniastrasse elevation was given extra stories (1947), the offices were added (1957) and the north-west wing (Seidengasse/Uraniastrasse) was remodelled by Roland Rohn (1961).
Schweizerische Bauzeitung, 115, 1940; W. Baumann, Zürich-Bahnhofstrasse, Zurich 1972; Guide to Swiss Architecture 1920–1990, vol. 1, 716, p. 173.

Zurich
Kappeli School
Badenerstrasse 618
1935–37
Alfred and Heinrich Oeschger

This design is based on an L-shaped layout set amid spacious lawns with games and sports areas, and an abundance of trees. Both wings have two storeys with flat roofs but their functions are different: the north-south section contains classrooms and the assembly hall, the east-west part two gymnasiums with ancillary rooms. The cubic construction with its light-coloured, painted walls and elegant rows of windows follows the dictates of modern architecture. All the classrooms face east and away from the road, the entrances and the outdoor facilities, thus ensuring ideal teaching conditions.

Schweizerische Bauzeitung, 110, 1937; Werk, 7, 1938; 55/198; Max Bill et al., Moderne Schweizer Architektur 1925–1945, Basel 1947; G.E. Kidder Smith, Switzerland Builds, New York-Stockholm 1950; Um 1930 in Zürich, exhibition catalogue, Zurich 1977; Guide to Swiss Architecture 1920–1990, vol. 1, 724, p. 178.

Zurich
Hauser House
Schreberweg 8
1937–38
Albert Heinrich Steiner
with G. Ammann

The three main ground-floor day areas - dining room, hall and living room - all have plate-glass windows facing onto the garden, while the night area is on the first floor. The search for fluid spaces and flexible links was partly made possible by technical innovations, such as the air-conditioning plant on the ceiling, the sliding metal windows and the steel pillars supporting the roof in the south-east wing. Another notable Zurich work by Steiner is the Housing, Billrothstrasse 14 (1963).

Landschaften und Bauten - Neues Bauen und Wohnen, Basel 1947; Die neue Stadt, 3, 1950.

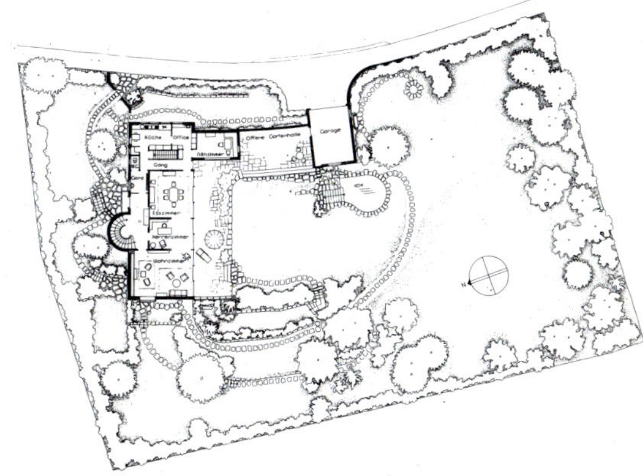

Opposite page:

Jelmoli Department Store

Kappeli School

Hauser House, period photo

Hauser House, site plan

Zurich
Housing and Kindergarten
Zentralstrasse 105/Zurlindenstrasse
1928–32
Hans Hofmann and Adolf Kellermüller

Well integrated into the urban context, this cooperative scheme draws on the classic model of courtyard housing with three- to five-room rented accommodation. The outcome of a 1928 competition, the L-shaped kindergarten establishes the north-east boundary of the complex, while the classroom design followed the most advanced teaching and sanitary research results.

Baumeister, 11, 1932; Werk, 10, 1932; 6, 1935; Um 1930 in Zürich, exhibition catalogue, Zurich 1977; Parametro, 140, 1985; Guide to Swiss Architecture 1920–1990, vol. 1, 718, p. 174.

Zurich
Doldertal Housing
Doldertal 17–19
1935–36
Alfred and Emil Roth
with Marcel Breuer and Carl Hubacher

Built in Doldertal to coincide with a housing exhibition in 1936, the three-story multi-occupancy blocks met all the requirements of the client: the art historian and CIAM Secretary Sigfried Giedion (1888–1968). White cubes with extensive window areas and terraces, apartments with variable layouts thanks to the structural steel frame – in line with the concept of modern international architecture. Each of the two buildings provides one bedsit, one 5–room and one 6–room apartment (plus kitchen and bathroom) on each of the main floors plus two studio apartments in the inset top story as well as garages and storage rooms at ground floor level. Turning the buildings at an angle to the building line means that the living rooms, with their large windows, face south, while the bedrooms are kept away from the road.

In the same neighborhood is the house of Alfred Roth (Bergstrasse 67) with its studio and student accommodation, built in 1960–61, and the house of Rudolf and Peter Steiger (Bergstrasse 71), dating from 1959. Another interesting building is the Wohnbedarf AG offices, Talstrasse 11, converted from a bar and restaurant in 1932–33 by Marcel Breuer in collaboration with Robert Winkler.

Max Bill et al., Moderne Schweizer Architektur 1925–1945, Basel 1947; G.E. Kidder Smith, Switzerland Builds, New York-Stockholm 1950; L'Architecture d'aujourd'hui, 103, 1962; L'Architettura, cronache e storia, 541, 1962; A. Altherr, New Swiss Architecture, Teufen 1965; Um 1930 in Zürich, exhibition catalogue, Zurich 1977; Werk, Bauen und Wohnen, 5, 1983; Parametro, 140, 1985; E. Blättler (ed), Neue Architektur in Zürich, Heiden 1989; Guide to Swiss Architecture 1920–1990, vol. 1, 723, p. 177.

Opposite page:

Doldertal Housing, view and section

Roth Studio-House, view and floor plan

Housing and Kindergarten

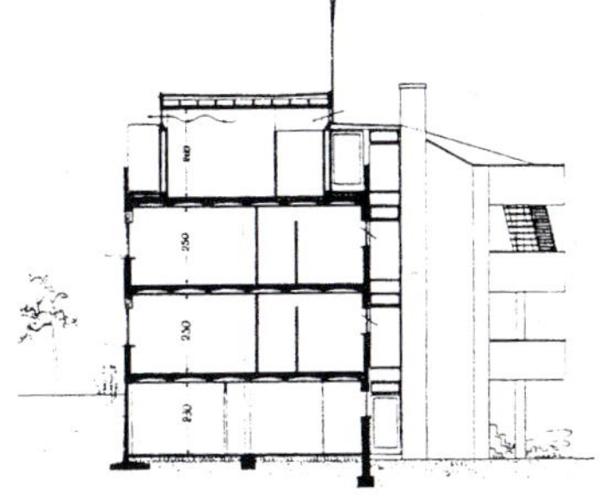

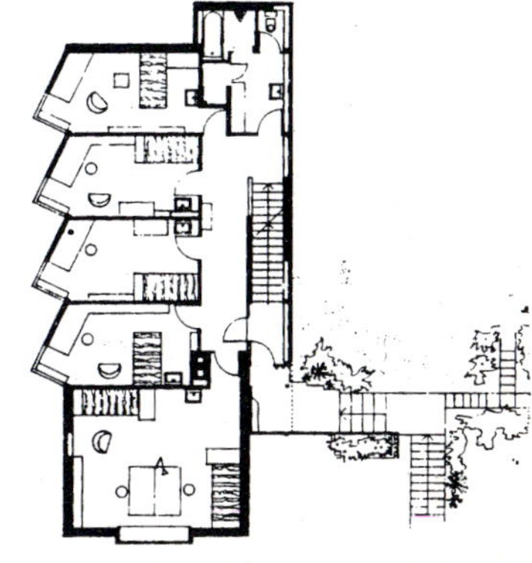

First Church of Christ, Scientist

Merkurstrasse 2–4
1937–38
Hans Hofmann and Adolf Kellermüller

The trapezoid-plan church has no lateral aisles, while the steel structure sets a vertical rhythm of pillars rising lightly and elegantly round the volume.
See also Hans Hofmann's AIAG Administrative Building, Klausstrasse 5 (1955–56).

Werk, 1, 1940; G. E. Kidder Smith, Switzerland Builds, New York-Stockholm 1950; H. Volkart, Schweizer Architektur, Ravensburg 1951; Guide to Swiss Architecture 1920–1990, vol. 1, 725, p. 178.

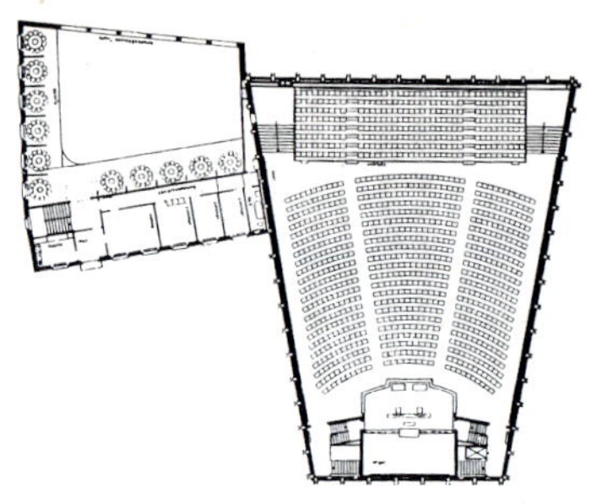

Zurich

Conference Center

Claridenstrasse 3–7
1936–39
Max Ernst Haefeli, Werner Max Moser and Rudolf Steiger

Built for the Swiss national exhibition of 1939, the Conference Centre was erected on a prominent site by Lake Zurich. The client specified that part of the old Tonhalle (1895) had to be incorporated in the new building. The architects were able to satisfy the diverse requirements of this large complex (including several conference and banqueting halls) but still create a harmonious relationship between the structure and its surroundings by breaking up and staggering the various sections of the building on the banks of the lake. The architecture of the existing building was simplified and there is a smooth transition to the new construction on two sides. The travertine cladding panels and bronze door and window frames give the elevations a simple but festive exterior. The Conference Center reflects the attempt to find a representative form for the architecture of the modern age in a "popular" language. Parts of the Conference Center were modified in the 1980s.
Other interesting works in Zurich by Haefeli, Moser and Steiger include the Hohenbühl housing development (1951–53), Hohenbühlstrasse 2–8, and the Monkey House (1954–59) in the Zoological Gardens – renovated in 1985 by Rudolf Zürcher. M.E. Haefeli and W. M. Moser were responsible for the Farbhof housing development, Badernerstrasse 742, built in 1956–57.

Werk, 3, 1937; 5, 1939; 3, 1951; Schweizerische Bauzeitung, 109, 1937; 22 and 26, 1943; G.E. Kidder Smith, Switzerland Builds, New York-Stockholm 1950; H. Volkart, Schweizer Architektur, Ravensburg 1951; J. Gubler, Nationalisme et Internationalisme dans l'Architecture Moderne de la Suisse, Lausanne 1975; Archithese, 2, 1980; 1, 1983; Werk, Bauen und Wohnen, 3, 1981; Parametro, 140, 1985; Guide to Swiss Architecture 1920–1990, vol. 1, 728, p. 180.

First Church of Christ, Scientist, view and, opposite page, floor plan

Conference Center, views

Zurich
Allenmoos Swimming Baths
Ringstrasse 79
1938–39
Max Ernst Haefeli and Werner Max Moser
with G. Ammann

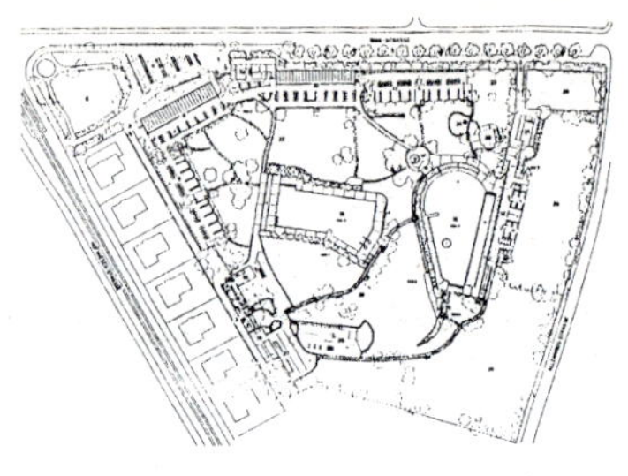

Situated around a green area of over 20,000 square meters, the functions of the various buildings in the Allenmoos complex may be clearly read, while their unity is achieved through the handling of the materials. This project was the outcome of a competition held by the city three years earlier; Haefeli and Moser had already tackled the theme in 1935, when together with R. Steiger and S. Giedion, they organized an exhibition entitled *Swimming Baths, Past and Present* at the Zurich Kunstgewerbemuseum.
The architects returned to the subject in 1948, when they designed the Im Moos Swimming Pool at Schlieren, Schulstrasse 8, while other significant examples of swimming facilities are Max Frisch's Letzigraben Baths, Dennlerstrasse (1947–48), and the Oberer Letten Baths, Lettensteg, built by Ernst and Elsa Burckhardt in 1951–52

A. Roth, Die Neue Architektur, Zurich 1940; Moderne Schweizer Architektur 1925–1945, Basel 1947; Werk, 7, 1947; 9, 1950; G. E. Kidder Smith, Switzerland Builds, New York-Stockholm 1950; Archithese, 2, 1980; E. Blättler (ed), Neue Architektur in Zürich, Heiden 1989; S. von Moos (ed), Das Neue Bauen in der Ostschweiz, Sankt Gallen 1989; Guide to Swiss Architecture 1920–1990, vol. 1, 730, p. 182.

Zurich
Altstetten Protestant Church
Pfarrhausstrasse
1937–41
Werner Max Moser

The Protestant Church stands beside an existing thirteenth-century church, establishing fresh spatial relations by the creation of a new square. The dialogue of contrasts is generated by the modern building's asymmetric plan and materials (reinforced concrete and silicon-limestone brick cladding). The excellent acoustics are partly due to the window screening (also softening internal light), and the absence of right angles, both in the walls and ceiling.

Schweizerische Bauzeitung, 120, 1942; Werk, 2, 1943; Moderne Schweizer Architektur 1925–1945, Basel 1947; G. E. Kidder Smith, Switzerland Builds, New York-Stockholm 1950; Archithese, 2, 1980; Guide to Swiss Architecture 1920–1990, vol. 1, 727, p. 179.

Allenmoos Swimming Baths, view and, opposite page, plan

Altstetten Protestant Church, view and section

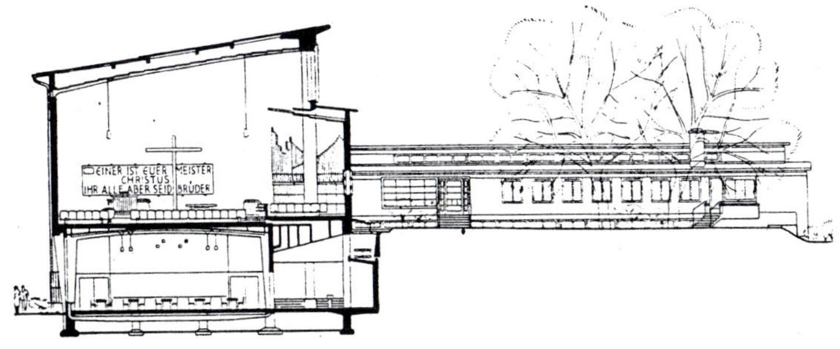

Zurich
Salvisberg House
Restelbergstrasse 97
1930–31
Otto Rudolf Salvisberg
Children's Hospital Outpatients' Wing
Steinwiesstrasse 75
1937–39, 1964–68
Otto Rudolf Salvisberg
Rudolf and Peter Steiger
Bleicherhof Offices
Bleicherweg 18–20
1939–41
Otto Rudolf Salvisberg

Built on the steep south-west slope of the hill overlooking the city, the main section of Salvisberg's own house projects a few meters out over the supporting masonry to provide a breathtaking view from the seemingly freely suspended living room. The lower side wings run parallel with the slope, opening out in the direction of the swimming pool in the garden, accessed via a loggia.

Only part of the original Children's Hospital has survived renovation work and extensions. In his contribution to this series of modifications, Salvisberg tried to create a hospital building which would be totally sympathetic to the size and psyche of children. The ward building was the work of Rudolf and Peter Steiger in the 1960s.

Salvisberg's last work (he died in 1940) was the Bleicherhof office building. The gently curving structure with its shop fronts behind a colonnade along the street, a glazed mezzanine floor above, a grid-like front to the office floors and a roof story set back from the main line of the building pioneered the way for the office and commercial developments of the post-war years.

Baumeister, 3, 1932; Schweizerische Bauzeitung, 99, 1932; Werk, 8, 1932; 11, 1941; 7, 1970; G.E. Kidder Smith, Switzerland Builds, New York-Stockholm 1950; Hochparterre, 4, 1990; Guide to Swiss Architecture 1920–1990, vol. 1, 726, p. 179; 734, p. 184.

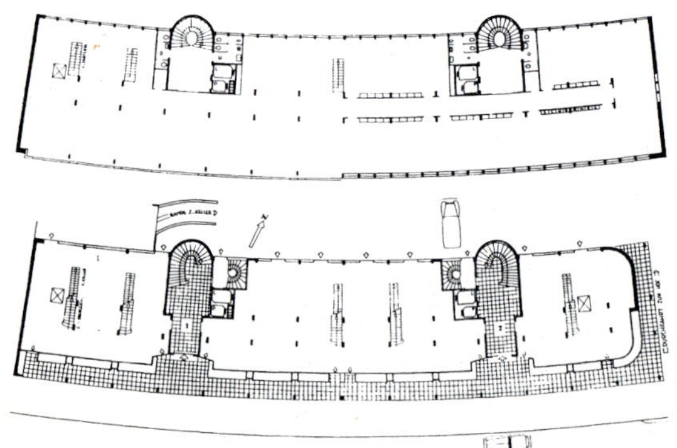

Bleicherhof Offices, floor plans

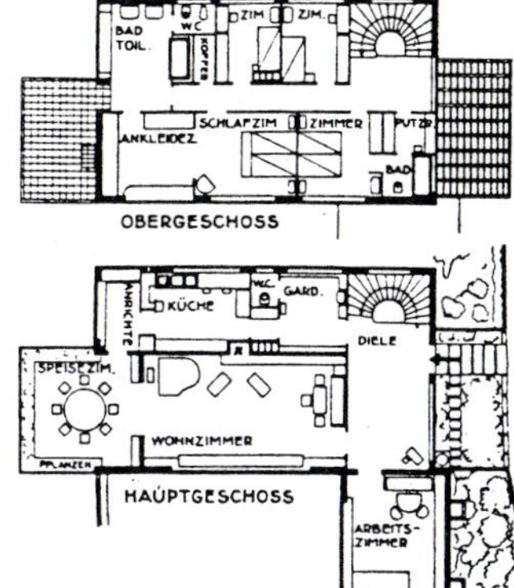

Salvisberg House,
view and plan

Children's Hospital

Bleicherhof Offices

Zurich
Cantonal Hospital
Rämistrasse 100
1942–53
AKZ Architects' Collective: Rudolf Steiger, Hermann Fietz, Max Ernst Haefeli, Hermann Weideli, Josef Schütz, Werner Max Moser, August Arter & Martin Risch, Robert Landolt, and Gottlieb Leuenberger & Jakob Flückiger

Built during the Second World War, this hospital complex was based on an organic conception as a means to creating a patient-centered but efficient approach to hospital design. The direct access to the grounds - through loggias and balconies - and the distribution of the buildings - in single blocks or independent wards - are on a well-balanced scale, without, however, obscuring the importance of technical details and equipment. The hospital has been renovated and extended several times, and now only the main nucleus and the Rämistrasse wing survive from the original building.
Nearby is the Nurses' Home, Plattenstrasse 10 (1957–59), designed by Jakob Zweifel.

Schweizerische Bauzeitung, 117, 1941; 67, 1949; Werk, 4, 1944; 11, 1946; 11, 1953; G. E. Kidder Smith, Switzerland Builds, New York-Stockholm 1950; H. Volkart, Schweizer Architektur, Ravensburg 1951; Baumeister, 8, 1953; Archithese, 2, 1980; Parametro, 140, 1985; Guide to Swiss Architecture 1920–1990, vol. 1, 736, p. 185.

Zurich
Mandrot/Roth House
Hadlaubstrasse 59
1943–44
Alfred Roth

Preserved in its original condition, this wooden house was commissioned as a winter residence by Hélène de Mandrot, owner of La Sarraz Castle and a promoter of the first CIAM (1929). The layout and hexagonal plan reflect the owner's ideas about terrestrial radiation. Ceded to Alfred Roth only a year

Cantonal Hospital

Mandrot/Roth House

after its completion, the house was occupied by the architect until 1961.
Werk, 7, 1944; Schweizerische Bauzeitung, 125, 1945; G. E. Kidder Smith, Switzerland Builds, New York-Stockholm 1950; H. Volkart, Schweizer Architektur, Ravensburg 1951; R. Winkler, Das Haus des Architekten, Zurich 1955; Bauen und Wohnen, 11, 1957; Parametro, 140, 1985; A. Roth, Amüsante Erlebnisse, Zurich 1988; Guide to Swiss Architecture 1920–1990, vol. 1, 738, p. 188.

Zurich-Seebach
Saint Mark's Reformed Church
Höhenring 54–58
1946–55
Albert Heinrich Steiner
Responding to the new liturgical needs of the Reformed Church and precise planning premises, the architect designed the central body concentrically round the pulpit. As befits the occasion, this space can be enlarged through a system of mobile partitions which, when open, makes use of the adjoining public room. To the north, the other parts of the building are arranged to form an entrance court. The facade is defined by a reinforced-concrete grid skeleton with a sandstone block infill.
Another Zurich work by Steiner is the Nordheim Crematorium, Käferholzstrasse 101 (1963–93).
Ferd. Pfammater, Betonkirchen, Einsiedeln 1948; Baumeister, 7, 1950; Schweizerische Bauzeitung, 2, 1950; H. Volkart, Schweizer Architektur, Ravensburg 1951; Werk, 2, 1952; World's Contemporary Architecture, Tokyo 1953; Bauen und Wohnen, 11, 1958; Guide to Swiss Architecture 1920–1990, vol. 1, 739, p. 188.

Saint Mark's Reformed Church

Zurich
Church of St Felix and St Regula
Hardstrasse 76
1949–51
Fritz Metzger

A close relationship between congregation and altar was the aim with this building. The altar area broadens to face the body of the church – a transverse oval in plan, the central axis of which lines up exactly with the altar. A balanced composition characterizes the external appearance of the rounded structure and so, despite its modest height, forms a distinct contrast to the housing in the area.

Metzger also designed the church of St Francis at Riehen in the canton of Basel-Land (1948–50). In that church, a segment-shaped area for the congregation merges into the transverse oval of the choir.

Werk, 8, 1951.

Zurich
Siedlung Sunnige Hof
Moosacker and Sunnige Hof, Probsteinstrasse
1943
Karl Kündig

E. Reinhard (ed), Neues Bauen und Wohnen, Basel-Olten 1946; G. E. Kidder Smith, Switzerland Builds, New York-Stockholm 1950; Guide to Swiss Architecture 1920–1990, vol. 1, 737, p. 186f.

Dreispitz Housing Colony
Wallisellenstrasse/Saatlenstrasse, Dreispitz
1945–55
Gottlieb Leuenberger, Jakob Flückiger, Josef Schütz, Max Steiger, and Carl Rathgeb

Church of Saints Felix and Regulus

Siedlung Sunnige Hof

Dreispitz Housing Colony

J. Maurizio, Der Siedlungsbau in der Schweiz 1940–1950, Erlenbach 1952; Werk, 1, 1957; Guide to Swiss Architecture 1920–1990, vol. 1, 757, p. 186f.

Siedlung Heiligfeld

Brahmsstrasse 60–92/
Letzigraben 5–11
1954–55

Albert Heinrich Steiner

Werk, 9, 1953; 1, 1956; Baumeister, 10, 1956; L'Architecture d'aujourd'hui, 66, 1956; 50 Jahre Wohnungspolitik der Stadt Zürich, Zurich 1957; I. Noseda and M. Steinmann, Zeitzeichen, Schweizer Baukultur im 19. und 20. Jh., Zurich 1988; Guide to Swiss Architecture 1920–1990, vol. 1, 757, p. 186.

In 1934 the Zurich municipal authorities redesigned the city boundaries, and included nine different peripheral areas. The 1940s witnessed a housing boom in these areas, financed by the public authorities and coordinated at planning level by the municipal building department, directed by A. H. Steiner. An organicist approach was adopted in the new housing complexes, arranged in "neighborhood units" in green areas with suitable infrastructures and community facilities. The Siedlung Sunnige Hof develops the model of the linear village, whereas the Dreispitz scheme consists of both single-family houses and three- to four-apartment blocks. A similar solution was adopted in the Heiligfield estate along with other housing types, such as the corridor-type building and the apartment tower. See also the Siedlung In der Au, Opfikonstrasse, Auzelg (1950–54), by Cramer, Jaray and Paillard in collaboration with Baerlocher & Unger.

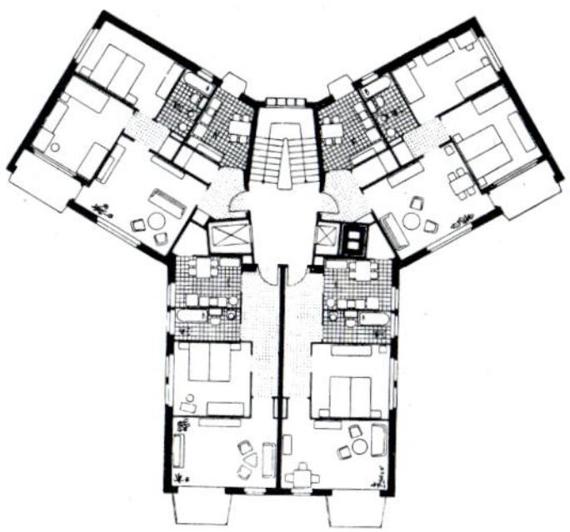

Siedlung Heiligfeld

Zurich
Zur Bastei Mixed-Use Building
Bärengasse 29, Bleicherweg, Talstrasse
1954–55
Werner Stücheli

This nine-story building on the banks of a stream is turned slightly away from the water to create a small forecourt. This integrates the stream into the group consisting of office block, low-rise appartment block and promenade with a flight of steps down to the water. The stylish aluminium and glass facade, with generous window openings and spandrel panels of dark-blue Carrara glass, lends the building a light transparency and the typical weightlessness of 1950s architecture.

Bauen und Wohnen, 6, 1955; Deutsche Bauzeitschrift, 10, 1955; Werk, 10, 1955; Archithese, 5, 1986; Guide to Swiss Architecture 1920–1990, vol. 1, 746, p. 192.

Zurich
Mixed-Use Building
Bahnhofstrasse 46
1956–57
Rudolf Zürcher

With its modular aluminium-and-glass curtain wall, this six-story building for offices and shops stands out forcefully from the uniform street front in the Bahnhofstrasse. It was inspired by SOM/Gordon Bunshaft's Lever House in New York (1952).

Bauen und Wohnen, 6, 1957; Werk, 11, 1957; A. Altherr, New Swiss Architecture,

Zur Bastei Mixed-Use Building

Mixed-Use Building

Teufen 1965; I. Noseda, Bauen an Zürich, Zurich 1992; Guide to Swiss Architecture 1920–1990, vol. 1, 750, p. 195.

Zurich

Freudenberg Cantonal School

Steinentischstrasse 10/
Gutenbergstrasse 15
1954–60
Jacques Schader
with W. Blaser, W. Dubach, R. Ellenrieder, R. Hofer, R. Mathys, and E. Kägi

One of the most celebrated postwar Swiss school designs, the Freudenberg complex is organized on a plateau making the most of the mountainous conditions of the site. The teaching spaces – junior high school and commercial college, laboratories, gymnasia and auditorium – are distributed in differentiated volumes. The sober handling of the exterior with exposed concrete and stone cladding is underscored by the horizontal rhythm of the fenestration providing optimal natural lighting.

Schweizerische Bauzeitung, 72, 1954; Bauen und Wohnen, 9, 1960; Architecture, formes + fonction, 8, 1961; Werk, 1, 1961; 1, 1962; A. Altherr, New Swiss Architecture, Teufen 1965; L'Architecture d'aujourd'hui, 121, 1965; E. Blättler (ed), Neue Architektur in Zurich, Heiden 1989; I. Noseda, Bauen an Zürich, Zurich 1992; Guide to Swiss Architecture 1920–1990, vol. 1, 752, p. 196.

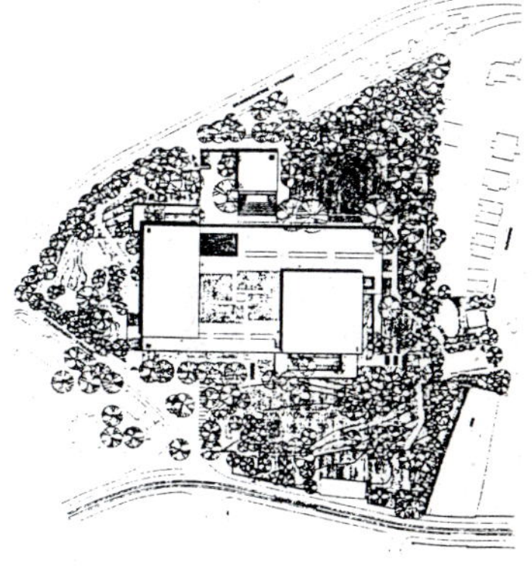

Freudenberg Cantonal School, view and site plan

Zurich
Letzi School
Espenhofweg 60
1953–59
Ernst Gisel
Youth Hostel
Mutschellenstrasse 114
1960–66
Ernst Gisel
with G. Erdt
Atelier Gisel
Streulistrasse 74a
1970–73
Ernst Gisel

The works of Ernst Gisel are the result of research which has made a significant contribution to the development of contemporary Swiss architecture. Although always highly individual and self-contained, his designs have a precise urban meaning and a number of constant features: integration into the context, an organic compositional matrix, the use of rudimentary natural materials, a complete control over the building process, and careful detailing. Among his other fine school designs is the Steinboden School, Rhihaldenstrasse 60 (1977–80), in Eglisau, while of his more recent output, see the Stampfenbach Rest Home, Lindenbachstrasse 1 (1983–88), and the World Trade Center, Leutschenbachstrasse, begun in 1989.

Werk, 3, 1954; 5, 1958; 3, 1960; 3, 1967; 1, 1976; Architektur-Wettbewerbe, 21, 1957; A. Roth, Das neue Schulhaus, Zurich 1957; K. Otto, Schulbau, Beispiele und Entwicklung, Stuttgart 1961; G. E. Kidder Smith, Moderne Architektur in Europa, München 1964; L'Architecture d'aujourd'hui, 121, 1965; Baumeister, 7, 1966; Casabella, 319, 1967; B. de Sivo, Architettura in Svizzera oggi, Naples 1968; a + u, Architecture and Urbanism, 8, 1977; W. Blaser, Architecture 70/80 in Switzerland, Basel 1981; Abitare, 206, 1982; Rivista Tecnica, 1, 1982; Guide to Swiss Architecture 1920–1990, vol. 1, 745, p. 191; 765, p. 203.

Zurich
Rämibühl Cantonal School
Freiestrasse 26
1966–70
Eduard Neuenschwander
with D. Köhler, B.C. Thurston, and A. Biro

Despite the comprehensive specification and the need to accommodate about 2,000 pupils, a solution was found which integrates the school complex into its environment consisting of old villas and a copious stock of trees. Secondary school, grammar school and natural sciences department with assembly hall were placed in three separate blocks. A uniform facade layout enabled a completely flexible division by means of windows and columns so that despite lively variations, overall unity is maintained.

Schweizerische Bauzeitung, 48, 1960; 19, 1965; J. Bachmann and S. von Moos, New Directions in Swiss Architecture, New York 1969; Bauwelt, 7, 1971; Werk, 8, 1971; Werk, Bauen und Wohnen, 1–2, 1980; Guide to Swiss Architecture 1920–1990, vol. 1, 760, p. 200.

Letzi School

Bottom left: Youth Hostel

Bottom right: Atelier Gisel, view and axonometric

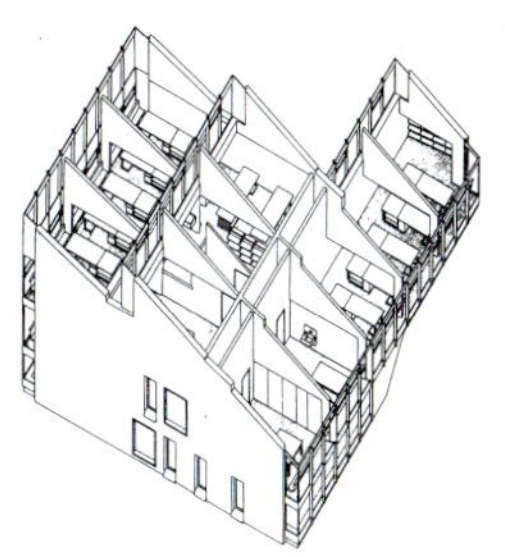

Upper left: Stampfenbach Rest Home

Rämibühl Cantonal School

Zurich
Riedhof School Complex
Riedhofstrasse 42–46
1965–67
Alfred Roth
with E. Schubiger
The study of school typologies was one of Roth's favorite research themes, and in this case he came up with a very successful solution. The various buildings - a nursery school, primary-school classrooms plus recreation room, and gymnasium - are arranged in parallel, thus forming terraces along the contours of the sloping land facing southeast.
Deutsche Bauzeitschrift, 3, 1964; Werk, 6, 1964; L'Architecture d'aujourd'hui, 121, 1965; Werk, Bauen und Wohnen, 5, 1983; Guide to Swiss Architecture 1920–1990, vol. 1, 756, p. 198.

Zurich
Housing
Eierbrechtstrasse 16
1958–60
Claude Paillard and Peter Leemann (Atelier Cramer-Jaray-Paillard)
with H. Tissi

Saatlen Protestant Church and Center
Saatlenstrasse 240
1961–64
Claude Paillard (Atelier Cramer-Jaray-Paillard-Leemann)

Opernhaus Restoration and Extension
Theaterplatz
1975–84
Claude Paillard, Peter Leemann and Associates (C. Paillard and W. Rafflenbeul)

Riedhof School Complex

Eierbrechtstrasse Housing

The unusually shaped Eierbrechtstrasse Housing accommodates independent apartments (including the architects' studio), developed down a series of terraces in order to adapt to the very steep lot. The Saatlen Protestant Center is a further exploration of a theme already tackled by the same architects in the Horgen Parish Center, Kelliweg 21 (1958–65): the design of a religious complex, which by hosting cultural activities becomes a reference point for the whole quarter. In renovating the Zurich Opera House - built in 1890–91 by the Viennese studio Fellner & Helmer - the architects were fully aware of the delicate nature of the task, and consequently adopted a very prudent approach. A new service wing with the Bernhardtheater was also added on this occasion.

The same studio also designed the Swisscontrol Tower of Kloten Airport (1979–91), of which the third phase of works was realized in the 1990s.

Werk, 2, 1961; Architecture, formes + fonction, 8, 1961–62; Deutsche Bauzeitschrift, 2, 1962; A. Altherr, New Swiss Architecture, Teufen 1965; L'Architecture d'aujourd'hui, 121, 1965; Werk, Bauen und Wohnen, 3, 1986; Guide to Swiss Architecture 1920–1990, vol. 1, 753, p. 197; 777, p. 209.

Saatlen Protestant Church and Center

Opernhaus and extension

Zurich

Mixed-Use Building

Seefeldstrasse 152

1957–60

Jakob Zweifel with Heinrich Strickler with L. Flotron and B. Pfister

The prism-shaped volume of this office and apartment block is patterned by the complex play of the apertures and the alternating of different surface textures (exposed-concrete bands and silicon-limestone bricks), highlighting the functional organization of the plan. A central stair serves three apartments of two, four and six rooms on each floor, while the ground floor is for use by shops, offices and studios.

Bauen und Wohnen, 3, 1962; Guide to Swiss Architecture 1920–1990, vol. 1, 754, p. 197.

Zurich

Zur Palme Building

Bleicherweg 33

1957–64

Max Ernst Haefeli, Werner Max Moser, Rudolf Steiger and André Studer with H. Dussy, M. Gut, F. Staub and O. Caretta

Situated on an important east-west axis through Zurich city center, this block fills a whole square and embodies two key motifs of urban development in the 1950s and 1960s: open construction rejecting roadside, linear developments, and the differentiation between low-rise shopping levels and high-rise office space. The two-story commercial zone runs along the street frontage and forms public pedestrian passageways through and within the building. Vehicles reach the parking levels by way of spiral ramps. The 11–story office block with its aluminum and glass facade has apartments on the top floor with rooftop gardens.

Werk, 3, 1957; 12, 1964; L'Architettura cronache and storia, 12, 1964; A. Altherr, New Swiss Architecture, Teufen 1965; Architektur und Wohnform, 2, 1965; Schweizerische Bauzeitung, 50, 1965; Archithese, 2, 1980; I. Noseda and M. Steinmann, Zeitzeichen, Schweizer Baukultur im 19. und 20. Jh., Zurich 1988; I. Noseda, Bauen an Zürich, Zurich 1992.; Guide to Swiss Architecture 1920–1990, vol. 1, 755, p. 198.

Zurich

Le Corbusier Center

Höschgasse 8

1964–67

Le Corbusier

Commissioned by gallery-owner Heidi Weber, this exhibition pavilion is situated in Zurichhorn Park. Le Corbusier designed it like a house, working out the proportions through the *modulor*. The spaces are organized in a *promenade architecturale*, protected by two large umbrellas forming the metal structure of the roof.

Werk, 12, 1967; S. von Moos, Der Corbusier-Pavillon, Neue Zürcher Zeitung, 16 July 1967; J. Bachmann and S. von Moos, New Directions in Swiss Architecture, New York 1969; Abitare, 206, 1982; A. Roth, E. Miltcheu, Le Corbusier und Zürich, Zurich 1987; Guide to Swiss Architecture 1920–1990, vol. 1, 758, p. 199.

Mixed-Use Building

Zur Palme Building

Le Corbusier Center

Zurich

Zentner House

Aurorastrasse 56

1964–68

Carlo Scarpa

Building regulations required that parts of the former single-family residence dating from 1914 had to be preserved. The architect then used them as the basis for his own independent design. The southern elevation consists of a series of terraces, while the plain street frontage has been enhanced by the use of different materials. On the whole, the building exhibits the fine detailing so typical of Scarpa.
Werk, 1, 1968; Archithese, 4, 1983.

Zurich

Herden Telecommunications Center

Aargauerstrasse 10, Herdern

1972–78

Theo Hotz

Marti AG Offices

Thurgauerstrasse 56, Oerlikon

1982–85

Theo Hotz

with Franz Romero

Apollo Office Building

Stauffacherstrasse 41

1989–91

Theo Hotz

with P. Berger, T. Fausch

Office Building

Seidengasse 20, Löwenplatz

1989–93

Theo Hotz

Machine and sculpture embodied in one, the vast aluminium facades of the telecommunications center dominate

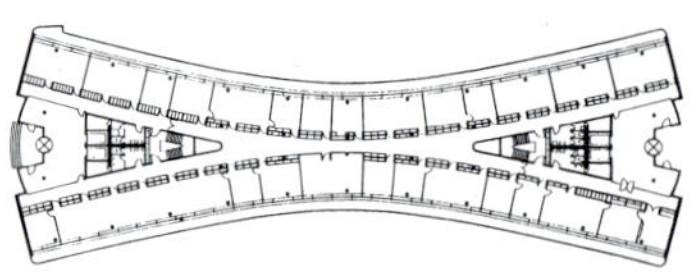

Zentner House

Telecommunications Center

Marti AG Offices, view and floor plan

the industrial estate on the western edge of Zurich. The type of construction adopted is intended to show how architecture can overcome its role of being a mere container, attaining quality with the help of state-of-the-art engineering.

Optimum use of the site and the technical finesse of the metal facade distinguish the office building in the Oerlikon district of Zurich. Its double-concave plan shape lends the building an unmistakable character in an otherwise anonymous environment.

In contrast, the office building in the Stauffacherstrasse holds its own by way of its inset wall following the line of the street, while the metal and glass front gradually cantilevers out into the street as it rises.

Other interesting works by Theo Hotz are the Raussmüller/Welti apartment block, Schneckenmannstrasse 25 (1986–87), the Grünenhof Banking Conference Center, Nüschelerstrasse 2 (1987–91), and the Feldpausch office building, Bahnhofstrasse 88 (completed in 1995).

Werk, Bauen und Wohnen, 1–2, 1980; 4, 1980; 11, 1987; 3, 1994; Abitare, 206, 1982; W. Blaser, Architecture 70/80 in Switzerland, Basel 1981; Rivista Tecnica, 1, 1982; 1–2, 1986; Archithese, 1, 1986; E. Blättler (ed), Neue Architektur in Zürich, Heiden 1989; Faces, 13, 1989; R. Schilling, Architektur in Zürich 1980–90, Zurich 1990; P. Disch (ed), L'architettura recente nella Svizzera tedesca, Lugano 1991, p. 179, 181; Hochparterre, 3, 1992; I. Noseda, Bauen an Zürich, Zurich 1992; GSA I, 766, p. 203; 7779, p. 210; 789, p. 215.

Apollo Building

Löwenplatz Office Building

Zurich
Manessehof Housing
Uetlibergstrasse 20/
Hopfenstrasse 11
1977–84
Arcoop (Ueli Marbach and Arthur Rüegg)
with T. Schonbächler and P. Steiner

The architects' intention to adapt the type of the traditional urban block clearly emerges in the corner element, highlighting the different urban characters of the adjacent streets. The two wings enclose an internal court, isolating the rooms of the apartments from street noise.

The same architects also designed the Housing at Balberstrasse 47 (1984–91).

Archithese, 1, 1980; 4, 1984; Werk, Bauen und Wohnen, 12, 1981; 10, 1984; 3, 1994; H. and M. Bofinger, Junge Architekten in Europa, Stuttgart 1983; Baumeister, 5, 1985; Rivista Tecnica, 1–2, 1986; R. Schilling, Architektur in Zürich 1980–90, Zurich 1990; P. Disch (ed), L'architettura recente nella Svizzera tedesca, Lugano 1991, p. 184; I. Noseda, Bauen an Zürich, Zurich 1992; Guide to Swiss Architecture 1920–1990, vol. 1, 774, p. 207.

Manessehof
Housing

Limmat REZ
Housing

Zurich

Limmat REZ Housing

Hardeggstrasse 17–23

1981–86

Benno Fosco, Jacqueline Fosco-Oppenheim, and Klaus Vogt with A. Peissard

Built following a private competition, this estate is situated on the banks of the river Limmat. Partly through the use of traditional materials, the uniform facade fits in well with the context. The rows of apartment blocks for dwellings or studios have wide roof terraces.

Aktuelles Bauen, 4, 1984; Archithese, 2, 1985; Schweizer Architektur, 80, 1987; Werk, Bauen und Wohnen, 1–2, 1987; E. Blättler (ed), Neue Architektur in Zurich, Heiden 1989; R. Schilling, Architektur in Zurich 1980–90, Zurich 1990; P. Disch (ed), L'architettura recente nella Svizzera tedesca, Lugano 1991, p. 203; Guide to Swiss Architecture 1920–1990, vol. 1, 783, p. 212.

Zurich

Juchhof Barn

Bernerstrasse 301

1982–84

Willi E. Christen with M. Weibel

This traditional wooden structure stands in a country estate belonging to the City of Zurich. Constructed in only five months after the previous building had been destroyed by fire, the prefabricated building system in no way limited the scope for careful detailing. Willi Christen also designed the Principal Pavilion (1986–89) in Zurich Zoological Gardens.

Holz Bulletin, 13, 1985; Werk, Bauen und Wohnen, 3, 1985; Schweizer Architektur, 72, 1986; R. Schilling, Architektur in Zürich 1980–90, Zurich 1990; P. Disch (ed), L'architettura recente nella Svizzera tedesca, Lugano 1991, p. 204; Guide to Swiss Architecture 1920–1990, vol. 1, 778, p. 209.

Juchhof Farmhouse, view and elevation

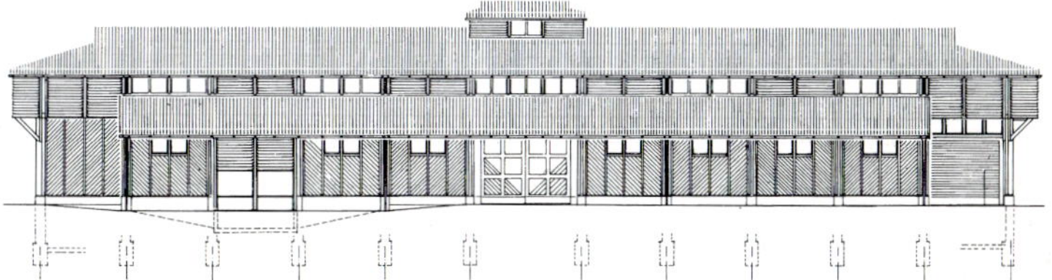

Zurich
Villa Meyer
Südstrasse 41
1985–86
Dolf Schnebli
with P. Kölliker, M. Meili, and M. Wassmer

Situated in a housing estate surrounded by green in the Riesbach area, this small villa is the outcome of an erudite exercise in style. The classic villa scheme is handled in proportions which immediately bring to mind Le Corbusier's *modulor*, especially as regards the heights. The harmoniously proportioned cubic volume is articulated starting from the glazed cylindrical entrance structure. The most significant contemporary features are the roof garden over the atrium, the prefabricated top and the choice of materials (reinforced concrete, silicon-limestone bricks, and gneiss slabs from the Val Maggia).

Rivista Tecnica, 3, 1987; Werk, Bauen und Wohnen, 3, 1987; Detail, 1, 1988; Architecture et Techniques, 380, 1988; a+u. architecture and urbanism, 221, 1989; R. Schilling, Architektur in Zürich 1980–90, Zurich 1990; The Architectural Review, 1, 1991; F.A. Cerver, Architectural Houses: Country Houses 7, Barcelona 1991; P. Disch (ed), L'architettura recente nella Svizzera tedesca, Lugano 1991, p. 197; du, 5, 1992; Guide to Swiss Architecture 1920–1990, vol. 1, 784, p. 212.

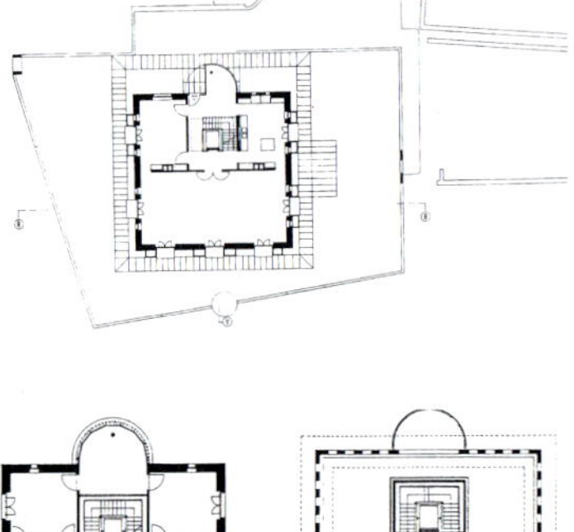

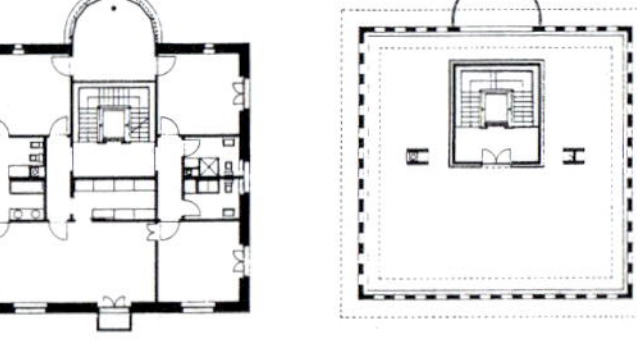

Villa Meyer, view
and plans

Zurich

Renovation and Extension of Stadelhofen Station

Stadelhoferplatz

1983–91

Santiago Calatrava, Werner Rüeger, and Arnold Amsler

Following a 1983 invitation competition, the city-center station of Stadelhofen was renovated and extended. The complex forms of Calatrava's structure - large metal ribs for the platforms and external passages as well as the imposing organic-inspired reinforced concrete roof for the commercial underpass - forge links with the existing urban context. In the same neighborhood are a number of other interesting works from the 1980s, such as the Stadelhofer Passage, Stadelhoferstrasse 18–28, built in 1977–84 by Ernst Gisel and Martin Spühler, and the Mixed-Use Building, Stadelhoferstrasse 10 (1989), by Arnold and Vreni Amsler.

Detail, 5, 1987; Archithese, 2, 1990; Hochparterre, 5, 1990; Architettura Svizzera, 94, 1990; Schweizer Ingenieur und Architekt, 48, 1990; P. Disch (ed), L'architettura recente nella Svizzera tedesca, Lugano 1991, p. 186–191; Werk, Bauen und Wohnen, 3, 1991; I. Noseda, Bauen an Zürich, Zurich 1992; Guide to Swiss Architecture 1920–1990, vol. 1, 786, p. 213.

Stadelhofen Station

Zurich-Wiedikon
Home for the Elderly
Sieberstrasse 22
1984–94
Martin Spühler
with C. Oberholzer
Redevelopment of the Selnau Station Area
Selnaustrasse/Sihlhölzlistrasse/
Sihlamtsstrasse
1985–95
Martin Spühler
with D. Munz

The Home for the Elderly and its grounds are housed in a re-converted former brick-manufacturing works. Divided into two halves, the new structure fully exploits the excellent orientation of the old building, while a central atrium is the key reference point in defining the internal spaces. Spühler also redesigned the area of the former station of Selnau, which required redeveloping after the Sihltal-Uetliberg railway line was moved: sixty-two dwellings with common spaces are planned on a triangular lot.
The same architect was also responsible for the Mixed-Use Building (begun in 1985) near the Uster Railway Station, Bankstrasse.
I. Noseda, Bauen an Zürich, Zurich 1992.

Zurich
Brahmshof Housing
Brahmstrasse 22–24
1989–91
Walter Fischer and Associates
(Kuhn, Fischer, Hungerbühler)
with K. Arn, M. Widmer, and M. Comte

Home for the Elderly

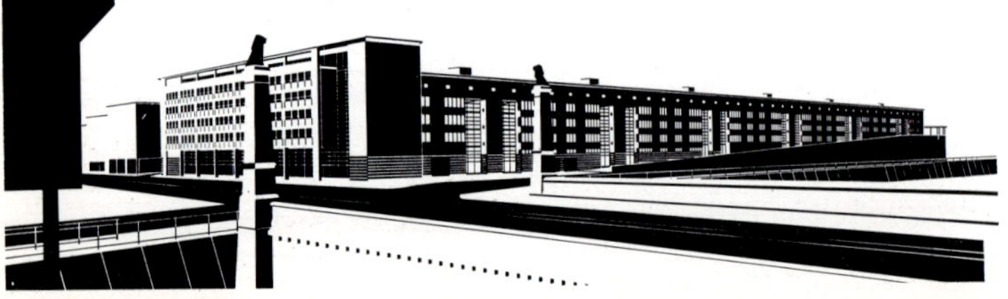

Selnau Station Redevelopment, perspective drawing

Hochparterre, 3, 1992; I. Noseda, Bauen an Zürich, Zurich 1992; Werk, Bauen und Wohnen, 3, 1992; Faces, 28, 1993; Abitare, 327, 1994; Guide to Swiss Architecture 1920–1990, vol. 1, 791, 216; P. Meyer (ed), Wohnbauten im Vergleich, vol. 18: Brahmshof, Zurich 1994.

Hellmutstrasse Housing

1989–91

Hellmutstrasse/Hohlstrasse 86 abc/ Brauerstrasse 75

ADP (Walter Ramseier, Beat Jordi, Caspar Angst, Peter Hofmann)

Werk, Bauen und Wohnen, 5, 1989; P. Disch (ed), L'architettura recente nella Svizzera tedesca, Lugano 1991, p. 192; Hochparterre, 10, 1991; Guide to Swiss Architecture 1920–1990, vol. 1, 791, p. 216; P. Meyer (ed), Wohnbauten im Vergleich, vol. 16: Hellmuthstrasse, Zurich 1993.

These very recent examples of publicly assisted housing developments have a high occupant density by Swiss standards. In both schemes, open walkways and courtyards characterize the transition between public and private areas. The layout on the Hellmutstrasse is noteworthy for it allows different combinations of rooms and subsequent changes to the sizes of the apartments between 2 and 7 rooms (excluding kitchen and bathroom).

Top: Brahmshof Housing

Hellmutstrasse Housing, view, section and elevation

Zurich
Technopark
Pfingstweidstrasse 30
1986–93
Itten + Brechbühl Ag, Ruggero Tropeano with H. Gessler, and G. Bölstelli

Built on an area of 20,000 square meters to the west of the city, the Zurich technology park has three primary functions organized in different areas: research, production and meetings. Respectful of the surroundings, the park is the key element in an overall development plan. The various buildings are arranged according to a double-comb plan connecting the main volume, intended for common functions, to the working spaces, separated by four courts used as workshops. Set on a concrete base, the blocks are curved inwards towards the principal facade, while their ends rest on pilotis. The contrast in the use of materials (Eternit-clad facades, aluminum window frames, and iron balconies) provides a suitable architectural quality to a complex intended to be a public place.

P. Disch (ed), L'architettura recente nella Svizzera tedesca, Lugano 1991, p. 201; Faces, 24, 1992; I. Noseda, Bauen an Zürich, Zurich 1992; Domus, 751, 1993; Werk, Bauen und Wohnen, 11, 1993.

Zurich
IBM Offices
Bernerstrasse
1988–95
Mario Campi and Franco Pessina

This large cuboid structure is designed as a block completely surrounding an internal courtyard which serves as a communications center. Austere perforated facades face the inhospitable surroundings of an industrial estate, those on the motorway side being given a formal and more expressive aspect through the two slightly taller corner columns.

Rivista Tecnica, 1–2, 1990; 10, 1992; K. Feireiss (ed), Mario Campi, Franco Pessina, Berlin 1994.

Technopark

Technopark,
external and internal
views

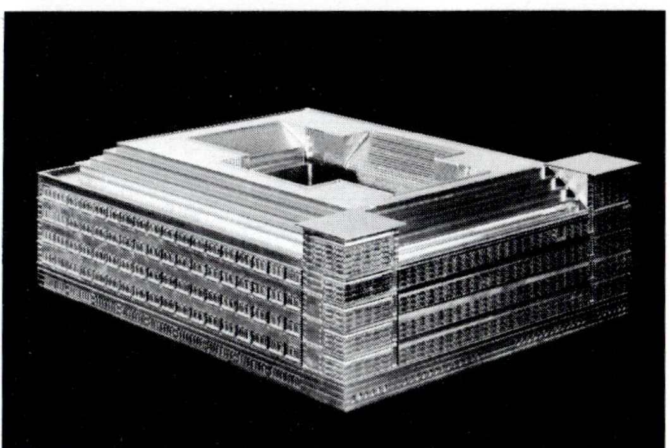

IBM Offices, model
view and section

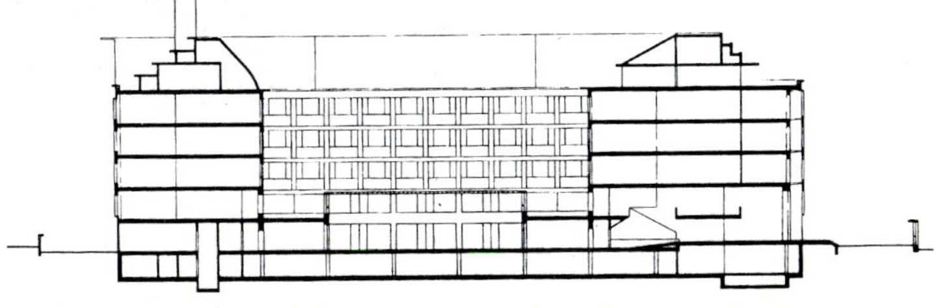

Schaffhausen

Schaffhausen
Georg Fischer AG Industrial Plant
Mühlentalstrasse/Amsler-Laffon-Strasse
1929, 1939–61, 1943–44, 1958–62
Karl Moser; Paul Mebes and Rudolf Bäny; Adolf Kellermüller

Curjel & Moser's work for the engineering firm Georg Fischer AG began before the First World War. Those projects concerned the design of housing for workers, a director's villa (1908–09) and, primarily, the conversion of the administration building (1912). Although these projects remained faithful to a regional style, Moser registered his shift to modern architecture with the second administration building in 1929.

Georg Fischer AG continued to employ challenging architecture as a means of corporate identity in its successive extensions to the production facilities from the end of the 1930s onwards. The steel casting foundry (1939–41) and gas plant (1943–44), by Paul Mebes from Berlin and the manager of the company's Building Dept, Rudol Bäny, achieved a monumental effect with smooth, cubic, overall forms and flat clay-brick elevations.

In two subsequent buildings, the laboratories (1958) and an office block (1962), Kellermüller chose uniform grid facades with a fine, light character as a contrast.

Werk, 1, 1968; Wilfried Rössling, Curjel & Moser, Karlsruhe 1986; S. von Moos u.a., Das Neue Bauen in der Ostschweiz, Sankt Gallen 1989; Guide to Swiss Architecture 1920–1990, vol. 1, 010, p. 22.

Schaffhausen

Cantonal School

Munotstrasse/Pestalozzistrasse 8

1960–66

Walter M. Förderer and Hans Zwimpfer

Sculptural handling of concrete masses is the hallmark of Förderer's works. As in the Im Gräfler School, Stettmerstrasse (1969–74), the use of a free plan and the emphasis on the volumetric arrangement does not exclude standardized solutions, while the handling of the stair as a light-sensitive element, gives the main hall a special spatial feel. Nearby is the Munot Nursery School, Munothaldenweg 1 (1932–33), designed by Wolfgang Müller.

Werk, 9, 1965; L'Architecture d'aujourd'hui, 9, 1965; 53, 1966; Schweizer Journal, 3, 1975.

Schaffhausen

Extension of Home for the Elderly

Stokarbergstrasse 21

1985–90

Rainer and Leonhard Ott with P. Studer

A heterogeneous complex made up of a fifteenth-century hospice – later converted to a home for the elderly – and the remains of a Neo-Gothic church, destroyed by fire in 1944, were renovated and extended in a design sensitive to the topographic features of the site.

A similar emphasis on the importance of the site can also be read in the Housing, Surbeckstieg 2–16 (1981–85), built by the same architects.

Cantonal School

Home for the Elderly

Opposite page: Georg Fischer Ag: Overall view with Kellermüller buildings, Moser building, Bäny building

Thurgau

Amriswil

School Complex

Egelmoosstrasse 8

1960–62

Cedric Guhl, Max Lechner, Walter Philipp, and Paul Kollbrunner

Comprising a kindergarten, secondary school and gymnasium, the Egelmoos complex is organized round a green atrium, the focal point of the composition. Technical difficulties forced the designers to raise the whole building and organize the functions on various levels.

Werk, 6, 1964; Guide to Swiss Architecture, 1920–1990, vol. 1, 001, p. 17.

Arbon

Adolph Saurer AG Headquarters

Schlossgasse 2

1942–43

Georges Pierre Dubois and Jakob Eschenmoser

This office building has a highly articulated volumetric character, while the facade is measured in effect through the use of natural materials. Having worked several times for the same clients, twenty years later, Dubois built the computer section (Weitegasse) and housing financed by the Saurer pension funds (Brühlstrasse 63). These works show evident influences from Le Corbusier's Brutalist vocabulary in the radical expressive tension of the reinforced-concrete structure.

Schweizerische Bauzeitung, 124, 1944; Werk, 6, 1944; Moderne Schweizer Architektur 1925–1945, Basel 1947; H. Volkart, Schweizer Architektur, Ravensburg 1951; I. Noseda and M. Steinmann, Zeitzeichen, Schweizer Baukultur im 19. und 20. Jh., Zürich 1988; Guide to Swiss Architecture 1920–1990, vol. 1, 003, p. 18.

Frauenfeld

Auen High School

Thurstrasse 23

1967–68, 1991–92

Alfons Barth and Hans Zaugg assisted by U. Wildi and H. Scheibler

The freely arranged glass and steel cubes were suitably complemented in the 1990s. Noble simplicity, also in the quality of the detailing, characterizes the overall ambience. Flexibility and clarity determine the interior layout and design.

Bauen und Wohnen, 10, 1967; Werk, 7, 1969; Detail, 2, 1970; Schweizerische Bauzeitung, 20, 1970; Guide to Swiss Architecture 1920–1990, vol. 1, 005, p. 19

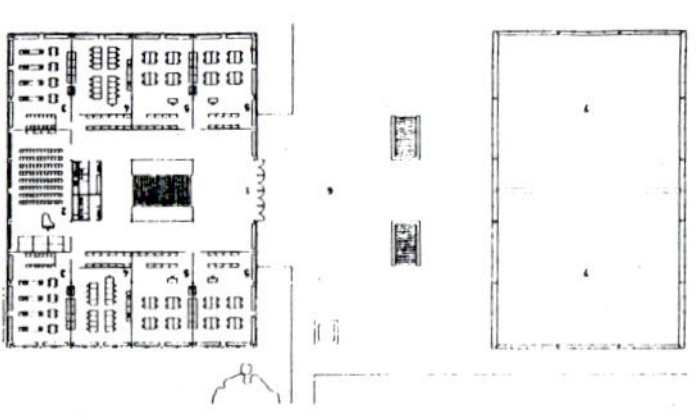

Auen High School, floor plan

School Complex

Adolph Saurer AG,
period photo

Auen High School,
model view

Mammern
Holiday Cottage
Spannacker
1937
Alfred Roth

As a building designed purely as a summer retreat, this elongated timber-framed construction only has to satisfy a modest demands. However, it still exhibits clever, functional details: for example, upon leaving, the windows can be easily secured with folding shutters and a glass wall on the covered patio protected behind a lattice screen.
Among other significant works dating from the 1930s in the Thurgau canton is the house at Rudwies 21a, Egnach, completed by Ernst Schindler in 1932.

Schweizerische Bauzeitung, 117–144, 1941; Moderne Schweizer Architektur 1925–1945, Basel 1947; G.E. Kidder Smith, Switzerland Builds, New York-Stockholm 1950; Werk, 1, 1968; Guide to Swiss Architecture 1920–1990, vol. 1, 008, p. 21.

Romanshorn
Multipurpose Center
Alleestrasse/Hafenstrasse/
Sternenstrasse
1987–93
Martin Spühler
with P. Trachsler

The design was conceived in keeping with the new urban plan for the town. The central space in the complex is a court open to the south with an "artificial garden" set above the parking and

Holiday Cottage, period photo

Multipurpose Center, court

flanked by accommodation for the elderly. Shops and offices are arranged on the street fronts, while the court is connected to the two wings by a passageway.

Warth

Ittingen Carthusian Monastery Conference Center and Museum

1978–92

Overall plan and conference center: Esther and Rudolf Guyer

Museum: René Antoniol and Kurt Huber

This monastery, founded in 1152 and taken over by the Carthusian order in 1461, was bought in 1977 by a foundation with its High-Baroque church in a very poor state of repair. In conjunction with the Listed Buildings Dept, the former utility buildings, the "external property of the Carthusian monastery", were converted into a training and conference center. The only completely new building is an elongated guesthouse. The northern wing of the cloisters with seven monk cells, erected on the old foundations, houses the Thurgau Art Gallery.

Holz Bulletin, 9, 1983; Deutsche Bauzeitschrift, 7, 1985; Detail, 2, 1986; P. Disch, L'Architettura recente nella Svizzera tedesca 1980–1990, Lugano 1991, p. 241; Guide to Swiss Architecture 1920–1990, vol. 1, 020, p. 28.

Multipurpose Center, internal view

Cantonal Fine Arts Museum and Study Center

Sankt Gallen

Henau

Felsegg Bridge over the River Thur

between Henau and Uzwil

1933

Robert Maillart

Spanning 72 meters, the Felsegg Bridge is Maillart's first open hollow box-girder design on a pointed arch. The same temporary works were used for both girders. Maillart provided open balustrading instead of solid parapets.

Max Bill, Robert Maillart, Zürich 3. Aufl. 1969; David Billington, Robert Maillart and the Art of Reinforced Concrete, New York and Zurich 1990; Guide to Swiss Architecture 1920–1990, vol. 1, 201, p. 51; Peter Marti und Emil Honnegger, Robert Maillart – Betonvirtuose. exhibition catalogue ETH, Zurich 1996.

Oberuzwil

Catholic Church

Neugasse 14

1934–35

Fritz Metzger

The imposing volume of the pitched-roof church towers up above the rest of the Oberuzwil complex (curia, cloister, and cemetery). The nave is entirely made of reinforced concrete, while the extensive lateral stained-glass windows providing natural lighting are the outcome of collaboration between the architect and artist C. Roesch.

Werk, 4, 1937; Moderne Schweizer Architektur 1925–1945, Basel 1947; G.E. Kidder Smith, Switzerland Builds, New York-Stockholm 1950; S. von Moos et al., Das Neue Bauen in der Ostschweiz, Sankt Gallen 1989; Guide to Swiss Architecture 1920–1990, vol. 1, 206, p. 54.

Sankt Gallen

House

Sonnenhaldenstrasse 65

1931

Arthur Kopf

A compact cube with a roof terrace, this single-family house is characterized by a suspended external stair and the complete absence of any ornamentation. With various influences from the architecture of Adolf Loos and Le Corbusier's Pessac works, the house is a significant example of Rationalist architecture in Sankt Gallen.

Das ideale Heim, 11, 1937; S. von Moos et al., Das Neue Bauen in der Ostschweiz, Sankt Gallen 1989; Guide to Swiss Architecture 1920–1990, vol. 1, 102, p. 36.

Felsegg Bridge

Catholic Church

House

Sankt Gallen

Housing

Dianastrasse 15

1933

Housing

Falkensteinstrasse 92–96b

1934–35

Moritz Hauser

By applying the esthetics of the essential while aware of the new models for dwellings, in the rented accommodation on Dianastrasse Moritz Hauser designed small units in a balconied apartment block with terrace-solariums and common services. The Falkensteinstrasse Housing, on the other hand, consists of three parallel rows of houses with the same plan (day zone on the ground floor and night zone on the first floor). Both works exalt utility as the main design criterion.

Among Hauser's late works in Sankt Gallen is the Housing, Kapellenstrasse 3 (1952–53).

S. von Moos et al., Das Neue Bauen in der Ostschweiz, ein Inventar, Sankt Gallen 1989; Guide to Swiss Architecture 1920–1990, vol. 1, 103, p. 36; 104, p. 37.

Dianastrasse Housing

Falkensteinstrasse Housing

Sankt Gallen

School of Economic and Social Sciences

Dufourstrasse 50

1957–63

Walter M. Förderer, Rolf Otto, and Hans Zwimpfer

Bruno Gerosa

The complex is made up of various buildings grouped round the main volume according to a free plan. The four lecture halls and administrative department are reached by crossing the entrance atrium with its striking freestanding sculptural stairway. Although inevitably built with standardized components, their effect is attenuated through an expressive architectural quality, at times integrated with elements from the figurative arts. Sculptures and paintings by various artists (including Arp, Calder, Giacometti, Miró, and Tápies) are arranged in a series of special spaces both inside and outside the buildings. Designed to fit in harmoniously with the rest of the complex, the Library (1986–89) was built by Bruno Gerosa.

Werk, 4, 1962; 8, 1963; 12, 1964; Architecture, formes + fonction, 10, 1963–64; A. Altherr, New Swiss Architecture, Teufen 1965; Guide to Swiss Architecture 1920–1990, vol. 1, 112, p. 41.

Sankt Gallen

Municipal Theater

Museumstrasse 24

1961–68

Claude Paillard (Cramer-Jaray-Paillard) with H. Gügler

Situated in a city park beside a concert hall and Museum of Fine Arts, the Municipal Theater is an imposing dynamic building entirely constructed in exposed concrete. The hexagonal plan opens up to the surroundings, providing easy access towards the foyer. The main auditorium is reached by a spiral stair with a series of rhythmically arranged landings. The asymmetric shape of the auditorium ensures a high degree of flexibility for viewing the stage.

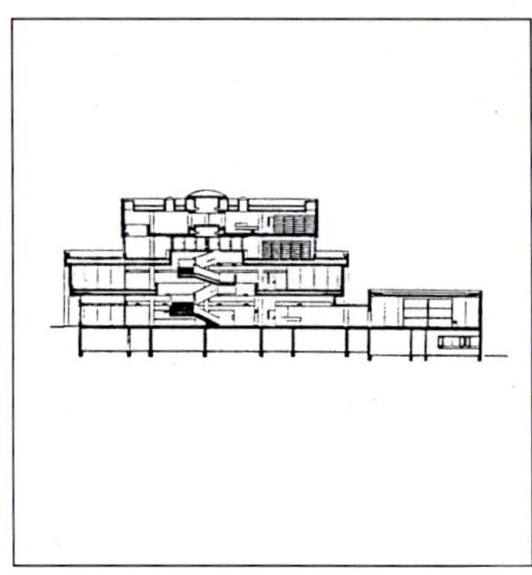

Bauen und Wohnen, 12, 1968; Werk, 12, 1968; Bauwelt, 1969, 17; J. Bachmann and S. von Moos, New Directions in Swiss Architecture, New York 1969; Architettura Svizzera, 9, 1973; Werk, Bauen und Wohnen, 1–2, 1980; Guide to Swiss Architecture 1920–1990, vol. 1, 115, p. 43.

School of Economic and Social Sciences, view and, opposite page, section

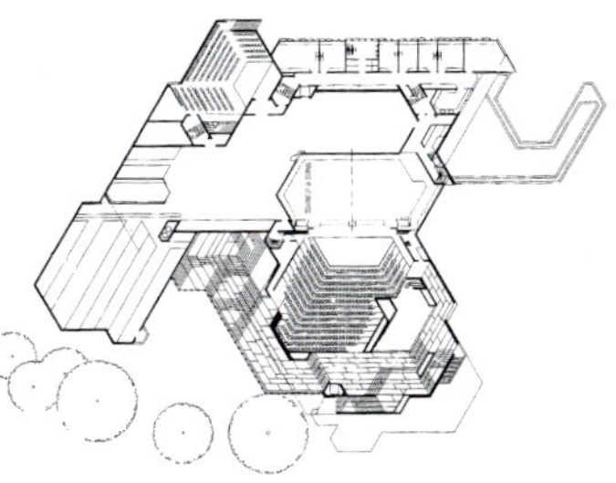

Municipal Theater, exterior view, stairway, and floor plan

Sankt Gallen
Renovation and Extension of the Museum of Natural History and Fine Arts
Museumstrasse 32
1981–87
Marcel Ferrier with C. Simmler and A. Sommer

After a long debate over whether the City Museum – built by Christoph Kunkler in 1877 – should be pulled down or preserved, a competition was held to renovate the building. The winning design proposed a critical re-interpretation of the existing structure. The former hall, situated on the west, becomes the main entrance linking the semi-underground wings housing the natural history collections and the twentieth-century art department. The new extension was added along the longitudinal axis of the building, whereas on the sides, two semi-circular spaces (for temporary exhibitions and multipurpose rooms) seem to rise up out of the ground, redefining the overall shape of the complex.

Archithese, 1, 1986; Werk, Bauen und Wohnen, 5, 1988; 12, 1989; Rivista Tecnica, 1–2, 1988; Schweizer Architekten, Winterthur 1990; Abitare, 296, 1991; P. Disch (ed), L'architettura recente nella Svizzera tedesca 1980–1990, Lugano 1991, p. 246; Guide to Swiss Architecture 1920–1990, vol. 1, 119, p. 45.

Sevelen-Werdenberg
Highway Service Station and Footbridge
Highway N13
1988–90
Quintus Miller, Paola Maranta, and Christoph Mathys, Walter Bieler with M. Schmid

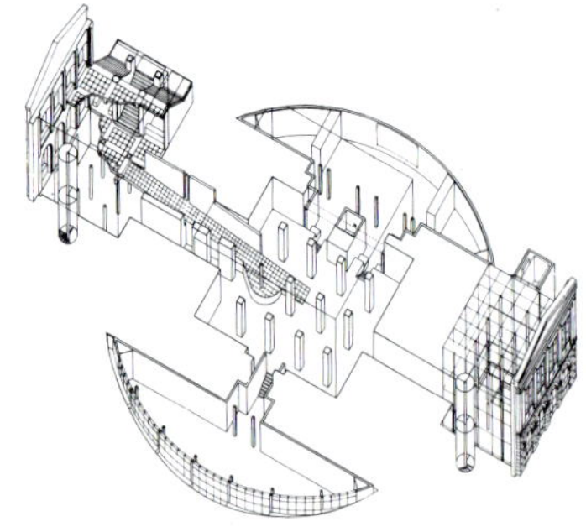

Museum of Natural History and Fine Arts

A wooden footbridge resting on reinforced-concrete supports over the highway alludes to traditional covered bridges joining up old watchtowers. The project must be credited with providing an elegant design for an often banally handled theme; the architectural effect is achieved with simple building elements.

Hochparterre, 6, 1990; W. Stadelmann, Holzbrücken der Schweiz, Chur 1990; Holz Bulletin, 32, 1992; Werk, Bauen und Wohnen, 3, 1992; Guide to Swiss Architecture 1920–1990, vol. 1, 212, p. 57.

Wattwil

Heberlein & Co. Industrial Plant

Bahnhofstrasse / Ebnaterstrasse 79

1925, 1969–71

Ziegler & Balmer

Walter Custer, Fred Hochstrasser and Hans Bleiker

With its high-format, transomed windows and column heads inside the building, this textiles factory dating from 1925 reminds the observer of a nineteenth-century establishment. In complete contrast to this, the production and administration buildings (1969–71) of this expanding business marked a peak in the evolution of the industrial architecture of their time: the internal layouts are flexible and the aluminum facades exhibit grid-like peripheries with integral solar protection which lend the building a lightness in the manner of Egon Eiermann.

Baumeister, 12, 1971; Schweizerische Bauzeitung, 34, 1971; 10, 1971; Architettura Svizzera, 9, 1973; Werk, Bauen und Wohnen, 1–2, 1980; S. von Moos et al., Das Neue Bauen in der Ostschweiz, Sankt Gallen 1989; Guide to Swiss Architecture 1920–1990, vol. 1, 216, p. 60.

Highway Service Station and Footbridge

Heberlein Industrial Plant

Wattwil

House and Studio

Volkshausstrasse 24

1930

Fritz Engler

Fritz Engler attracted great attention in Wattwil in 1930 with his "roofless" house and office completed in just 3½ months. Economic with both space and material, designed with function in mind and omitting any decorative ingredients, it is the first example of modern architecture in the region.

Another interesting work in Wattwil is Heberlein House, Eichhofstrasse 6, built in 1940–41 by Max Ernst Haefeli.

S. von Moos et al., Das Neue Bauen in der Ostschweiz, Sankt Gallen 1989; Guide to Swiss Architecture 1920–1990, vol. 1, 217, p. 61.

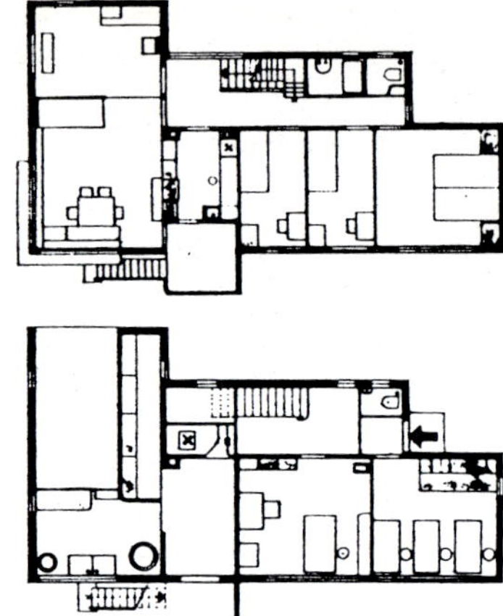

Widnau

Beldona Textile Factory

Nöllenstrasse 13

1985–87

Suter & Suter

The outcome of a invitation competition, the building was designed to meet the brief criteria of functionality, flexibility and efficiency. The volumes are strongly characterized by the sloping structure of the shed-style roofing echoing the glazed-wall fronts.

Werk, Bauen und Wohnen, 10, 1989; Guide to Swiss Architecture 1920–1990, vol. 1, 220, p. 62.

Wil

Hürlimann Works

Churfirstenstrasse 54

1937–39, 1947, 1967

Paul Truniger and Fritz Vogt

This factory was built in various stages from the 1930s on and shows the sober and pragmatic approach of the owner-client and former craftsman Hans Hürlimann. The original layout can be read in the symmetrical entrance front containing the offices, and houses of the owner and managing director. The plan highlights the underlying early industrial notion of controlling production. The subsequent extensions attempt to continue the original matrix to meet new requirements.

S. von Moos et al., Das Neue Bauen in der Ostschweiz, Sankt Gallen 1989.

House and Studio, view and, opposite page, floor plans

Beldona Textile Factory

Hürlimann Works, period photo

Appenzell

Herisau
Cantonal Psychiatric Clinic
Krombach 1–15
1906–08
Rittmeyer & Furrer

The architects responded to the functional needs of the clinic using the well-tried solution of the pavilion building type. In keeping with the widespread nineteenth-century conception of health and hygiene, the clinic is isolated in a green area on the outskirts of the city. The various pavilions for treatment or wards are handled in the *Heimatstil.*

Schweizerische Bauzeitung, 56, 1910; INSA. Inventario Svizzero di Architettura 1850–1920, vol. I, Berne 1984.

Cantonal Psychiatric Clinic

Herisau
Cantonal Bank
Obstmarkt 1
1977–84
Ernst Gisel
with P. Meyer, R. Cremer, and W. Schlaf

Standing at the end of the Obstmarktplatz, the new bank alludes to the traditonal character and proprotions of Appenzell architecture through the treatment of the facades. The upper floors projecting out over the base strengthen the portico, while the roof is on a similar scale to neighboring constructions. The attempt to establish a relation with the local context is reflected in the use of materials, which acquire patinas over time (such as the copper for the pillar cladding, and lead

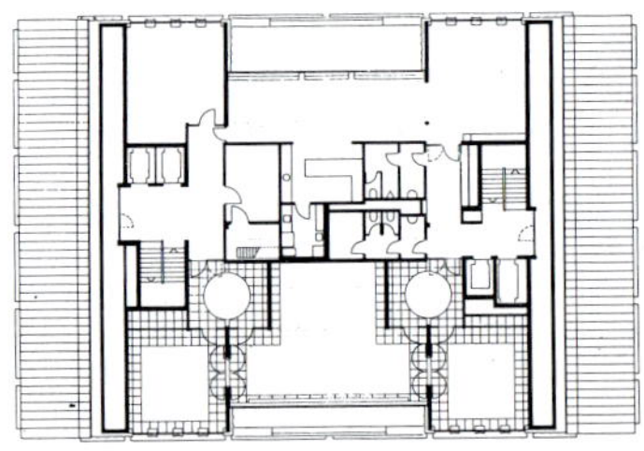

Cantonal Bank, view and plan

in the fronts) and the design of the inclined elements protecting the windows.

Werk-archithese, 25–26, 1979; Archithese, 1, 1986; Detail, 4, 1986; Rivista Tecnica, 1–2, 1986; Guide to Swiss Architecture 1920–1990, vol. 1, 204, p. 53.

Trogen

Pestalozzi Village

1946–49, 1959–60, and 1967–68

Hans Fischli

Max Graf

Ernst Gisel

Founded immediately after the Second World War by the Swiss philanthropist, Walter Robert Corti, this village became the model for many similar foundations which offer hospitality to orphans or refugees no matter what their race or nationality. Following an invitation competition, Fischli built the first-phase housing, then in the 1950s Graf added the schools and staff accommodation. The complex was completed with Gisel's wooden chapel, whose plastic form makes it a fitting place for ecumenical worship.

Schweizerische Bauzeitung, 128, 1946; 45, 46, and 47, 1949; L'Architecture d'aujourd'hui, 25, 1949; H. Volkart, Schweizer Architektur, Ravensburg 1951; J. Maurizio, Der Siedlungsbau in der Schweiz 1940–1950, Erlenbach 1952; Werk, 3, 1961; 3, 1969; Guide to Swiss Architecture 1920–1990, vol. 1, 213, p. 58.

Pestalozzi Village, aerial view

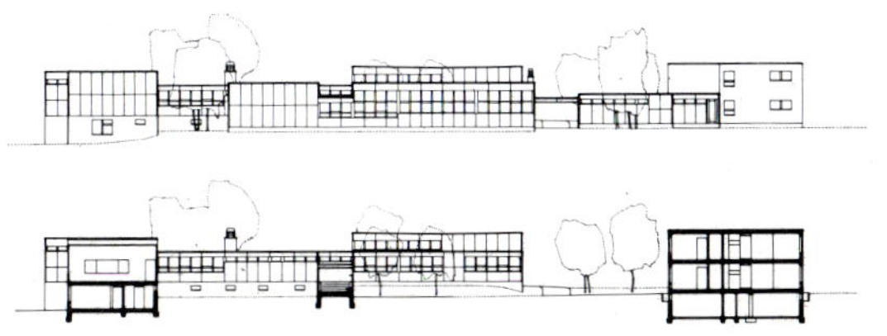

Pestalozzi Village Schools, elevation and section

Principality of Liechtenstein

Schaan

School and Recreation Center

1973–76

Walter Schindler

This complex for a school and various recreation facilities is grouped round three central areas connected by partially covered passages. The alternation of high and low buildings, the fan-like arrangement of the windows and the mobile partitions are all combined to obtain optimal natural lighting and the greatest spatial flexibility – the starting point for educational experimentation.

Schellenberg

Catholic Church

1958–63

Eduard Ladner

with G. Malin, F. Weigner, and R. Galizia

Situated on a plateau overlooking a valley, the church's soberly arranged volumes combine with the internal spiraling itinerary to heighten the spiritual dimension of the architecture.

Werk, 1, 1965; Guide to Swiss Architecture 1920–1990, vol. 1, 211, p. 56.

Vaduz

Mühleholz School Complex

Marianumstrasse 45

1968–90

Ernst Gisel

with C. Zweifel

Built following a 1968 competition and extended in the 1980s, this school complex includes grammar and scientific high schools, a gymnasium, a library, chapel and accommodation for the clergy who run the school. The free plan organizes the functions in various buildings, joined up by collective passages and places.

In addition to the Vaduz Terrace Housing, Schalunstrasse 1–9, in Liechtenstein, see also Gisel's Schaan Theater, Reberastrasse 12, (1972).

Architettura razionale, exhibition catalogue, Milan 1973; Architectural Design, 8, 1977; A + u, architecture and urbanism, 8, 1977; Costruire, 109, 1978; Werk-Archithese, 13–14, 1978; W. Blaser, Architecture 70/80 in Switzerland, Basel 1981.

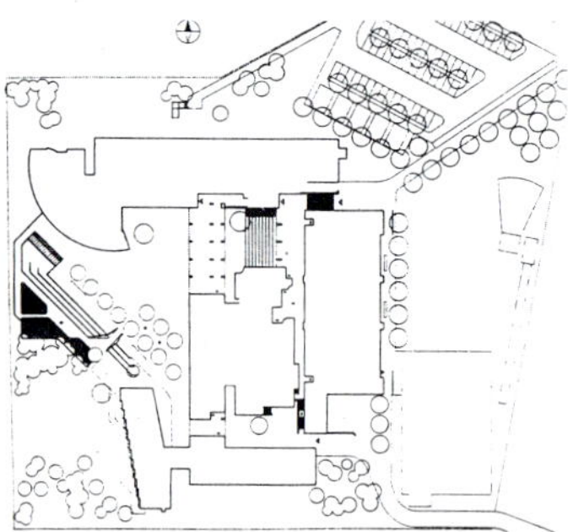

School and Recreation Center, site plan

School and Recreation Center, view

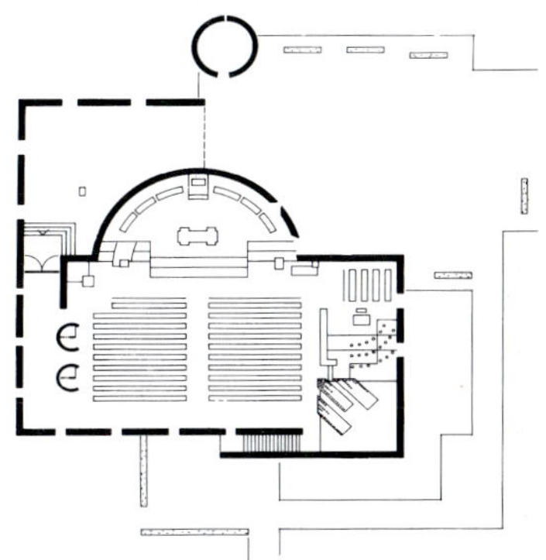

Catholic Church, internal view and floor plan

Mühleholz School Complex

Aargau

Aarau
Outdoor Swimming Baths
Uferpromenade/Schützenhausweg
1952
Max Ernst Haefeli, Werner Max Moser, and Rudolf Steiger
The Aarau Baths were designed using similar elements to the Allenmoos Baths (see p. 60), built in Zürich by the same architects before the war. Located on the bank of a river, the complex consists of swimming pools and various pavilions with dressing rooms and restaurant set in green suroundings.
L'Architecture d'aujourd'hui, 121, 1965.

Aarau
Office Building
Laurenzenvorstadt 11
1987–92
Urs Burkard, Adrian Meyer and Max Steiger
with D. Krieg, H. Nienhaus, M. Blatter, and W. Tehlar
The round-shaped building becomes a key orientation point for the diverse buildings arranged along the perimeter of the area. The excellent functional organization is combined with the successful articulation of the volumes and careful detailing, highlighting each individual element in the project.
P. Disch (ed), L'architettura recente nella Svizzera tedesca 1980–1990, Lugano 1991, p. 110.

Outdoor Swimming Baths, period photo

Office Building, court and internal view

Baden

NOK Building

Parkstrasse 23

1927–28

Otto and Werner Pfister

The administrative building of the NOK (the electric company for north-east Switzerland) is a squat three-floor volume, characterized by mansard roofs and an imposing granite cornice. The apertures interrupted by projecting string courses give the facades a tight geometric rhythm. The same architects had previously built a dam for NOK in the canton of Schwyz (Wäggital, 1923–24).

50 Jahre Nordostschweizerische Kraftwerke AG Baden, Zurich 1965; INSA. Inventario Svizzero di Architettura 1850–1920, vol. I, Berne 1984.

Baden

Post Office

Bahnhofstrasse 3

1929–31

Karl Moser

A prototype for post offices both in terms of functional organization and constructional features, Moser's building arranges the various offices round an atrium. The structural skeleton is in reinforced concrete, while the facades are clad in artificial stone. Among the many works built by Curjel & Moser at Baden at the turn of the century, see Villa Boveri, Ländliweg 5 (1895–97), Villa Langmatt, Römerstrasse 30 (1899–1906) and Villa Burghalde, Mellingerstrasse 34 (1904–05).

INSA. Inventario Svizzero di Architettura, vol. I, Berne 1984.

NOK Building

Post Office

Baden
Municipal Services Headquarters
Haselstrasse 15
1931–34
Robert Lang and Hans Loepfe
Renovation
1987–89
Eppler, Maraini and Associates
This building is one of the most interesting architectural works in Baden from the 1930s. The outcome of a joint project by Robert Lang and Hans Loepfe (who had come first and second in a 1931 competition with Otto Salvisberg in the jury), the complex is organized in a series of exposed reinforced-concrete buildings carefully divided into the main volume, workshops and commercial wing. The impressively balanced composition of the facades is achieved by large glazed sections and ribbon windows modulated by metal profiles.
Neues Bauen in der Schweiz, Führer zur Architektur der 20er und 30er Jahre, Blauen 1985; Guide to Swiss Architecture 1920–1990, vol. 2, 213, p. 100.

Baden
Brown Boveri Industrial Complex
Haselstrasse/Bruggerstrasse/
Wiesenstrasse
1942–46
Roland Rohn
The industrial complex of Brown Boveri, a major Swiss manufacturer of electric machinery, dates from the late

Above left:
Municipal Services
Headquarters

Brown Boveri
Industrial Complex,
aerial view and
period photo of
offices

nineteenth century and was a fundamental element in the urban growth of Baden. The buildings added by Rohn in the 1940s are organized as pure volumes. The two buildings on Haselstrasse (workshops and offices) are marked by restrained vertical apertures which, in the Bruggerstrasse building, are combined with the horizontal emphasis of the ribbon windows.

H. Volkart, Schweizer Architektur, Ravensburg 1951; Werk, 7, 1954; INSA. Inventario Svizzero di Architettura 1850–1920, vol. I, Berne 1984; Guide to Swiss Architecture 1920–1990, vol. 2, 209, p. 96.

Baden
Chapel and Crematorium
Liebenfels Cemetery
1957
Edi and Ruth Lanners
with Res Wahlen

Beside an old cemetery on a south-facing slope, a path in the landscape, marked out by suitably religious bare and severe architectural elements, leads to a rectangular church-square with a large bronze fountain, the chapel and crematorium. The sloping chapel roof and concrete portal solemnly rise up above perimeter walls defining an enclosure.

The same architects also designed the Catholic Church (1965), situated alongside the Windisch Roman amphitheater.

Schweizerisches Baublatt, 7, 1957; Werk, 10, 1959; Deutsche Bauzeitschrift, 8, 1960; A. Altherr, New Swiss Architecture, Teufen 1965; Guide to Swiss Architecture 1920–1990, vol. 2, 215, p. 101.

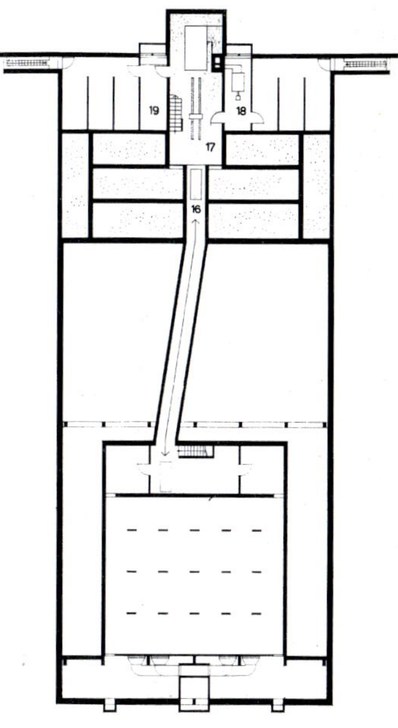

Chapel and
Crematorium

Baden
Cantonal School
Seminarstrasse 3
1960–64
Fritz Haller
with E. Meier, A. Rigert, and J. Iten
Well-known for his studies on steel structural systems, Fritz Haller applied the results of industrialisation in the building sector to architecture. Fully aware of the importance of the production process and the specific properties of materials, Haller seeks to establish a neutral relationship between building and function with flexible uses and scope for redevelopment. The criteria informing his modular research range from the definitions of individual buildings to the overall site plan arrangements. In this case various parallelepipeds contain the classrooms, gym and administration.
Bauen und Wohnen, 10, 1964; 7–8, 1981; 7–8, 1992; Domus, 695, 1988; Guide to Swiss Architecture 1920–1990, vol. 2, 216, p. 101.

Baden
Multipurpose Building
Bahnhofstrasse 40–42
1979–83
Urs Burkard, Adrian Meyer, and Max Steiger
with Y. Morin, R. Dietiker, H. Nienhaus, and P. Süsstrunk
Höchi Center
Höchi, Dättwil
1984–88
Urs Burkard, Adrian Meyer, and Max Steiger
with W. Arnold, H. Nienhaus, P. Zimmermann, C. Schweizer, and R. Tedeschi
Mixed-Use Building
Martinsberstrasse 40
1989–92
Urs Burkard, Adrian Meyer, and Max Steiger
with R. Ganz, W. Knecht, and D. Bannwart
Located in the station area, the Multipurpose Building accommodates a Cantonal Bank, department store, shops and apartments. The main focus in the design is a modular clinker element intended to create not simply a large container but an integrated piece of the urban fabric. The urban situation is tackled at various levels. A plaza, road, and portico are related by perspective views between the various floors and staggered levels. In the works of Burkard, Meyer and Steiger, architecture is conceived of as the "art of building". Through this process the specific character of each building and its original urban matrix are given shape.
The same Aarau studio designed the Crédit Suisse at Lenzburg, Bahnhofplatz (1987–91).
Rivista Tecnica, 1–2, 1984; Domus, 657, 1985; Werk, Bauen und Wohnen, 3, 1989; P. Disch (ed), L'architettura recente nella Svizzera tedesca 1980–1990, Lugano 1991, p. 124 and 127; Guide to Swiss Architecture 1920–1990, vol. 2, 218, p. 102; 222, p. 104; 219, p. 103.

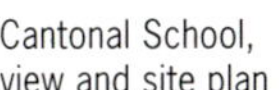

Cantonal School, view and site plan

Middle left: Multipurpose Building

Middle right: Mixed-Use Building

Höchi Center

Baden-Dättwil

Housing

Pilgerstrasse

1985–87

Werner Egli and Hans Rohr with U. Müller, J. Meyer, and R. Hofmann

Situated in the environs of Baden, the scheme consists of six rows of houses and a five-unit apartment block forming the south-eastern corner. The designers have attempted to overcome the anonymous aspect of peripheral city life by making the dwellings highly individual, creating external spaces and introducing roof gardens.

The same studio also designed the extension to the Burghalde District School (1982–86).

Werk, Bauen und Wohnen, 6, 1988; Ideales Heim, 3, 1991; P. Disch (ed), L'Architettura recente nella Svizzera tedesca 1980–1990, Lugano 1991, p. 123; Guide to Swiss Architecture 1920–1990, vol. 2, 222, p. 104f.

Baden

History Museum

Landvogteischloß

1988–92

Wilfrid and Katharina Steib

Soberly integrated into a river landscape, the History Museum is shaped like a convex element clinging to the mountain by means of a reinforced-concrete structure, while on the old-city side the horizontal emphasis of the facade is underscored by ribbon windows. There are pedestrian walkways round the perimeter walls. Simple materials were chosen: exposed concrete, zinc for the roof, copper, glass and wood.

Housing

History Museum

P. Disch (ed), L'Architettura recente nella Svizzera tedesca 1980–1990, Lugano 1991, p. 132; Werk, Bauen und Wohnen, 12, 1992; Hochparterre, 12, 1992; Bauwelt, 35, 1993; C. Affolter, Unsere Kunstdenkmäler, Berne 1993; Guide to Swiss Architecture 1920–1990, vol. 2, 221, p. 106.

Baden
Extension to the Kappelerhof School Complex
1991–92
Kornfeldweg
Dolf Schnebli
with S. Häuselmann, D. Bastianello, B. Trinkler, M. Sollberger, P. Stäuble, and P. Vollenweider

The designers' initial concern was to integrate a small new local school into an existing complex. Two geometrical systems – the perpendicular grid of the roads and the oblique position of the existing school facing south east – led to the classrooms being arranged along an arc of the complex circumference. Access to the entrance – a large atrium situated between the road and a multipurpose room – runs between a rear wall protecting from street noise and the classrooms. Simplicity in the choice of materials and details is contrasted by the spatial experience in the rich play of light on the walls as well as the interesting rhythms and relations between the whole and its parts. Another significant example of the new being integrated in a historical context is the House and Shop, Alte Zürcherstrasse 13, built by Schnebli and Isidor Ryser in 1989–90.

The Architectural Review, 1, 1991; du, 5, 1992; Werk, Bauen und Wohnen, 3, 1994.

History Museum, interior view

Extension to the Kappelerhof School Complex

Bremgarten
Barracks
north-western town outskirts
1959–68
Esther and Rudolf Guyer, and Manuel Pauli
with F. Zwahlen

Designed to provide accommodation for around 700 soldiers, the Bremgarten barracks were constructed using innovative prefabrication techniques. Although the repeated elements are uniformly arranged, the overall effect is surprisingly plastic.

Schweizerische Bauzeitung, 10, 1960; Schweizerische Journal, 11, 1966; Werk, 8, 1968.

Brugg
Stahlrain Mixed-Use Building
Stahlrain 2/am Perron
1985–93
Metron
(Ueli Rüegg, Franz Roth, and Gioconda De Min)

This triangular-plan building for offices and appartments overlooks Brugg station. The plan round a central court – the vertical links and common services are situated at the top of the building – leaves two wings free for offices and the third eastern wing for apartments. The handling of the windows highlights the sinuous Eternit-clad facades. Among other recent works by this Aarau studio is the Cantonal Hospital (1984–92).

Hochparterre, 9, 1993; Architektur & Technik, 1, 1994.

Brugg-Windisch
Technical College
Klosterzelgstrasse
1962–66
Fritz Haller
with A. Rigert, and J. Iten

The tendency to seek universal solutions, based on a vision of the building as an object in the production process, leads Haller to adopt a modular system. In this way he creates free spatial relations, leaving it up to the user to organize the internal surfaces according to specific functional requirements. In the Brugg-Windisch Technical College the various educational facilities are organized in two simple volumes: the principal cubic volume houses a showroom, administrative offices and lecture hall, while the workshops are situated in a parallelepiped.

Bauen und Wohnen, 8, 1968; 7–8, 1981; 7–8, 1992; Detail, 1, 1969; J. Bachmann and S. von Moos, New Directions in Swiss Architecture, New York 1969; Archithese, 1, 1982; Fritz Haller bauen und forschen, Solothurn 1988; Guide to Swiss Architecture 1920–1990, vol. 2, 253, p. 123.

Oppposite page:
Technical College

Barracks

Stahlrain Mixed-Use Building, view and section

Laufenburg
Professional School
Winterthurerstrasse 3
1985–92
Marianne Burkhalter and Christian Sumi with C. Amrein and A. Froelich
The school building is part of a global project dating from a 1985 competition, which included a home for the elderly and the raising of a shopping center. The single volume of the school is designed in three functional layers. The southern front facing the road contains the entrance, public library and staff rooms. Separated from the horizontal distribution and oriented to north, the third layer contains the classrooms organized on two levels. The rich internal solution includes the anti-naturalistic use of materials providing the basis for sensual plays of light.
Werk, Bauen und Wohnen, 12, 1992; Hochparterre, 11, 1992; Lotus international, 73, 1992; Faces, 27, 1993; Domus, 754, 1993; Guide to Swiss Architecture 1920–1990, vol. 2, 234, p. 112.

Lenzburg
Parish Center
Bahnhofstrasse
1983–94
Luigi Snozzi with Bruno Jenni with C. Buetti, E. Domenighini, R. Cavadini, and M. Arnaboldi
The key idea in the project is the creation of a plaza, linked to Bahnhofstrasse, and of a park towards Turnerweg, containing a children's home similar to the typical villas in the quarter. The urban context includes a number of existing buildings: a church with bell-tower and the parish community house, an old chapel (renovated with the addition of a new bell-tower marking the entrance to the plaza) and housing along Bahnhofstrasse. The area behind the common spaces provides a link between plaza and park.
Rivista Tecnica, 11, 1983; T. Boga, Tessiner Architekten, Zürich 1986.

Möhlin
Bat'a Colony
along the Rhine, west of Basel
1930–60
Hannibal Naef
The colony was founded in 1930 by the Czech shoe manufacturer Tomás Bat'a (1876–1932). From Zlín he promoted workers' villages throughout the world even involving Le Corbusier in various projects for Bat'a factories and shops. Designed for both shoe manufacturing and dwellings with leisure activities, the Möhlin complex has considerable architectural qualities. Moreover, it highlights a corporate strategy in keeping with the enlightened entrepreneurial ideas of the day, combining ethical and social principles with production incentives. Working alongside the company architects, who decided the main lines of the various projects using well-defined models, Hannibal Naef dealt with the Colony in the 1940s and '50s.
Another interesting work by the same architect is the Schelling Paper Factory at Rümlang, Oberglatter-

strasse 13 (1949–51), in the canton of Zürich.

Rassegna, 3, 1980; J. L. Cohen, Article Bat'a in: Le Corbusier (Centre Pompidou publication), Paris 1987; Die Bata-Kolonie in Möhlin, exhibition catalogue, Basel 1992; Guide to Swiss Architecture 1920–1990, vol. 2, 239, p. 115.

Laufenburg School

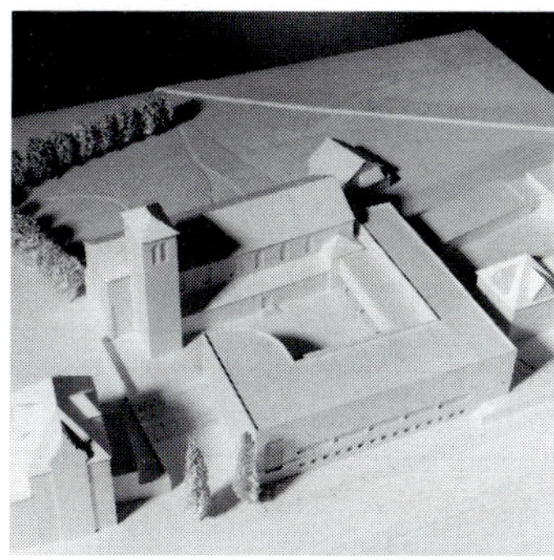

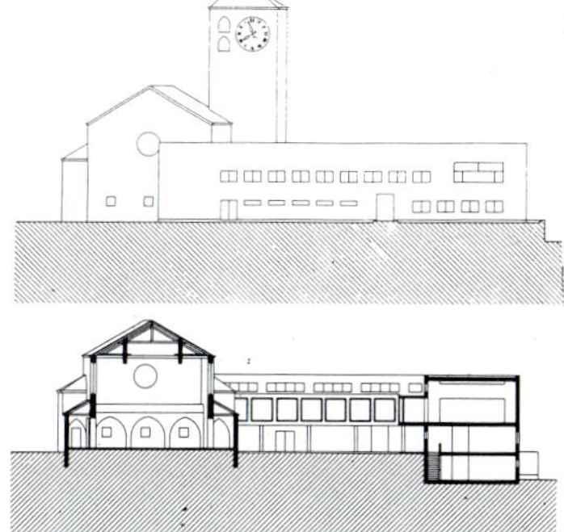

Parish Center, model view, elevation and section

Bat'a Colony

Mülligen
Siedlung Loh
1985–87
Metron
(Ueli Rüegg, Franz Roth, and Gioconda De Min)
with J. Kleiner

The Metron studio has contributed a number of significant works testifying to its successful design experience in the field of housing. Characterized in the 1960s by the attempt to make architecture a truly inter-disciplinary profession and inspired by constructivist realism, their research focuses on rationalizing uses, forms and materials in relation to the specific context in question.

Among Metron's other housing schemes in the canton of Aargau are the Siedlung Zelgli at Windisch, Zelgliacherstrasse (1979–81), and Oepfelbaum at Stetten, Baumgartenstrasse (1984–86).

J. Bachmann and S. von Moos, New Directions in Swiss Architecture, New York 1969; Werk-archithese, 21–22, 1978; Aktuelles Bauen, 8, 1980; Archithese, 2, 1985; Werk, Bauen und Wohnen, 12, 1985; 10, 1989; P. Disch (ed), L'architettura recente nella Svizzera tedesca 1980–1990, Lugano 1991, p. 122.

Siedlungen Loh, Zelgli and Oepfelbaum

Suhr

Shopping Center

Bernstrasse-West

1984–86

Santiago Calatrava and Peter Frey

Bärenmatte Community Center

1984–88

Santiago Calatrava with G. Herting

Calatrava's flair for creating sculptural forms has produced extraordinary structural inventions in these two successful experiments. The roof of the concert hall in the Bärenmatte Community Center is shaped like a stringed instrument: the V-section box girders rest on perimeter pillars with steel traction cables covering an area of 25 x 40 meters; the longitudinal walls, inclined at 45 degrees, help stabilize the structure. The Shopping Center, on the other hand, is shaped like a huge cylinder. The fronts supported by precast concrete elements are characterized by continuous rings of metal balconies. Inside, overhead natural lighting enhances the central space.

Domus, 705, 1989; P. Disch (ed), L'architettura recente nella svizzera tedesca, Lugano 1991, p. 111.

Shopping Center, view and section

Bärenmatte Community Center, internal view

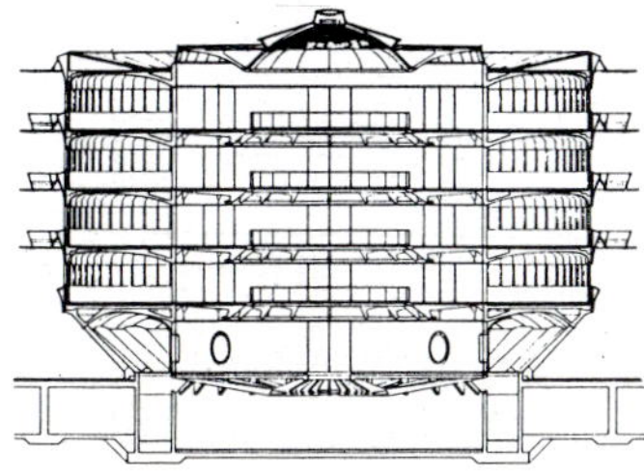

Wohlen

Cantonal School

Allmendstrasse

1983–88

Urs Burkard, Adrian Meyer, Max Steiger and Santiago Calatrava with D. Krieg, R. Gisiger, and H. Binggeli

Four parts of the design for this School built at Wohlen by Burkard, Meyer, and Steiger – an entrance canopy, library, atrium and main hall – bear the unmistakable hallmark of Calatrava's formal language. The library roof consists of four concrete vaults all resting on a single central support. The main hall has a V-section box-beam system, while the large canopy stretching from the atrium outwards, supported by beams and steel cables, conjures up the image of a tent as meeting place for students.

P. Disch (ed), L'architettura recente nella svizzera tedesca, Lugano 1991, p. 125; Guide to Swiss Architecture 1920–1990, vol. 2, 257, p. 125.

Würenlingen

Unter der Halde Housing

Steinbruchweg

1983–88

Dolf Schnebli and Paolo Kölliker with J. Pfyl and C. Gautschi

Developed in three stages, this housing scheme is integrated into the urban context as a series of apartment blocks to be used as low-rent accommodation. The logic of the design – highlighted by the plan and building techniques involved – does not neglect the overall quality, and includes com-

Cantonal School

mon recreation spaces as well as private gardens and terraces. The same architects also designed a significant piece of school architecture in Aarau: the Bünzmatt School at Wohlen (1966).
Detail, 4, 1984; 2, 1988; Archithese, 2, 1985; Parametro, 141, 1985; Docu Bulletin, 2, 1989; Werk, Bauen und Wohnen, 12, 1989; 12, 1990; 3, 1993; P. Disch (ed), L'architettura recente nella svizzera tedesca, Lugano 1991, p. 121; du, 5, 1992; Guide to Swiss Architecture 1920–1990, vol. 2, 261, p. 127.

Zofingen
Showroom and House
Luzernerstrasse 7
1989–93
Mario Botta
This building not only closes a gap on the avenue front, it also dialogues with a twentieth-century villa to the rear. The brief was highly unusual: on the ground floor and suspended platform on the first level is a spacious exhibition area characterized by vertical natural lighting filtered through rooflights; on the third floor, on the other hand, is a small dwelling, protected by side loggias. The symmetric layout is highlighted in the facade by a bold central cut (a typical Botta gesture), while two compact empty elements on the edges are sunk into the green of the surrounding park.
a + u, architecture and urbanism, 279, 1993; Raum und Wohnen, 11, 1993.

Top:
Unter der Halde Housing

Showroom and Dwelling, front and internal view

Basel-Stadt

Basel

Badischer Bahnhof Station

Schwarzwaldallee 200

1909–13

Karl Moser

The founding father of modern Swiss architecture, Karl Moser designed the new Basel station bearing in mind the example of Saarinen's Helsinki Station (1904–14). At the same time he elegantly reinterprets Schinkel's neoclassicism. A continuous cornice follows the articulation of the various bodies, while an overall uniform character is created through use of only one material.

W. Stutz, Bahnhöfe der Schweiz, Zurich 1976; U. Jehle-Schulte Strathaus, Bauten im 20. Jahrhundert, Basel 1977; INSA. Inventario Svizzero di Architettura 1850–1920, vol. II, Berne 1986; D. Huber, Architekturführer Basel, Basel 1993, S. 144–146.

Basel

Granary

Hafenstrasse 3–7/Kleinhüningen

1924

Hans Bernoulli and Oskar Bosshardt

Among the structures most praised by the radical historians in the Modern movement – and even mentioned by Le Corbusier in *Vers un'architecture* as a practical example of the modern age – were the utilitarian granaries which sprang up at the turn of the century in major European and American ports (London, Hamburg, Chicago, Buenos Aires, etc.). This huge building for storing grain built by Bernoulli in 1924 is characterized by its allusions to the traditional formal heritage: a great brick "nave", patterned by small apertures and the Neo-Romantic rhythm of the arches, ends in a "bell-tower".

U. Jehle-Schulte Strathaus, Bauten im 20. Jahrhundert, Basel 1977; INSA. Inventario Svizzero di Architettura 1850–1920, vol. II, Berne 1986.

Badischer Bahnhof Station

Granary

Basel

Church of St Antonius

Kannenfeldstrasse 35

1925–27

Karl Moser with Gustav Doppler and son

Restauration 1981–91

Thedy Doppler, Engineering Office Eglin Ristic AG

This is the most significant work in Moser's historicist approach to religious architecture, which also produced buildings such as the Church of St Antonius in Zurich, 1905–08, and the Church of St Paulus, Steinenring 20, 1898–1901, in Basel. The first exposed reinforced-concrete church in Switzerland (the engineer was Otto Ziegler), St Antonius was built just after Auguste Perret's Notre Dame at Raincy (1922–23). The geometric synthesis of the volumes and rough treatment of the materials are heightened by the design of the great windows (Hans Stocker and Otto Steiger) and the form of the bell-tower.

See also the house by Moser and Curjel at Schützenmattstrasse 49–55 (1905–06).

Werk, 5, 1927; Max Bill et al., Moderne Schweizer Architektur 1925–1945, Basel 1947; U. Jehle-Schulte Strathaus, Bauten im 20. Jahrhundert, Basel 1977; Die Antoniuskirche in Basel: ein Hauptwerk von Karl Moser, Basel 1991; D. Huber, Architekturführer Basel, Basel 1993, S. 298 f.; Guide to Swiss Architecture 1920–1990, vol. 2, 002, p. 23.

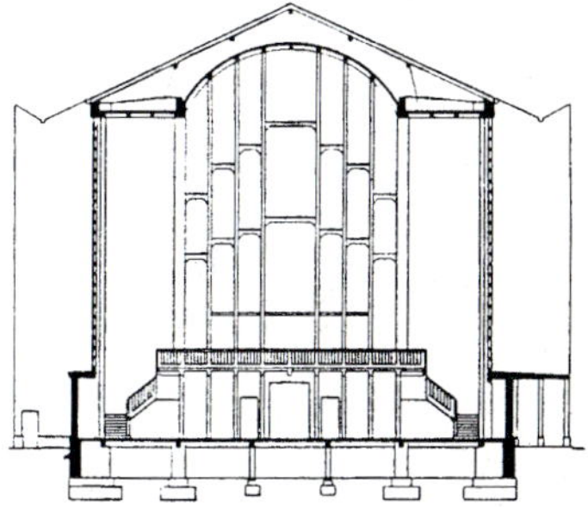

Church of St Antonius, view and section

Basel

Siedlung Im Vogelsang

Eugen Wullschlegerstrasse 1–65, 2–60

1924–26

Hans Bernoulli and August Künzel

Siedlung Hirzbrunnen

Hirzbrunnenschanze 1–93, 2–92/ Kleinriehenstrasse 50–76

1924–30

Hans Bernoulli, August Künzel, Paul Oberrauch, and Hans von der Mühll

One of the most celebrated examples of low-cost popular housing, the Siedlung Im Vogelsang reveals a number of the principles of "social architecture" cherished by Bernoulli. The ideals of the garden city are expressed in rows of single-dwelling houses exploring the theme of *existenzminimum* with a street front (conceived as the typical public place) and gardens to the rear. The use of exposed brick gives the whole row a domestic feel. The Hirzbrunnen estate, built almost at the same time, occupies the area to the east of the large urban block of the St Clara Hospital. In the same scheme there is a row of houses built on Tüllingerstrasse by Bernoulli in 1934.

Schweizerische Bauzeitung, 72, 1918; Werk, 4, 1929; 17, 1930; Habitation, 3–4, 1945; U. Jehle-Schulte Strathaus, Bauten im 20. Jahrhundert, Basel 1977; Archithese, 6, 1981; Parametro, 140, 1985; INSA. Inventario Svizzero di Architettura 1850–1920, vol. II, Berne 1986; D. Huber, Architekturführer Basel, Basel 1993, S. 250–252; Guide to Swiss Architekture 1920–1990, vol. 2, 001, S. 24f.

Riehen

Sandreuter House

Wenkenhofstrasse 29

1924–25

Rudolf Steiger and Flora Steiger-Crawford

Built using a mixed system (wood, reinforced concrete and masonry) the house expresses the postulates of the Swiss Modern movement as regards the theme of the individual house: namely, great respect for the site conditions and orientation, the use of natural materials in authentic forms, and, most importantly, experimentation in new building techniques.

ABC, 1924, series I, 5; Schweizerische Bauzeitung, 91, 1928; J. Gubler, Nationalisme et internationalisme dans l'architecture moderne de la Suisse, Lausanne 1975; Archithese, 2, 1980; Guide to Swiss Architecture 1920–1990, vol. 2, 054, p. 59.

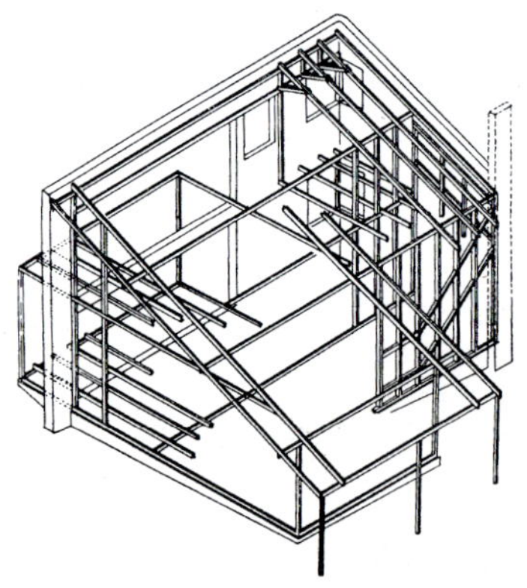

Sandreuter House, axonometric with indications for assembly

Siedlung Im Vogelsang

Siedlung Hirzbrunnen

Sandreuter House

Basel
Siedlung Schorenmatten
In den Schorenmatten 1–95
1927–29
Hans Schmidt, Paul Artaria, and August Künzel
Siedlung Eglisee (Woba)
Im Surinam 108–138/Am Bahndamm/Gotterbarmweg
1929–30
A. Kellermüller and H. Hofmann, H. von der Mühll and P. Oberrauch, E. F. Burckhardt, A.P. Steger and K. Egender, M. Braillard, E. Mumenthaler and O. Meier, K. Scherrer and P. Meier, H. Schmidt and P. Artaria, A. Hoechel, H. Bernoulli and A. Künzel, H. Baur, F. Gilliard and F. Godet, W. Moser, and E. Roth.

These two housing schemes are emblematic examples of how the major Swiss avant-garde architects focused on a new concept of dwelling linked to the housing reform explored in the Weimar republic. Consisting of six rows of houses plus a kindergarten, the Siedlung Schorenmatten provided a great opportunity to develop models for the

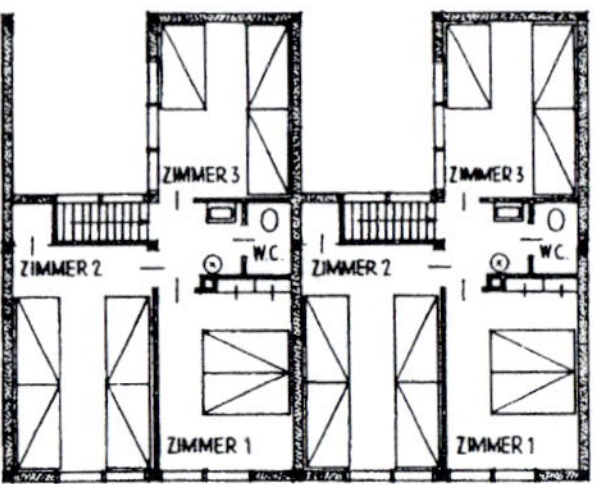

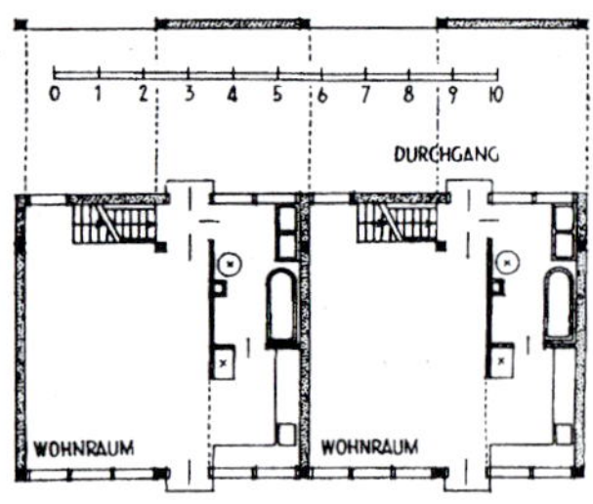

Siedlung Schorenmatten

mass-production of dwellings, called for by Schmidt in the pages of *ABC*. Opposite and to the west, is the Siedlung Eglisee, built as part of the Basel building exhibition promoted by the Swiss Werkbund. The involvement of many architects and studios led to wide-ranging experiments in building types, which can still be seen today, despite restoration works.
See also, the Eglisee Municipal Swimming Pool, east of Schorenmatten Siedlung, Egliseestrasse 85, built in 1930–31 by Julius Maurizio, who also designed the Psychiatric Hospital, Schaffhauserrheinweg (1938).

Das Wohnen, 12, 1929; 1, 3, 7, and 9, 1930; Woba-Führer durch die Ausstellungs-Siedlung Eglisee, Basel 1930; Baumeister, 11, 1930; Schweizerische Bauzeitung, 96, 1930; Werk, 6, 1930; 10, 1972; H. Baur, Das Wohnungswesen in der Schweiz, Stuttgart 1932; U. Jehle-Schulte Strathaus, Bauten im 20. Jahrhundert, Basel 1977; Werk, Bauen und Wohnen, 5, 1981; Archithese, 5, 1982; Parametro, 140, 1985 D. Huber, Architekturführer Basel, Basel 1993, p. 259–263; Guide to Swiss Architecture 1920–1990, vol. 2, 003, p. 26; 006, p. 28.

Woba-Siedlung Eglisee, facade detail

Site plan of both estates

Eglisee Municipal Swimming Pool

Riehen
Colnaghi House
Wenkenstrasse 81
1927
Hans Schmidt and Paul Artaria
Restoration 1990–93
T. Osolin and P. de Meuron (consultant)

Schmidt constantly tried out new building types and construction techniques for middle-class housing. The metal frame – used here for the first time in Switzerland – and the small concrete blocks are a paragon of simplicity, rationality and economy in organizing the work-site. See also, at Riehen, the Im Schlipf House, Schlipfweg 22 (1924–25) and the Wenk Studio-House, Mooshaldenweg 5 (1926), by the same architects.

Werk, 10, 1972; J. Gubler, Nationalisme et internationalisme dans l'architecture moderne de la Suisse, Lausanne 1975; J. Gubler (ed), ABC. Architettura e avanguardia 1924–1928, Milan 1983; S. von Moos, Estetica industriale, Disentis 1992; D. Huber, Architekturführer Basel, Basel 1993, p. 273; Guide to Swiss Architekture 1920–1990, vol. 2, 055, p. 60.

Basel
Single Women's Residence
Speiserstrasse 98
1927–29
Hans Schmidt and Paul Artaria

The L-shaped plan of the dwellings includes collective spaces open towards the garden on the ground floor, while the two upper floors have small one- to three-room apartments with balconies or loggias. The structure is an iron skeleton with concrete infill and standardized metal window frames. This building opportunity was used as an experiment to try out theoretical ideas about a prototype suitable for the industrialization of building components.

Schweizerische Bauzeitung, 12, 1929; Das Wohnen, 5, 1930; P. Artaria, Fragen des Neuen Bauens, Winterthur 1933; Max Bill et al., Moderne Schweizer Architektur 1925–1945, Basel 1947; Werk, 10, 1972; U. Jehle-Schulte Strathaus, Bauten im 20. Jahrhundert, Basel 1977; Archithese, 4, 1980; D. Huber, Architekturführer Basel, Basel 1993, p. 275 f.; Guide to Swiss Architekture 1920–1990, vol. 2, 004, S. 27.

Single Women's Residence

Colnaghi House, views and floor plan

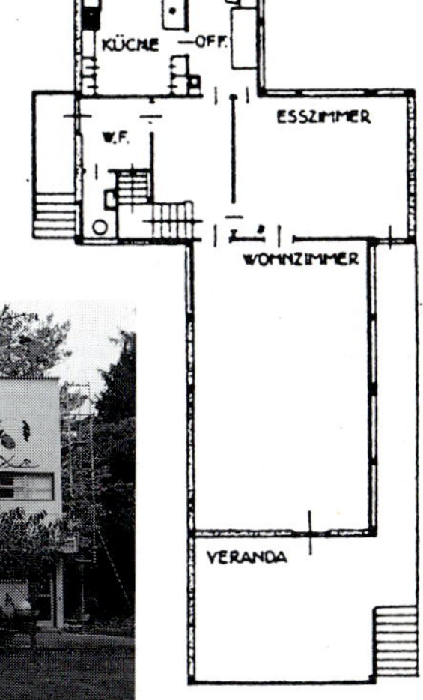

Single Women's Residence

Riehen

Schaeffer House
Sandreuterweg 44
1927–29
Hans Schmidt and Paul Artaria
Restoration 1990
Jacques Herzog and Pierre de Meuron

Huber-Zweifel House
Hackbergstrasse 29
1928–30
Hans Schmidt and Paul Artaria

Two single-dwelling houses provided the opportunity to try out cell types and tackle the problems of mass production, enthusiastically advocated by the more radical wing of Neues Bauen. In the Schaeffer House the bedrooms are designed with a circulation corridor (several times used by Schmidt as an alternative to Le Corbusier's "train-carriage-house"). A well-defined layout of public and private spaces which could be indefinitely repeated in rows of house is neatly formulated in the Huber-Zweifel House.

See also by Artaria and Schmidt: Riesen House, Eisenbahnweg 19 (1929–30), the Siedlung Haslerain, Seidenmannweg/Friedhofweg (1945–47) and the Siedlung Im Höfli, Hörnli-Allee/Kohlistieg/Rauracherstrasse (1946–54), both in the Riehen area.

Baumeister, 5, 1930; Werk, 1, 1930; Das Wohnen, 6, 1930; Max Bill et al., Moderne Schweizer Architektur 1925–1945, Basel 1947; J. Gubler (ed), ABC. Architettura e avanguardia 1924–1928, Milan 1983; Baukonstruktion der Moderne aus heutiger Sicht, Basel-Boston Berlin 1990; A. Rüegg, Artaria & Schmidt – Wohnhaus Schaeffer, Riehen, Basel 1927/1928, Zurich 1993; D. Huber, Architekturführer Basel, Basel 1993, p. 274; Guide to Swiss Architecture 1920–1990, vol. 2, 055, p. 60f.

Schaeffer House

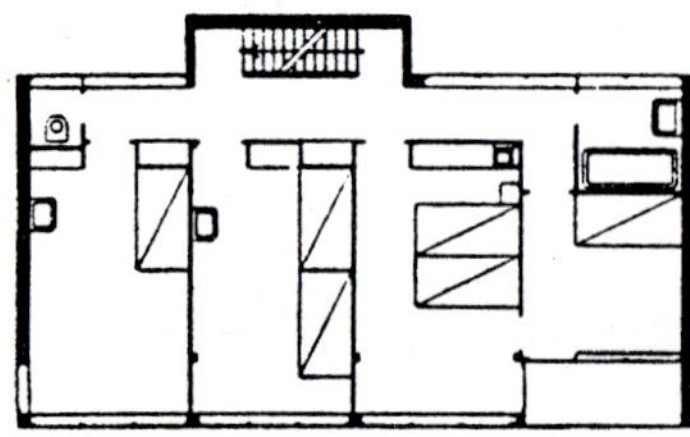

Huber-Zweifel House, view and floor plan

Basel
Corner Building
Klybeckstrasse 83/Bläsiring 50
1927
Hans Weissenborn
Well-known because of its red-plaster fronts, the Corner Building has some typical features of 1930s architecture, such as the prominent corner balconies and the small tower on the roof. The tower was originally intended as a base for a statue of St Blasius but is, however, also a traditional element in Basel architecture.
U. Jehle-Schulte Strathaus, Bauten im 20. Jahrhundert, Basel 1977.

Basel
Housing
Riehenring 5–25
1931
Emil Bercher and Eugen Tamm
The housing scheme is built along a curve in the road, while the overall scale is modulated by the regular volumetric rhythm, underscored by the projecting entrance and stairway volumes.
Bercher & Tamm also built the Rialto Indoor Swimming Pool, Birsigstrasse 45 (1934–35).
Schweizerische Bauzeitung, 1, 1935; Werk, 1, 1968; D. Huber, Architekturführer Basel, Basel 1993, p. 285.

Corner Building Housing

Basel
Fine Arts Museum
St Albangraben 16
1931–36
Paul Bonatz and Rudolf Christ
The design was the outcome of a controversial 1929 competition, held following a number of lost opportunities. A significant work in the debate on the theme of monumentality (raised by Peter Meyer in 1937 in the review *Werk*), the Basel Kunstmuseum has a renewed classical character achieved through the axial layout of the *court d'honneur* (containing sculptures by Rodin, Arp and Calder), while elements in the facade allude to the Doge's Palace in Venice. The granite pillars and the use of a variety of stones in the cladding convey a vision of the museum as a fortress guarding over its art treasures.
Werk, 3, 1937; U. Jehle-Schulte Strathaus, Bauten im 20. Jahrhundert, Basel 1977; Werk-Archithese, 11–12, 1978; Parametro, 140, 1985; Archithese, 1, 1993; D. Huber, Architekturführer Basel, Basel 1993, p. 300–302; Guide to Swiss Architecture 1920–1990, vol. 2, 013, p. 32.

Riehen
Children's Home
Im Baumgarten, Riehen
1933
Ernst Mumenthaler and Otto Meier
Situated on a sloping site, the building has communal spaces facing south east and open onto a garden as well as general services on the ground floor, while the upper floor contains the bedrooms arranged along a corridor characterized by a strip of windows. The structure is a metal skeleton combined with exposed brickwork.
The same architects also designed the Neuweg House, Bäumlihofstrasse 39 (1933), and the Zu den drei Linden, Augsterweg, Giebenacherweg, a *Siedlung* built together with August Künzel in 1944, both in Basel.
Moderne Schweizer Architektur 1925–1945, Basel 1947; U. Jehle-Schulte Strathaus, Bauten im 20. Jahrhundert, Basel 1977.

Basel
Barell House
Rennweg 62
1932–34
First Church of Christ, Scientist
Dufourstrasse 27/Picassoplatz 2
1935–36
Hoffmann-La Roche Laboratories
Grenzacherstrasse/Schaffhauser-Rheinweg
1935–37
Otto R. Salvisberg
Extension
1953–54
Roland Rohn
After working in Germany and going through an Expressionistic phase, as early as the 1930s, began Salvisberg elaborating an essential vocabulary stripped of any historicist elements. Without forgoing the sense of refined opulence characterizing the Barell House, Salvisberg's architecture took on plastic connotations, which are highlighted in the volumetric character of the Christian Science Church. He then achieved extreme plastic elegance in the Hoffmann-La Roche Laboratories, where the horizontality in the

facades is emphasized by continuous windows alternated with strips of white exposed concrete.

Moderne Bauformen, 1, 1936; 9, 1937; Werk, 4, 1936; 7, 1937; L'Architecture d'aujourd'hui, 6, 1939; Schweizerische Bauzeitung, 4, 1939; Moderne Schweizer Architektur 1925–1945, Basel 1947; U. Jehle-Schulte Strathaus, Bauten im 20. Jahrhundert, Basel 1977; D. Huber, Architekturführer Basel, Basel 1993, p. 303–306.

Barell House

Right:
Fine Arts Museum

Children's Home

First Church of Christ, Scientist

Hoffmann-La Roche Laboratories

Basel

Church of Johannes

Metzerstrasse 52/Mülhauserstrasse 145

1934–36

Karl Egender and Ernst F. Burckhardt

A stone's throw from Karl Moser's church of St Antonius (1925–27 – see p. 121), Johannes' is the first modern Swiss Protestant Church. The main body with the nave in reinforced concrete and iron is lit by a glass brick side wall. The basement floor accommodates meeting rooms and ancillary premises. The south-eastern wing hosts other parish activities (classrooms, conference room, and the minister's lodgings). The use of new materials is emphasized by the sculptural metal skeleton of the bell tower.

Moderne Schweizer Architektur 1925–1945, Basel 1947; U. Jehle-Schulte Strathaus, Bauten im 20. Jahrhundert, Basel 1977; Werk-archithese, 11–12, 1978; D. Huber, Architekturführer Basel, Basel 1993, p. 279; Guide to Swiss Architecture 1920–1990, vol. 2, 014, p. 33.

Basel

University College

Peterplatz 1

1937–39

Roland Rohn

The overall design follows the course of the road in a U-shaped plan enclosing a garden belonging to a neighboring building to the rear. The continuous projecting cornice, the use of travertine for the cladding and the sharp definition of the apertures combine to give the building a stately bearing.

U. Jehle-Schulte Strathaus, Bauten im 20. Jahrhundert, Basel 1977; Werk-archithese, 1978, 11–12 D. Huber, Architekturführer Basel, Basel 1993, p. 307–308; Guide to Swiss Architecture 1920–1990, vol. 2, 017, p. 35.

Church of Johannes

University College

Basel
Bruderholz Grammar School
Reservoirstrasse
1938–39
Hermann Baur
Arts and Crafts School
Vogelsangstrasse/Riehenstrasse/
Peter-Rot-Strasse
1953–61
Hermann Baur, Franz Bräuning, and Arthur Dürig
with H. P. Baur

Mentioned by Alfred Roth in *Constructions scolaires en Suisse, hier et aujourd'hui* as the first pavilion-type educational facility built in Switzerland, the Bruderholz School consists of a series of classrooms organized in a herring-bone structure open towards the southeast in an interesting play of spaces. The Arts and Crafts School, the much criticized outcome of a 1940 competition, was only actually begun in 1953. The administrative block and arts building on Vogelsangstrasse define the entrance, while the workshops are aligned along Riehenstrasse. The use of precast concrete slabs characterizes the facade, while sculptures and paintings attest to the educational importance of the figurative arts.

H. Volkart, Schweizer Architektur, Ravensburg 1951; Architecture, formes + fonction, 9, 1962–63; L'Architecture d'aujourd'hui, 121, 1965; B. De Sivo, L'architettura in Svizzera oggi, Naples 1968; U. Jehle-Schulte Strathaus, Bauten im 20. Jahrhundert, Basel 1977; D. Huber, Architekturführer Basel, Basel 1993, p. 329 f.; Hermann Baur – Architektur und Planung in Zeiten des Umbruchs, exhibition catalogue, Basel, 1994; Guide to Swiss Architecture 1920–1990, vol. 2, 018, p. 35; 030, p. 42.

Bruderholz School

Arts and Crafts School

Basel
Bürgerspital
Spitalstrasse
1938–45
Hermann Baur; Bräuning, Leu, Dürig; Ernst and Paul Vischer
Infectious Diseases Ward
Schanzenstrasse
1939–46
Hans Schmidt

Situated in a city-center area of around 28,000 square meters, the hospital's overall layout was conditioned by the desire to orient the inpatient wards to the southeast This means the rooms overlook a park and services are organized on the northern side of the corridor. A separate building contains the medical departments, the operating theaters and polyclinic as well as classrooms and research labs. Four small blocks with therapeutic facilities for outpatients link the two main sectors. The low volume on Schanzenstrasse (built at a later stage by Hans Schmidt) contains the infectious diseases department.

Werk, 6, 1948; H. Volkart, Schweizer Architektur, Ravensburg 1951; U. Jehle-Schulte Strathaus, Bauten im 20. Jahrhundert, Basel 1977; Werk-archithese, 11–12, 1978; D. Huber, Architekturführer Basel, Basel 1993, p. 308–310; Guide to Swiss Architecture 1920–1990, vol. 2, 019, p. 36.

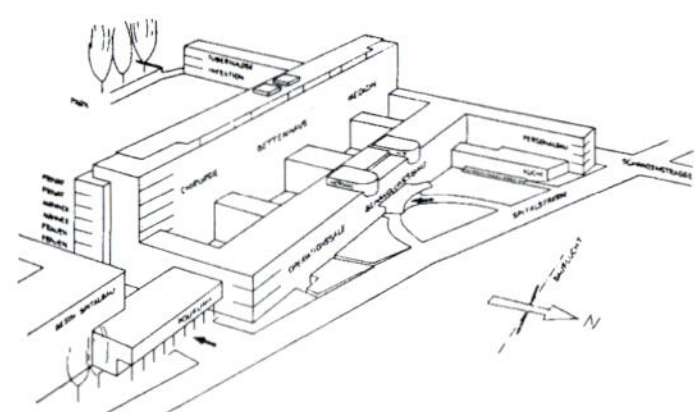

Bürger Hospital, front view and perspective drawing

Infectious Diseases Ward

Basel
Lonza Tower
Münchensteinerstrasse 38
1959–62
Suter & Suter

By now a Basel landmark, this office tower is characterized by the ribbing

pattern on the corners (clad in aluminum sheets) and a row of artificial lights running up the spine. The vertical circulation system leaves the nineteen floors free for the company's administrative offices, while the telephone system, archives and storerooms are in the basement levels.
Architecture, formes + fonction, 9, 1962–63; L'Architecture d'aujourd'hui, 121, 1965; U. Jehle-Schulte Strathaus, Bauten im 20. Jahrhundert, Basel 1977.

Basel
Ciba Administration and Laboratories
Unterer Rheinweg
1963–66
Suter & Suter
Situated in an area of 26,000 square meters on the river waterfront, this tower block contains the Ciba biology research laboratories and administrative offices. The uniform metal grid of the window frames highlights the neutral character of the prismatic volume, which through the use of standard equipment meets the functional requirements of the company in a flexible way.
In 1966–67 the same architects built the Ciba Canteen, Ecke Gärtnerstrasse/Maurerstrasse. More recently they were responsible for the interior renovations for the Basel Bourse, Aeschenplatz 7 (1982–86).
U. Jehle-Schulte Strathaus, Bauten im 20. Jahrhundert, Basel 1977; Guide to Swiss Architecture 1920–1990, vol. 2, 031, p. 44f.

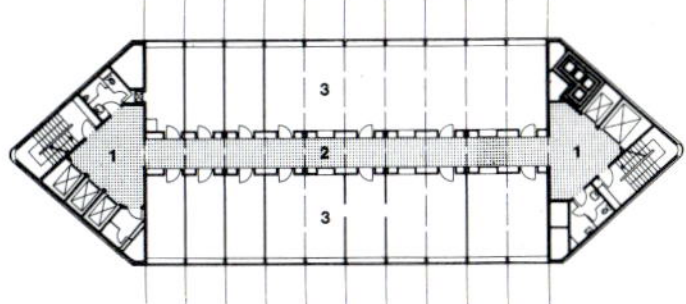

Lonza Tower, view and floor plan

Ciba Administration and Laboratories

Basel
Wasgenring School
Welschmattstrasse/Blotzheimer-strasse 82
1951–62
Fritz Haller
with M. Streicher
The school complex was built in two phases: the grammar school (1953–54) and the secondary school (1960–62). Organized on a free layout, the various pavilions of the grammar school are joined up by semi-covered passages, leaving an overall effect of transparency.

Bauen und Wohnen, 5, 1955; 11, 1962; Werk, 4, 1956; D. Huber, Architekturführer Basel, Basel 1993, p. 326–328; Guide to Swiss Architecture 1920–1990, vol. 2, 026, p. 40.

Basel
Furniture Cooperative Building
Güterstrasse 133
1956–57
Hans Fischli
with F. Eichholzer and E. Franz
Constructed on the site of the previous demolished building, the Furniture Co-operative Building for shops, offices and storerooms consists of two blocks arranged perpendicularly, but distinguished by the handling of materials.

Wasgenring School

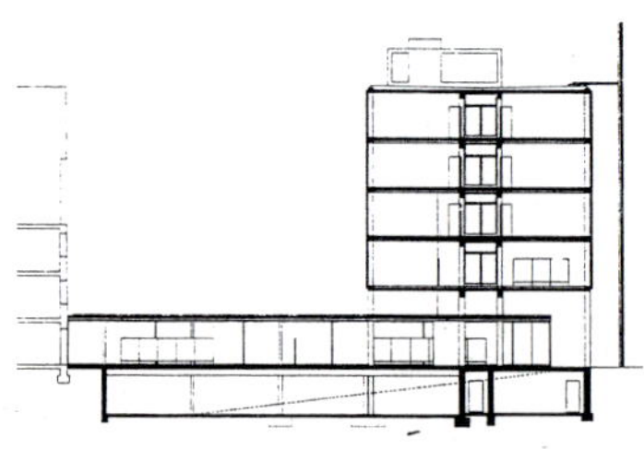

Furniture Cooperative Building, section and exterior view

The main four-story office block on Güterstrasse is in reinforced concrete, while a one-story salesroom, linked to the storerooms, is supported by a light metal structure.

Bauen und Wohnen, 8, 1958; Werk, 7, 1958.

Basel

University Library

Schönbeinstrasse 20

1962–68

Otto H. Senn

Built in two stages so that the existing facility could continue to function, the new Library stands at the edge of the old botanical gardens. Defined by a crossroads, the limited site meant the two wings had to be set within a 60-degree angle. In the first stage the administrative building was constructed, arranged as a symmetric wing to the old library building. The domed reading room was then added, and, lastly, the corner entrance volume renovated. Among Otto H. Senn's most significant works are the "Parkhaus Zossen" Housing in Basel, St Alban-Anlage 37, built with Rudolf Mock in 1934–35, and the Riehen House, Schnitterweg 40, designed with Walter Senn in 1934.

L'Architecture d'aujourd'hui, 121, 1965; Werk, 11, 1966; D. Huber, Architekturführer Basel, Basel 1993, p. 334f.; Guide to Swiss Architecture 1920–1990, vol. 2, 035, p. 47.

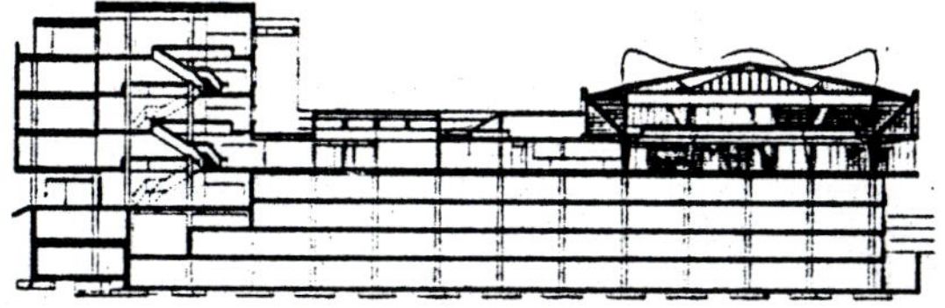

University Library

Basel

Housing and Bank

Missionsstrasse 86/St Johanns-Ring
1982–85
Diener & Diener (Roger Diener, Dieter Righetti, Andreas Rüedi, Paul Langlotz, and M. Stingelin)

Mixed-Use Buildings

St Alban-Rheinweg 94–96
1984–86
Diener & Diener (M. Buser, Roger Diener, Dieter Righetti, and E. Rysler)

Fides Offices

Innere Margarethenstrasse 5/Steinentorberg 8–12
1984–90
Diener & Diener (Roger Diener, Jens Erb, Dieter Righetti, Andreas Rüedi, Wolfgang Schett)

Administrative Building

Picassoplatz
1990–93
Diener & Diener (Roger Diener, Jens Erb, Dieter Righetti, Mireille Blatter)

The concept of the city as the sum of individual interventions and the definition of its spaces in a hierarchic and interdependent way (from public to private) have always informed the prolific design activity of the Basel-based Diener & Diener studio. The comparison of various spatial qualities – in the quarter, street, court or house interior – determine the functional organization of a building, while the self-contained nature of individual projects never violates the rules governing the historical context into which they must be inserted.

Among this studio's many works in Basel see also: Hammer I and II Housing, Hammerstrasse/Bläsiring (1978–

Housing and Bank

Housing with Studio

Fides Offices

Adminstrative Building

81) and Riehenring/Amerbachstrasse (1980–85), the Offices on Hochstrasse (1986–88) and the training center of the Swiss Bank Company, Viaduktstrasse 45 (1990–94). The studio was also responsible for the interesting interior design of the Domus-Haus by Max Rasser and Tibère Vadi (1958) which they converted into the Architectural Museum, Pfluggässlein 3 (1985).

Werk, Bauen und Wohnen, 12, 1982; 12, 1983; 1–2 1987, 1–2; Casabella, 535, 1987; Quaderns d'Arquitectura i Urbanisme, 173, 1987; Abitare, 2, 1990; A. Rüegg, Diener & Diener Architekten. Wohnhäuser St Alban-Tal, Basel 1982–1986, Zurich 1993; D. Huber, Architekturführer Basel, Basel 1993, p. 370f., 402–406; Guide to Swiss Architecture 1920–1990, vol. 2, 044, p. 54; 043, p. 52f.; 049, p. 56; 050, p. 57.

Basel

Mixed-Use Building

Spalenvorstadt 11

1981–85

Ueli Marbach and Arthur Rüegg

with C. Zürcher

In a deep narrow lot, typical of Basel's historic urban fabric, this project for housing and shops effortlessly solves the problems set by the brief. The position of the stair on the side of the building frees the ground floor space, making it suitable for shops, while the upper floors are available for housing.

Werk, Bauen und Wohnen, 1–2, 1986; C. Fingerhuth (ed), Bauten in Basel, Basel 1988; Holz Bulletin, 24, 1990; D. Huber, Architekturführer Basel, Basel 1993, p. 372f.

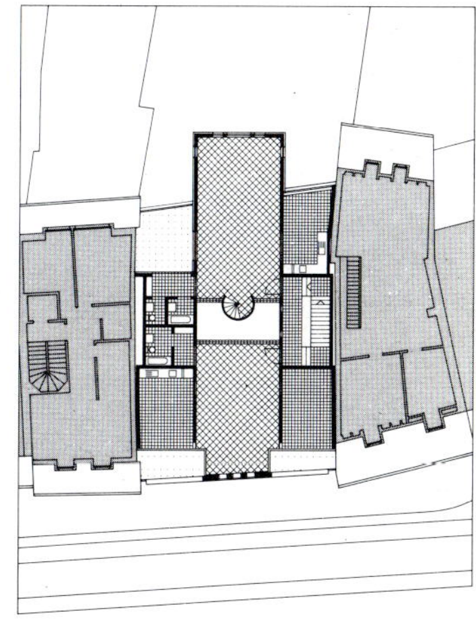

Basel
Wiesengarten Housing
Wiesendamm/Altrheinweg/Giessliweg, Kleinhüningen
1983–86
Wilfrid and Katharina Steib,
Bruno Buser, Jakob Zäslin
with R. Schaub and U. Gramelsbacher

Built in a former industrial zone beside the railway line, the Wiesengarten Housing makes good use of its own volumetric presence to give a new identity to the whole area. The buildings are gradually set back from the line of the front through a play of terraces and balconies, considerably enhancing the local urban character. Wilfrid and Katharina Steib also designed the Basel Contemporary Art Gallery, St Alban-Rheinweg 60 (1978–80) and the Home for the Elderly in the Riehen area, Inzlingerstrasse 230 (1986–88).

C. Fingerhuth (ed), Bauten in Basel, Basel 1988; P. Disch (ed), L'architettura recente nella Svizzera tedesca 1980–1990, Lugano 1991, p. 30, 34, 36; D. Huber, Architekturführer Basel, Basel 1993, p. 410.

Basel
Apartment Building along a party wall
Hebelstrasse 11
1984–88
Jacques Herzog and
Pierre de Meuron
with M. Meier

Schwitter Mixed-Use Building
Allschwilerstrasse 90
1985–88
Jacques Herzog and
Pierre de Meuron
with A. Gigon

Alteration and Extension to the SUVA Mixed-Use Building
St Jakobstrasse 24

Hebelstrasse House

Wiesengarten Housing

Opposite page:
Top left: Schwitter Building
Bottom left: SUVA Extension
Right: Mixed-Use Building

1988–93
Jacques Herzog and Pierre de Meuron
Mixed-Use Building
Schützenmattstrasse 11
1992–93
Jacques Herzog and Pierre de Meuron

The house in Hebelstrasse court recovers the traditional Basel building criteria as regards both distribution and construction (masonry for the street front and wood – here oak – for the secondary volumes at the back). The projecting wooden loggia rests on a series of oak supports highlighting the serial character of the structure. The form of the Schwitter Building emerges from the complex interplay of two curved lines of different radii determined by the course of the street and the geometry of the court to the rear. The Schützenmattstrasse Housing was strongly conditioned by the Gothic lot, leaving very little room for maneuver. The architects thus focused on the facade for which they proposed an experimental, abstract curtain.
In addition to the extension and alteration of the apartment and office building of the Swiss accident insurance company SUVA, where a glass envelope wraps round both old and new buildings, other interesting works by Herzog and de Meuron are the House in Therwil, Lerchenrainstrasse 5 (1985–86), and the major Railway engine depot and emblematic copper-clad Auf dem Wolf signal box in Basel (1988–96).

Abitare, 206, 1982; 11, 1983; Parametro, 11, 1985; du, 5, 1992; Lotus international, 73, 1992; Domus, 747, 1993; 756 and 761, 1994; Werk, Bauen und Wohnen, 1993; Casabella, 612, 1994; D. Huber, Architekturführer Basel, Basel 1993, p. 407–409; Guide to Swiss Architecture 1920–1990, vol. 2, 046, 047, p. 55.

Riehen

Vogelbach Housing

Friedhofweg, Riehen

1989–92

Michael Alder with Hanspeter Müller and Roland Naegelin with A. Rüdisühli and C. Blessing

Luzernerring Housing

Bungestrasse 10–28

1989–93

Michael Alder with Hanspeter Müller with A. Hindemann

Both of these developments are on the urban scale of a whole quarter and reveal principles tried out by Michael Alder in previous works. The Vogelbach Housing at Riehen is a classic example of his clear and simple language, while the housing block in the Luzernerring scheme is aligned with the street, thus creating an urban promenade enhanced by the rhythm of the entrances and the volumetric play of the balconies.

Elegant solutions on a smaller scale can be seen in the workshops, studios and a converted industrial building in St Alban-Tal 40A and 42 in Basel (1986–87).

Baumeister, 12, 1993; Guide to Swiss Architecture 1920–1990, vol. 2, 059, p. 63; 052, p. 58.

Basel

Renovation of the Tabourettli Cabaret

Spalenberg 12

1986–88

Santiago Calatrava and Beda Küng

This project is part of the restoration of the sixteenth-century Spalenhof, included in the redevelopment scheme for the historic center begun by the Basel municipal authorities in 1976. A new stair, resting on a steel "egg" solves the static problems of the existing building, concentrating all the forces in a single point. The new element has a twofold function in plan and structure and has the aspect of a sophisticated machine modifying the layout and form of the spaces.

Bauten für Basel, Basel 1988; Domus, 697, 1988; Holz Bulletin, 24, 1990; D. Huber, Architekturführer Basel, Basel 1993, p. 364..

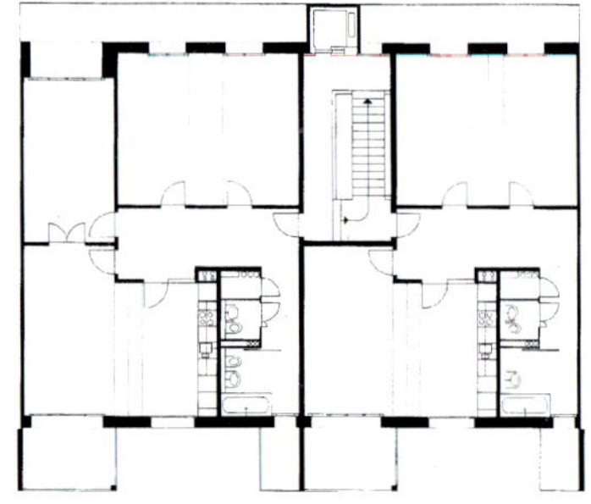

Luzernerring Housing, floor plan

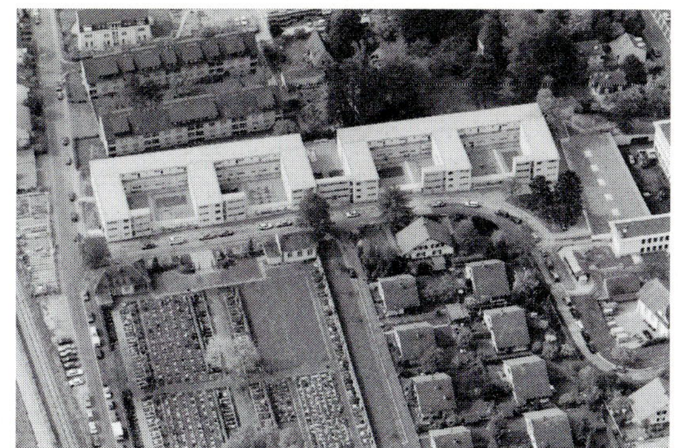

Vogelbach Housing

Luzernerring Housing

Tabourettli Cabaret

Basel
Union Bank of Switzerland (UBS) Headquarters
Aeschenplatz 1
1986–1995
Mario Botta
with Burkhardt & Partner (site management)

The project tackles the problems of reconciling contrasting features in the surrounding urban fabric – the continuously built-up Aeschengraben and the open layout on St Jakobstrasse. The solution is an independent object separating and differentiating the two contrasting existing urban developments. A large cylinder opens up towards the ground floor with the entrance atrium, pedestrian passage and various public functions. Through the resultant high degree of transparency the continuity between street and internal space is highlighted.

Botta also designed the Tinguely Museum in Solitude Park, Grenzacherstrasse (1992–96).

Emilio Pizzi, Mario Botta. The Complete Works, Vol. 3, Basel Boston Berlin 1997.

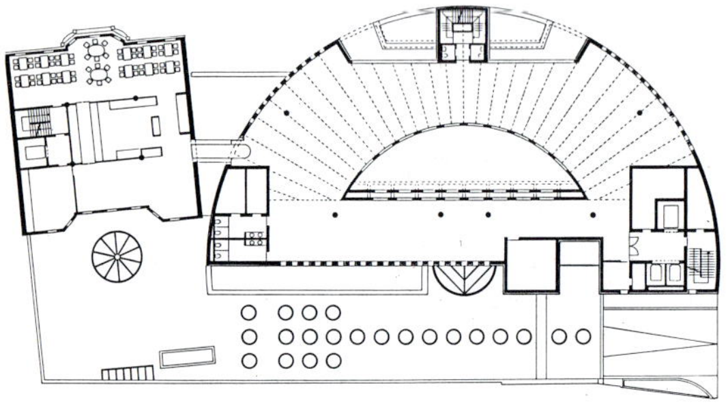

Schweizerische Bankgesellschaft Headquarters, floor plan and view

Basel
Housing
Müllheimerstrasse 138–140
1989–93
Meinrad Morger and Heinrich Degelo with L. Egli

This building – a compact red concrete prism for subsidized housing – was the outcome of a competition held by the municipal authorities in 1989. The volume fits in perfectly with the chessboard fabric of Matthaus, a traditional Basel working-class quarter on the right bank of the Rhine. A critical reinterpretation of postwar housing, the project explored building types as a response to new social issues. The result is that the collective spaces are given prominence and special care is taken over the number of circulation centers and the exit spaces by placing a multipurpose room and kindergarten on Amerbachstrasse.

Rivista Tecnica, 4, 1992; Detail, 1, 1993; Faces, 281, 1993.

Müllheimerstrasse Housing

Basel-Land

Biel-Benken
Spittelhof Housing
Spittelhofstrasse/Schulgasse
1990–96
Peter Zumthor
with T. Durisch and J. Bumann
Situated on the outskirts of Biel, this housing scheme consists of various buildings: a house for several families at the top of a slope and two rows of houses arranged down the slope. The rhythm of the window and door frames gives the whole scheme a uniform character.

Binningen
Schmidt-Kohl House
Hölzlistrasse 15
1929, 1947, and 1954
Hans Schmidt and Paul Artaria
Hans Schmidt found himself with a rather unusual client for this house – his brother Georg, art-historian and critic, director of the Basel Kunstmuseum, and a fervent believer in the principles of Modern architecture. This "architectonic essay" was intended to prove that the rationalization of building components would lead not only to industrialized building systems but to the mass production of low-cost housing. The standard plan and components generate a bare essential language. The house was later extended when Schmidt designed a new volume with a less radical semicircular aperture.
Artaria also built the house on Rebgasse 32 (1931) at Binningen.

U. Jehle-Schulte Strathaus, Bauten im 20. Jahrhundert, Basel 1977; Archithese, 5, 1985; Guide to Swiss Architecture 1920–1990, vol. 2, 105, p. 73.

Birsfelden
Power Station on the Rhine
Hofstrasse 60/Grenzacherstrasse
1955
Hans Hofmann
This power station is elegantly integrated into the river landscape without having to resort to any mimetic expedients. The main features of the building are the corrugated silhouette of the roof and the skillful use of color, while the large structural spans ensure a fair degree of transparency. The rhythm of the small volumes of the control cabins seems intended to play down the expressive force of the whole.
For another interesting work by Hofmann, see his round courtyard building for the Basel Trade Fair, Hallen 10–21/Rosentalstrasse (Messeplatz, 1953–54).
Werk, 7, 1954; D. Huber, Architekturführer Basel, Basel 1993, p. 314f.; Guide to Swiss Architecture 1920–1990, vol. 2, 107, p. 74.

Birsfelden
Vitra Adminstrative Building and Shop
Klünenfeldstrasse
1993–94
Frank O. Gehry
Having designed the Vitra Design Museum for a major collection of modern furniture at Weil am Rhein in Germany, close to the Swiss and French borders, Frank Gehry then tackled a project for the company's administrative offices,

showroom and shop. The continual building up and breaking down of the volumes, the play of interpenetrations, juxtapositions and shifts of spaces and building elements, so typical of the Californian architect, are used here to invent suitable forms for a high-quality corporate image.

Werk, Bauen und Wohnen, 7–8, 1993; Hochparterre, 6–7, 1994; Guide to Swiss Architecture 1920–1990, vol. 2, 109, p. 75.

Vitra Adminstrative Building and Shop, model view

Schmidt-Kohl House

Power Station on the Rhine

Spittelhof Housing, model view

Bottmingen
House and Studio-Theater
Rappenbodenweg 6
1984–85
Jacques Herzog and Pierre de Meuron

The specific details of the program (the client's house and a small puppet theater) induced the designers to handle the building with the same kind of care as if it were a piece of furniture or a musical instrument. Entirely made of wood, the building is raised from the ground, highlighting its independence from the surrounding gardens.

Rivista Tecnica, 1–2, 1986; P. Disch (ed), L'architettura recente nella Svizzera tedesca, Lugano 1991; du, 5, 1992; D. Huber, Architekturführer Basel, Basel 1993, p. 391.

Bottmingen
House
Kirschbaumweg 27
1987–88
Michael Alder

As in the Itingen House, Hinter den Gärten 23 (1983–84), Alder returns to and develops rudimentary forms from the domestic tradition, using wood as the principal material. The rationality of this "simple" architecture lies in the relations between forms, use and the technique which is their practical application through craftsmanship.

The Ziefen House (1969) is another significant example of Alder's research into the architecture of the house.

Archithese, 1, 1980; Holz Bulletin, 24, 1990; P. Disch (ed), L'architettura recente nella Svizzera tedesca, Lugano 1991; du, 5, 1992.

Muttenz
Siedlung Freidorf
St Jakobstrasse
1919–21
Hannes Meyer with A. Künzel

In the Swiss socio-political context of the day, this project was seen as being of a revolutionary character. It was the first cooperative village to put into practice the Pestalozzi-inspired reformist ideology of its promoters. A convinced advocate of the initiative, considered a new model of working-class life, Hans Meyer designed the quarter by superimposing a classic matrix on a triangular lot. The community activities – school, library, theater and market – are concentrated in a single building in the central square, while the 150 dwellings with gardens are arranged linearly on three parallel axes. The return to nature was intended to free the inhabitants from urban slavery, while building according to dwelling types and the use of standard materials met the need for optimal savings in construction costs.

J.F. Schär, H. Faucherre, and H. Meyer, Die siedlung Freidorf, Basel 1921; Werk, 12, 1925; J. Gubler, Nationalisme and internationalisme dans l'architecture moderne de la Suisse, Lausanne 1975; U. Jehle-Schulte Strathaus, Bauten im 20.Jahrhundert, Basel 1977; Parametro, 140, 1985; D. Huber, Architekturführer Basel, Basel 1993, p. 256f.; Guide to Swiss Architecture 1920–1990, vol. 2, 115, p. 80.

House and Studio-Theater, view and section

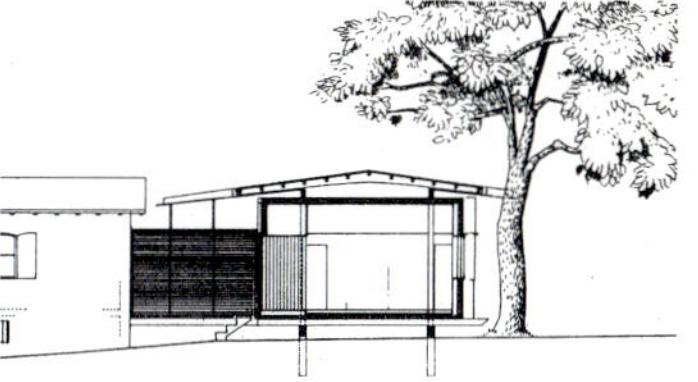

Kirschbaumweg House

Siedlung Freidorf, elevation and view

Solothurn

Dornach
Goetheanum
Rüttiweg 45
1924–28
Rudolf Steiner
Concentrated in the anthroposophic village of Dornach, Rudolf Steiner's works are an attempt to translate into architecture a cosmological vision inspired by Goethe's theory of color and natural metamorphoses. Starting from his own anthroposophic ideas, the founder of the movement designed tectonically-molded reinforced-concrete forms, rich in expressionist tensions generating a very dynamic internal spatiality.
Architettura, 55–58, 1960; Architectural Association Journal, 6, 1963; W. Pehnt, Rudolf Steiner, Goetheanum, Dornach, Berlin 1991; Guide to Swiss Architecture 1920–1990, vol. 2, 111, p. 76.

Grenchen
Park Theater
Bahnhofplatz
1949–55
Ernst Gisel
Built in a U-shape round a small entrance plaza, the complex consists of several volumes accommodating the theater, a wing with a hotel, and a restaurant. The use of materials – red brick and copper – brings to mind the works of Alvar Aalto.
Werk, 10, 1949; 3, 1951; 5, 1956; Schweizerische Bauzeitung, 4, 5, 34, 1950; L'Architettura, 10, 1956; L'Architecture d'aujourd'hui, 71, 1957; Edilizia Moderna, 63, 1958; B. de Sivo, L'Architettura in Svizzera oggi, Naples 1968; J. Bachmann

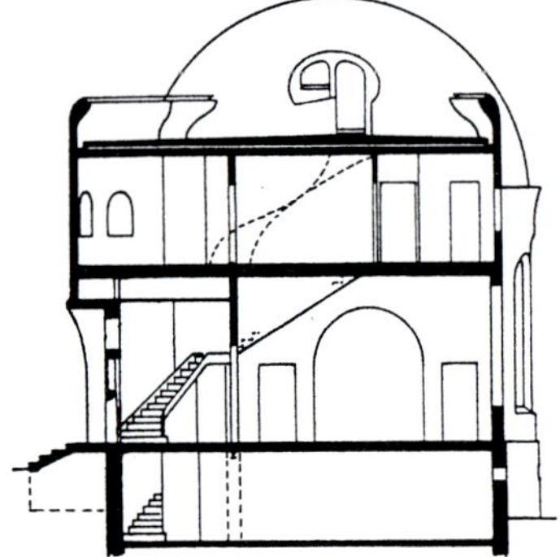

Goetheanum, period photo and section

Park Theater

and S. von Moos, New Directions in Swiss Architecture, New York 1969; Guide to Swiss Architecture 1920–1990, vol. 2, 306, p. 136.

Mümliswil
Children's Home
1938–39
Hannes Meyer
Situated on a hill to the north of the village, the small colony for children was commissioned by the foundation created by Bernhard Jäggi, a pioneer in the Swiss cooperative movement. Designed by Meyer during a brief spell back in Switzerland (after his Moscow experience and prior to his move to Mexico), the building reveals a number of the architect's favorite themes: the relation with the landscape, the use of forms from local architecture, the modern use of traditional materials, and standardization. Dominating the whole panorama and forging a link between two wings, a cylindrical volume – later raised by a further story – accommodates the collective facilities.
See also the two housing blocks built in 1921 and 1930 as workers lodgings for the Balsthal Factory, Hofmattweg 8–30.
Arquitectura, 8, 1941; Werk, 7, 1953; 10, 1954; Rivista Tecnica, 10, 1954; M. Kieren, Hannes Meyer: Dokumente zur Frühzeit 1919–27, Teufen 1990.

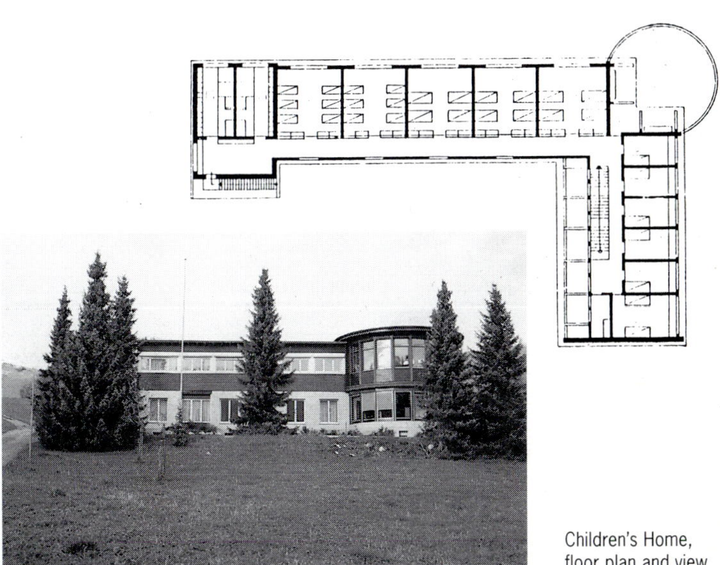

Children's Home, floor plan and view

Oensingen

Vebo Rehabilitation Center

Werkhofstrasse 8

1980–84

Alfons Barth and Hans Zaugg with U. Wildi and H. Scheibler

In addition to the Säli School at Olten (1964–68) and the more recent extension (library and refectory) of the Solothurn Cantonal School, Herrenweg 18 (1986–90), Barth and Zaugg built this facility for the disabled – a free composition with four parallelepipeds round a central square.

See also the Zaugg House at Olten, Fustlighalde 92 (1956).

Werk, 1, 1968; J. Bachmann and S. von Moos, New Directions in Swiss Architecture, New York 1969.

Olten

Public Baths

Schützenmatte 3

1937–39

Hermann Frey & Ernst Schindler

Situated on the beaches of the Aare near the historic center, this sports complex has typical features from the architectural tradition of this kind of Swiss institution: a rationalist vocabulary, the use of reinforced concrete, and highly functional services and facilities.

Moderne Schweizer Architektur 1925–1945, Basel 1947; Guide to Swiss Architecture 1920–1990, vol. 2, 314, p. 139.

Solothurn

Schweizerische Volksbank Building

Wengistrasse 2

1926–28

Otto R. Salvisberg

Although not considered particularly modern by orthodox historians of architecture, Salvisberg must be credited with having paved the way for a moderate transition from the old to the new. The Solothurn bank reveals his skill in reconciling antithetical elements in a homogenous whole. The gray granite-clad prismatic volume is characterized by the regular rhythm of apertures and the arches of the entrance loggia.

Schweizerische Bauzeitung, 25, 1926; Werk, 7, 1929; Werk-archithese, 10, 1977.

Vebo Rehabilitation Center

Public Baths

Solothurn

School

Allmendstrasse

1956–59

Fritz Haller with F. Müller

Cantonal School Extension

Herrenweg

1984–93

Fritz Haller with H. Weber

A comparison of the Allmendstrasse School built in the 1950s (concrete volumes and metal-profile structures) with the more recent extension to the Cantonal School (built using a modular system with large steel load-bearing girders) highlights Haller's technical-constructional development.

This kind of research and his typical vocabulary are further illustrated by other works, such as the Hafler House, Fegetzallee 7 (1976).

Werk, Bauen und Wohnen, 7–8 1981; 7–8, 1992; 3, 1994; Domus, 695, 1988; Guide to Swiss Architecture 1920–1990, vol. 2, 320, p. 144.

Solothurn

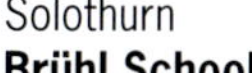

Brühl School

Brunngrabenstrasse

1988–92

Markus Ducommun

with W. Kamber and A. Jenni

The outcome of a 1988 competition, the project meets the requirements of the brief in a single elliptical building. The classrooms and administration are located in an outer band, while the gymnasium and amphitheater are at the center.

P. Disch (ed), L'architettura recente nella Svizzera tedesca 1980–1990, Lugano 1991, p. 70.

Volksbank

Allmendstrasse School

Cantonal School Extension

Brühl School

Berne

Biel
Volkshaus
Rue de la Gare 11/Rue d'Aarberg 112
1930–32
Eduard Lanz
Renovation 1986–89
Andry & Habermann, Henry Mollet
One of the most significant examples of Modern architecture in Biel, this "house of the people" bears witness to the social-democratic ideals pursued by the municipal authorities in the 1930s. Famed for his theoretical writings and a member of the planning commission for the station area, Eduard Lanz met the requirements of the brief by designing a long wing on Rue d'Aarberg (consisting of one large room) and an eight-story volume (originally intended for offices and lodgings). The corner solution is highlighted by a circular element reflecting the shape of the lot.
E. Lanz, Das neue Bieler-Volkshaus, Biel/Bienne 1933; Werk-archithese, 23–24,1978; Guide to Swiss Architecture 1920–1990, vol. 2, 803, p. 220 f.

Biel
General Motors Assembly Shed
Rue de la Gabelle 21–27
1935–36
Rudolf Steiger
with C. Hubacher

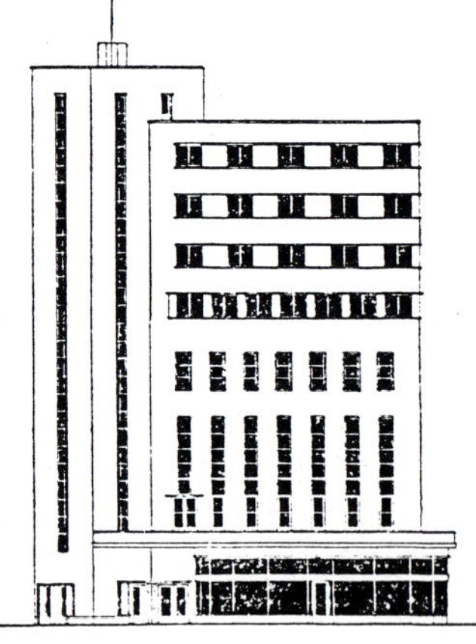

Volkshaus, view and elevation

Situated to the south-west of the station, the complex includes an assembly shop, modulated according to production needs, and an administrative building, whose main facade contains the showroom and is characterized by a projecting stair shaft. An itinerary through the complex enables visitors to admire the production cycle.
Schweizerische Bauzeitung, 110, 1937; Max Bill et al., Moderne Schweizer Architektur 1925–1945, Basel 1947; Archithese, 2, 1980; Guide to Swiss Architecture 1920–1990, vol. 2, 804, p. 219.

Biel
Congress Center
Silbergasse/Zentralstrasse
1957–66
Max Schlup
The result of a showy structural architecture using exposed concrete as the principal material, the building has a balanced stereometric play between the tower incorporating the offices and the lower building (swimming-pool and theater) with its dynamically rising roof.
Schlup has also designed other significant works in Biel, such as the Champagne School, Champagneallee (1960), and the Office Building, Leugenestrasse 6 (1984–85).
B. de Sivo, L'architettura in Svizzera, Naples 1968; Guide to Swiss Architecture 1920–1990, vol. 2, 807, p. 224.

General Motors Works Offices and period aerial view

Congress Center

Biel
Training College for the Timber Industry Extension
Solothurnerstrasse 102
1990–
Marcel Meili and Markus Peter with U. Schönenberger
The School extension is a wooden prismatic volume characterized by the horizontal rhythm of the apertures and an attic crowned by extended eaves. The architects' skillful detailing has made an important contribution in continuing the Swiss wooden building tradition.
Construction. Intention. Detail. Five Projects from Five Swiss Architects, London-Zürich 1994.

Berne
Volkshaus
Zeughausgasse 9
1913–14
Otto Ingold
Situated in a downtown area, the building designed by Otto Ingold has a monumental character, expressed through the giant orders comprising the three upper floors, together with a semi-circular tympanum crowning the entrance. This early work is a very significant stage for understanding Ingold's future development in works such as the Housing at Buchserstrasse 2–4 (1933–35).
Schweizerische Bauzeitung, 5, 1913; INSA. Inventario Svizzero di Architettura 1850–1920, vol. II, Berne 1986.

Berne
Lory Hospital
Freiburgstrasse 18
1924–29
Otto R. Salvisberg and Otto Brechbühl
Elfenau Clinic
Elfenauweg 68
1929–30
Otto R. Salvisberg and Otto Brechbühl
Extensions
1948 and 1967
Otto Brechbühl
Built following a 1924 competition, the Lory Hospital is the extension of an existing complex. The longitudinal volume with the patients' rooms is south-oriented and has partly open balconies and partly a glass facade with semicircular rooms at both ends. This solution was used again in the Elfenau Cantonal Clinic, where sliding windows can create open-air rooms. The building was later extended and raised by one floor under the direction of Brechbühl. See also the District Hospital of St-Imier, in the canton of Jura, built by Salvisberg in 1933–34.
Schweizerische Bauzeitung, 87, 1926; 97, 1931; 97, 1930; Werk, 13, 1926; 7, 1929; Moderne Bauformen, 9, 1930; L'Architecture d'aujourd'hui, 2, 1939; Werk-archithese, 10, 1977; 11–12, 1978; Guide to Swiss Architecture 1920–1990, vol. 2, 701, p. 189.

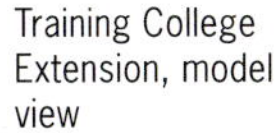

Training College Extension, model view

Volkshaus

Elfenau Clinic

Lory Hospital

Berne

University Institutes of Natural Sciences

Bühlstrasse 20/Sahlistrasse 6–10
Baltzerstrasse/Muesmattstrasse
1928–31

Otto R. Salvisberg and Otto Brechbühl

With carefully balanced proportions, this longitudinal exposed concrete block is shaped by the serial repetitions of elements. It contains laboratories and lecture halls for various institutes. Projecting comb-like bodies create side courts towards south, while the sequence of curved volumes of the amphitheaters sets the rhythm for the entrances.

Schweizerische Bauzeitung, 4, 1929; Werk, 7, 1929; 8, 1932; Moderne Bauformen, 9, 1930; 2, 1933; Werk-archithese, 10, 1977; Parametro, 140, 1985; Guide to Swiss Architecture 1920–1990, vol. 2, 704, p. 192.

Berne

SUVA Building

Laupenstrasse 11/Seilerstrasse
1930–31

Otto R. Salvisberg and Otto Brechbühl

Just after returning from Berlin Salvisberg was commissioned (following a competition) to build what was to be the most important Berne architectural work of the 1930s – the SUVA-Haus. Clearly influenced by Erich Mendelsohn's Schocken Department Stores at Chemnitz (1928–29), the building's projecting vertical stair shafts balance the horizontality of the curved travertine-clad front with ribbon windows.

In 1936 Salvisberg built the Favre House, Alpenstrasse 64, at Biel.

Schweizerische Bauzeitung, 96, 1930; Werk, 8, 1932; Moderne Bauformen, 2, 1933; Werk-archithese, 10, 1977; 11–12 1978; Guide to Swiss Architecture 1920–1990, vol. 2, 706, p. 193.

Berne

Swiss National Library

Hallwylstrasse 15
1928–31

Alfred Oeschger, Josef Kaufmann, and Emil Hostettler

Built following a national competition, the library design has a symmetric plan and responds to specific functional requirements (offices, reading rooms, book storage, etc.) through the articulation of blocks of various heights, further differentiated by the handling of the apertures.

Nearby is the Museum of Natural History, Bernstrasse 15, built by Krebs and Müller (1932–33), and subsequently extended three times (1938, 1960, and 1970).

Werk, 11, 1931; Moderne Schweizer Architektur 1925–1945, Basel 1947; H. Volkart, Schweizer Architektur, Ravensburg 1951; Werk-archithese, 11–12, 1978; Guide to Swiss Architecture 1920–1990, vol. 2, 705, p. 191.

University Institutes of Natural Sciences

SUVA Building, front view and section

Swiss National Library

Berne
Stapfenacker School
Brünnenstrasse 40, Bümpliz
1929–32
Karl Indermühle
Extension
1946
Peter Indermühle

The competition-wining project was completely revised at the executive stage. The L-shaped plan with the classrooms in the north-west wing – broken up into groups of three by stair blocks – leaves the area to the south free for games.

Among other interesting works by Karl Indermühle, see the Friedenskirche, Kirchbühlweg 25 (1917–20), and the Reformed Church of Grenchen in the canton of Solothurn, Zwinglistrasse 9 (1914).

Werk, 10, 1932; Werk-archithese, 11–12, 1978; Guide to Swiss Architecture 1920–1990, vol. 2, 707, p. 193.

Berne
Housing
Hallerstrasse 49–55
1934–35
Ernst W. Ebersold

Situated on a slope overlooking the main Berne railway station, the apartments in this housing are organized in a single curved block with an entrance court at the rear side.

Werk-archithese, 11–12, 1978.

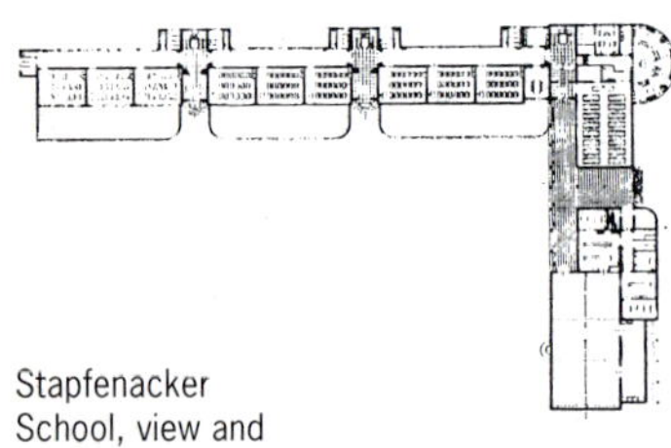

Stapfenacker School, view and floor plan

Hallerstrasse Housing

Berne

Arts and Crafts School

Lorrainestrasse 1

1935–39

Hans Brechbühler

Situated parallel to the river beside the Lorraine Bridge, Brechbühler's Arts and Crafts School – a reinforced concrete parallelepiped supported by pilotis and flanked by independent towers of stairs – has clearly been influenced by Le Corbusier. The worshops also have their own volume, stretching along the main building on the slope towands the river Aare.

Schweizerische Bauzeitung, 106, 1935; Werk, 7, 1940; Werk-archithese, 11–12, 1978; Guide to Swiss Architecture 1920–1990, vol. 2, 712, p. 196.

Berne

Amthaus Extension

Hodlerstrasse 7

1976–81

Atelier 5

Although the Amthaus (district judicial offices) was entirely renovated and extended to house new workspaces, the nineteenth-century street facade was preserved. The extension juxtaposed to the rear of the building closely follows the corner shape and creates small covered courts. It constitutes a sensitive modern counterpoint to the existing building through the use of glass and steel.

Baumeister, 3, 1978; Guide to Swiss Architecture 1920–1990, vol. 2, 724, p. 207.

Arts and Crafts School

Amthaus, detail of court facade

Berne
Art Museum Extension
Hodlerstrasse 12
1976–83
Atelier 5
with C. Bartenbach, H. Eichenberger, and R. Zaugg

Backed onto the existing building with its proportions and orientation, but in a clearly contrasting architectural language, the extension to the Kunsthaus inverts the conventional view of the museum by creating a "machine for perception" with subtle technical devices blending natural and artificial light.

Baumeister 3, 1978; Docu Bulletin, 1, 1980; Architettura Svizzera, 4, 1984; Archithese, 1, 1984; Rivista Tecnica, 1, 1984.

Berne
Wittigkofen Nursing Home
Jupiterstrasse 65
1983–85
Atelier 5

The Nursing Home consists of two L-shaped buildings characterized by a

Art Museum and Extension

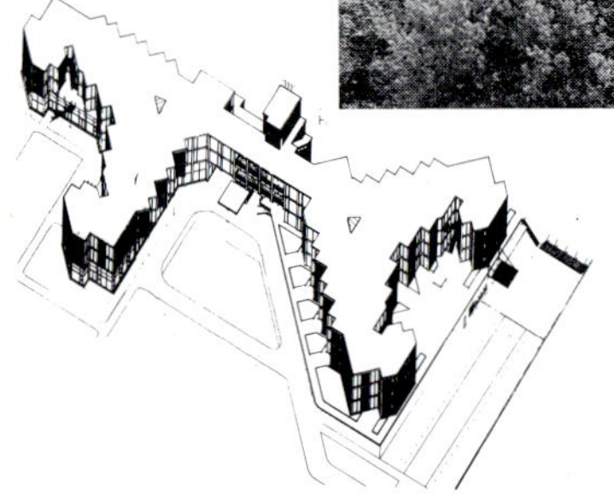

Wittigkofen Nursing Home, axonometric and view

series of balconies and terraces making optimal use of natural lighting. In this way the carefully designed plan meets the complex needs of an institution caring for the chronically ill.
Baumeister, 2, 1985; Werk, Bauen und Wohnen, 12, 1989; Architettura Svizzera, 7–8, 1990; Architectural Review, 1, 1991; P. Disch (ed), L'architettura recente nella Svizzera tedesca 1980–1990, Lugano 1991, p. 77; Deutsche Bauzeitung, 5, 1992; Guide to Swiss Architecture 1920–1990, vol. 2, 732, p. 211.

Berne
Unitobler Human and Social Sciences Center
Länggasstrasse/Lerchenweg/Muesmattstrasse
1987–93
Pierre Clemençon, Daniel Herren, and Andrea Roost
with G. Hofman
The aim of the project was to redevelop the heterogeneous urban fabric created by the uneven growth of the Tobler chocolate factory (1898–1957) as a university center for the human and social sciences. The load-bearing structure of the existing building is left intact – as a memory of the factory's history – and the main focus is on the core of the complex, where a central space for the library is created in the old courtyard. The various university institutes are located in the former production areas, while the classrooms face onto a new plane-tree-lined court along Lerchenweg.
P. Disch (ed), L'architettura recente della Svizzera tedesca, Lugano 1991, p. 85; Guide to Swiss Architecture 1920–1990, vol. 2, 734, p. 212.

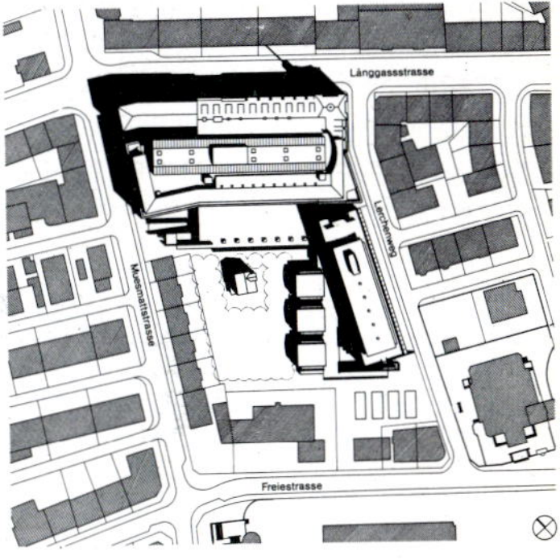

Unitobler Human and Social Sciences Center, interior and site plan

Berne

Bühlplatz Student Center

Gertrud-Woker-Strasse 3

1988–91

Regina and Alain Gonthier with B. Schenk and E. Bischoff

Not far from the University Institutes of Natural Sciences, Bühlstrasse 20, by Otto R. Salvisberg and Otto Brechbühl (see p. 158), the new student center is conceived as a formally independent structure meant as a single element in the orthogonal fabric of the university quarter. At the same time, as a meeting place and recreation facility, the complex is an important part of the university. Built up from clear geometric principles, the building joins up the public sector (cafeteria and services), based on a radial structure open to the exterior, with the technical installations to the rear. The same architects also designed Housing at Hünibach-Thun, Wartbodenstrasse 27 (1985–88).

P. Disch (ed), L'architettura recente nella Svizzera tedesca 1980–1990, Lugano 1991, p. 80; Hochparterre, 1992, 6; Architettura Svizzera, 1993, 6; Werk, Bauen und Wohnen, 1993, 7–8.

Brügg

Siedlung Rainpark

Rainpark

1968–71

Halen

Siedlung Halen

Halenbrücke/Länggasse

1955–61

Herrenschwanden

Siedlung Thalmatt I and II

Mettlenwaldweg

1967–74 and 1981–85

Atelier 5

Of the many housing schemes built by Atelier 5 from the 1950s on, the

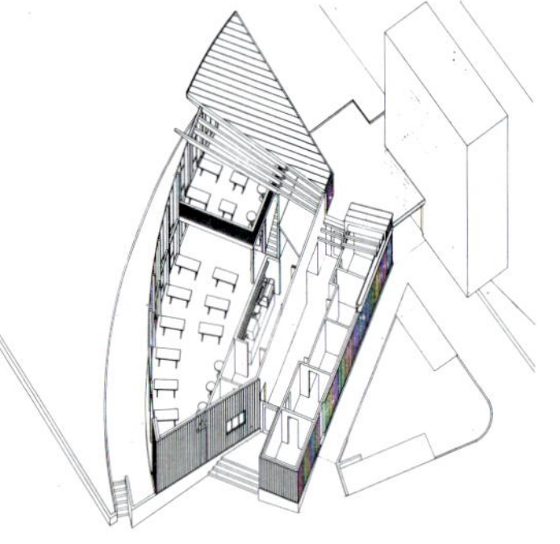

Bühlplatz Student Center, view and axonometric

Siedlung Halen widely came to be seen as one of the most significant postwar residential works. The 79 houses in rows arranged on terraces (two building types and four variations) with common facilities (swimming pool, sports center, restaurant and services), reflect the attempt to give a compact urban feel to the scheme but with all the advantages of the natural setting. This typological solution is further developed in the Siedlung Rainpark and the Thalmatt I and II schemes, which include a rational separation of circulation flows.
Similar criteria inform the design for the Siedlung Ried, Brüggbühlstrasse (1983–91) at Niederwangen by the same architects. Another interesting work is their Thalmatt Shopping Center, Mettlenwaldweg (1985–88), at Herrenschwanden.

G.E. Kidder Smith, The New Architecture of Europe, New York 1961; Architectural Design, 2, 1963; Werk, 2, 1963; 7, 1971; 4, 1974; 3, 1975; L'Architecture d'aujourd'hui, 121, 1965; 11–12, 1973; 252, 1987; R. Banham, The New Brutalism, London-New York 1966; J. Bachmann and S. von Moos, New Directions in Swiss Architecture, New York 1969; Architettura Svizzera, 1, 1972; 10, 1974; a + u, architecture and urbanism, 10, 1975; Werk-archithese, 9–10, 1978; Abitare, 206, 1986; Faces, 2, 1986; P. Disch, L'Architettura recente nella Svizzera tedesca 1980–1990, Lugano 1991, p. 88; Guide to Swiss Architecture 1920–1990, vol. 2, 812, p. 226; 602, p. 177; 603, p. 178.

Siedlungen:
Rainpark
Halen
Thalmatt I and II

Münsingen

USM Manufacturing Plant

Thunstrasse 55

1961–87

Fritz Haller

with R. Steiner, H. Weber, J. Luterbacher

In response to the need to build this manufacturing plant in four stages, Haller developed a new construction system with steel elements providing the maximum flexibility. This approach was also of fundamental importance in his "system-designs" for office furniture developed for the same project.

Bauen und Wohnen, 11, 1962; 10, 1964; Detail, 2, 1967; J. Bachmann and S. von Moos, New Directions in Swiss Architecture, New York 1969; F. Haller, Bauen und Forschen, Solothurn 1988.

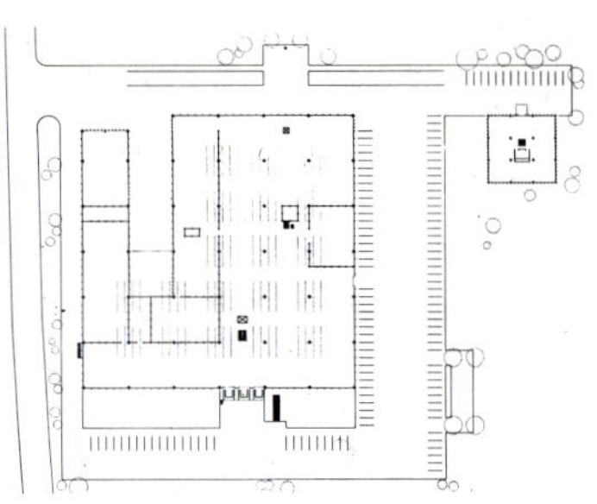

USM Manufacturing Plant, site plan

Schwarzenburg

Rossgraben Bridge

Schönentannen-Hinterfultigen road

1932

Robert Maillart

In exploring new possibilities for reinforced concrete, Maillart designed this triply articulated box girder bridge to supersede the old pillar-beam constructional system, as he did with the neighboring stiffened bar arch bridge, the famous Schwandbach Bridge (1933). This effectively paved the way to a new aesthetics of reinforced concrete based on the relations between form, structure and cost.

Max Bill et al., Moderne Schweizer Architektur 1925–1945, Basel 1947; Werk, Bauen und Wohnen, 12, 1983; D. P. Billington, Robert Maillart and the Art of Reinforced Concrete, Zurich and Munich 1990.

Steffisburg

Studio-House

Kirchbühlweg 15

1928

Arnold Itten

The close collaboration between the architect and the client-artist clearly shows through in this studio-house, a significant project on the Modern Swiss architectural scene of the 1920s. Still preserved in its original condition, the building's articulated volumes, and the marked horizontality in the facades, are reminiscent of the hotels designed by Itten at Mürren, now unfortunately completely altered.

Neues Bauen in der Schweiz, Führer zur Architektur der 20er und 30er Jahre, Blauen 1985.

USM Manufacturing Plant

Rossgraben Bridge, view and section

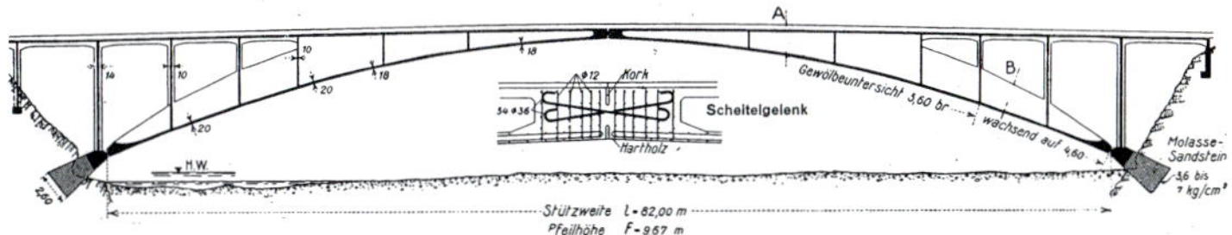

Studio-House, exterior views

Villeret

Cartier Factory

1990–92

Jean Nouvel, Emmanuel Cattani and Associates

with J. Chapelet and E. Maria

Contractors: IMZA

Situated in the valley of Saint-Imier, traditionally famed for its clock and watch production, the building of the *Compagnie des technologies de luxe* emerges from a landscape of industrial sheds in the form of a glass parallelepiped characterized by the strength of its architectural ambition. Although abstraction is the principle used to define and separate the structure from the context, paradoxically its transparency creates a play of reflections integrating the building into the Jura scenery. The explicit functional inner organization reveals the building's derivation from a given typology.

Architecture romande, 4, 1991; Faces, 28, 1993; Guide to Swiss Architecture 1920–1990, vol. 2, 826, p. 234.

Zollikofen

Mixed-Use Building

Industriestrasse 1

1987–91

Atelier 5

Starting from the need to provide an adequate response to the overall urban condition as well as to make optimal use of the site, the building follows the lines of the lot and meets the various functional requirements for offices, storerooms and craft workshops.

Of the many works by Atelier 5 in the canton of Berne, see the small factory, Bernstrasse 19 (1958–59) and the Seminary, Äussere Ringstrasse (1977–86) at Thun, the psychiatric hospital at Münsingen (1984–91) and the Vaucher Building, Hallmattstrasse 4 (1980–83), at Niederwangen.

Werk, Bauen und Wohnen, 12, 1992; Architettura Svizzera, 5, 1993; Guide to Swiss Architecture 1920–1990, vol. 2, 611, p. 182.

Cartier Factory

Mixed-Use Building: Street facade, floor plan, and aerial view

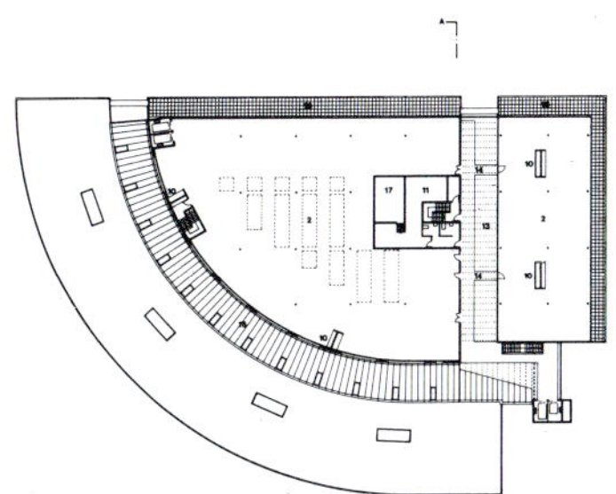

Mixed-Use Building: Workshops

Glarus

Glarus
Art Gallery
Oswald-Heer-Strasse 2
1951–52
Hans Leuzinger

Leuzinger's ensemble is convincing because of its simplicity: the two cube-shaped, distinct buildings with solid, yellow-brick elevations and glass pitched roofs are linked via a flat entrance pavilion to form an L-shape which opens out towards the park.

Leuzinger also designed what was at the time classed as an example of "new mountain architecture": the Ortstockhaus alpine refuge built in 1931 at Braunwaldalp at an altitude of 1,700 meters. Unfortunately, it has since been remodeled.

Werk, 9, 1952; Guide to Swiss Architecture 1920–1990, vol. 1, 405, p. 99.

Glarus
Cantonal Hospital Staff Lodgings
Buchholzstrasse/Asylstrasse
1950–53, 1967–69
Jakob Zweifel
with C. Hoffmann

The complex was built in various stages involving the use of different building types. Both the tower building, flanked by a group of four nurses' lodgings, and the annexed row of houses with terraces for the medical staff were designed with the focus on finding the most suitable solution for residential requirements.

Werk, 1, 1952; 1, 1954; 5, 1955; Werk, Bauen und Wohnen, 7–8, 1989; Guide to Swiss Architecture 1920–1990, vol. 1, 404.

Niederurnen
Eternit AG Headquarters
Eternitstrasse
1953–54
Max Ernst Haefeli and Werner Max Moser
with F. van Kuyk
For reasons of corporate image, Eternit tiles were chosen as the principal cladding material on the exterior of this building. The two functional areas of the structure are clearly distinguished by the rows of windows and spandrels of the offices as well as the enclosed staircase tower extended to act as a showroom.
A similar relationship between architectural appearance and product can be seen in Eternit's Payerne Factory, rue Bovière, Vaud Canton, by Paul Waltenspühl (1956–57).
Werk, 6, 1956; Deutsche Bauzeitschrift, 5, 1958; Archithese, 2, 1980; 5, 1993; Guide to Swiss Architecture 1920–1990, vol. 1, 408, p. 102.

Niederurnen
Village Hall
1955–56
Hans Leuzinger and Hans Howald
Positioned on a natural rise cut out of a stone base leading to the entrance area, the village hall has a hexagonal plan and a pitched roof raised on the front axis.
At Niederurnen, together with Jean Graf, Leuzinger also built the School on Pestalozzistrasse (1953–54).
Werk, 4, 1957; Deutsche Bauzeitschrift, 10, 1961; Guide to Swiss Architecture 1920–1990, vol. 1, 409, p. 102.

Eternit Headquarters

Village Hall

Opposite page:
Art Gallery

Cantonal Hospital Staff Lodgings, exterior views

Schwyz

Buttikon
Parish Center
Dorfplatz
1964–70
Joachim Naef, Ernst Studer, and Gottfried Studer

The outcome of a 1964 competition, the church was part of an overall project to redevelop the town center (town hall, shops and housing). The central-plan building with an exposed reinforced-concrete structure has natural lighting from skylights. The three entrances all have external towers. The spiral circulation guides the members of the congregation towards the altar. The flexible interior may be adapted to various parish community events (concerts, lectures and meetings).

Well-known for their long experience in the field of religious architecture, the architects also designed the Buchrain Church, canton of Lucerne (1970–72), and the Parish Center of St Martin at Thun (1971), canton of Berne.

Rivista Tecnica, 24, 1971; Werk, 12, 1971; Werk, Bauen und Wohnen, 1–2, 1980.

Parish Center

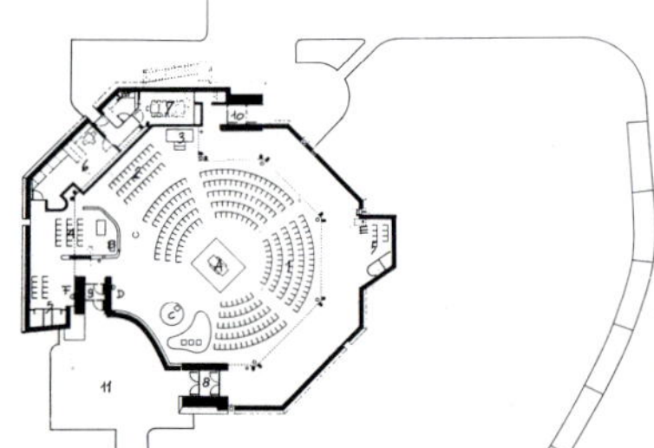

Zug

Baar

Büel Housing

Büelstrasse 21–27

1983–86

Dolf Schnebli and Tobias Ammann

with Werner Egli and Hans Rohr

with V. Brändli, and F. Vogel

Situated near a railway line, the Siedlung Büel groups various housing blocks round a plaza in an open scheme. A closed building on the western side contains the access passages for the residential units and also provides acoustic protection. The main dwelling type is a duplex with individual entrances and access to roof-terraces for the upper-floor units, while the ground-floor apartments have private gardens.

Archithese, 2, 1986; 3, 1986; Rivista Tecnica, 1–2, 1986; Faces, 14, 1989; Architettura Svizzera, 2, 1990; Detail, 1, 1990.

Büel Housing

Oberägeri
van de Velde Houses I and II
Holderbachweg 1a/
Alte Landstrasse 4a
1939 and 1957
Alfred Roth

The first of these two houses was designed by Alfred Roth in the 1930s as a holiday house for a celebrated client: Henry van de Velde. In old age he was no longer able to go along the path to reach the house, so Roth designed a second house for him nearby. Here van de Velde spent his last years writing his memories which, incidentally, mentions the wooden bungalows magnificently set in the landscape and inspired by the early houses of Frank Lloyd Wright.

Werk, 11, 1962.

Oberägeri
House
Müslirain 9
1990–92
Mario Campi and Franco Pessina

The sloping zinc roof elements, chosen because of local building regulations, becomes – along with the smooth natural stone – the main feature in this design for a single-family house by Campi and Pessina. The marked projection of the roof conveys a sense of great lightness. The circulation leads to the house from the garage – half underground beneath the entrance – to the living room on the first floor. It then comes to a dramatic climax in the double-height space overlooking the landscape – the real fulcrum of the house.

Rivista Tecnica, 10, 1992; Domus, 751, 1993; A + u, architecture and urbanism, 3, 1993.

Steinhausen
Ecumenical Center
Chilematt
1976–81
Ernst Gisel
with Heinz Schmid, P. Steiner, and J. M. Bovet

The aim of the project for this fast-growing dormitory town not far from Zürich was to create an urban identity and provide suitable social facilities. In addition to a Catholic Church and an Evangelical Church, the center has various rooms for community activities organized in a single building deliberately stripped of any hierarchical elements but articulated in differentiated volumes. The use of exposed concrete in the exteriors with copper, wood and natural stone claddings breaks up and defines the masses, while inside the white walls are brightened by overhead lighting.

Abitare, 206, 1982; Werk, Bauen und Wohnen, 7–8, 1982; Detail, 4, 1983.

van de Velde
Houses I and II

House in Oberägeri

Ecumenical Center

Unterägeri

Former Children's Hospital (Nurses' lodgings)

Heimeilistrasse

1935–38

Dagobert Keiser and Richard Bracher with E. Steiger and P. Trüdinger

Conceived in the Rationalist tradition of hospital designs, the Heimeli hospital, with its characteristic metal structure anchored to a massive concrete base, is completely faced in wood.

Moderne Schweizer Architektur 1925–1945, Basel 1947; Werk, 9, 1954.

Zug

Protestant Church

Alpenstrasse

1903–06

Karl Moser

with Jacques Kehrer and Friedrich Wehrli

Like the Church of St Michael (Zugerbergstrasse) or the Church of St Paulus in Lucerne (Moosmattstrasse 2), built by Curjel & Moser in 1892–1902 and 1911–12, respectively, this Protestant church is an example of how Moser explored the most suitable sty-

Children's Hospital

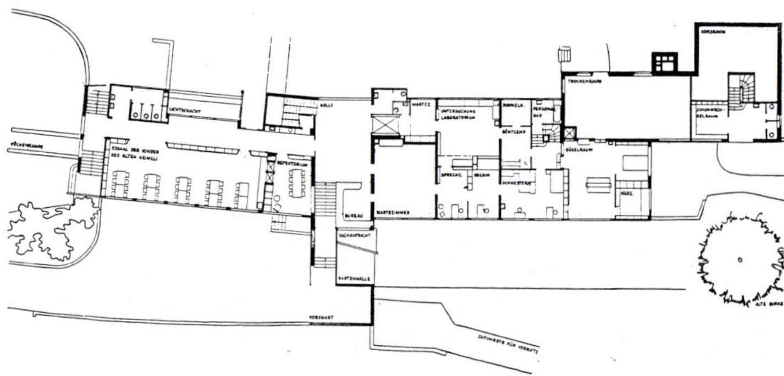

listic possibilities in the many religious buildings he designed at the turn of the century. At this time Moser showed considerable leanings towards Romanesque forms. He used them to experiment with anti-Classical proportions and detailing as well as in creating unorthodox spaces.

Schweizerische Bauzeitung, 47, 1906; ISNA. Inventario Svizzero di Architettura 1850–1920, vol. 10, Berne 1992.

Zug
Housing
Bleichimattweg 11
1931
Heinrich Peikert

The adoption of terraced type housing with continuous verandahs stressing the horizontality of the whole scheme highlights not only the importance of the orientation, exposure to the sun, and building rationality, but also a concern with the central themes in the Modern debate on new approaches to housing.

I. Noseda, Kulturobjekte der Stadt Zug, Zug 1990.

Protestant Church

Housing

Zug
Cantonal Bank
Bahnhofstrasse 1
1949–58
Leo Hafner and Alfons Wiederkehr

In the clearly organized plan the building is arranged round a central atrium (modified in 1985). The design of the facade re-elaborates traditional elements of the *palazzo*, such as the loggia and crowning, but does so in a functionalist key, using lighter materials – aluminum, steel and glass.

Werk, 5, 1959; A. Altherr, New Swiss Architecture, Teufen 1965; Guide to Swiss Architecture 1920–1990, vol. 1, 843, p. 246.

Zug
Terrassenweg Housing
Terrassenweg 1–9
1957–60
Fritz Stucky and Rudolf Meuli

Pioneers in developing a particularly popular building type in Switzerland, Stucky and Meuli designed blocks of dwellings arranged in step-like fashion on a fifty-one-degree slope. Each block consists of five superimposed stories of apartments, with the services further uphill and the living rooms overlooking large terraces. Another example of this kind of housing is the Mühlehalde scheme, at Brugg-Umiken, can-

Cantonal Bank

Terrassenweg Housing

ton of Aargau (1962–71), designed by Scherer, Strickler and Weber (Team 2000).

Werk, 2, 1961; 10, 1964; Architecture, formes + fonction, 8, 1961; L'Architecture d'aujourd'hui, 100, 1962; A. Altherr, New Swiss Architecture, Teufen 1965; J. Bachmann and S. von Moos, New Directions in Swiss Architecture, New York 1969; Guide to Swiss Architecture 1920–1990, vol. 1, 844, p. 246.

Zug

Herti V Housing

General-Guisanstrasse 22–30

1989–94

Kuhn, Fischer and Associates (W. Fischer and G. Scherrer) with P. Winistörfer, P. Meichtry, and C. Späti

The complex is organized in two sectors, separated by a pedestrian passage, characterized by the rhythm of the vertical circulation shafts. The main building block, which ends towards General-Guisanstrasse, accommodates the apartments, while a comb-like structure contains various service areas and collective facilities.

Schweizer Ingenieur und Architekt, 50, 1989; Hochparterre, 10, 1990.

Herti V Housing

Lucerne

Baldegg
Sonnhalde Crèche, Kindergarten and Nursing Home
Sonnhaldenstrasse 2
1968–72
Marcel Breuer and Beat Jordi

This basically inward-looking complex is built to an H-shaped plan with passages giving onto courtyards. The highly plastic feel of the horizontally-patterned buildings is achieved through the use of prefabricated concrete elements (creating deep windows) and natural materials (stone and wood), whose texture is evidenced by the play of light.

In collaboration with Herbert Beckardt and Eberhard Eidenbenz, Marcel Breuer also designed the Staehelin House, Im Hausacker 35 (1957), at Feldmeilen, canton of Zürich, which today still is a private home.

Werk, 4, 1973; Bauen und Wohnen, 9, 1975; Architettura Svizzera, 38, 1979.

Eggen
Erni Studio-House
Kreuzbuchstrasse
1957 and 1966
Hans Erni, Josef Gärtner, and Paul Gässner

Painter and sculptor Hans Erni designed his own studio-house on a hill overlooking the lake. The handling of the volumes and evident search for a "human scale" reveal the artist's admiration for the work of Le Corbusier.

H. Ineichen and T. Zanoni (eds), Luzerner Architekten 1920–1960, Zurich-Berne 1985.

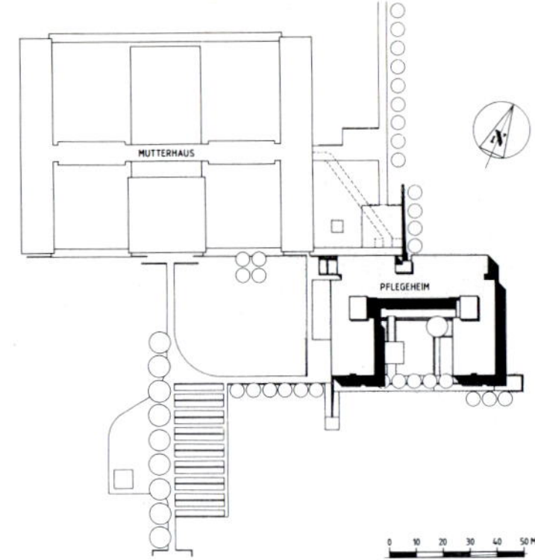

Emmenbrücke
Kraan-Lang House
Oberriffig 7
1992–93
Daniele Marques and Bruno Zurkirchen
with S. Mauthe and F. Ritter

The highly heterogeneous peripheral context consisting of various buildings, such as industrial structures and housing schemes, led the designers to create a kind of container whose handling clearly implies its provisional nature. The use of light materials – a prefabricated wooden system and metal sheet cladding – creates a counterpoint to a neighboring massive reinforced-concrete volume.

Hochparterre, 5, 1994; Werk, Bauen und Wohnen, 5, 1994.

Sonnhalde Crèche, Kindergarten and Nursing Home, view and, opposite page, site plan

Erni Studio-House

Kraan-Lang House

Littau

Ruopigen Center

Ruopigenplatz 4–20

1962–87

Dolf Schnebli, Tobias Ammann and Isidor Ryser

with R. Matter, P. Huber, M. Meili, A. Fickert and J. Kubli

Primary school

Ruopigen Center

1974

Dolf Schnebli

with K. Dolder and Dommann-Plüss

The subject of an ideas competition held in 1962, the Ruopigen Center in the Lucerne conglomerate required a twenty-year planning process aimed at giving an anonymous area an urban character. The plan included a settlement of 9,000 inhabitants on an area of 530,000 square meters and defined the overall spatial order with a hierarchical scheme of inter-relations between public and private spaces explicitly drawing on the models of the British new towns and the ideas of Le Corbusier.

Ruopigen Center

After the project had been revised several times, building work – planned in various stages – began in 1974 with the construction of a primary school, followed in the 1980s by the completion of the housing center.

The urban structure based on "organically" articulated settlements with separate networks for road and pedestrian traffic is innovative both for the Lucerne building rules and in terms of the architectural definition of the individual elements.

Archithese, 2, 1980; Abitare, 206, 1982; Werk, Bauen und Wohnen, 11, 1985; Architektur und Technik, 3, 1987; Rivista Tecnica, 7–8, 1987; Detail, 6, 1988; The Architectural Review, 1, 1991; du, 5, 1992; Guide to Swiss Architecture 1920–1990, vol. 1, 826, p. 236; 825, p. 237.

Lucerne

SUVA Offices

Fluhmattstrasse 1

1914–15

Otto and Werner Pfister

Winners of a 1914 competition (the members of the jury were leading architects of the day, such as Maurice Braillard, Karl Indermühle, and Robert Rittmeyer), the Pfister brothers met the functional requirements of the brief by proposing a *palazzo* type. The organization of the main building body, with a solid volume acting as the head, crowned by a Neo-Baroque dome, gives the overall construction a monumental dimension.

Werk, 10, 1916; INSA. Inventario Svizzero di Architettura 1850–1920, vol. VI, Berne 1991; Archithese, 3, 1993.

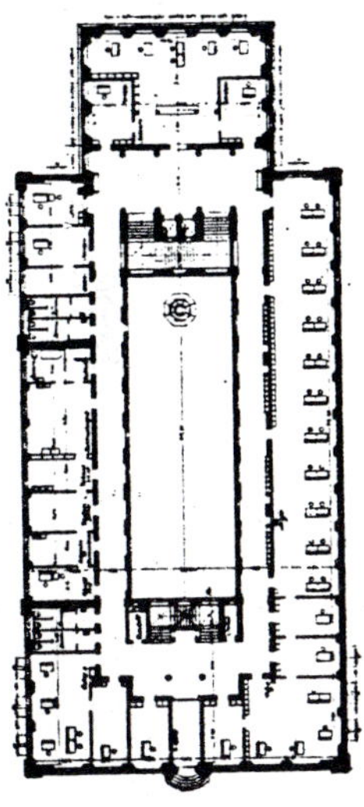

SUVA Offices, view and floor plan

Lucerne
Schweizerische Kreditanstalt Headquarters
Schwanenplatz 8
1922
Karl Moser and Emil Vogt
Swiss National Bank
Pilatusstrasse 10
1922
Hermann Herter
Both of these bank buildings constitute monumental edifices in the cityscape. However, while Karl Moser and Emil Vogt resorted to massive pier and column arrangements, the tried-and-tested formula for noble status, Hermann Herter employed thrifty, classical stylistic means so that his liking for the elemental cubic form already becomes apparent here.
H. Ineichen and T. Zanoni (eds), Luzerner Architekten 1920–1960, Zurich-Berne 1985; Guide to Swiss Architecture 1920–1990, vol 1, 901, p. 255.

Lucerne
Crematorium
Friedental
1923–26
Albert Froelich
Situated on the north-west periphery of the city, the symmetric and monumental crematorium is set on a terraced area of the cemetery. The architect, who also built the crematoriums in Zürich and Aarau, organizes the building in a central cylindrical volume,

Schweizerische Kreditanstalt Headquarters

Swiss National Bank

Crematorium

crowned by a dome, and two wings containing the columbaries.

Lucerne
Siedlung of the Allgemeine Baugenossenschaft
Neuweg/Blücherstr./Bundesstr./ Claridenstr./Heimatweg/Tödistr.
1926, 1931
Otto Schärli snr, Werner Dolder
Siedlung Geissmatt
Spitalstr. 26–27–29/ Spitalweg 6
1935–36
Carl Mossdorf

The ABL development was built in two phases and made use of two types of building. Otto Schärli's 1926 scheme (Neuweg/Blücherstrasse) was based on blocks completely surrounding an enclosed garden court, whereas five years later Werner Dolder designed three curved, six-story blocks on the Bundesstrasse in a north-south direction (PTT head building, Augusto Guidini, 1932).

The Geissmatt estate evolved out of a self-help response on the part of the construction industry. Four low-cost, parallel blocks with open walkways were erected on cheap land on the former edge of the town. All apartments have loggias facing west. The pitched roofs convey the image of a tempered Modern style.

Siedlung of the Allgemeine Baugenossenschaft

Siedlung Geissmatt

Lucerne
Mixed-Use Building
Burgerstrasse 33
1930–31
Art and Conference Center
Bahnhofplatz 2
1930 (destroyed)
Allmend Barracks
Murmattweg 6
1935
Armin Meili

Meili's Center was situated on the banks of the lake next to the railway station. Directly opposite stands Meili's delicate metal landing stage dating from 1935. The traditional facade of the Burgertor mixed office and housing scheme conceals the advanced technologies in the interior. The coherent architecture, the rough-formwork finish to the reinforced concrete and the regimented rows of identical windows lend the barracks a powerful expressive quality.

Guide to Swiss Architecture 1920–1990, vol. 1, 906, p. 258; 904, p. 257; 908, p. 260.

Lucerne
Cultural and Congress Center
Bahnhofplatz
1989/1993–2001
Jean Nouvel

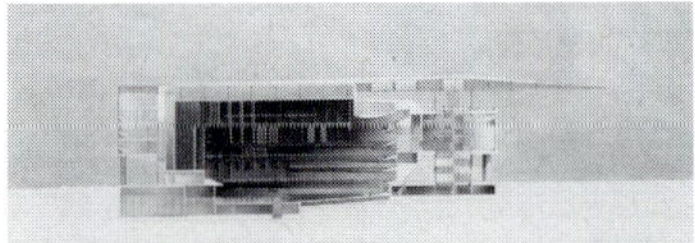

Mixed-Use Building

Top: J. Nouvel, Cultural and Congress Center

Middle: A. Meili, Art and Conference Center

Allmend Barracks

Replacing Meili's former Art and Conference Center, the new complex is formed by three parallel concert and performance halls connected by a transverse structure.
Olivier Boissière, Jean Nouvel, Basel/Berlin/Boston 1996.

Lucerne
Dula School
Bruchstrasse 78
1931–33
Albert Zeyer
Blaesi House and Studio
Adligenswilerstrasse 31
1938
Albert Zeyer
Zeyer won the competition held in 1930 to design the Dula School and thereby received his first major and public contract; the result became one of the best-known Functionalist works in Lucerne. Besides classrooms, the building had to accommodate various common facilities. Unfortunately, the gymnastics and sunbathing area on the roof of the gymnasium were sacrificed in favor of extra stories in 1969.
The house and studio designed by Zeyer for his friend and sculptor August Blaesi is a modest affair. The studio forms a rectangle parallel to the slope with the living accommodation in the two stories above forming a rectangle perpendicular to that so that a covered working area is created in front of the studio and a lateral terrace "on" the studio.
H. Ineichen and T. Zanoni (eds), Luzerner Architekten 1920–1960, Zurich-Berne 1985; Guide to Swiss Architecture 1920–1990, vol. 1, 905, p. 257; 911 and 910, p. 261.

Dula School

Blaesi Studio-House

Lucerne
Church of St Karl
St.-Karlistrasse 23
1930–34
Fritz Metzger

Metzger's imposing reinforced concrete structure with its entrance section dominating the river represents an outstanding urban solution and chronicles the importance attributed to sacred buildings by modern architecture (a trend started in Switzerland by Karl Moser's Church of St Anthony in Basel). The new formal elements (a loadbearing structure consisting of freestanding columns, rows of windows which reveal that the walls are not loadbearing components but an envelope) amalgamate with classical allusions in the monumental narthex, decorated with sculptures by August Blaesi.

Werk, 4, 1937; G.E. Kidder Smith, Switzerland Builds, New York-Stockholm 1950; Docu Bulletin, 5, 1984; H. Ineichen and T. Zanoni (eds), Luzerner Architekten 1920–1960, Zurich-Berne 1985; Guide to Swiss Architecture 1920–1990, vol. 1, 907, p. 259.

Lucerne
Church of St Lucas and Parish Hall
Morgatenstrasse 16
1935
Alfred Möri and Karl Krebs

Radically revised compared to the competition-winning design of 1924, the relationship between parish hall and church reflects the orthogonal structures of the neighborhood. The vertical, soaring, open bell-tower forms the entrance facade.

Werk, 3, 1938; Docu Bulletin, 5, 1984; H. Ineichen and T. Zanoni (eds), Luzerner

Church of St Karl

Church of St Lukas

Architekten 1920–1960, Zurich-Berne 1985 Guide to Swiss Architecture 1920–1990, vol. 1, 909, p. 260.

Lucerne
Parish Church of St Joseph, Maihof
Weggismattstrasse
1941–51
Central Library
Sempacherstrasse 10
1949–52
Otto Dreyer

Otto Dreyer was one of the most important exponents of modern Swiss church-building during the 1930s and 1940s. His characteristic features were the use of exposed concrete, reducing the architecture to its typical primary elements and an overall economy of form. The Church in Maihof forms an independent solution since a wide, open staircase separates the bell-tower from the nave.

The design for the Central Library is based on a competition design of 1944 and was intended to be built at the Jesuits' Church. However, it was erected at its present location without any modifications. Three of the wings open to the public and the five-story storage section enclose a rectangular internal courtyard. The design and details reflect the Modernist revival in the 1950s.

H. Volkart, Schweizer Architektur, Ravensburg 1951; H. Ineichen and T. Zanoni (eds), Luzerner Architekten 1920–1960, Zurich-Berne 1985; Guide to Swiss Architecture 1920–1990, vol. 1, 912, p. 262; 914, p. 263; 918, p. 265.

Church of St Joseph Maihof

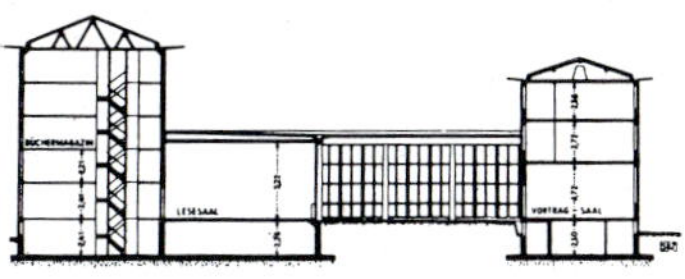

Central Library, view and section

Lucerne
Felsberg School
Felsbergstrasse 10–12
1944–48
Emil Jauch and Erwin Bürgi
Winning the competition for the Felsberg School in 1944 (built 1944–48) gave the architects the opportunity to open a practice in Lucerne. Three separate classroom pavilions each intended for a different age group are laid out in a row along a broad arc, opening out towards the park. The entrance to the school is denoted by the gymnasium. The repetition of simple forms and the simple materials can be traced back to Jauch's period in Sweden (1936–39).
This work has a number of features in common with the Matt School at Hergiswil, Baumgartenweg 7, in the canton of Nidwalden.
Werk, 7, 1949; H. Volkart, Schweizer Architektur, Ravensburg 1951; H. Ineichen and T. Zanoni (eds), Luzerner Architekten 1920–1960, Zurich-Berne 1985; Guide to Swiss Architecture 1920–1990, vol. 1, 913, p. 262.

Lucerne
Professional Training College
Heimbachweg 12
1954–58
Josef Gasser and Gottfried Wielandt
In contrast to the conventional linear plan for schools, Gasser came up with a square central building in the 1954 competition for this school design. In the center there is a circular inner court spanned by a delicate framework. The exciting combination of square and circle determines the overall room layout and manifests itself on the exterior in a round attic story. In designing this college, the architect advocated Wright's ideas in the Swiss architecture debate of the 1950s.
Archithese, 3, 1985; H. Ineichen and T. Zanoni (eds), Luzerner Architekten 1920–1960, Zurich-Berne 1985 Guide to Swiss Architecture 1920–1990, vol. 1, 916, p. 264.

Lucerne
Schönbühl Tower
Langensandstrasse 37
1965–68
Alvar Aalto, Karl Fleig and Max Wandeler
Shopping Center
Langensandstrasse 23
1965–67
Alfred Roth
with R. Arni and A. Maurer
The sixteen-story tower is the Finnish architect's only building in Switzerland and a further development of his Neue Vahr in Bremen, 1958–62. Its ground plan shows a fan solution. Together with Roth's nearby shopping center, the entire development is an emblematic example in the urban plan controlling the city's southward expansion towards the lake. In addition to attracting an interest in American models of peripheral urban growth, the quality of Aalto's project and Roth's elegant handling of parking access both demonstrate how interesting approaches can be adopted to these often banal kinds of projects.
Werk, 10, 1968; J. Bachmann and S. von Moos, New Directions in Swiss Architecture, New York 1969; Rivista Tecnica, 4, 1982; Guide to Swiss Architecture 1920–1990, vol. 1, 920, p. 267.

Felsberg School

Professional Training College

Schönbühl Tower, view

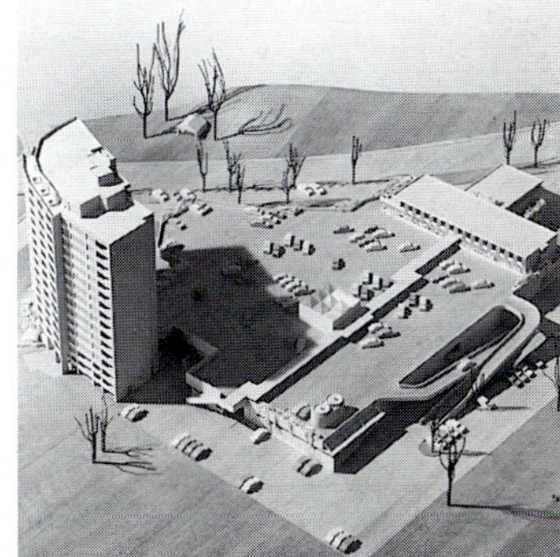

Shopping Center, model view

Lucerne

Redevelopment of the Station Area

Bahnhofplatz

1975–91

Hans-Peter Ammann, Peter Baumann and Santiago Calatrava with R. Borchert, M. Bosshard, M. Burkhalter, H. Cometti, F. Fischer, K. Gallati, D. Geissbühler, R. Hergert, G. Hindalov, P. Höing, E. Imhof, E. Kurze, R. Leimenstoll, A. Linke, E. Lüthi, H. Portmann, T. Portmann, A. Renner, P. Stöckli, G. von Wartburg, and H. Weibel

The outcome of a 1971 competition following the destruction of the old station by fire, the overall project was for several buildings: a passenger arrivals hall with administrative offices; a shopping area; parking; an arts and crafts school building; a postal center and a multistory car park, behind the Fine Arts Museum; and the Inseliquai mixed-use building, overlooking the lake. Calatrava's project for the new station entrance building (reinforced-concrete portico towards the lake and a glazed roof suspended by steel cables) makes the main facade on the station square a powerful architectural presence.

Werk-archithese, 9–10, 1979; Werk, Bauen und Wohnen, 12, 1983; 12, 1988; 6, 1990;

Lucerne Station, aerial view and station elevation

3, 1991; Archithese, 3, 1985; 3, 1986; Quaderns d'Arquitectura i Urbanisme, 6, 1987; 1–2, 1992; Detail, 6, 1988; Architectural Record, 8, 1991; Hochparterre, 1, 1991; P. Disch (ed), L'architettura recente nella Svizzera tedesca 1980–1990, Lugano 1991, p. 144; du, 5, 1992; Guide to Swiss Architecture 1920–1990, vol. 1, 922, p. 268f.

Lucerne
Offices
Rösslimattstrasse 40
1982–87
Hans Eggstein and Walter Rüssli with H. Bühlmann and F. Schnyder

Designed for an unfavorable urban situation due to the triangular shape of the lot bounded by access roads, the building consists of two volumetrically separate buildings joined by a glazed stair shaft, highlighting the contrast between the parts but also providing overall architectural unity. The functional division in the internal organization reflects the external volumetric arrangement with the offices in the parallelepiped and archives in the semi-cylinder.

Archithese, 2, 1988; Werk, Bauen und Wohnen, 12, 1988; P. Disch (ed), L'architettura recente nella Svizzera tedesca 1980–1990, Lugano 1991, p. 150; Architettura Svizzera, 101, 1992; Guide to Swiss Architecture 1920–1990, vol. 1, 923, p. 270.

Lucerne Station

Offices

Lucerne

Mixed-Use Building

Fluhmattweg 4

1988–94

Daniele Marques and Bruno Zurkirchen

Situated in the same areas as the SUVA Building, this shopping and residential complex stands on a steeply sloping site between two roads with different gradients. The stairway joining the two roads and the geometry of the supporting walls become the distinctive features of the complex. In its formal characteristics the complex echoes a number of elements from existing buildings such as the rhythm of the mansard roof contrasting with the monolithic reinforced-concrete structure. At the same time, through the proportions, the project seeks to create a new architecture for the area.

P. Disch (ed), L'architettura recente nella Svizzera tedesca 1980–1990, Lugano 1991, p. 151.

Meggen

Catholic Church and Parish Center

Schlösslistrasse

1964–66

Franz Füeg

The Meggen church is contained in a large closed parallelepiped, characterized by the rhythm of the metal profiles. The constructional system combines prefabricated steel elements with marble panels. Because the panels are very thin, light filters through the veins in the marble, creating a suitable atmosphere for meditation and prayer.

Bauen und Wohnen, 12, 1966; J. Bachmann and S. von Moos, New Directions in Swiss Architecture, New York 1969; R. Gieselmann, Neue Kirchen, Stuttgart 1972.

Catholic Church

Mixed-Use Building, model view and floor plan

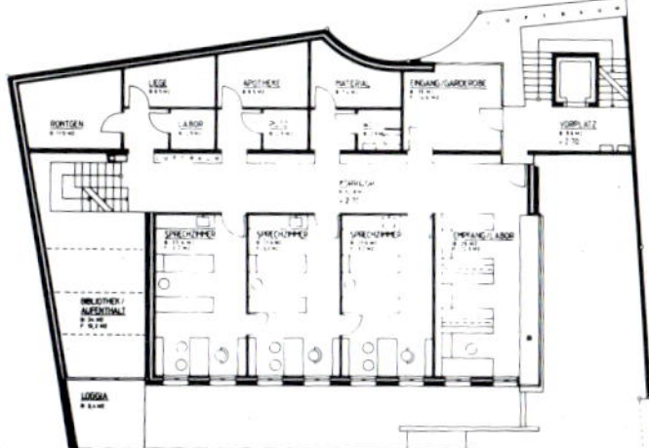

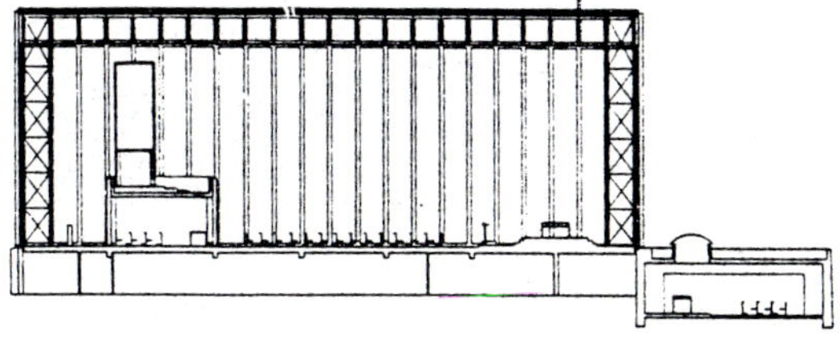

Catholic Church, internal view and section

Meggen

Hodel House

Blosseggrain 2

1984–85

Daniele Marques and Bruno Zurkirchen

with J. Grunder

Hodel House is the architects' first completed commission. Tight building regulations and the adjacent house dating from the nineteenth-century allowed them to design a structure intact on the side facing the road, fragmented facing the garden, the oblique angles making it seem larger than it actually is. The house opens out onto a south-facing slope, appearing to float above it due to the sizeable cantilevers. A number of elements, such as the box-type windows of the living room, are reminiscent of the 1950s Modernist revival.

Marques and Zurkirchen also designed a detached house at Sursee, Seehäusernstrasse 25, in 1985–86.

Archithese, 5, 1985; 5, 1986; Rivista Tecnica, 1–2, 1986; Quaderns d'Arquitectura i Urbanisme, 173, 1987; Häuser, 1, 1988; Bulletin ETH, 225, 1990; P. Disch (ed), L'architettura recente nella Svizzera tedesca 1980–1990, Lugano 1991, p. 159; du, 5, 1992; Guide to Swiss Architecture 1920–1990, vol. 1, 828, p. 237.

Nottwil

Swiss Paraplegic Center

Wilfrid and Katharina Steib

1987–90

The outcome of an ideas competition, this health center was designed according to a medical and therapeutic brief which included in-patient bed areas as well as sports facilities suitable for rehabilitation requirements. Despite a centrifugal site plan, the complex has a continuous front on the lake side, characterized by a sinuous volume with the patients' bedrooms and the metal frame of the terrace in a style reflecting the modern approach to this theme.

Werk, Bauen und Wohnen, 5, 1990; P. Disch (ed), L'architettura recente nella Svizzera tedesca 1980–1990, Lugano 1991, p. 160 f.; Guide to Swiss Architecture 1920–1990, vol. 1, 832, p. 240.

Hodel House

Rigi-Kaltbad

Reformed Church

Unterer Firstweg

1960–63

Ernst Gisel and Louis Plüss

Ernst Gisel designed religious architecture on several occasions. In the late 1950s, however, he began a period of intense activity on this theme, producing a number of fine churches. Whereas the churches he built together with Louis Plüss at Effretikon, Am Rebbuck (1956–61), and Oberglatt, Rümlangstrasse 5 (1960–64), in the canton of Zürich, and at Reinach (1958–63), in the canton of Basel-Land, explore the sculptural potential of concrete, the small chapel at Rigi-Kaltbad is the emblematic outcome of a poetic use of natural materials, producing an architecture that is integrated into the landscape without losing its own formal autonomy.

A. Altherr, New Swiss Architecture, Teufen 1965; Werk, 1, 1965; L'Architecture d'aujourd'hui, 126, 1966; Rivista Tecnica, 1, 1982; Guide to Swiss Architecture 1920–1990, vol. 1, 834, p. 241.

Swiss Paraplegic Center, lakeside front and interior view

Reformed Church

Obwalden

Engelberg
Convent School
Aeschiweg 2
1961–67
Ernst Gisel
assisted by C. Zweifel

Situated on a cramped, steeply sloping site below the convent church, the rooms of the school are spread like terraces over five levels, and the roof of the gymnasium serves as the school yard. Sharply articulated, heavy concrete cubes lend the school sculptural qualities. Only inside does facing brickwork relieve the harshness of the materials used.

Architektur Wettbewerbe, 55, 1968; 7–8, 1982; Baumeister, 11, 1968; Werk, 7, 1968; J. Bachmann and S. von Moos, New Directions in Swiss Architecture, New York 1969; A + u, architecture and urbanism, 8, 1977; Rivista Tecnica, 1, 1982; Guide to Swiss Architecture 1920–1990, vol. 1, 813, p. 230.

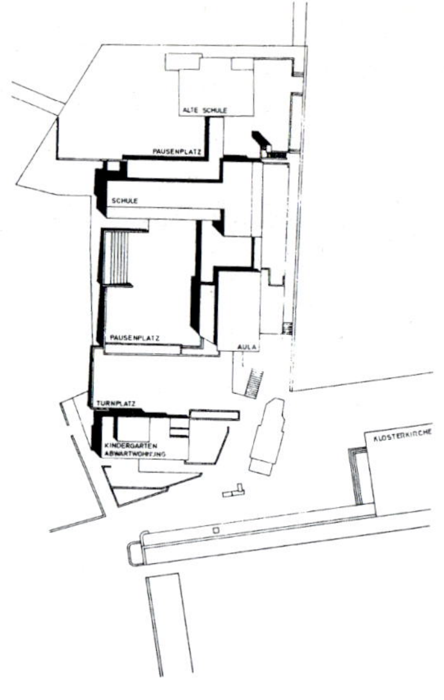

Sarnen
Collegiate Church
Brünigstrasse 177
1964–66
Joachim Naef, Ernst Studer and Gottfried Studer
with G. Zimmermann

The highly sculptural appearance of the church is due to both the spatial continuity of the masses, modeled with nuances of shade and light, and the tactile aspect of the rough surfaces contrasting with the gently fluid lines. The altar is the liturgical focal point in the central floor plan. It is reached by a maze-like itinerary broken up by the side chapels and enclosed by the perimeter walls.

The same architects designed the Sachseln School and Community Center, Mattli 24 (1969–74).

Werk, 2, 1967; J. Bachmann and S. von Moos, New Directions in Swiss Architecture, New York 1969; R. Gieselmann, Neue Kirchen, Stuttgart 1972; Guide to Swiss Architecture 1920–1990, vol. 1, 837, p. 243.

Convent School, view and, opposite page, site plan

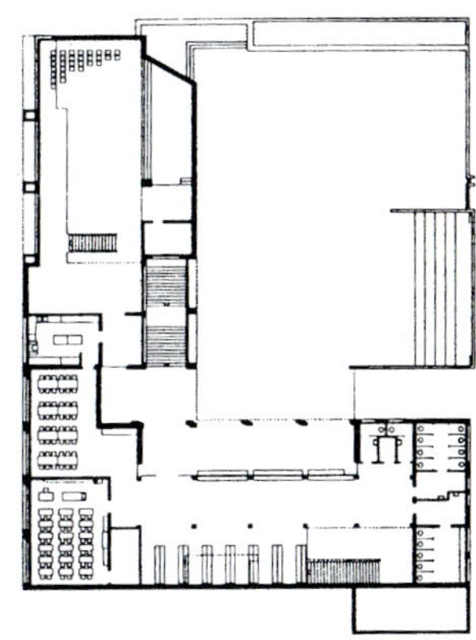

Collegiate Church, floor plan and internal view

Nidwalden

Büren
School Extension
Büren Village Center
1989–92
Daniele Marques and Bruno Zurkirchen
with H. van der Meijs and J. Wals

Following a similar compositional pattern to that of the buildings in the center of the village, where the existing school is situated, the new buildings in the school extension form a complex round the main square. The free pavilion-like arrangement of the various volumes ensures they are harmoniously blended into the landscape. The facades and use of materials reflect the attempt to reinterpret the local architectural traditions.

P. Disch (ed), L'architettura recente nella Svizzera tedesca 1980–1990 Lugano 1991, p. 165; Werk, Bauen und Wohnen, 3, 1994.

Büren School Extension

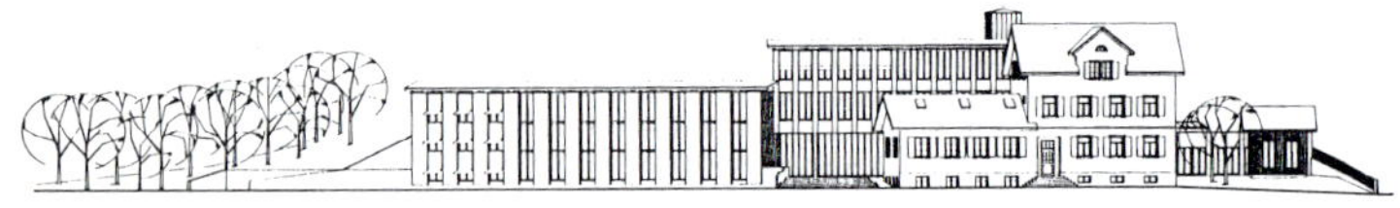

Hergiswil

Matt School

Baumgartenweg 7

1952–54

Walter Schaad and Emil Jauch

The outcome of a competition, this project heralded a new pedagogic vision of the relation between children's education and their environment. The design seeks a mimetic relationship with the landscape, without forgoing geometry as a compositional tool. The simplicity of the materials and the stress laid on natural lighting reveal the controlled nature of the intervention.

Werk, 3, 1955; H. Ineichen and T. Zanoni (eds), Luzerner Architekten 1920–1960, Zurich-Berne 1985; I. Noseda and M. Steinmann, Zeitzeichen, Schweizer Baukultur im 19. und 20. Jh., Zurich 1988; Guide to Swiss Architecture 1920–1990, vol. 1, 814, p. 230.

Matt School

Uri

Altdorf
Dätwyler Ag Headquarters
Gotthardstrasse 31
1939–40, 1951–65
Otto R. Salvisberg
Roland Rohn

For over thirty years the wire and rubber production company (Kabel-, Gummi- und Kunststoffwerke; Dätwyler since 1946) developed its own industrial complex with lodgings and facilities for its staff in collaboration with leading architect Salvisberg. In order to create a suitable corporate image for the company, in 1939–40 he designed a building with a street front. From the 1950s Roland Rohn took over as the company's main architect. Well-known for his experience in industrial architecture (see, for example, the Schindler Center at Ebikon, 1953–57, in the canton of Lucerne, built in collaboration with W. Gattiker, C. Mossdorf, F. Zwicky and A. Boyer), he designed the new production plant (1951), and the social center (1964–65).

INSA. Inventario Svizzero di Architettura, vol. I, Berne 1984; Guide to Swiss Architecture 1920–1990, vol. 1, 802, p. 224.

Altdorf
Confederation Granaries
Eyschachen
1912–13
Eduard Züblin and Robert Maillart
Renovation
1989–91
Max Germann and Bruno Achermann with M. Tremp

Numerous interventions and various renovations have modified the original structure of the Altdorf granaries, described by Giedion as an example of coherence between form and function in industrial architecture. Recently the studio of Germann & Achermann have restructured the buildings in the complex, and have rebuilt the end tower.

Heimatschutz, 8, 1913; Sigfried Giedion, Space,Time and Architecture, Cambridge, Mass. 1941; Schweizerische Bauzeitung, 74, 1956; INSA. Inventario Svizzero di Architettura, vol. I, Berne 1984.

Altdorf
Health and Pedagogic Center
Gotthardstrasse 14
1974–79
Joachim Naef, Ernst Studer, and Gottfried Studer

The outcome of a 1974 competition, this complex houses various cantonal institutions (children's home, health center and school). The new building blends in with the existing structures, while the principal functions are concentrated in a linear block. The volumes open up to the surrounding area and each individual formal element is designed to underline the regular geometry of the porticos characterizing the complex.

Archithese, 3, 1980.

Schattdorf
Gotthard-Raststätte Staff Lodgings
Bötzligerstrasse
1988–92
Max Germann and Bruno Achermann with P. Aregger
The outcome of a 1988 competition, this building provides accommodation for seasonal workers employed in a highway restaurant managed by Gotthard-Rastätte. The stylistic choices (use of color, definition of the volumes, contrasting materials, and frame details) all combine to give this building an original architectural identity.

Confederation Granaries

Health and Pedagogic Center

Dätwyler Ag Headquarters

Gotthard-Raststätte Staff Lodgings

Jura

Fontenais

Parish Church of Saints Pierre et Paul

Rue du Collège

1935

Fernand Dumas

Having designed several churches in French-speaking Switzerland, and especially in the canton of Fribourg (at Orsonnens, Bussy, Murist and Mézières), Dumas adopted a basilica type for the church of Fontenais with a bare essential language, while the limits imposed by traditional forms are superseded through the use of geometric inventions.

L'artisan liturgique, 27, 1932.

Rossemaison

Annaheim House

Les Grands-Champs 139

1979–80

Vincent Mangeat

with J. Chappuis and S. Cerato

This single-family dwelling is not conceived as an architectural object but

Parish Church of Saints Pierre et Paul

Annaheim House

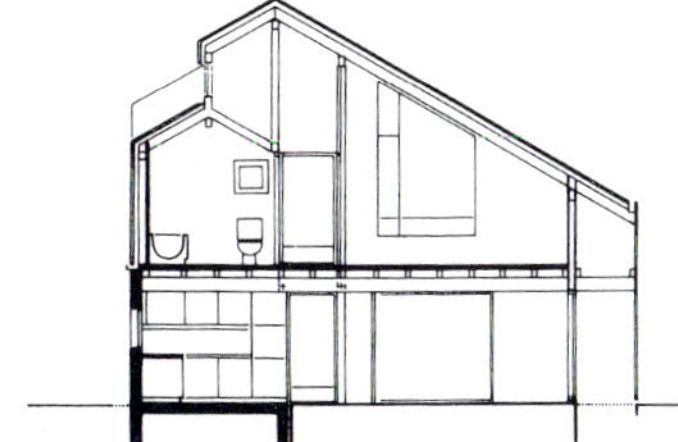

as a reconstruction of an area: a light wooden skin is shaped round the dwelling overlapping the massive walls forming the northern confine. The fluid spatiality of the interior corresponds with the rhythm of the structure of cross walls and recesses.

Architettura Svizzera, 48, 1981; Lignum, 12, 1984; Werk, Bauen und Wohnen, 9, 1985; Techniques et Architecture, 8–9, 1989; Hochparterre, 5, 1991; Rivista Tecnica, 11, 1992; Guide to Swiss Architecture 1920–1990, vol. 2, 824, p. 233.

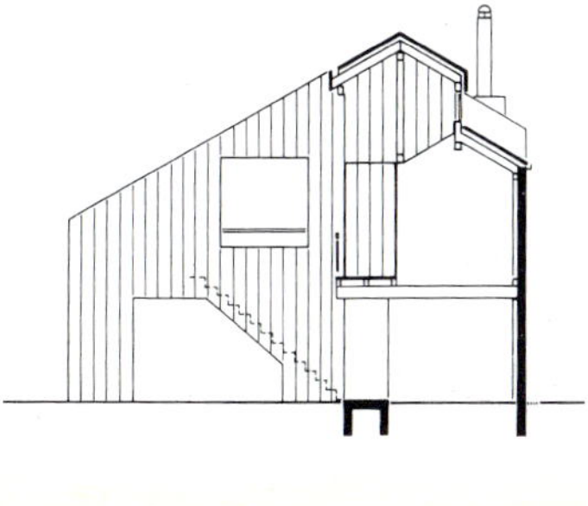

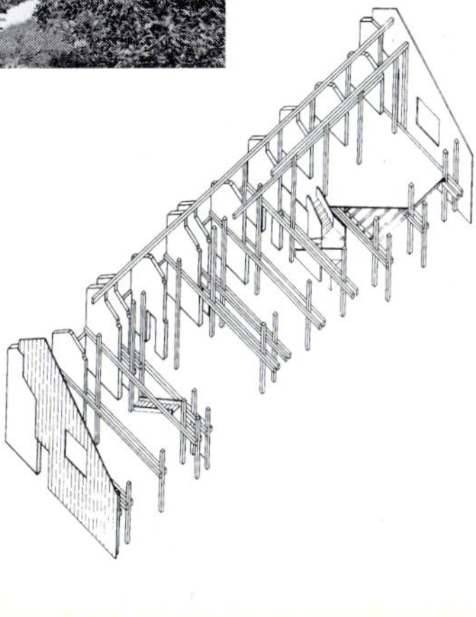

Neuchâtel

Cortaillod
Sferax Factory
Route de Boudry 1
1978–82
Marie Claude Bétrix, Eraldo Consolascio and Bruno Reichlin with P. Huber

The distinctive element employed in transforming and extending the existing factory is the shed-style roofing. The materials (brick, iron, aluminum and glass) are used as a function of their formal potential, highlighting the awareness of the conditions of the building process.

The same architects also designed the Berani Warehouses, Ackerstrasse 50 (1981–82), at Uster in the canton of Zürich.

Archithese, 1, 1980; 4, 1993; Werk, Bauen und Wohnen, 9, 1981; 3, 1988; Abitare, 206, 1982; Domus, 647, 1984; Baumeister, 6, 1986; Guide to Swiss Architecture 1920–1995, vol. 3, 013, p. 36.

La Chaux-de-Fonds
Villa Fallet
Chemin de Pouillerel 1
1905–07
Charles-Edouard Jeanneret (Le Corbusier) and René Chapallaz with the Atelier L'Eplattenier

"When I was seventeen I had the good fortune to meet a client who, with no preconceptions whatsoever, commissioned me to build a house" – that was how Le Corbusier described his first

Sferax Factory

professional design experience together with René Chapallaz, procured thanks to the good offices of his design master L'Eplattenier. The small chalet is situated to the north of the town on the slopes of the Jura, not far from the villa L'Eplattenier built for his own family (1902–04). The rooms are rationally arranged in relation to a double-height space, drawing on the nineteenth-century model of the bourgeois villa and prefiguring a type Le Corbusier was to develop in future works. The villa may effectively be set in the local tradition of Art Nouveau. However, a number of the picturesque ornamental details translate natural forms into rigorous geometries.

Werk, 1963, 12; M. Sekler, The Early Drawings of Charles-Edouard Jeanneret, New York-London 1977; P. Turner, The Education of Le Corbusier: a Study of the Development of Le Corbusier's Thought 1900–1920, New York 1977; J. Gubler, The Temperate Presence of Art Nouveau, in Art Nouveau Architecture, London 1979; INSA. Inventario Svizzero di Architettura 1850–1920, vol. III, Berne 1982; Abitare, 206, 1982; Archithese, 2, 1983; W. Curtis, Le Corbusier: Ideas and Forms, Oxford 1986; G. Baker and J. Gubler, Le Corbusier. Early Works by Charles Edouard Jeanneret-Gris, London 1987; S. von Moos, Estetica industriale, Disentis 1992; Guide to Swiss Architecture 1920–1995, vol. 3, 002, p. 28 f.

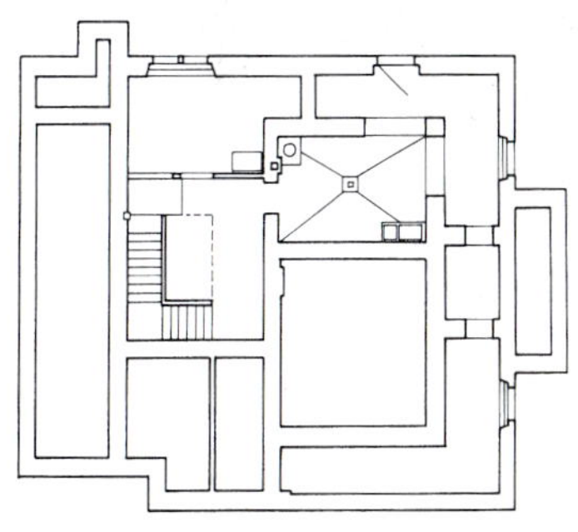

Villa Fallet

La Chaux-de-Fonds
Villa Jaquemet
Chemin de Pouillerel 8
1908–09
Charles-Edouard Jeanneret (Le Corbusier) and René Chapallaz
Villa Stotzer
Chemin de Pouillerel 6
1908–09
Charles-Edouard Jeanneret (Le Corbusier) and René Chapallaz
Villa Jeanneret-Perret
Chemin de Pouillerel 12
1912
Charles-Edouard Jeanneret (Le Corbusier)

The clients who commmissioned Jeanneret's early works came from L'Eplattenier's circle of friends and belonged to the bourgeoisie associated with clock industry at La Chaux-de-Fonds. With Chapallaz as consultant, Jeanneret designed Villa Jaquemet and Villa Stotzer on a trip to Italy and during his Viennese stay. In both two-family dwellings the arrangement of the interiors is subordinated to the external form of the villa and basically similar plans are adopted. Although using reinforced concrete (the Hennebique system), Jeanneret continued to develop decorative elements in the

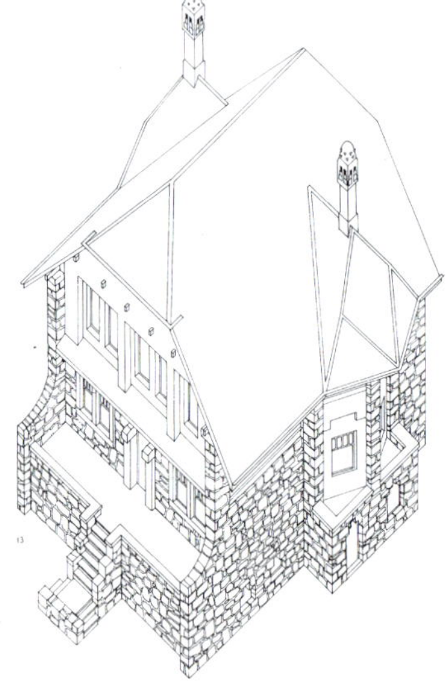

Villa Jacquemet

Art Nouveau tradition in an effort to create a regional style inspired by the local flora and fauna. In the intense formative period from 1908 to 1911 Jeanneret drew on a rich variety of sources: he trained with Perret in Paris and Behrens in Berlin as well as developing contacts with the Werkbund during a Munich stay and traveling to the East. In 1912 on returning home, he took up the *profession libérale*. In the design for his parents' house he abandoned decorative themes and explored new compositional possibilities in the plan, starting from the core of the house – a music room marked out by four central pillars.

For literature see p. 207.

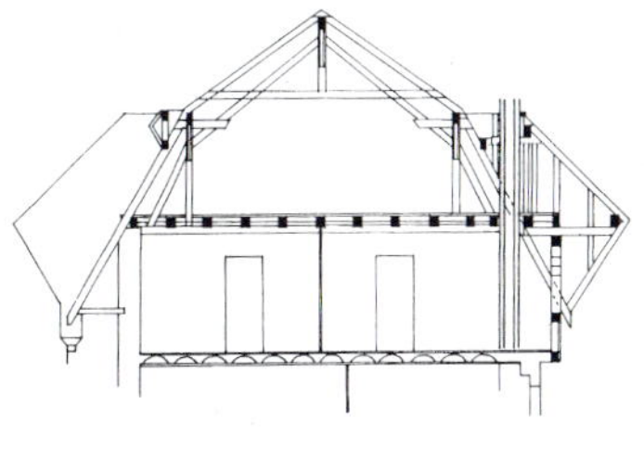

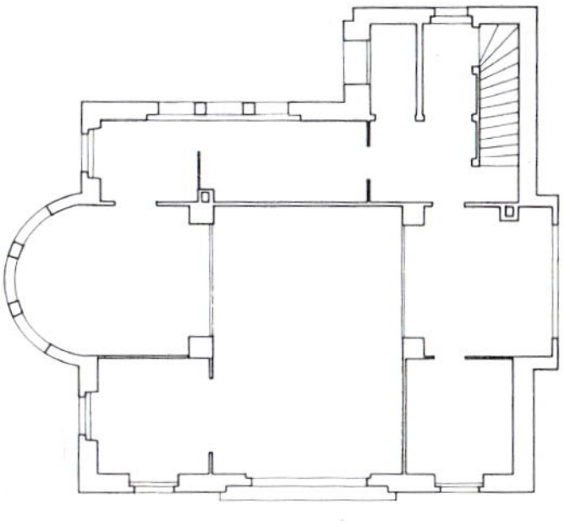

Villa Stotzer

Villa Jeanneret-Perret

La Chaux-de-Fonds
Villa Schwob
Rue du Doubs 167
1916–17
Charles-Edouard Jeanneret (Le Corbusier)

Inspired by a previous project designed during his first Parisian sojourn, Villa Schwob has a number of elements used by Jeanneret in the house for his parents (Villa Jeanneret-Perret), such as the large front window and the apse-like volumes. In addition to the influence of Auguste Perret, critics have also identified illustrious precedents in the architecture of Frank Lloyd Wright and Josef Hoffmann. Designed for an important entrepreneur in the clock industry, Villa Schwob may be seen as a kind of epilogue to Jeanneret's formative period. It reveals his ability to make very personal use of hetereogenous elements, the outcome of his interest in highly varied trends on the architectural scene of the day. In addition to the presence of reinforced concrete, we already find a concept that was to be a key feature of his future architecture. The center of the design is the double-height central space which expands into the semicircle side premises and links day and night zones. Unlike the previous houses, Villa Schwob was published in *L'Esprit Nouveau,* although Jeanneret – who in the meantime had moved to Paris – did not really supervise the work on site.
For literature see p. 207.

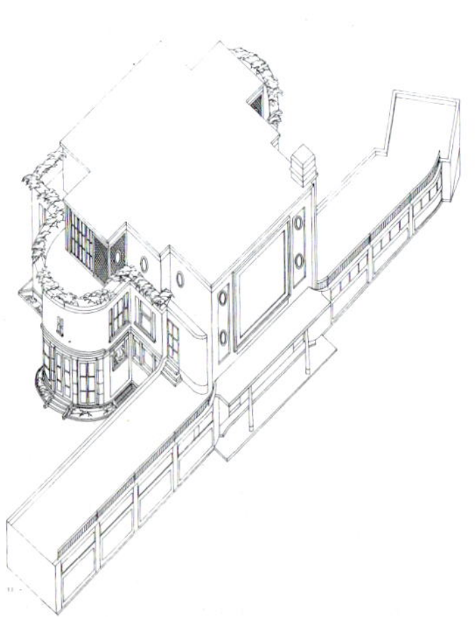

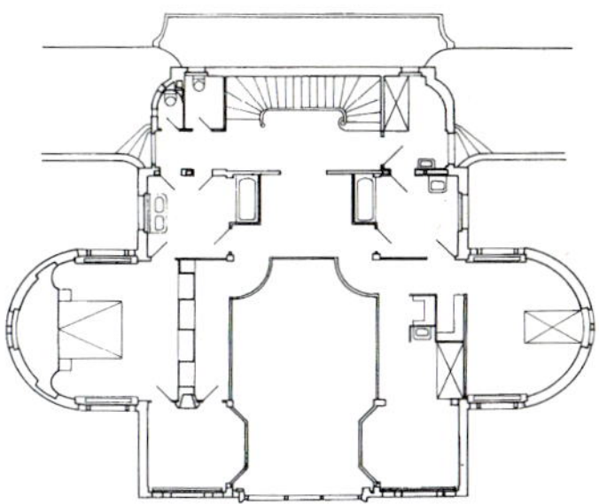

Villa Schwob

La Chaux-de-Fonds
La Scala Cinema
Rue de La Serre 52
1916
Charles-Edouard Jeanneret (Le Corbusier)

The structure of the cinema auditorium – six wooden arches resting on concrete pillars – was built by a specialist Zurich firm. Jeanneret's task (after the row with Chapallaz, who had been given the commission) was to design classic facades in Louis XVI style but by drawing on models from Behrens' architecture. Partially destroyed by fire in 1971, the cinema was rebuilt, and the only surviving section of the original is the rear.

For literature see p. 207.

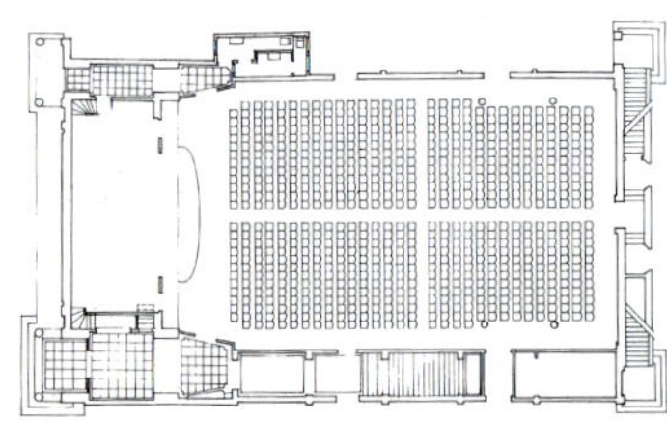

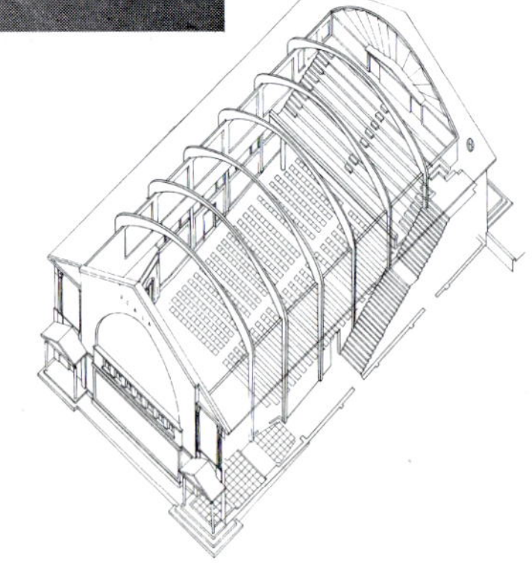

La Scala Cinema

La Chaux-de-Fonds
Espacité Complex
Avenue Léopold Robert
1987–94
Jacques Richter and Ignacio Dahl Rocha
with K. Ross

This was the winning design in a 1987 ideas competition for the layout of Place Sans-Nom, part of the redevelopment program planned for the town center by the local authorities to celebrate the centenary of Le Corbusier's birth. The multipurpose complex consists of a plaza, a long building on the northern edge of the site and a tower. In addition to accommodating offices, dwellings and a shopping zone, the complex also creates a number of public spaces – a forum, terraces and green areas. The whole is integrated into the urban structure of La Chaux-de-Fonds by reconstructing the grid layout where it merges with the fabric of the historic center. With its top-floor gallery, the tower is a local landmark.

Baumeister, 1, 1990; Archithese, 4, 1993; Construction et énergie, 9, 1993.

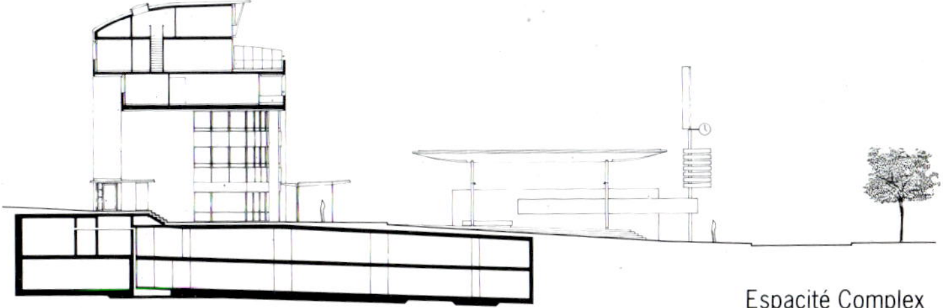

Espacité Complex

Le Locle
Villa Favre-Jacot
Côte des Billodes 6
1912
Charles-Edouard Jeanneret (Le Corbusier)

Commissioned by Georges Favre-Jacot, a magnate in the Neuchâtel clock-making industry, this villa provided Jeanneret with the opportunity to experiment various themes free from rigid financial constraints: the *cour d'honneur*, asymmetry, superimposed forms curved with respect to orthogonal geometry, classic moldings and the garden and terraces conceived as extensions to the home interior. Among the various possible influences in this design exercise – in addition to Behrens' Classicism, Hoffmann's decorativism and the Mediterranean-style *Romande* regionalism – is Loos' design of the Villa Karma at Clarens near Montreux in the canton of Vaud, which was being completed by Hugo Ehrlich in 1912 (see p. 223).

For literature see p. 207; Ingénieurs et architectes suisses, 21, 1987.

Villa Favre-Jacot

Neuchâtel

House

Trois-Portes 3

1933–34

François Wavre and Louis Carbonnier

Situated on a steeply sloping lot, this single-dwelling house is one of the best-known 1930s buildings in Neuchâtel. Through the strict volumetric organization, the design exploits the natural features of the site, with terraces and balconies facing out towards a wood.

Werk, 1, 1968; Guide to Swiss Architecture 1920–1995, vol. 3, 021, p. 40.

Neuchâtel

Cantonal Police Headquarters

1993

Aubry et Monnier and Associates with P. Schmid, L. Geninasca, C. Gerster, P. Bourquin, and R. Dalla Costa

The formal solution to the building is a response to a particularly unfavorable urban context: the site is in fact a complicated road junction with a crossroads, tunnel and passageway. The self-contained nature of the building is the logical consequence of this situation and its powerful image gives a high-quality urban character to an otherwise anonymous setting.

Among the most recent works of the Robert Monnier studio is Les Deux Thielles School and Sports Center at Le Landeron (1991).

Archithese, 4, 1993.

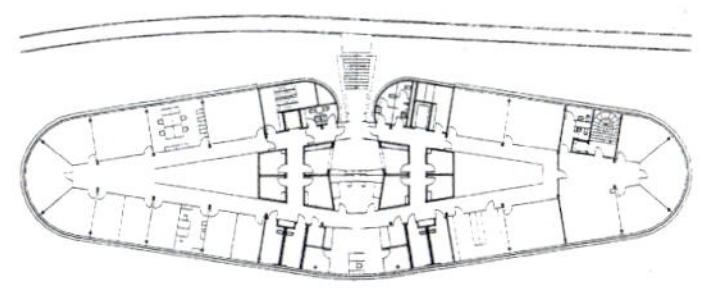

House at Trois-Portes

Cantonal Police Headquarters, floor plan and view

Fribourg

Flamatt

Flamatt I, II, and III Housing

Neueneggstrasse 6–8–10

1957–58, 1960–61, and 1984–88

Atelier 5

Built over thirty years, these three housing schemes reveal the evolution of Atelier 5's design ideas in the field of housing. Built at the time when the more celebrated Siedlung Halen was being designed, Flamatt I (six terraced houses raised on pilotis and a block with ateliers covered by a roof-garden) is the prototype of all such schemes. Flamatt II is a continuous aggregation of duplex buildings (each dwelling unit with studio is oriented westwards with independent access, roof-garden and loggia), while Flamatt III consists of thirteen dwellings organized in articulated volumes.

In the canton of Fribourg, the Berne studio of Atelier 5 also built the Merz House at Môtier, Route du Lac 301(1958–59).

Werk, 11, 1958; L'Architecture d'aujourd'hui, 87, 1959–60; 103, 1962; Casabella, 258, 1961; Architectural Design, 9, 1962; Bauen und Wohnen, 4, 1962; a + u, architecture and urbanism, 12, 1971; 9, 1993; GA Global Architecture, 23, 1973; Baumeister, 9, 1990; Faces, 17, 1990; Architectural Review, 1, 1991; Guide to Swiss Architecture 1920–1990, vol. 2, 907, p. 246.

Flamatt I, II, and III

Fribourg

Cantonal Library

Sentier Guillaume Ritter 18

1905–10

Bracher, Widmer and Daxelhoffer

with Leon Hertling (site management)

Renovation and Extension

1967–75

Otto H. Senn

The winning project in a 1905 international competition divides the volumes into three functionally different sectors: a reading room with overhead natural lighting flanked by oval-shaped rooms, the store in Rue Saint-Michel, and a curved administrative wing linking the main entrance and the side building. For the facades a Neo-Baroque style modulated by local influences was adopted. A new wing (1967–75) in the area of the old storage premises was added by Otto Senn.

Schweizerische Bauzeitung, 48, 1906; 55 and 56, 1910; La Bibliothèque cantonale et universitaire, Fribourg 1909–1976, Fribourg 1976; INSA. Inventario Svizzero di Architettura 1850–1920, vol. IV, Berne 1982.

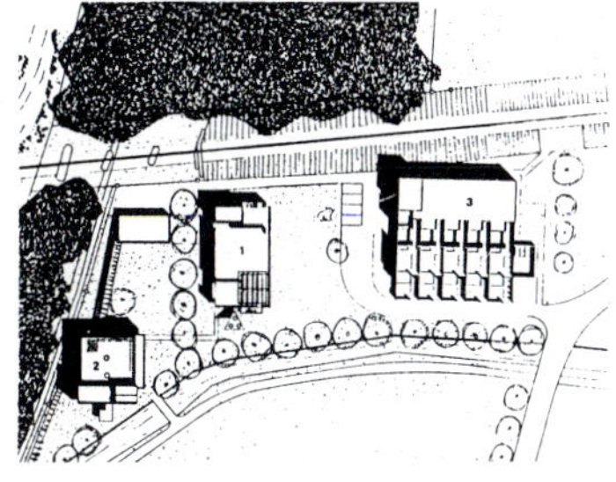

Flamatt I, II, and III, site plan

Cantonal Library

Fribourg
La Bâloise Building
Avenue de la Gare
1950
Ernst and Paul Vischer
The rhythm of the facade is established by the structural elements, while the travertine cladding provides a continuous street front respecting the alignment of the existing facades. The orthogonal grid containing the windows is brought into relief by a loggia on the top floor.
H. Volkart, Schweizer Architektur, Ravensburg 1951.

Fribourg
Miséricorde University
Route du Jura
1938–41
Denis Honegger and Fernand Dumas
One of the most important works in Swiss architecture of the 1930s, the

La Bâloise Building

Miséricorde University

university complex is situated in a green area. It houses three faculties (arts, theology and law) distributed in three separate buildings: a central volume with entrance foyer, main lecture hall, museums and general services; a building for general courses, with an amphitheater and classes facing south east; and a wing for musicology with workshops, reading room and chapel. The reinforced-concrete structure has a glass-brick infill alternated with prefabricated panels, forming a series of geometric textures and patterns.

Vie, art et cité, 1941 (special issue); Max Bill et al., Moderne Schweizer Architektur 1925–1945, Basel 1947; Werk, 1, 1968; Parametro, 140, 1985; Guide to Swiss Architecture 1920–1990, vol. 2, 909, p. 248.

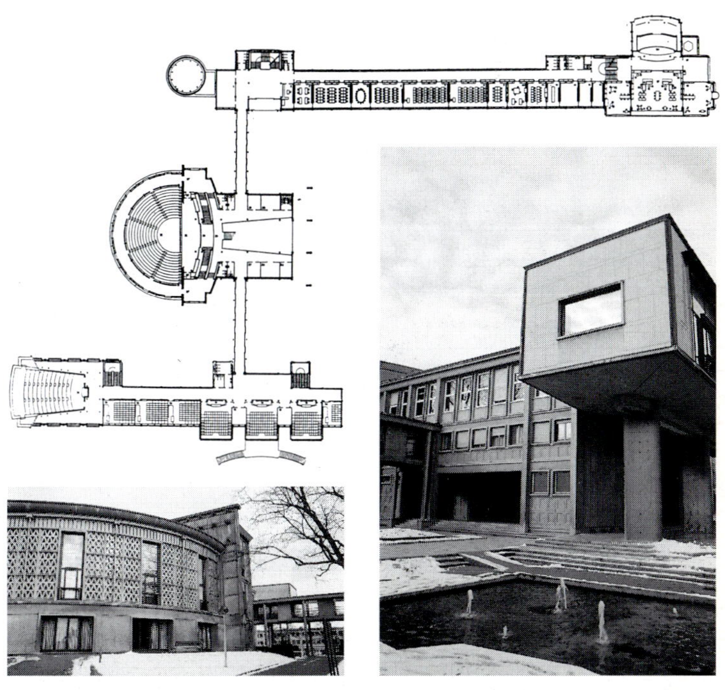

Miséricorde
University, plan and
views

Fribourg
State Bank
Boulevard Pérolles 1
1977–82
Mario Botta
with E. Hutter, T. Urfer, A. Gonthier, T. Hoehn, J.M. Ruffieux, E. Ryser, G. Schaller, and C. Schroeter

The design for the Fribourg State Bank paradoxically fits in with the rules governing the urban context by the way it focus attention on its own exceptional nature. The volumes of the building are articulated in a cylinder dialoguing with the plaza and in two lateral wings with street fronts. The entrances and pedestrian passages function as a hinge at the point where the cylindrical volume is detached from the whole. The different handling of the facades in the side apertures reflects the character of the surrounding buildings, while the curtain wall gives the central cylinder a monumental look. The choice of green granite as the cladding (applied with various criteria) underlines the unity of the building. The basement floors even host a discotheque where the geometry of the plan is reproposed in plays of light and mirrors.

Lotus International, 15, 1977; a + u, architecture and urbanism, 105, 1979; Werk-Archithese, 25–26, 1979; Abitare, 206, 1982; Casabella, 484, 1982; Progressive Architecture, 7, 1982; Archithese, 1, 1983; Baumeister, 6, 1983; GA Document, 6, 1983; Werk, Bauen und Wohnen, 1–2, 1983; GA Architect, 3, 1984; Guide to Swiss Architecture 1920–1990, vol. 2, 915, p. 252.

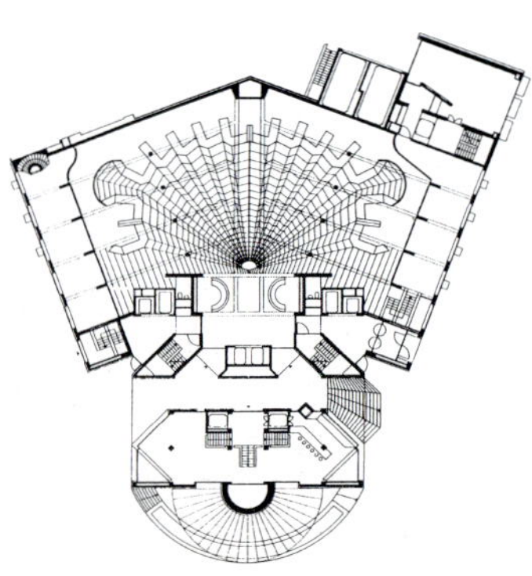

Fribourg State Bank

Murten

Swiss Railway Training Center

Löwenberg

1978–82

Fritz Haller, Alfons Barth, and Hans Zaugg

Educational activities, lodgings, a restaurant and services are contained in four separate volumes – two different sized prisms and two cylinders. The Center's overall image, however, is uniform, since the parts are simple functional containers built through assembling prefabricated components. Following the example of Mies van der Rohe, the architects – leading designers of modular construction systems – explore purely technological architecture.

Werk, Bauen und Wohnen, 7–8, 1981; W. Blaser, Architecture 70/80 in Switzerland, Basel 1981; Detail, 3, 1984; 7–8, 1992; Rivista Tecnica, 1–2, 1986; Guide to Swiss Architecture 1920–1990, vol. 2, 920, p. 254.

Swiss Railway Training Center

Vaud

Chavannes

Cantonal Archives

Rue de la Mouline 32

1980–84

Atelier Cube (Guy and Marc Collomb, and Patrick Vogel)

with M. Chavanon

The winning design in a 1980 competition divides the complex according to morphologically different sectors: the public premises, administration, and semicircular reading room face south, while a modular system expanding northwards houses the storerooms. The overall size of the building has been kept fairly compact since the sloping site meant that the access could be placed on an intermediate level and two of the four stories with storage rooms are underground (documents are thus protected from the light).

Archithese, 4, 1983; Werk, Bauen und Wohnen, 7–8, 1985; Architettura Svizzera, 7–8, 1986; Rivista Tecnica, 4, 1989; Guide to Swiss Architecture 1920–1995, vol. 3, 107, p. 60.

Cantonal Archives

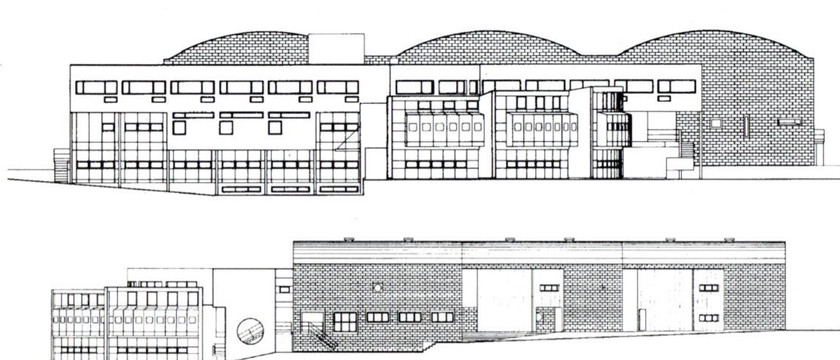

Clarens

Villa Karma

Rue St Moritz 352

1904–12

Adolf Loos, Henri Lavanchy, and Hugo Ehrlich

The Viennese psychiatrist Theodor Beer commissioned Henri Lavanchy to convert this old country-estate house on the northern shores of Lake Leman into his residence. Adolf Loos was brought in to deal with the interiors – *Innendekoration* – in what was his first commission in private building. Loos tackled the project by developing Lavanchy's initial design, which had raised the original building by a floor and added a new envelope on three sides with a double gallery superimposed on the south-east and south-west fronts. In Loos's design a small panoramic tower was added and the pergolas at the top of the corner prisms extended. The oval double-height lobby leads into refined living spaces enhanced with a variety of colors and luminosity, typical of Loos (unfortunately the interior is closed to the public). Work was interrupted in 1906 because of arguments with the owner, but then completed in 1912 by Hugo Ehrlich, an assistant in the Viennese studio of Josef Hoffmann.

Formes et Couleurs, 4, 1944; Architectural Review, 3, 1969; Alte und moderne Kunst, 113, 1970; Werk-archithese, 6, 1977.

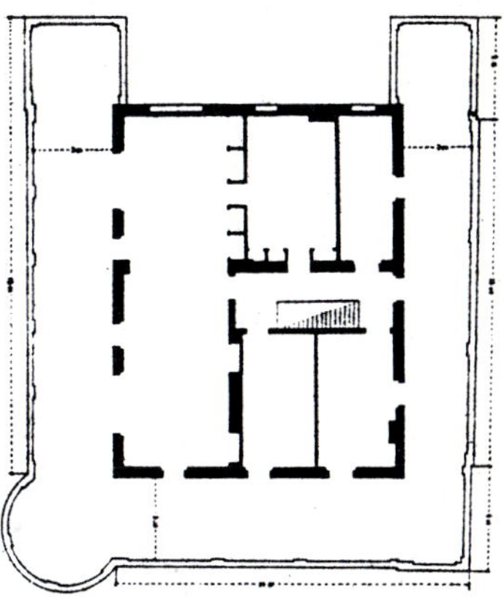

Villa Karma

Corseaux-Vevey

Villa Jeanneret (La petite maison)

Route de Lavaux 21

1922–25

Le Corbusier and Pierre Jeanneret

The *petite maison* built by Le Corbusier for his parents is situated on the shores of Lake Geneva in the Vevey area. According to Le Corbusier, the strictly functional project was designed before the site was chosen. This situates the design in the perspective of the dwelling as a "machine for living in" that Le Corbusier explored in the 1920s. The house has a number of features dear to the architect: the roof-garden, ribbon windows and simple materials. The northern front, parallel to the road, is characterized by metal cladding to protect from the weather, while the southern front has an aperture framing the landscape in a stone wall. This surreal gesture paradoxically proves that this architectural "machine" is actually one of the most successful manifestos for Le Corbusier's poetics.

Le Corbusier, Une petite maison, Zurich 1954; Werk-archithese, 6, 1977; Abitare, 206, 1982; Le Corbusier a Genève 1922–1932, exhibition catalogue, Lausanne 1987; Lotus international, 60, 1989; F. Vaudou, La petite maison de Le Corbusier, Nyon 1991; Guide to Swiss Architecture 1920–1995, vol. 3, 112, p. 64.

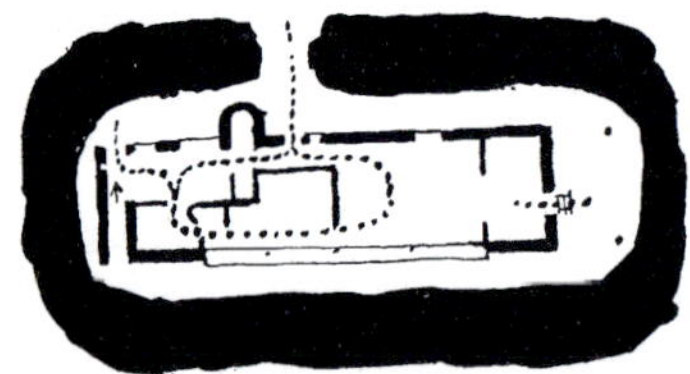

Corseaux
De Grandi Studio-House
Chemin d'Entre-deux-villes 7
1937–39
Alberto Sartoris

Situated on slightly sloping ground among vineyards above Lake Leman, this house is the realized project of the last in a series of studio-houses designs for the De Grandi brothers, who were both painters. Three elements characterize the facades: the large studio window to the north; the full-height cut so large canvases can be transported in and out, to the west; and the sightseeing balcony to the south. Inside, the architect organizes the minimum for living based on fixed furniture mainly in whites, yellows, grays and greens (the entrance floor and the stair are clad in green marble), while outside white plaster prevails.
An extension made by the owners to the south-east corner has destroyed the original volumetric character of the building.
In 1935 Sartoris designed the interior of the Cercle de l'Ermitage, Café Au Vieux-Moulin, Route Cantonale, Epesses, in the Vaud, unfortunately also modified. A color drawing of the axonometric section (published in the *Architectural Review* in 1936) and a serigraph (made from the same drawing and published in Milan in 1982) have survived as evidence of the original design.

Alberto Sartoris, Lisbon 1980; G. Remiddi (ed), Sartoris. Casa de Grandi 1937–1939, Rome 1987; Guide to Swiss Architecture 1920–1995, vol. 3, 113, p. 63.

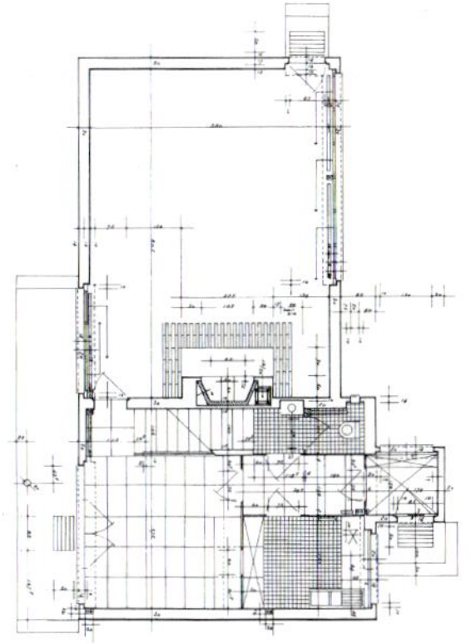

De Grandi Studio-House

Cully

Former Motel Les Blonnaisses (now Intereurope)

Route Cantonale

1963–65

Alberto Sartoris

The motel is in a panoramic position on the shores of Lake Leman between Lausanne and Vevey. The building has three floors above ground. The road level contains bars, parking, garage and local services. The bedrooms on the upper floors face south towards the lake or north towards a hill, and are served by an internal circulation passage and two stairs. The original white color of the plaster and metal balustrade has been replaced. Exploiting and highlighting the sloping terrain, the design was also to have included a second set-back volume linked by a hanging garden with the existing building.

Alberto Sartoris, Lisbon 1980; Controspazio, 2, 1988.

Ecublens

Federal Polytechnic School of Lausanne (EPFL)

University Campus

1970–

Jakob Zweifel, Robert Bamert and Alexander Henz

with H. U. Glauser, M. Schellenberg, D. Badic, A. Berler, R. Dèzes, K. Hosp, H. Kurth, P. Simond, and U. Van Molivan

The new building for the EPFL is modulated in a spatial system generated by several overlapping orthogonal grids. The external access axes determine the position of the high-density constructions. The university campus consists of several faculty buildings designed over the last thirty years by noted Swiss architects: Max Richter and Marcel Gut, Physical Sciences (1969–73); Frédéric Brugger, Social Sciences I (1977); Fonso Boschetti, Jean-Jacques Alt, Gérald Iseli and François Martin, Biology (1983); Mario Bevilacqua, Jacques Dumas, and Jean Luc Thibaud, Social Sciences II (1987); Mondada & Giorgis, Pharmacology (1991). The Chemistry faculty complex designed by the Atelier Cube in collaboration with Ivo Frei in 1991 is located on the western edge of the campus and includes various research and teaching facilities. The same architects also designed the Plasma Physics Research Center (1981–96).

Werk, 10, 1970; Bauen und Wohnen, 5, 1978; Detail, 1, 1984; 4, 1985; Rivista Tecnica, 1–2, 1989; Archithese, 4, 1993; Guide to Swiss Architecture 1920–1995, vol. 3, 252, p. 124 f.

Federal Polytechnic School, aerial view

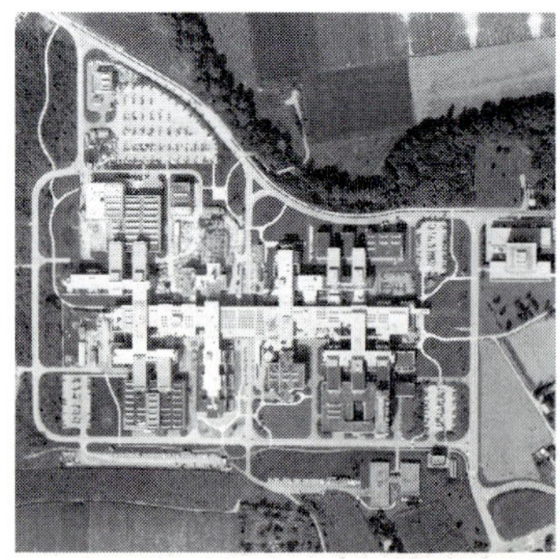

Motel Les Blonnaisses

Federal Polytechnic School, views

Ecublens

PTT Radio-Communication Building

Avenue Forel

1987–94

Rodolphe Luscher

with D. Linford

Situated on the eastern edge of the EPFL campus, the radio-communication center is a landmark characterizing the site. Resting on a half-moon-shaped base, the building consists of three volumes rotated in such a way as to give the three functional areas different orientations. The central sector organizes the circulation, while to the east are the entrance, administration and, on the upper floor, very-high-frequency laboratories; to the west are the technical premises. On a central reinforced-concrete "blade", the tower rises up with the reception aerials facing the stations of La Dôle and Mont Pélerin.

Werk, Bauen und Wohnen, 5, 1988; Hochparterre, 12, 1988; Edilizia, 211, 1989; Rivista Tecnica, 1, 1989; Guide to Swiss Architecture 1920–1995, vol. 3, 254, p. 126.

Gland

Grand-Champ Secondary School

Rue du Collège

1985–92

Patrich Mestelan and Bernerd Gachet

The complex consists of two buildings containing the school and collective structures (theater, gymnasium and restaurant) arranged round a porticoed court or plaza, open to the landscape. Highlighting the institutional nature of the center, the design creates an urban microcosm based on social dialogue: the plaza, atriums and porticoes are the places intended for meeting and communicating.

Faces, 22, 1991; Rivista Tecnica, 3, 1991; Controspazio, 3, 1993; Guide to Swiss Architecture 1920–1995, vol. 3, 118, p. 67.

La Dôle

Swisscontrol Building

1990–92

Vincent Mangeat

with H. Jaquiery, S. von Alvensleben, and M. Toscan

Inspired by the example of Jean Prouvé, Mangeat adopted a clear constructional method to tackle the problems involved in building on an inhospitable site (1,670 meters up) in extreme meteorological conditions and with no access roads. The work-site operations were reduced to a minimum: a concrete foundation was constructed *in situ* to provide a base on which to dry assemble precast modules small enough to be transported by helicopter.

Hochparterre, 11, 1992; Rivista Tecnica, 11, 1992; Deutsche Bauzeitschrift, 5, 1993; Journal de la construction, 1–2, 1993; Werk, Bauen und Wohnen, 3, 1993; Guide to Swiss Architecture 1920–1995, vol. 3, 109, p. 61.

PTT Radio-Communications Building, model view

Grand-Champ Secondary School, views

Swisscontrol Building

Lausanne

Villa La Sauvagère

Avenue Verdeil 6

1905

Alphonse Laverrière and Eugène Monod

Central Station

Place de la Gare

1908–16

Alphonse Laverrière, Eugène Monod, Jean Taillens and Charles Dubois

Bel-Air Métropole Tower

Place Bel-Air 1

1929–32

Alphonse Laverrière

Renovation 1996–97

Devanthéry & Lamunière

Having trained at the Ecole des Beaux-Arts in Paris, Laverrière worked on many of the most important pre-First World War buildings in Lausanne. The Chauderon Bridge (1902–05) is characterized by a sculptural Art Nouveau vocabulary – also explored in picturesque Sezessionist key in the almost contemporary Villa La Sauvagère – suitable for celebrating its technical image and urban importance. The Central Station, on the other hand, drew on a typology used in the design for Leipzig Station by W. Lossow and M. H. Kühne (1902–15).

In the 1930s the massive complex of the Bel-Air Métropole, the first metal-structure Swiss skyscraper (with hundreds of apartments, offices, 1,600-capacity cinema-theater – renovated in 1996 by Devanthéry & Lamunière –, dancing hall and shops) introduced a metropolitan-scale building into the city. Among Laverrière's many other Lausanne works, see the Bois-de-Vaux

Villa Sauvagère

Central Station

Bel-Air Métropole Tower

Cemetery (1924), and the Mixed-Use Building for offices and shops, Avenue de Rumine 4–8 (1927–28).
Also worth noting is the Public Elevator (1990–93), added to the Chauderon Bridge by Atelier Cube in collaboration with engineer Jean Marc Duvoisin.
Schweizerische Bauzeitung, 51, 1908; 59, 1912; 71, 1918; 100, 1932; Journal de la Construction, 11, 1930; E. Scotoni, Bel-Air Métropole, Lausanne: 1929–1931, Lausanne 1933; Werk, 20, 1933; J. Gubler, Nationalisme et internationalisme dans l'architecture moderne de la Suisse, Lausanne 1975; Werk-archithese, 11–12, 1978; Parametro, 140, 1985; INSA. Inventario Svizzero di Architettura 1850–1920, vol. V, Berne 1990; Faces, 18, 1990; Guide to Swiss Architecture 1920–1995, vol. 3, 207, p. 97.

Lausanne
Prélaz Quarter
Avenue de Morges 45–117
1921
Frédéric Gilliard and Frédéric Godet
In line with the ideas of Bernoulli and the Swiss housing reformers, the Prélaz Cooperative garden city combines individual dwellings with collective housing, organizing various multi-dwelling blocks in a symmetric plan round a central plaza.
Nearby is the Ecole des Métiers, Rue de Genève 73, built in 1929 by the same architects in collaboration with Charles Dubois and Jacques Faverger.
Habitation, 6, 1969; J. Gubler, Nationalisme et internationalisme dans l'architecture moderne de la Suisse, Lausanne 1975; Werk-archithese, 11–12, 1978; INSA. Inventario Svizzero di Architettura 1850–1920, vol. V, Berne 1990; Guide to Swiss Architecture 1920–1995, vol. 3, 201, p. 92.

Chauderon Bridge
Public Elevator

Prélaz Quarter,
housing block

Lausanne
Montchoisi Mixed-Use Building
Avenue Montchoisi 4–10
1931
Charles Trivelli and Joseph Austermayer

In the Montchoisi complex, situated in a peripheral quarter, Trivelli and Austermayer accepted the street alignments dictated by the triangular shape of the lot and arranged the volumes round a court open to the avenue. A pavilion containing shops and the garages is situated on the central axis of the composition. Around the same time the two architects also tackled city-center problematics in the design for the Sainte-Luce Shopping Galleries, Rue du Petit-Chêne, Avenue de Sainte-Luce (1931–34).

Werk, 6, 1937; Neues Bauen in der Schweiz, Führer zur Architektur der 20er und 30er Jahre, Blauen 1985.

Lausanne
La Chandoline Housing
Rue de Chandolin
1932–34
Henri Robert von der Mühll

A founder of the first CIAM at La Sarraz in 1928 and a contributor to the review *ABC*, von der Mühll was a theoretician committed to promoting Modern ideals, but who also designed numerous works. After Villa Foetisch (1930–31), he built La Chandoline Housing, his best-known complex. In a rigorously functionalist language, the facades are characterized by a large glazed area to the south, and ribbon windows with projecting cylinder-shaped balconies to the north. Von der Mühll's explorations on the theme of low-cost housing may also be admired in the Valency Quarter, Prilly (1949–53).

A.Sartoris, Gli elementi dell'architettura funzionale, Milan 1941; J. Gubler, Nationalisme et Internationalisme dans l'architecture modern de la Suisse, Lausanne 1975; Werk-archithese, 23–24, 1978; Archithese, 1, 1982; 4, 1993; Neues Bauen in der Schweiz, Führer zur Architektur der 20er und 30er Jahre, Blauen 1985; Guide to Swiss Architecture 1920–1995, vol. 3, 210, p. 98.

Lausanne
Selhofer Bookstore
Rue du Petit-Chêne
1934
Alberto Sartoris

The bookstore facade has an L-shaped vermilion-red metal cladding enclosing the door and window. The entrance is characterized by a glass door (again with a red metal frame) and two thin columns, one yellow, the other black. Sartoris also chose the white letters for the signs. Inside is a single large room with a gallery in the upper section, while the services are in the rear of the shop. The right-side strip of cladding was removed during renovation works on the shop next door.

Montchoisi Mixed-Use Building

La Chandoline Housing, views

Selhofer Bookstore

Lausanne
Bellerive Plage
Avenue de Rhodanie 23
1934–37
Marc Piccard
Renovation
1990–93
Devanthéry & Lamunière

A favorite summer spot in the city, the Bellerive swimming baths was the first municipal building to be designed in a functionalist style. The entrance building – the pivot in the composition – also contains the restaurant. It is a cylindrical volume with a central court containing stairs. One wing with cabins and dressing rooms is developed longitudinally, marking off the area for the solarium. In the recent restoration work the concrete was renovated and the window and door frames repaired, while the potential of the original design was further developed to meet new needs and uses.

Habitation, special issue, 1937; Werk, 5, 1938; Max Bill et al., Moderne Schweizer

Bellerive Plage

Architektur 1925–1945, Basel 1947; Werk-archithese, 11–12, 1978; Rassegna, 49, 1992; Archithese, 4, 1993; Construction, 11, 1993; Faces, 29, 1993; Werk, Bauen und Wohnen, 3, 1994; Guide to Swiss Architecture 1920–1995, vol. 3, 212, p. 100.

Lausanne
Cantonal Bank Extension
Rue de la Grotte / Rue de Beau Séjour
1947
Ch. Thévenaz, Ch. Brugger, and M. Maillard

The addition to the Cantonal Bank of an extension linking the existing building in such a way as to occupy the neighboring urban block created one of the most important Lausanne works of the 1940s. Adapted to the features of the site, the new building is organized round a central court with carefully modulated facades.

H.Volkart, Schweizer Architektur, Ravensburg 1951.

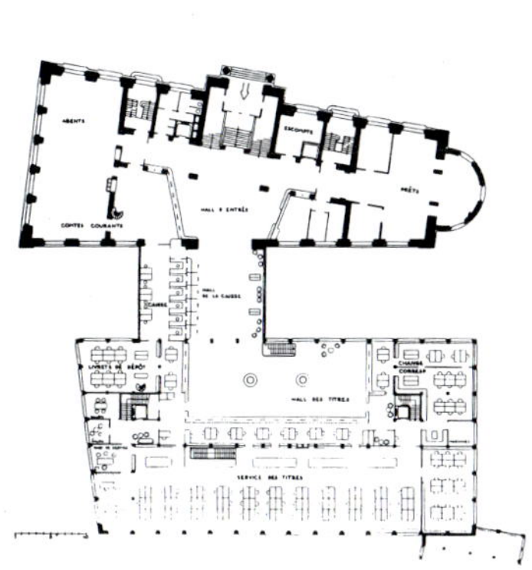

Cantonal Bank
Extension

Lausanne
Professional Institute
Rue de Genève 55 / Rue de la Vigie
1953–55
Charles and Frédéric Brugger
with Jean Perrelet, Laurent Stalé, and Pierre Quillet
Kodak Building
Avenue de Rhodanie 50
1960–62
Frédéric Brugger
with W. Blaser
Elysée Secondary School Complex
Avenue de l'Elysée
1961–64
Frédéric Brugger
with J. Mutrux and J. P. Borgeaud

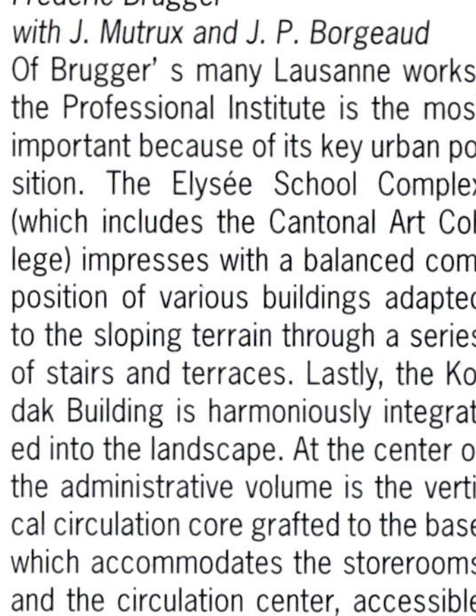

Of Brugger' s many Lausanne works, the Professional Institute is the most important because of its key urban position. The Elysée School Complex (which includes the Cantonal Art College) impresses with a balanced composition of various buildings adapted to the sloping terrain through a series of stairs and terraces. Lastly, the Kodak Building is harmoniously integrated into the landscape. At the center of the administrative volume is the vertical circulation core grafted to the base which accommodates the storerooms and the circulation center, accessible

Professional Institute

Kodak Building

Elysée School Complex

by pedestrian ramps. All three buildings demonstrate Brugger's skill in tackling site conditions.

L'Architecture d'aujourd'hui, 121, 1965; B. De Sivo, L'architettura in Svizzera, Naples 1968; Werk, 1, 1968; J. Bachmann and S. von Moos, New Directions in Swiss Architecture, New York 1969; Guide to Swiss Architecture 1920–1995, vol. 3, 218, p. 103; 231, p. 110; 229, p. 109.

Lausanne

Valmont Girls' Boarding School

Route d'Oron 47

1961–64

Max Richter and Marcel Gut

Situated on a hill overlooking the city and facing towards the lake, the building exploits the features of the site in a horizontal development. Organized in three stories round two internal courts (services in the basement floor, collective activities on the ground floor and dormitories on the upper floor), the complex is given unity by the handling of the facades, defined by repeating prefabricated reinforced-concrete elements. Joined to a wood above by a pedestrian bridge, the roof-garden contains special teaching rooms and the elegant technical services volumes.

L'Architecture d'aujourd'hui, 121, 1965; Werk, 1, 1968; Guide to Swiss Architecture 1920–1995, vol. 3, 230, p. 109.

Valmont Girls' Boarding School

Lausanne
Vidy Theater
Vidy Park
1963–64
Max Bill
Extension 1996
Rodolphe Luscher
Constructed for the 1964 National Exposition, the theater is the only surviving building of the various pavilions and facilities specially designed for the event. Situated on the shores of the lake in Vidy Park, the 400–capacity auditorium was part of the exhibition section entitled "Art and Life", and was built using a system of prefabricated elements. The organization of the low building, with a vertical volume for the stage, shapes the profile of the complex, which is also suitable for open-air shows thanks to the layout of the external spaces.

J. Bachmann and S. von Moos, New Directions in Swiss Architecture, New York 1969; Abitare, 206, 1982.

Lausanne
Boissonet Housing 1 and 2
Chemin de Boissonet 32, 34–46
1982–85 and 1984–90
Atelier Cube (Guy and Marc Collomb, and Patrick Vogel)
with D. Horber and M. Pidoux
Mixed-Use Building
Route Aloys-Fauquez 87 / chemin d'Entrebois 2
1984–87
Atelier Cube (Guy and Marc Collomb, and Patrick Vogel)
with M. Chavanon
Jeunotel
Chemin Bois-de-Vaux 36
1991–93
Atelier Cube (Guy and Marc Collomb, and Patrick Vogel)

Vidy Theater

Boissonet Housing

Atelier Cube has tackled the theme of subsided housing in several projects, including in the La Grande Borde complex, Rue de la Borde 16–23 (1985–92). The Boissonet council housing – with simplex dwellings in a cylindrical volume and duplexes in a long building – makes up the southern edge of a terraced scheme built in two stages by a cooperative. The program for the Mixed-Use Building on Route Aloys-Fauquez, on the other hand, was for apartments and shops arranged in two functionally differentiated blocks. Lastly, in the hotel facility of Jeunotel the volumes are organized round four courts.
Lit.: Habitation, 3, 1986; Werk, Bauen und Wohnen, 5, 1986; 12, 1989; 7–8, 1991; Architettura Svizzera, 2, 1987; 12, 1993; Techniques et architecture, 10–11, 1988; Rivista Tecnica, 1–2, 1989; Faces, 18, 1990; 26, 1992; Baumeister, 2, 1993; Guide to Swiss Architecture 1920–1990, vol. 3, 241, p. 117; 247, p. 120.

Boissonet Housing

Mixed-Use Building

Jeunotel

Lausanne

Kindergarten

Chemin Champrilly 21 A, Parc de Valency

1983–89

Rodolphe Luscher

with S. Rouvinez, P. Schmidt, and R. Zoss

The design for the Valency Children's Day Center reveals an unusually acute awareness of children's specific needs. Going beyond the traditional model of a kindergarten approached along the rigid lines of the form-function relationship, the design divides the space according to the rhythm of the structures making use of sliding surfaces and natural lighting. Each part of the building is intended to arouse curiosity: from the technical installations (colored pipes mean that the children can follow the route taken by water to reach the tap) and the colors and textures of materials, making the building itself a playful universe waiting to be explored as the children move from open to closed areas – from a protective interior world to contact with nature.

Abitare, 290, 1990; Detail, 6, 1990; Habitation, 7, 1990; Rivista Tecnica, 4, 1990; Techniques et Architecture, 390, 1990; Werk, Bauen und Wohnen, 10, 1990; Architectural Review, 9, 1991; Modulo, 190, 1993; A. Hablützel and V. Huber, Architecture d'interieur en Suisse 1942–1992, Sulgen 1993; Guide to Swiss Architecture 1920–1995, vol. 3, 243, p. 118.

Lausanne

Ulysse Mixed-Use Building

Rue de Genève

1987–94

Aurelio Galfetti

with A. Spitsas and T. Estoppey

Kindergarten

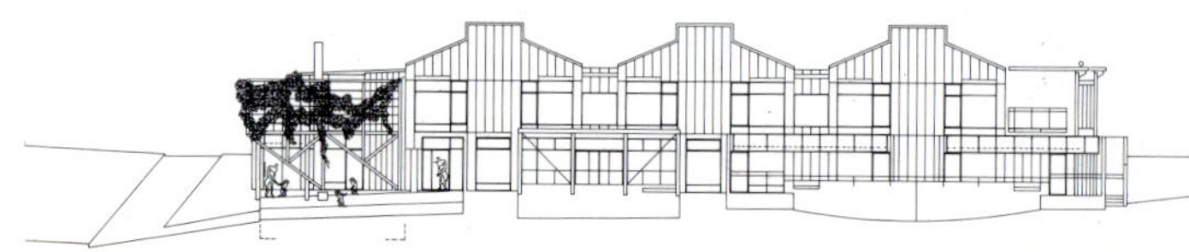

Built following a 1987 competition, the Ulysse Multipurpose Center addresses a problem tackled by Galfetti on several occasions: how to rebuild the urban fabric. The adopted solution with three prominent corners (three towers) alludes to the pre-existing order, but the main focus of the work is a self-contained cylindrical volume. Shunning all forms of mimesis, the central building supported by rendered pillars presents a continuous stone facade only interrupted by the large cut marking the entrance to the complex.

Journal de la Construction, 7, 1993; Guide to Swiss Architecture 1920–1995, vol. 3, 249, p. 121.

Lutry

Toises Condominium

Route de la Conversion, Toises

1959

Alberto Sartoris

This building in a relatively isolated position was designed for middle-class housing. The overall complex consists of two independent volumes with staggered heights linked by the stair shaft and a spacious entrance. The galleries are completely glazed, while the roof, which was flat in the original design, is covered in tiles, in accordance with local building regulations.

Other noteworthy housing complexes built by Sartoris in the 1960s include the low-cost Chamaley Housing, Petite Corniche-Chamaley, Lutry (1961–66), and the Mixed-Use Building for offices and dwellings at La Tour-de-Peilz, Avenue Perrausaz 79 (1964), also in the canton of Vaud.

Alberto Sartoris, Lisbon 1980; Controspazio, 9–10 1988.

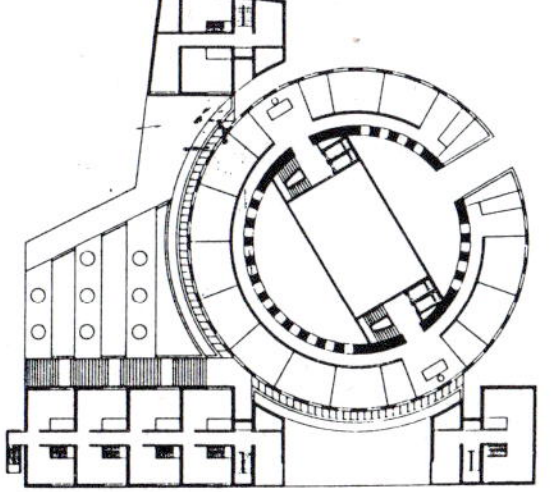

Ulysse Mixed-Use Building, view and floor plan

Les Toises Condominium

Montreux

Apartment Building

Rue du Théâtre 6

1962

Alberto Sartoris

This three-story house, closed on two sides, was designed for small- to medium-size rented apartments with ground-floor internal parking lots. The building's main facade has a series of deep balconies characterizing each apartment.

Controspazio, 9–10, 1988.

Nyon

High School

Route de Divonne 48

1984–88

Vincent Mangeat

with H. Jaquiery, C. Creissels, G. Mann, O. Pina, B. Verdon, and M. Freud

The features of the site – a deep valley on the edge of the town – determined the building types chosen by Mangeat in the project. The overall complex is shaped by the relation between a bridge-building, designed for collective activities, and a sloping building containing the classrooms. A plaza stretches across the two sides of the valley, while the course of the perimeter walls highlights the shored-up terrain. A detailed use of natural lighting characterizes and enhances the concrete structure.

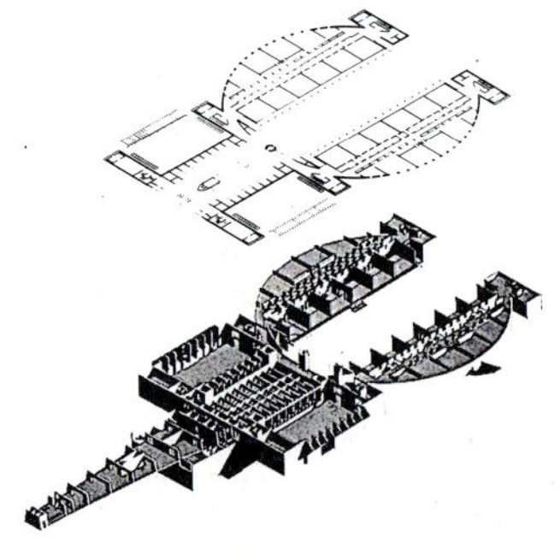

Archithese, 1, 1986; Werk, Bauen und Wohnen, 5, 1986; Techniques et Architecture, 8–9, 1989; Abitare, 240, 1990; Hochparterre, 5, 1991; Rivista Tecnica, 11, 1992; Guide to Swiss Architecture 1920–1995, vol. 3, 129, p. 73.

Renens
Siemens Center
Avenue des Baumettes 57
1989–92
Edouard Catella, Frédéric Brugger and Associates
with D. Monnier and P. A. Racine
Situated in a recently urbanized green area, the building houses the offices and laboratories in two long buildings joined by a central cylindrical volume – the dominating element in the design, intended for public areas and the circulation. The high-tech corporate image was created by the building solution generating the modular rhythm of the facades.

Saint-Prex
Keller Industrial Works
1959
Alberto Sartoris
Designed for the display, sales and repairs of industrial machines, the building is an aggregation of three volumes conceived according to a square module. Each volume has a different function, identifiable by the various kinds of windows adopted. Of particular interest are the specially designed large hinged glazed doors, which can be opened up completely, and the suspended stairs detached from the side walls.
Controspazio, 9–10, 1988.

Siemens Center

Keller Industrial Works

Opposite page:
Apartment Building

Nyon High School, view and axonometric

Saint-Sulpice
Villa Huber
Chemin du Bochet
1960–61
Alberto Sartoris
Also known as Villa Rodaniana, this house is the family home of an art collector. Arranged with the day area on the ground floor and the night area on the first floor, the house is connected to the garage building by a pergola. The structure is made of various materials (concrete, metal sections and brick), while the pitched roof, imposed by local building regulations, is covered with Catalan-style tiles.
Alberto Sartoris, Lisbon 1980; Casa Vogue, 4, 1982; 5, 1983; Controspazio, 9–10, 1988; Arte costruita, 1, 1988.

Tannay
School
1983–87
Vincent Mangeat
with H. Jaquiery, P. Bottlang, P. De Benoit, and O. Dalloz
The memory of place and of the theme – and therefore the typology – determined the design process for this school building in the park of Tannay castle, conceived as a pavilion modulated according to strict geometrical principles. The teaching areas are contained in a massive wall with the services and stairs. The classrooms are superimposed in twos and converge diagonally towards the external recreation portico, which opens towards a park with castle. Following the recommendations of Alfred Roth, *Das Neue Schulhaus*, the lighting is provided by lateral overhead natural lighting.
Aktuelles Bauen, 3, 1985; Rivista Tecnica, 1–2, 1989; Techniques et Architecture, 8–9, 1989; Architecture contemporaine, 11, 1989–90; Hochparterre, 5, 1991; Werk, Bauen und Wohnen, 3, 1991; Guide to Swiss Architecture 1920–1995, vol. 3, 140, p. 79.

Tolochenaz
FVE Institute of Building
Chemin de Riond-Bosson
1983–88
Patrick Mestelan and Bernerd Gachet with N. Baghdadi, J. L. Bujard, N. Cuccio, and M. Ruetschi
Situated in a large park, the institute complex has been designed starting from the right-angled intersection of two axes determining the entrances and direction of potential expansion. Great care has been taken to safeguard the natural setting. Organized round a central court with an ornamental pool, the building has two wings of atelier spaces with overhead natural lighting. They are flanked by the classrooms for theory, facing onto the court, and by storerooms (service areas facing outwards). The central volume houses the collective activities. The building is intended to be a teaching demonstration of the construction process.
Parametro, 141, 1985; Werk, Bauen und Wohnen, 1–2, 1988; Architettura Svizzera, 10, 1989; Hochparterre, 5, 1989; Rivista Tecnica, 1–2, 1989; Archithese, 4, 1993; Guide to Swiss Architecture 1920–1995, vol. 3, 141, p. 79.

Villa Huber

Tannay School, views and elevations

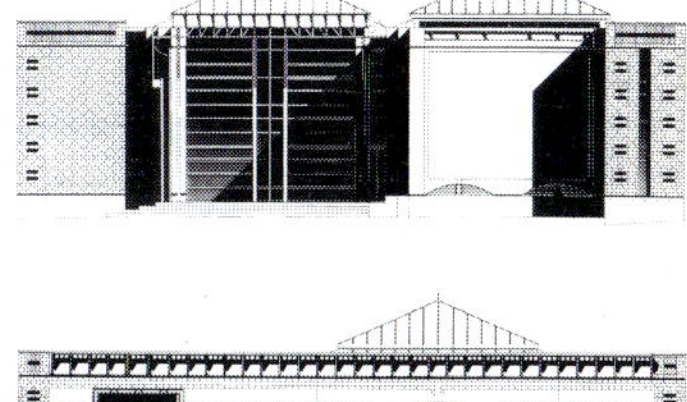

FVE Institute of Building

Vevey

Maison du Peuple

Rue de la Madeleine, Rue Rousseau

1932–33

Alberto Sartoris

In his second project for the complex, Sartoris had designed a cinema and shops on the ground floor, the Maison du People on the first floor and then five stories of apartments, slightly set back from the line of the street, and a laundry on the attic level. This project was modified in 1932 by Frédéric Widmer (Widmer & Gloor studio) because of real-estate problems. The official reason was so that the building could be adapted to local building regulations, safety rules and the industrial techniques used by the contractors involved in building the rest of the street block. But the outcome was that the land was fully exploited and the attic level eliminated.

Fillia (ed), Gli ambienti della nuova architettura, Turin 1935; R. Giolli, Alberto Sartoris, Milan 1936; Faces, 28, 1993.

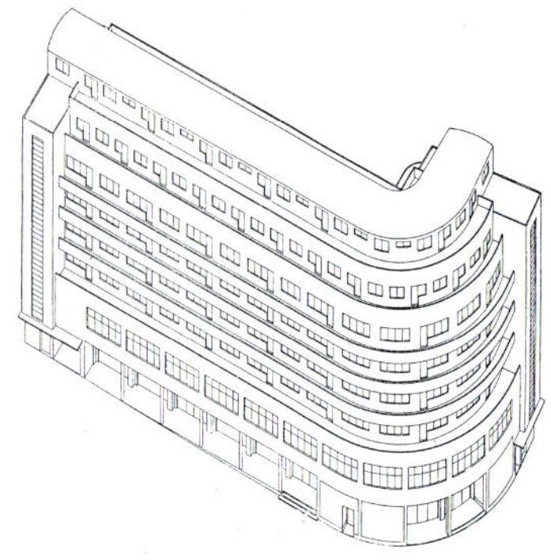

Maison du Peuple, axonometric

Vevey

Nestlé Head Office

Avenue Nestlé 55

1959–60

Jean Tschumi

The main features of Tschumi's architecture are a clear composition highlighting structure, a close correspondence between form and function, and the restrained use of materials according to logical criteria. These features were previously developed in the Assurance Mutuelle Vaudoise Administrative Building, Place de Milan, Lausanne (1953), and the WHO Headquarters at Pregny-Chambésy, Chemin de la Vie (1965–66), in the canton of Geneva, built in collaboration with Pierre Bonnard, but they are given their fullest expression in the Y-shaped office building designed for Nestlé on the shores of Lake Leman. Supported by massive polygonal pillars on a reinforced concrete platform (thus making the ground floor virtually transparent), the seven floors of offices are equipped with the latest technology, while the elegant facade infill consists of a glazed aluminum screen.

Architecture, formes + fonction, 9, 1962–63; Werk, 1, 1968.

Maison du Peuple, period photo

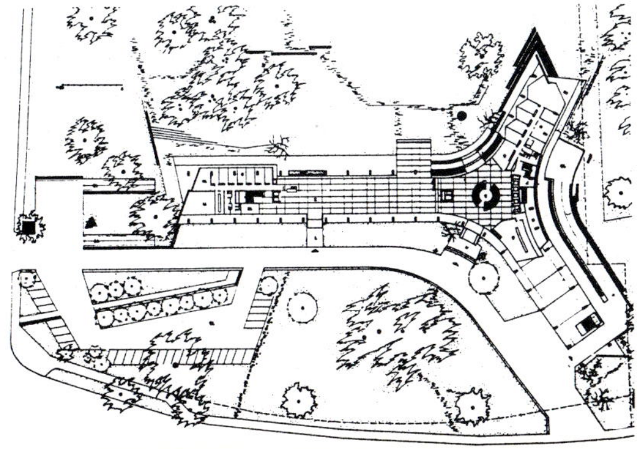

Nestlé Head Office, view and site plan

Geneva

Cologny
Jeanneret-Reverdin House
Chemin des Princes
1955–56
Jean Marc Lamunière and Pierre Bussat
Two duplex dwellings and a common area containing children's bedrooms and services are fitted into a prism, whose reinforced-concrete load-bearing structure is separate from the additional walls. This solution sets the living rooms facing the lake, while independent terraces are created.
The same architects also designed the Villa Bédat at Vandoeuvres, Chemin des Hauts-Crêts 64 (1960).
Architecture, formes et fonction, 5, 1958; Habitation, 9, 1958; Werk, 10, 1958; Arte Costruita, 1, 1988; Architettura Svizzera, 3, 1991.

Geneva
Maison du Paon
Avenue Pictet-de-Rochemont 7
1902–03
Eugène Cavalli and Ami Golay
One of the best-known Art Nouveau buildings in Geneva, the Maison du Paon was designed for shops and apartments. The sculptural details, the handling of the iron balcony railings, and the corner towers crowned with pinnacles are all inspired by contemporary Parisian models. Another interesting early twentieth-century building in Geneva is the Department Store, Rue du Marché 13–15 (1911–14), by A. Olivet, unfortunately now remodeled.
Art Nouveau Architecture, London 1979; INSA. Inventario Svizzero di Architettura, vol. IV, Berne 1982.

Geneva
House
Avenue de Gallatin 3, Saint-Jean
1911–13
Maurice Braillard
Montchoisy Housing
Rue de Montchoisy/Avenue William Favre (Square A)
Rue Montchoisy 62–72 (Square D), Eaux-Vives
1926–33
Maurice Braillard and Louis Vial
Maison Ronde
Rue Charles-Giron 11–19, Saint-Jean
1927–30
Maurice Braillard
One of Braillard's main concerns throughout his design career was to develop the theme of housing, always seen to the background of contemporary European architectural discourse. His wide-ranging interests included typological experiments with bourgeois housing closely linked to urban issues through the focus on the topological aspects of a project and the hierarchical configuration of public spaces. His rationalization of domestic spaces eschews any of the schematic divisions generated by strict functionalism. By designing plans with twofold orientations, transparency and good lighting are emphasized, while a strongly expressive vocabulary emerges in the detailing.
Of Braillard's public buildings, see the recently restored Onex Town Hall and

School (1908–09), the Mies School (1910–12) in the canton of Vaud, the Garage des Nations in Geneva, Rue de Montbrillant 99 (1935–36), and the Salève Cableway (1931–32) in neighboring French Haute-Savoie (only the transformed upper station is still intact).

Werk, 12, 1929; 10, 1931; Habitation, 1, 1931; A. Corboz, J. Gubler and J.M. Lamunière, Guide d'architecture moderne à Genève, Lausanne 1969; J. Gubler, Nationalisme et internationalisme dans l'architecture moderne de la Suisse, Lausanne 1975; Archithese, 2 and 3–4, 1984; Faces, 13, 1989; 16, 1990; Architecture de la raison, la Suisse des années vingt et trente, Lausanne 1991; Casabella, 604, 1993; Domus, 751, 1993; Werk, Bauen und Wohnen, 9, 1993; Guide to Swiss Architecture 1920–1995, vol. 3, 405, p. 151; 406, p. 157.

Maison du Paon

Jeanneret-Reverdin House

Montchoisy Housing

House on Avenue de Gallatin

Maison Ronde

Geneva
Aïre Garden City
Avenue d'Äire
1920–23
Camille Martin, Arnold Hoechel, and Paul Aubert
Vieusseux Garden City
Route des Franchises/Chemin de Vieusseux/Route de Lyon
1929–31
Maurice Braillard, Louis Vincent, Max Baumgartner, Frédéric Gampert, and Frédéric Mezger

Both of these housing schemes – unfortunately now partially demolished – drew on the Swiss version of the idea of the garden city. They were emblematic examples of the policy implemented by the Geneva cooperative movement to meet the housing shortage following the First World War. Having been preceded by the PIC-PIC competition, which had promoted the urban solution for low-cost housing, Hoechel designed ninety dwellings for a triangular lot on Avenue d'Äire, adopting the *maison familiale rangée* with vegetable-plot-garden as the main dwelling

Aïre Garden City

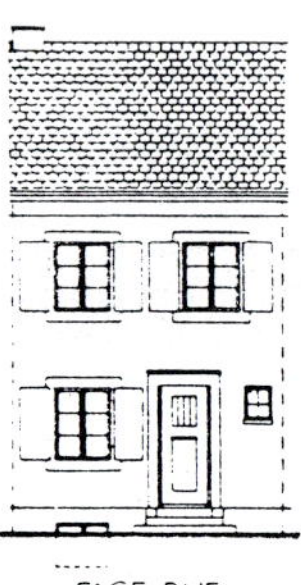

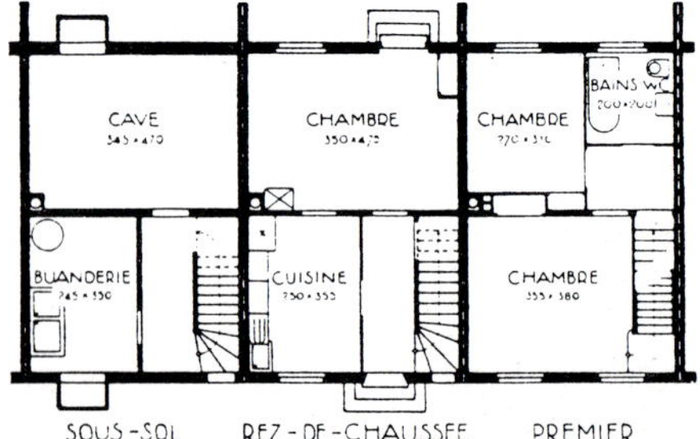

FACE JARDIN

type. Built by various architects to a master plan proposed by Braillard, the Cité Vieusseux consists of six housing blocks arranged on a symmetric plan perpendicular to the central avenue, the main axis of the composition and public heart of the quarter. Making good use of his in-depth knowledge of the avant-garde experiments in popular housing in Berlin and Frankfurt, Braillard here gives full vent to his vision of architecture as the practical expression of a social project. The Vieusseux complex includes accommodation for the elderly built by Frédéric Mezger in 1931–32 (Route des Franchises 22–28).

Braillard also designed the layout of the *rive droite* (1928–31) and the urban plan for the city of Geneva (1935).

Habitation, 3–4, 1945; J. Gubler, Nationalisme et internationalisme dans l'architecture moderne de la Suisse, Lausanne 1975; Werk-archithese, 11–12, 1978; Archithese, 2, 1984; Parametro, 140, 1985; Guide to Swiss Architecture 1920–1995, vol. 3, 403, p. 146 f.

Vieusseux Garden City

Geneva
Cornavin Station
Place Cornavin
1927–33
Julien Flegenheimer
Following a fire in 1909, the need to build a new station led to a national competition being held in 1925. To the background of considerable controversy – documented by Maurice Braillard's alternative design and Marc Stam's counter-project – Flegenheimer's Neoclassical project was chosen as representing the "essence" of the city. But the tower which was supposed to have crowned the axis along Rue du Mont-Blanc was never built. Opposite the station is the Hotel Cornavin constructed by Marc Camoletti in 1932. Despite the differences in style, Camoletti used the same structural system (metal elements) adopted by Adolphe Guyonnet and Louis Perrin for the contemporary Disarmament Conference Building on Quai Wilson, recently destroyed by fire.
Schweizerische Bauzeitung, 81, 1923; 19, 20 and 23, 1925; ABC, 6, 1925; Werk-archithese, 2, 1977; 11–12, 1978; Archithese, 2, 1984.

Geneva
League of Nations Building
Avenue de la Paix 8–14, Place des Nations
1926–36
Henri-Paul Nénot and Julien Flegenheimer, Carlo Broggi, Joseph Vago and Camille Lefèvre

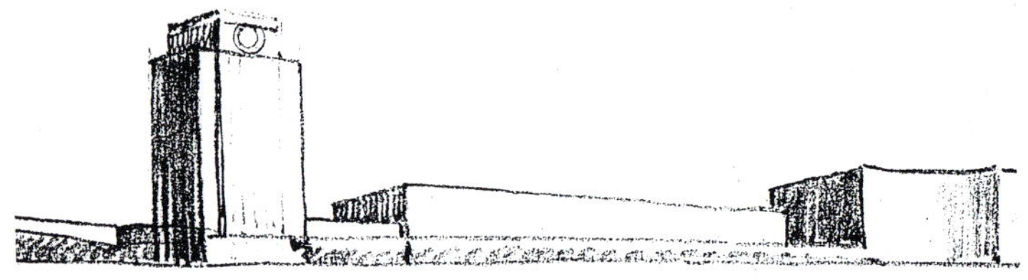

Cornavin Station, sketch by M. Braillard and front view

This building was the disappointing outcome of a competition organized by the League of Nations for its own headquarters. Radical historians of architecture consider it a bitter defeat for Modern architecture. Using a very unusual method the jury of nine – including Victor Horta, Josef Hoffmann, Karl Moser and Hendrik Petrus Berlage – awarded three groups of nine joint prizes, without indicating an outright winner (who would have been Le Corbusier), thus creating a good deal of official pressure and lobbies by those seeking to procure the commission. In the end an ad-hoc committee chose the Franco-Swiss group Nénot & Flegenheimer, proposing that they re-elaborate their project in collaboration with Broggi, Lefèvre and Vago but for a new site. Le Corbusier's various attempts – including the accusation of plagiarism – to promote the project he had designed with Pierre Jeanneret were to no avail. In 1932 the work site was opened in the park of Ariana, and the building was finally inaugurated in 1936.

S. Giedion, Space, Time and Architecture, the Development of a New Tradition, Cambridge Mass. 1941; B. Zevi, Spazi dell'architettura moderna, Turin 1973; Werk-archithese, 11–12, 1978; C. L. Anzivino and E. Godoli, Geneva 1927: il concorso per il palazzo della Società delle Nazioni e il caso Le Corbusier, Florence 1979; Archithese, 2, 1984; Parametro, 144, 1985; 7, 1986; Le Corbusier a Genève 1922–1932, exhibition catalogue, Lausanne 1987; Guide to Swiss Architecture 1920–1995, vol. 3, 404, p. 148–150.

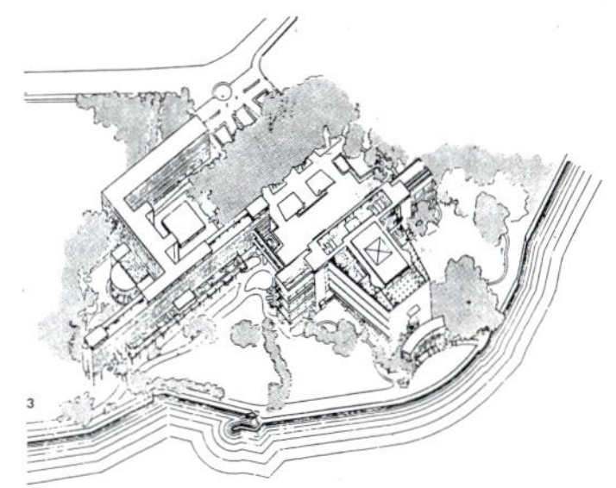

The League of Nations Building, view

Le Corbusier and P. Jeanneret, axonometric of competition design

Geneva

Maison Clarté

Rue St Laurent 2–4/Rue Adrien Lachenal

1928–32

Le Corbusier and Pierre Jeanneret with R. Maillart (foundations), J. Torcapel, F. Quétant, and B. Nazarief

Renovation

1976–78

Camoletti & Hauserman

The Clarté building was designed for the Geneva industrialist Edmond Wanner, who was also the building contractor. It is the first collective housing built by Le Corbusier in Switzerland. Having abandoned the passage circulation arrangement in the Immeuble-Villa for the innovative concept of the cell, the forty-five duplex apartments in this *maison de verre* are grouped in two self-contained units round the stairs. The light prefabrication system (standard structures in steel and dry assembling) meant work was completed in just thirty months. The designing of the facades only according to functional requirements was made possible by the absence of static problems.

Bauwelt, 37, 1932; Die Kunst in der Schweiz, 4–5, 1933; Werk-archithese, 11–12, 1978; Rassegna, 3, 1980; Abitare, 206, 1982; C. Courtiau, L'immeuble Clarté à Genève, Le Corbusier 1931/1932, Berne 1982; Archithese, 2, 1984; Le Corbusier a Genève 1922–1932, exhibition catalogue, Lausanne 1987; Immeuble-villa/plan libre/ maison à sec, Zurich 1989; Werk, Bauen und Wohnen, 6, 1989; The Footsteps of Le Corbusier, New York 1991; Guide to Swiss Architecture 1920–1995, vol. 3, 408, p. 159.

Maison Clarté

Geneva

Villa Ruf

Chemin des Manons, le Grand-Saconnex

1928–29

Housing

Chemin de Roches 1–3

1934–35

Francis Quétant

A member of the GANG (Groupe pour l'architecture nouvelle à Genève), Quétant worked with Le Corbusier in 1931 on the Maison Clarté, where he further explored the dry-assembly methods previously used in the Villa Ruf at Grand-Saconnex in 1928–29. For this small single-family villa he adopted a new building method: a metal skeleton with in-fill panels of compressed straw anchored to iron wiring. In the residential blocks in Chemin de Roches, on the the other hand, Quétant used reinforced-concrete structures and stone walls with special insulation elements. See also his Villa Meyer, Chemin Pré-Langard 5 (1936), at Cologny.

Moderne Schweizer Architektur 1925–1945, Basel 1947; J. Gubler, Nationalisme et internationalisme dans l'architecture moderne de la Suisse, Lausanne 1975; A. Rüegg, Le Corbusier, Edmond Wanner, Francis Quétant und die Villa Ruf, Zürich 1987; Guide to Swiss Architecture 1920–1995, vol. 3, 444, p. 180.

Villa Ruf

Chemin de Roches Housing

Villa Meyer

Geneva
Swiss Credit Bank
Place Bel-Air
1930
Maurice Turrettini and Robert Maillart
The outcome of a competition, this building created a great public outcry both because of its position in the city and its formal features. Drawing on the tradition of classical Roman art, the design emphasizes the vertical rhythm of the apertures in modeling the cubic volume. The building has been renovated several times and on the last occasion the glided aluminum sections were added.
Werk-archithese, 11–12, 1978.

Geneva
Les Pâquis Public Baths
Quai du Mont Blanc
1931–32
Service des Travaux de la Ville
Renovation
1993–94
Collectif d'architectes (Marcellin Barthassat, Claude Butty, Gabriele Curonici, and Jacques Menoud)
The Pâquis Public Baths – like the Plage de Reposoir, Route de Lausanne, Pregny, built by the Service d'Urbanisme de la Ville in 1937–38 – is an isolated but emblematic case of public works policy responsive to the developments in Modern architecture. Built to replace old wooden installations, the Baths are characterized by the use of reinforced concrete and a comb-like plan, parallel to the *quai* and open towards the lake, organizing the services and dividing the beach into two separate areas for men and women. In 1993–94 the complex was enlarged by a sports association and equipped with various facilities.
A. Corboz, J. Gubler and J. M. Lamunière, Guide d'architecture moderne de Genève, Lausanne 1969; Guide to Swiss Architecture 1920–1995, vol. 3, 409, p. 158.

Geneva
Housing
Route de Chêne 102
1932
Arnold Hoechel and Henry Minner
After the experience of Aïre Garden City (1920–23, see p. 250), Hoechel – architect and urbanist, a delegate to the first CIAM in 1928, lecturer, and member of the editorial staff of the review *Habitation* – tackled the theme of private housing in a block of six apartments, designed along strictly functionalist lines. Despite the limited financial resources, the plan – with two symmetrical units on the axis of the stairs – generates light and spacious rooms; the overall design is emphasized by the transparent vertical circulation elements.
Werk, 4, 1933; J. Gubler, Nationalisme et internationalisme dans l'architecture moderne de la Suisse, Lausanne 1975; Archithese, 2, 1984.

Swiss Credit Bank

Les Pâquis Public Baths, views

Route de Chêne Housing

Geneva
Frontenex Parc Housing
Route de Frontenex 53–57
1933–34
Louis Vincent and Jean Jacques Honegger

Having previously developed the theme of low-cost housing in the Housing at Avenue Weber 5–7 (1930–32), in this scheme the two architects had to follow the master plan for the Montchoisy quarter drafted by Vial and Braillard in 1928. Referring to Rationalist principles, they designed the facades in relation to the building system: an exposed concrete structure with the glazed modules of the window and door frames as infill. Of the many works by the Honegger brother in Geneva, see also the Deux-Parcs Housing, Avenue William Favre 32–34 (1947–49).

Habitation, 1, 1951; H. Volkart, Schweizer Architektur, Ravensburg 1951; A. Corboz, J. Gubler and J.M. Lamunière, Guide d'architecture moderne de Genève, Lausanne 1969; Werk-archithese, 11–12, 1978; Archithese, 3, 1984.

Geneva
Housing
Quai Gustave-Ador 28
1935–36
Atelier d'Architectes (Vincent, Schwertz, Lesemann, and Saugey)

The strong horizontal emphasis in this building for housing and a café (the

Frontenex Parc Housing

Quai Gustave-Ador Housing

Café des Marins) is created by strip balconies – a device previously used by the Atelier to highlight the volumetric character of the building in Chemin Krieg 3 (1933–36). In addition to the elegant play of the facade alignments, the other main features of the building are the rationale of the functional plan and the masterly detailing.
Archithese, 2, 1984.

Geneva
New Apostolic Church
Rue Liotard 14
1949
Werner Max Moser, Max Ernst Haefeli, Rudolf Steiger and Francis Quétant

Designed by Moser and built by the Zürich studio in collaboration with Francis Quétant, the New Apostolic Church on Rue Liotard is characterized by its monumental volumetric character, geometric organic forms and different textures for the various facades. This style was to spread and become the popular expression of postwar Swiss architecture.
Werk, 2, 1952; A. Corboz, J. Gubler and J.M. Lamunière, Guide d'architecture moderne de Genève, Lausanne 1969; Archithese, 2, 1980; Guide to Swiss Architecture 1920–1995, vol. 3, 413, p. 161.

New Apostolic Church

Geneva

Cantonal University Hospital

Rue Micheli-du-Crest

1949–53, 1959, and 1968–73

Arnold Hoechel, Pierre Nierlé, Jacques Lozeron and Jean Erb

The outcome of a 1945 competition, the new Cantonal Hospital was built in three stages, begun in 1949 and completed in 1973. The last work in Arnold Hoechel's many-faceted career, the complex introduced the influence of August Perret into French-speaking Switzerland. The same ideas were further developed by Pierre Nierlé in the project for the Beau-Sejour Hospital, Avenue Beau-Séjour (1961).

Archithese, 2, 1984.

Geneva

Malagnou-Parc Housing

Avenue Weber 34–36

1948–51

Hôtel du Rhône

Quai Turrettini

1950

Cantonal Hospital

Malagnou-Parc Housing

Mont Blanc Center and Plaza Cinema
Rue Chantepoulet 1–3
1953–54
Miremont-le-Crêt Housing
Avenue Miremont 6–8/Avenue Callas
1957
Marc Joseph Saugey

A member of the Study Commission for the Development of Geneva (created in 1945 by the Public Works Department) and the CIAM and GANG (Groupe pour l'architecture nouvelle à Genève), Saugey gradually broadened his professional experience and by the 1950s was one of the most innovative architects in the city. To the background of problems associated with an international city, his works tried out new technical possibilities in an attempt to find the right disciplinary tools to produce a qualitative response to the needs of a fast-growing building market. Other works in his intense design output are the well-known Terreaux du Temple, Rue de Cornavin (1951–55), Le Paris Cinema Avenue Mail 1 (1957), and the Offices at Rue du Rhône 21 (1963).

Werk, 1, 1951; 9, 1959; L'Architecture d'aujourd'hui, 45, 1952; 55, 1954; 121, 1965; Bauen und Wohnen, 5, 1953; Bulletin technique de la Suisse romande, 18, 1955; Architecture, formes + fonction, 4, 1957; 5, 1958; 8, 1961–62; Werk-archithese, 3–4, 1978; Faces, 21, 1991; Archithese, 4, 1993; Guide to Swiss Architecture 1920–1995, vol. 3, 417, p. 163; 423, p. 167.

Hôtel du Rhône

Mont Blanc Center and Plaza Cinema

Miremont-le-Crêt Housing

Geneva
Municipal Gymnasia
Rue du Stand/Rue du Tir
1951–52
Paul Waltenspühl
Parc Geisendorf School and Pedagogic Center
Rue de Lyon/Rue Liotard
1952–67
Paul Waltenspühl and Georges Brera with K. Kleiner
La Tourelle Housing
Chemin M. Duboule, Petit-Saconnex
1964–70
Paul Waltenspühl, Georges Brera, Georges Berthoud, and Claire and Oscar Rufer with J. Arnold

The partnership of Waltenspühl and Brera successfully blended the roles of engineer and architect to yield works characterized by a clear composition, responsive to the definition of site and particularly careful over the handling of materials (both traditional and modern). In the Parc Geisendorf complex, which was built in various stages, the architects introduced the pavilion-type school building – previously tried out in German-speaking Switzerland – into the French-speaking area.

Municipal Gymnasia

Parc Geisendorf School and Pedagogic Center

La Tourelle Housing

Tours de Carouge Housing

Waltenspühl systematically studied this theme (see, for example, Les Palettes School at Grand Lancy, Avenue des Communes Réunies, 1964–67). He also designed a number of low-cost housing projects: both the Tours de Carouge (1958–63, built in collaboration with G. Brera, R. Schwertz, L. Archinard, E. Barro, A. Damay, and J. J. Mégevand) and the La Tourelle scheme (1965–70) are coherent solutions to the problems of building in the outskirts of Geneva in the 1960s.

Architecture, formes + fonction, 6, 1959; 9, 1962–63; 10, 1963–64; A. Corboz, J. Gubler and J.M. Lamunière, Guide d'architecture moderne de Genève, Lausanne 1969; Guide to Swiss Architecture 1920–1995, vol. 3, 416, p. 163; 419, p. 164; 405.7, p. 155.

Geneva

Vernets Sports Center

Quai de Vernets

1956–58 and 1966–68

Albert Cingria, François Maurice, and Jean Duret

with E. Guex, P. Tremblet, and J. P. Dom

Built in several stages, the Vernets Sports Center is articulated in various volumes. The large 10,000–seat skating rink (1956–58) has a reinforced-concrete structure with a metal roof supported by posts; it has recently been modified to meet new regulations. The indoor swimming pool complex (1966–68), which was also to include an outdoor skating rink (only partly built), is characterized by the rhythm of the roof grid structure, patterned by alternating skylights. In addition to the usual technical installations, the center has an administrative sector and bar-restaurant.

Architecture, formes + fonction, 6, 1959; Bauen und Wohnen, 7, 1960; Bulletin technique de la Suisse Romande, 12, 1967; Werk, 9, 1968; Faces, 23, 1992; Guide to Swiss Architecture 1920–1995, vol. 3, 425, p. 168.

Vernets Sports Center Swimming Pool

Geneva
Aïre Housing
Chemin Nicolas Bogueret
1958–59 and 1960–61
François Maurice, Jean Duret, and Jean Pierre Dom
with G. Steinmann
Fédération des Syndicats Patronaux Headquarters
Rue St Jean 98
1965–67
Jean Pierre Dom and François Maurice

The outcome of many years of research into planning and low-cost housing (see also, for example, the Les Ailes Cooperative Complex, Avenue Louis Casaï 83, built by the same architects in 1958–59), the master plan for low-cost housing scheme at Aïre was for two groups of three housing blocks. In the first stage work was begun on a five-story north-south building. By using an entirely prefabricated system the whole quarter was completed by the early 1970s. The building in Rue St Jean, on the other hand, is an efficient and skillful response to the theme of the office building – as are the offices at Rue d'Italie 6 (1965–67) and Rue du Rhône 75 (1970–72).

Architecture, formes + fonction, 7, 1960; 14, 1968; Habitation, 3 and 7, 1961; Bauen und Wohnen, 3, 1962; L'Architecture d'aujourd'hui, 104, 1962; Bauwelt, 19, 1968.

Geneva
Parc de Budé Housing
Avenue de Budé, Petit-Saconnex
1958–64
Georges Addor, Dominique Julliard, Jacques Bolliger, Jean Jacques and Pierre Honegger
Le Lignon Housing
Chemin du Lignon, Aïre-Vernier
1962–71 and 1985
Georges Addor, Dominique Julliard, Jacques Bolliger, Louis Payot

Aïre Housing

Fédération des Syndicats Patronaux

Parc de Budé Housing, view and site plan

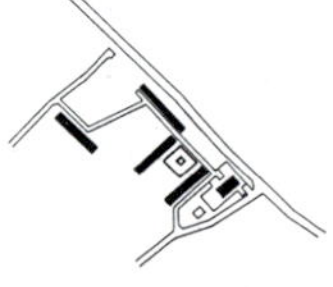

Meyrin Housing

Avenue de Feuillasse/Route de Mategnin/Rue des Boudines
1963–67
Georges Addor, Dominique Julliard, Jacques Bolliger, and Louis Payot

The housing schemes on the outskirts of Geneva are the result of an urban planning policy outlined as early as 1948 in the report by the Study Commission for the Development of Geneva. By recommending that the growth of the city should not exceed 200,000 inhabitants, the report paved the way to the creation of "satellite-cities". The urban planning solutions adopted sought to reconcile public and private interests and promoted housing blocks in large green areas (farmlands under neighboring town administrations). The various schemes had a number of common features: multi-story blocks of dwellings arranged around services and collective facilities, and the use of advanced prefabrication building systems.

One of the earliest results of this urban policy was the Vermont Quarter, Route de Montbrillant/Rue de Vermont (1948–54) built by André Bordigoni, Jean Gros, and Antoine de Saussure, with Eugène Beaudouin and Adolphe Guyonnet as consultants.

Bauen und Wohnen, 2, 1968; B. De Sivo, L'architettura in Svizzera, Naples 1968; A. Corboz, J. Gubler and J.M. Lamunière, Guide d'architecture moderne de Genève, Lausanne 1969; J. Bachmann and S. von Moos, New Directions in Swiss Architecture, New York 1969; Werk-archithese, 5, 1977; Archithese, 4, 1993; Guide to Swiss Architecture 1920–1995, vol. 3, 405.6 and 405.9, p. 154 and 156.

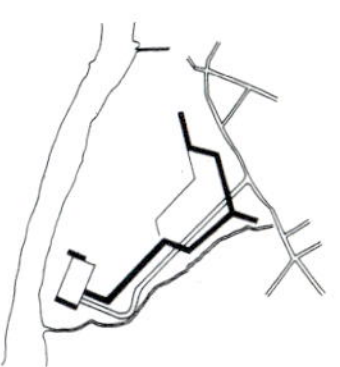

Le Lignon Housing, view and site plan

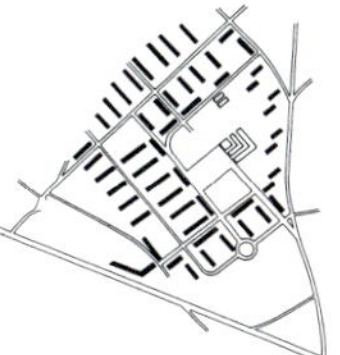

Meyrin Housing, view and site plan

Geneva
French School
Avenue Weber/Chemin de Roches/
Chemin de Vergers 4
1961–64
Arthur Bugna and Georges Candilis
Primary School
Place des Charmilles
1966
Edmond Guex and Gerd Kirchhoff

Based on the typical educational principles of the 1960s, the design for the French School organizes the volumes on an orthogonal grid, with terraces and spaces for open-air classes. The Charmilles Primary School owes its elegant appearance to the sculptural concrete massing and the refined handling of the materials.

J. Bachmann and S. von Moos, New Directions in Swiss Architecture, New York 1969; Guide to Swiss Architecture 1920–1995, vol. 3, 427, p. 169.

Geneva
New Headquarters of the International Labor Organization (ILO)
Route du Morillon 4
1965–69
Eugène Beaudoin, Alberto Camenzind and Pier Luigi Nervi
with J. Muller with the ILO Architectural Office (BABIT)
International Conference Center (CIGC)
Rue Varembé 15
1968–73
André and Francis Gaillard, and Alberto Camenzind
with the CICG Architectural Office

French School

Primary School

New Headquarters of the International Labor Organization

New Building for the Red Cross International Committee Central Research Agency (CICR)
Avenue de la Paix 17
1979–84
Mario Borges, Alain Burnier and André Robert Tissot
with Michel Girardet
Fondation des Immeubles pour les Organisations Internationales (FIPOI)
Geneva plays permanent host to several major international organizations, and, as a consequence, in recent decades the city has witnessed the growth of vast multipurpose complexes, consolidating its cosmopolitan image. The long curved prism containing the ILO is given plastic expression in the convex-concave handling of facades made of prefabricated elements, while the prestressed reinforced-concrete structure with faceted pillars bears the hallmark of Nervi in the design stage. The International Conference Center has an octagonal plan and a system of variable rooms (from 260 to 1,700 seats) modified by vertical sliding partitions. Lastly, the new building for the Red Cross Central Research Agency subordinates functional organization to the decision to locate the archives on the upper floor, while the requirements for thermal insulation have strongly influenced the external appearance of the building.

L'Architecture d'aujourd'hui, 121, 1965; Werk, 6, 1973; Parametro, 140, 1985; Werk, Bauen und Wohnen, 1–2, 1985; Architettura Svizzera, 7–8, 1986.

International Conference Center

New Building for the Red Cross International Committee

Geneva

United Nations School

Route de Pregny

1968–70 and 1973–76

Jean Marc Lamunière, Rino Brodbeck, Gérard Kupfer, and Georges Van Bogaert

Housing

Quai Gustave-Ador 64

1979–85

Jean Marc Lamunière and Georges Van Bogaert

Mixed-Use Building

Boulevard Carl-Vogt 2–4

1984–91

Jean Marc Lamunière, Georges Van Bogaert, and Bruno Marchand

Since the 1970s Lamunière – an architect, theoretician and town-planner involved in the debate on Rationalist architecture – has focused his research on the need to find a common language for designers and users, drawing on typological and semantic analysis as tools to

United Nations School

Quai Gustave-Ador Housing

enhance the vision of urban and architectural space. The works cited here, as well as the Tours de Lancy, Chemin de la Vendée 29 (1963–64), built by Lamunière in collaboration with Georges Van Bogaert and Bruno Marchand, testify to a rigorous design language suitable for prefabrication methods.
The Geneva Botanical Gardens Greenhouse (1984–88), entirely built in glass and steel, is another example from their prolific output.

L'Architecture d'aujourd'hui, 121, 1965; 166, 1973; J. Bachmann and S. von Moos, New Directions in Swiss Architecture, New York 1969; Werk, 2, 1972; Techniques et Architecture, 298, 1974; Architettura Svizzera, 8, 1975; 3, 1991; La presenza del passato, exhibition catalogue, Milan 1980; Werk, Bauen und Wohnen, 1–2, 1980; 3 and 6, 1986; 11, 1988; Architecture, 12, 1982; Architettura per il terzo millenio, Milan 1991; Archithese, 4, 1993; Guide to Swiss Architecture 1920–1995, vol. 3, 402, p. 145.

Mixed-Use Building

Tours de Lancy

Geneva
Les Pâquis School and Library
Rue de Berne/Rue de la Navigation/ Rue du Môle
1975–79 and 1978–81
Jean Jacques Oberson
with G. Curonici, M. Currat, R. Loponte
Ugo Brunoni

The school complex designed by Oberson is the first stage in an urban redevelopment scheme for the whole of the working-class quarter of Le Pâquis with the aim of creating social, cultural and sports facilities as well as housing. Respecting the local urban morphology, the individual parts tend to offer a clear interpretation of their solutions. This is the informing criterion in the complex with four reinforced-concrete volumes, arranged in pairs and linked by a suspended bridge passing through the building.

In Brunoni's project to convert a nineteenth-century primary school into a public library the external structure is preserved, while the new functions are organized around an iron staircase enclosed in a glazed shaft. The interior spaces are embellished by various figures taken from the vocabulary of contemporary architecture but also reflect the historical memory.

Werk-archithese, 9–10, 1978; 11–12, 1979; Architettura Svizzera, 12, 1981; Werk, Bauen und Wohnen, 10, 1981; 5, 1986; Abitare, 206, 1982; Rivista Tecnica, 1, 1982; Parametro, 141, 1985; Guide to Swiss Architecture 1920–1995, vol. 3, 433, p. 173.

Geneva
Mixed-Use Building
Rue de la Pélisserie 16–18/Rue Frank-Martin 8–10
1975–84
Janos Farago and Joseph Cerutti
with B. Cirlini

Situated on the northern side of the upper city and bordering on the lower edge of the historic center, this building for shops, offices and housing was designed as a contrasting point of contact between two different urban contexts. The complex plan with the functions superimposed is deliberately independent from the facades. The architectural composition, intended to evoke the multiple themes involved in the project, becomes a factor in overcoming the fragmentary nature of the space.

Architettura Svizzera, 1, 1984; L'Architettura, 10, 1987; Guide to Swiss Architecture 1920–1995, vol. 3, 434, p. 172.

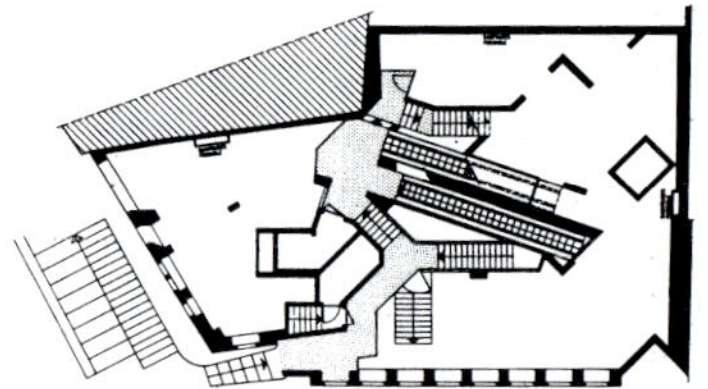

Mixed-Use Building, site plan and, opposite page, views

Les Pâquis School and Library, view, interior detail, and floor plan

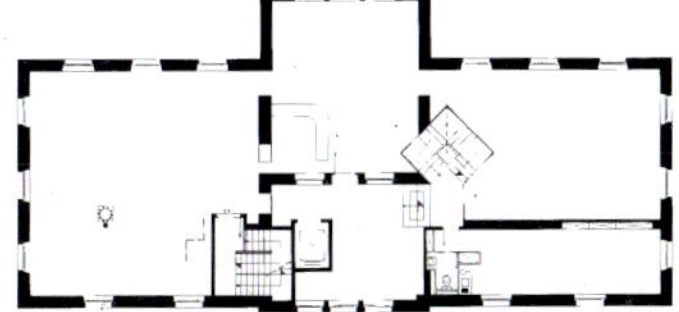

Geneva

Les Grottes I Housing

Avenue des Grands Prés/Rue Louis-Favre

1976–84

Christian Hunziker, Robert Frei and Georges Berthoud

with N. Barada, P. de Billaud, J.C. de Bortoli, E. Mohr, J. P. Stefani, S. Tchavgov, R. Schneider, and F. Olivet (sculptor)

After collaborating with Marc Saugey in the 1950s and working professionally with his brother Jacob, and Robert Frei, Christian Hunziker brought all his previous experience to bear on the design for this complex. The so-called "house of the *Stroumpfs*" (dwarves) is a strikingly unusual building on the Swiss architectural scene of low-cost housing. The building's highly organic forms aroused controversy over the urban renewal of the quarter. Following a mixed brief for housing, commercial facilities and craft activities, the design team abandoned the traditional isolated professional approach in favor of public participation.

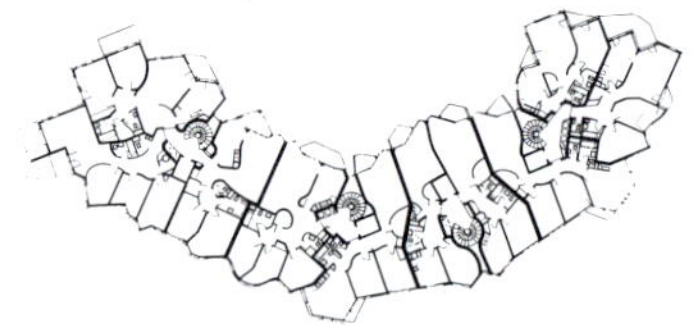

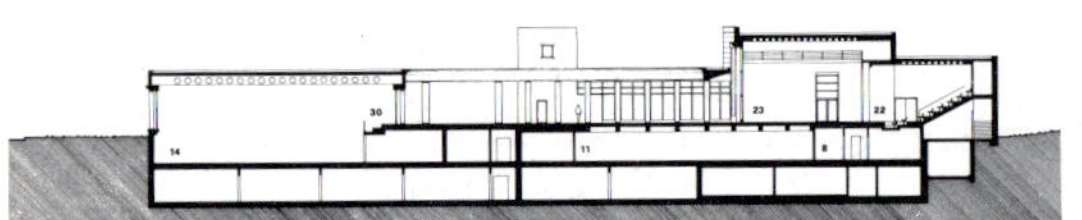

Les Grottes I Housing, view and floor plan
Le Corbusier School, view and sections

Aktuelles Bauen, 11, 1983; Domus, 657, 1985; Schweizer Journal, 1–2, 1985; Housing 2. I grandi quartieri come problema, Milan 1988; Guide to Swiss Architecturc 1920–1995, vol. 3, 435, p. 176.

Geneva
Le Corbusier School
Rue Le Corbusier 2–4–6, Malagnou
1980–85 and 1985–90
Ugo Brunoni
with Imré Vasas (site management) and J. Y. Ravier, J. Jebavy, and E. Muller

The design adopted an L-shaped plan, later modified to a U-shape through the construction of multipurpose community premises. The two fronts are differentiated: to the north, a compact wall protects the classrooms from traffic noise, while to the south the building opens up in a court, alluding to the features of Mediterranean architecture, making light and space the key elements in the recreation spaces. In Geneva Brunoni also designed the Church of the Holy Trinity (1986–94).
Architecture Romande, 4, 1986; Swiss Design, 10, 1986; Werk, Bauen und Wohnen, 11, 1986; Architettura Svizzera, 2, 1987; Controspazio, 3, 1993.

Geneva
Youth Hostel
Rue Rothschild 28–30
1982–87
Marie Christine and Pierre Kössler, Claude Morel, with Eric Lauper and Pierre Ruedin
with J. Bondallaz, L. Gentile, and P. Versteeg

The brief for the redevelopment of two buildings – the nineteenth-century Rothschild Hospital and the Barde Pavilion – also included the construction of a new building. The aim was to join up the existing buildings with a courtyard structure to be used as a youth hostel. The stylistic contrast between old and new is resolved by a gallery organizing the functional and spatial relations between the various parts of the complex.
Architettura Svizzera, 10, 1988.

Youth Hostel

Geneva
Multi-Use Building
Avenue Sainte Clotilde 18/Boulevard Carl-Vogt 29
1984–88
Chantal Scaler
with C. Kazian, F. Fossati, and T. Begat

The response to a mixed brief for car parks, ground-floor shops, a floor of offices and various apartments, the building is a classic "corner design" based on a plastic and functional architectural solution. The double facade traps sun through a greenhouse effect and also provides acoustic protection for the apartments (energy-saving installations are a feature of the complex). On the south facade two *maisonnettes* are reminiscent of the nineteenth-century buildings demolished to make way for the new complex.

Architettura Svizzera, 7–8, 1988; Guide to Swiss Architecture 1920–1995, vol. 3, 437, p. 176

Geneva
Hôtel de Police
Chemin de la Gravière/Quai d'Arve
1985–93
Carlo Steffen, André Gallay, Jacques Berger, and Jacques Bugna

The outcome of a 1985 competition, the police headquarters has a double comb plan stretching over the whole site. The official image of the building is stressed by the monumental volumes and the large metal structures, while the play of the glazed areas (internal central road and side glasshouses) breaks the monotony of the facades.
See also the Montbrillant Offices, Rue de Montbrillant/Avenue de France (1988–94) by Carlo Steffen in collaboration with André Gallay, Jacques Berger, Urs Tschumi and Michel Heurteux.

Geneva
Multi-Use Complex
Rue de la Coulouvrenière 19
1986–89
Olivier Archambault, Françoise Barthassat, and Enrico Prati
with P. Maréchal

The commission was for two works in the same urban block: the redevelopment of a waterfront structure to be used as a café and concert hall, and the construction of a mixed-use building for offices and dwellings on Rue de la Coulouvrenière. The solution in the plan for the intermediate spaces involved the creation of a fluid horizontal link on the first floor with the existing edifice. The facades of the two buildings respect the continuity of the neighboring built fabric but differ according to their urban contexts: an industrial zone characterized by the generators along the Rhône, and a street in a quarter partially redeveloped in the 1960s.
The same architects also designed the Place de l'Octroi at Carouge (1985–89).

Architettura Svizzera, 9, 1991.

Mixed-Use Building

Hôtel de Police

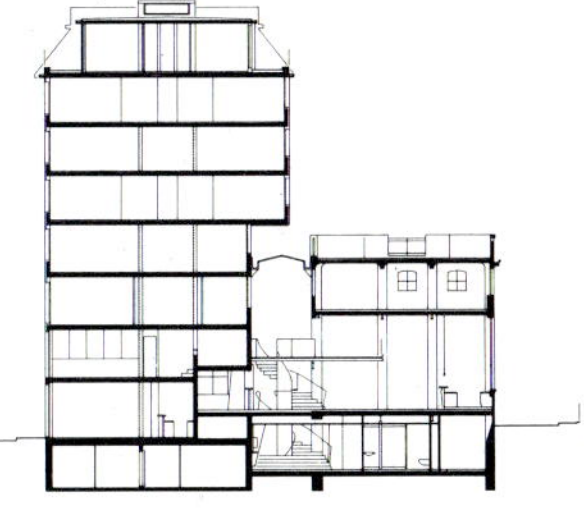

Multi-Use Complex, view and section

Geneva

Am Stram Gram Theater

Route de Frontenex 56

1987–92

Peter Böcklin and Predrag Petrovic with R. Fabra, N. Maeder, and B. Porcher

The decision to construct most of the building underground preserved the features of the place and the varied aspect of the urban fabric as well as leaving intact an existing park. Fully aware of the special features required, the architects designed a 325–seat Italian-style auditorium with a flexible stage. The fluid spatiality of the passage between entrance hall and main foyer is characterized by the gradual passage from daylight, which floods in from an upper glazed section, to the total darkness of the auditorium. The careful handling of the details and use of materials are evidence of a highly refined design sensibility.

Ingénieurs et Architectes Suisses, 26, 1992; Werk, 12, 1992; Docu Bulletin, 2, 1993; Habitation, 2, 1993; Guide to Swiss Architecture 1920–1995, vol. 3, 439, p. 177.

Geneva

Pre-Picot School Complex

Chemin Frank-Thomas 31/Plateau de Frontenex

1987–93

Fausto Ambrosetti, Laurent Chenu and Pierre Jéquier with M. Rollet, Y. Jacot, Y. Keller, A. Poussière, N. Pradervand, and P. Ambrosetti

Focusing on the concept of the school as the child's earliest social universe (both the material surroundings and spatial representation of childhood), the design proposed an open typology

Am Stram Gram
Theater

so as to establish an intense relation between classrooms and outside spaces. Articulated in three buildings grouped along a tree-lined avenue, the complex links two very different situations: an urbanized area and the countryside. Like the school building, the various facilities (gym, refectory, sports and recreation areas) are interconnecting and establish the coordinates for a new public space in the local quarter.

Bâtir une école. Groupe scolaire de Pré-Picot, Geneva-Cologny 1993; Archithese, 4, 1993; Faces, 29, 1993; Guide to Swiss Architecture 1920–1995, vol. 3, 440, p. 178.

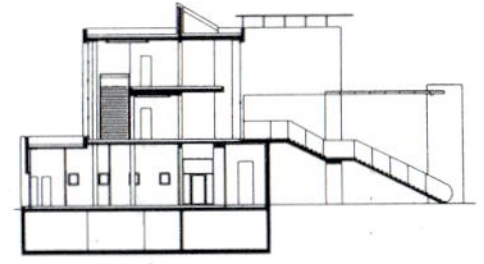

Geneva

Bruxelles Lambert Bank

Rue Frontenex

1987–96

Mario Botta

The unusual dimensions of the lot led to the adoption of a prism volume, open on three sides. The building is a precise response to the urban context, reconciling the internal spatial requirements with the necessary variations in the handling of the facades. A large central void (indicated externally by projecting bow windows and a long vertical slit) establish a fluid visual relation between the various functional levels.

See also Botta's House at Cologny, Chemin de Ruth 8 (1989–93).

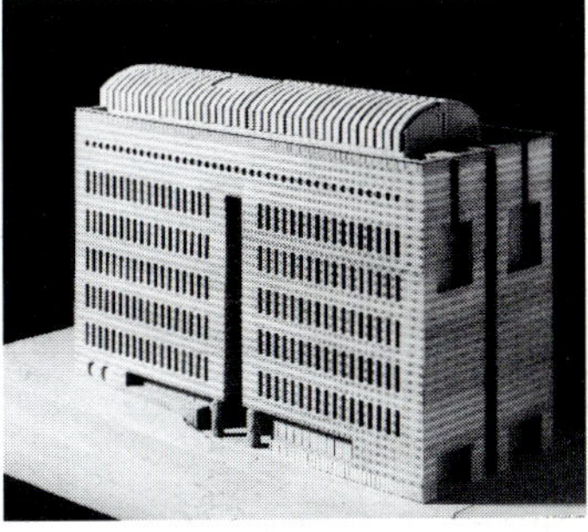

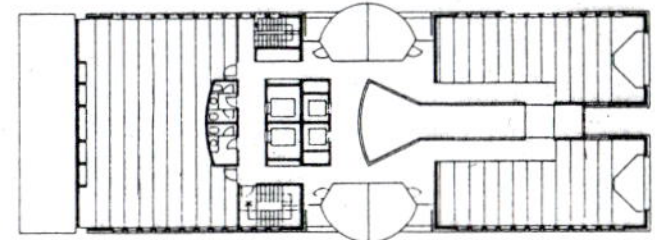

Pre-Picot School Complex, view and section

Bruxelles Lambert Bank, model view and floor plan

Geneva

Mixed-Use Building

Chemin Frank-Thomas 80

1988–91

Jean Marie Bondallaz

The design seeks to eliminate any residual spaces in the plan usually created when priority is given to functional aspects. The opening up of corners with balconies and conservatories lets light filter into the core of the building, while the typological choice, based on grouped spaces and uniform sizes, creates communal areas for residents. See also the building by Bondallaz in Place des Alpes 2–4 (1982–89).

Geneva

Uni Mail Building

Boulevard Carl-Vogt 102/Boulevard du Pont d'Arve

1988–92

ACAU (G. Châtelaine and G. Tournier)
Interiors: Max Bill, Jürg Bohlen, Alfredo Mumenthaler, Gilles Porret, and Philippe Spahni

This building is the first stage in a project to enlarge the university of Geneva. The overall urban plan was for the construction of the Social Sciences Faculty in a central area of the city. A completely glazed internal road – the axis connecting the accesses and public garden to be created on the banks of the Arve – organizes the composition in a quadrilateral built round four courts to be used for various functions (library, lecture rooms, multipurpose hall, and restaurant). The facades are designed to fit in harmoniously with the nineteenth-century context through the

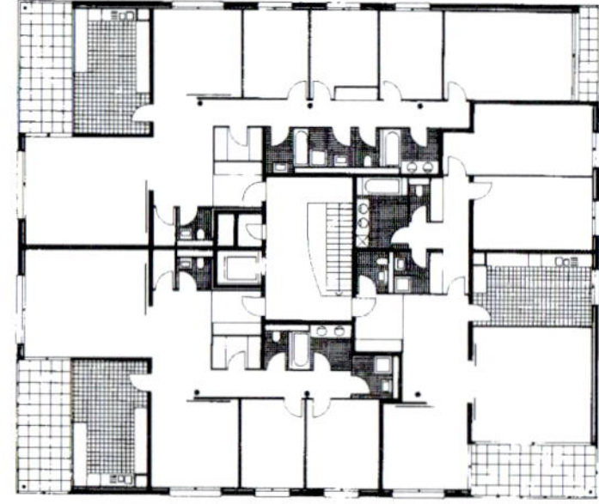

Mixed-Use Building, view and floor plan

Uni Mail Building, view

scale, window proportions and handling of materials. One of the key features in the design is the use of natural lighting to establish various internal spaces of different size and character. The central internal plaza is enhanced by art works from the group of Bill, Bohlen, Mumenthaler, Porret and Spahni.

Geneva

Student Residence

Boulevard de la Tour 1/Rue Micheli-du-Crest, Plainpalais

1988–93

Patrick Devanthéry and Inès Lamunière

with I. Charollais

This building for student accommodation with nineteen two- to five-room apartments has all the features of family dwellings. A clear articulation of the parts and an architectural language making sober use of Modernist elements are the response to an initial challenge to construct a building in tone with the volumes and materials of the context.

Techniques et Architecture, 380, 1988; Baumeister, 1, 1990; Archithese, 4, 1993; Guide to Swiss Architecture 1920–1995, vol. 3, 441, p. 178.

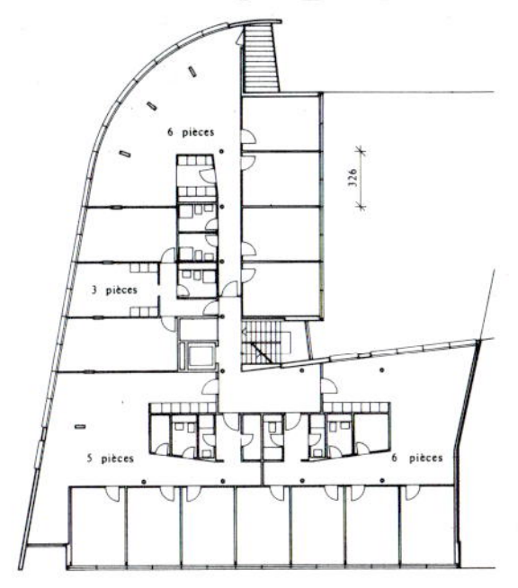

Uni Mail Building, interior view

Student Residence, view and floor plan

Lancy

Landscaping of the Parc En Sauvy

1980–85

Avenue du Curé Baud/Chemin des Semailles

Georges Descombes

with A. Léveillé, W. Weber, and J. Gebert

The itinerary consisting of a network of walkways takes the visitor to various isolated structures in search of lost traces from the local past: a paradoxical footbridge-tunnel, pergolas, a long fountain, a glass and metal covered structure, sand pits, and a small open-air theater. Formal restraint is a prerequisite in constructing the itinerary enabling visitors to perceive the spirit of the place. The materials – prefabricated pipes, corrugated sheets and concrete bricks – allude to elements in the history of the site.

Casabella, 515, 1985; L'Architecture d'aujourd'hui, 240, 1985; 262, 1989; Parametro, 141, 1985; Faces, 3, 1986; Georges Descombes. Il territorio transitivo, Rome 1988; Controspazio, 2, 1988; Abitare, 6, 1989; Domus, 706, 1989; Denatured visions. Landscape and Culture in the Twentieth Century, New York 1991; Guide to Swiss Architecture 1920–1995, vol. 3, 450, p. 183.

Parc En Sauvy, details

Landecy
Country Estate Housing
1982–85
Collectif d'architectes (Marcellin Barthassat, Marc Brunn, Claude Butty, and Jacques Menoud), with Groupe Y (first stage)
with D. Burnier, A. Conne-Borghini, L. Chenu, and P. Maréchal

This project to convert a typical nineteenth-century Geneva country estate building into housing is characterized by the organization of collective services and spaces kept separate from the internal layout of the dwellings, which are more conditioned by individual requirements. The external structure is left intact, while the new elements are handled boldly and freely.

Habitation, 7–8, 1987; Architettura Svizzera, 5, 1988; Ingenieurs et Architectes Suisses, 3, 1988.

1

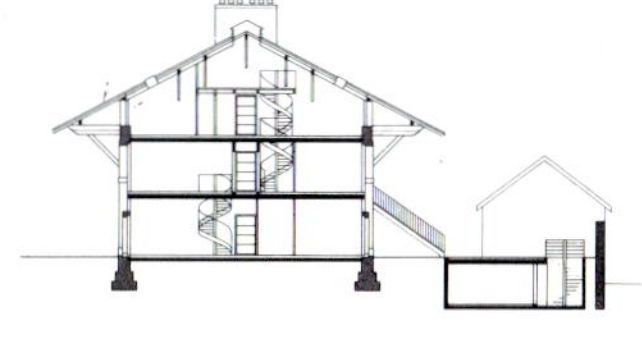

Country Estate Housing

Meyrin-Satigny
Hewlett-Packard III
Route Nant-d'Avril
1982
Jean Jacques Oberson with Janez Hacin
Firmenich Offices
Route Bergère 7
1985–90
Jean Jacques Oberson, Laurent Chenu, Maurice Currat, and Didier Jolimay
with P. Krahenbühl, A. Poussière, and C. Zihlmann

The headquarters of Hewlett-Packard is an open volume characterized by sober facades contrasting with a rich central space. The Firmenich manufacturing facility has a very different solution. The site in an industrial zone on the French border is associated with moves to decentralize the firms activities. The u-shaped court building contains the administrative sector. The building is situated at the edge of the laboratory area and thus directly connecting with the outside world. Also by Oberson, in collaboration with Laurent Chenu, Maurice Currat and the Offices des Constructions Fédérales (OCF) is the Bardonnex Customs Post (1986–91).

Werk, Bauen und Wohnen, 1–2, 1984; 12, 1989; Faces, 13, 1989; 22, 1991; Rivista Tecnica, 3, 1991; Guide to Swiss Architecture 1920–1995, vol. 3, 308, p. 133; 309, p. 134.

Hewlett-Packard III

Firmenich Offices

Bardonnex Customs Post

Opposite page: House at Puplinge

Puplinge
House
Christian and Jakob Hunziker, Robert Frei, Giancarlo Simonetti, and François Cuenod
1962–64
The same principles previously tried out in the Villa A Rajada at Gland (1957–62), canton of Vaud, and the Villa Frei at Vésenaz, Route d'Hermance 39 (1959), were applied to this single-family dwelling built on a small budget. The use of solar energy and economic constructional solutions paved the way for new design possibilities. The search for an intuitive architecture – with the aim of recovering the essential and primitive aspects of dwellings – informed the work-site developments, involving craftsmen and the clients themselves in the building process.
Architecture, formes + fonction, 9, 1962–63; L'Architecture d'aujourd'hui, 102, 1962; 121, 1965; a + u, architecture and urbanism, 72, 1984.

Vessy
Bridge over the Arve
1936
Robert Maillart
The outcome of Maillart's exploration of the technical and esthetic potential of reinforced concrete, the bridge over the Arve at Vessy is a three-hinged, hollow-box arch system. With its thrusting span and sober profile, this bridge is one of his finest constructions.
Moderne Schweizer Architektur 1925–1945, Basel 1947; Faces, 30, 1993–94.

Bridge over the Arve, view and section

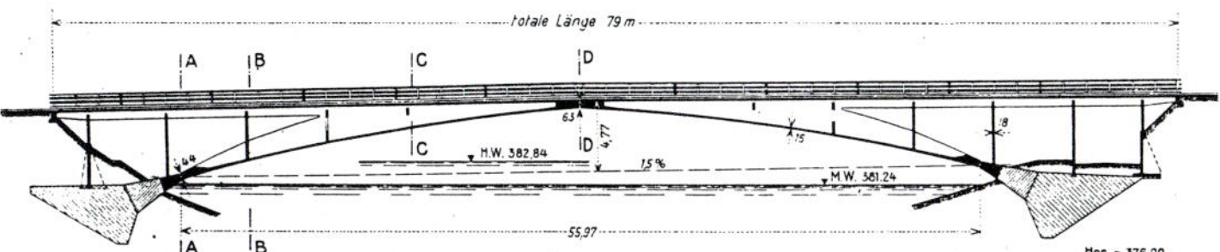

Valais

Crans-Montana
Bella Lui Sanatorium
1930–32
Rudolf Steiger, Flora Steiger-Crawford, and Arnold Itten
One of the most celebrated avant-garde buildings in the 1930s, the exclusive Bella Lui Sanatorium is a successful example of the application of innovative architectural principles: natural lighting, functionality, and standard furnishings. Inspired by similar works designed by Gaberel and Salvisberg, the building has a roof-solarium and bedrooms with individual balconies facing south, thus giving it the appearance of a luxury holiday hotel. The interesting mixed structure comprises a metal skeleton and concrete floors.
Schweizerische Bauzeitung, 96, 1930; Werk, 3, 1933; Moderne Schweizer Architektur 1925–1945, Basel 1947; Parametro, 141, 1985; Archithese, 3, 1991.

Finhaut
Le Châtelard Aqueduct
on the Eau-Noire
1925
Robert Maillart
The striking profile of the Le Châtelard Aqueduct, which carries water into the Barberine hydroelectric reservoir, makes it one of the most significant works in Maillart's early output. With a thirty-meter span, the structure con-

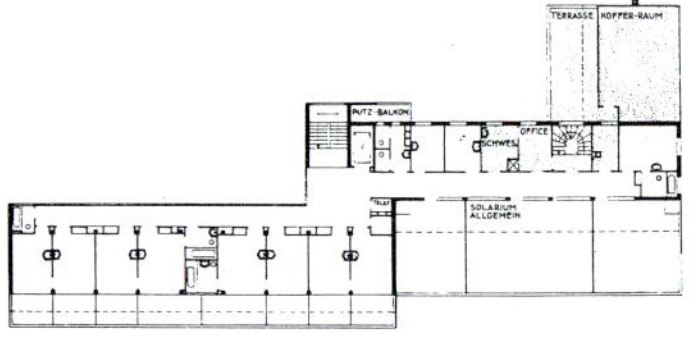

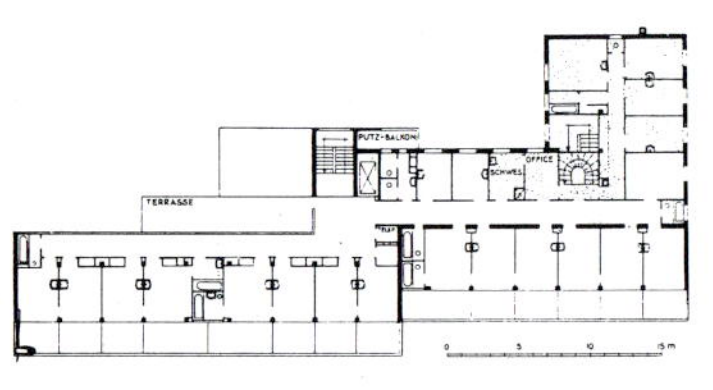

Bella Lui
Sanatorium, floor
plans and view

sisting of quadrangular caissons resting on supplementary pillars has the typical light feel of his boldest designs. There are also a number of engineering works by Alexandre Sarrasin in the canton of Valais: the Marécottes Regulating Reservoir at Salvan (1925–26), the Bridge over the Viège at Stalden (1928–30), and the Bridge over the Trient at Vernayaz (1931–33).
Schweizerische Bauzeitung, 10, 1927; Archithese, 3, 1991.

Les Evouettes
Multipurpose Building
1989–94
Christian Beck
with S. Cheasaux and P. Boschetti

The outcome of a 1989 competition, the building was designed for entertainment activities, sports facilities and various local and regional events. According to the use requirements, the stage, seating and gallery can be flexibly arranged around a principal space extending out towards the plaza. The overall image is determined by the use of exposed reinforced concrete.
See also Beck's Church of Sainte Marie Madeleine at Mase (1983).
Cahiers suisses de l'architecture et du design, 5, 1982; Werk, Bauen und Wohnen, 5, 1986; Baumeister, 1, 1990; Faces, 20, 1991; Rivista Tecnica 6, 1992.

Le Châtelard Aqueduct

Multipurpose Building

Lourtier

Church of Notre-Dame du Bon Conseil

1932 and 1955–68

Alberto Sartoris

This small mountain church created a great public outcry when the original structure was built in 1932. After undergoing modifications to the bell tower the same year, the church was later enlarged under the guidance of Sartoris himself and finally completed in 1968. The main changes involved moving the entrance further forwards and extending the nave, which was raised, while the monopitch roof was replaced by a pitched roof. Heated rain-pipes run along the pillars supporting the roof which, like the apse and entrance, are clad in local granite. The stained-glass windows are by Carla Prina.

E. Humeau, Légende in La chapelle de Lourtier, Geneva 1932; Le scandale de Lourtier ou la maison de Dieu peut-elle etre moderne? Exposition des pièces du procés, Lausanne 1933; Alberto Sartoris et le Valais, Martigny 1983.

Church of Nôtre-Dame du Bon Conseil, exterior and interior views

Martigny

Renovation of the Parish Church

Place du Midi

1986–93

John Chabbey, Michel Voillat, Raymond Coquoz and Jacques Faravel

with J. M. Rouiller, A. Fernández, and N. Carron

The principal historic monument in the town, this sixteenth-century church has undergone several restorations and modifications over the years. The

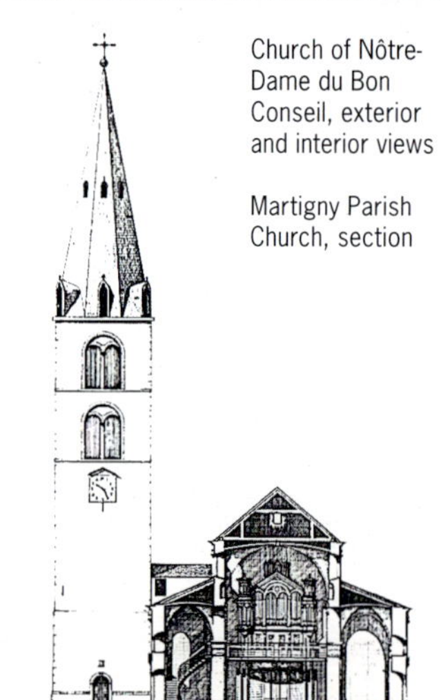

Martigny Parish Church, section

most recent restoration aimed to return the building to its original condition, at the same time giving it a modern interest. There are a number of highly refined design features: a new gallery, liturgical furnishings using iron as the strikingly contemporary main material, and a new lighting system.
Another work by Chabbey & Voillat is the Cretton House at Fully (1990–91).
Restauration de l'église paroissiale de Martigny, Martigny 1993.

Monthey
Du Crochetan Theater
Rue du Théâtre
1982–89
Jean-Luc Grobéty, Raoul Andrey and Christian Sottaz
with R. Gay, and Sneiders & Zinnernamm (site management)
For a small-sized lot near the city center, the architects adopted a concentrated plan with two superimposed rooms for theater shows. The vertical emphasis of the structure, intended to highlight the public nature of the building, is balanced by the articulated volumes of the parts, shaped as a shell protecting the theater space.
See also Grobéty's Porrentruy Sports Center (1985) in the canton of Jura.
Archithese, 3, 1991; Rivista Tecnica, 3, 1991; Guide to Swiss Architecture 1920–1995, vol. 3, 526, p. 211.

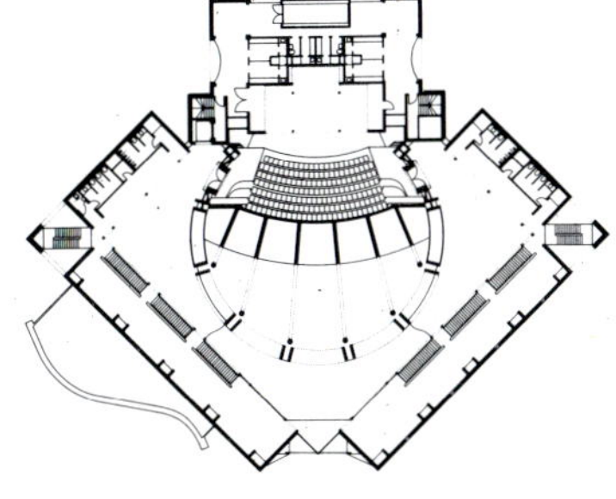

Crochetan Theater

Monthey
Ritz House
Rue du Coppet 7
1985–90
Vincent Mangeat
with G. Mann, O. Pina, and H. Ritz

Built after the widening of a mountain road, the house is the outcome of the contrast between a static space (the services sector backed onto the supporting wall), and a dynamic space – the metal volume containing the rooms, resting on reinforced-concrete-lamina foundations. The project is in keeping with the small traditional scale.

Rivista Tecnica, 3, 1991; 11, 1992; Werk, Bauen und Wohnen, 10, 1991; Futurismo-oggi, 9, 1992; Deutsche Bauzeitschrift, 5, 1993; Guide to Swiss Architecture 1920–1995, vol. 3, 527, p. 212.

Ritz House

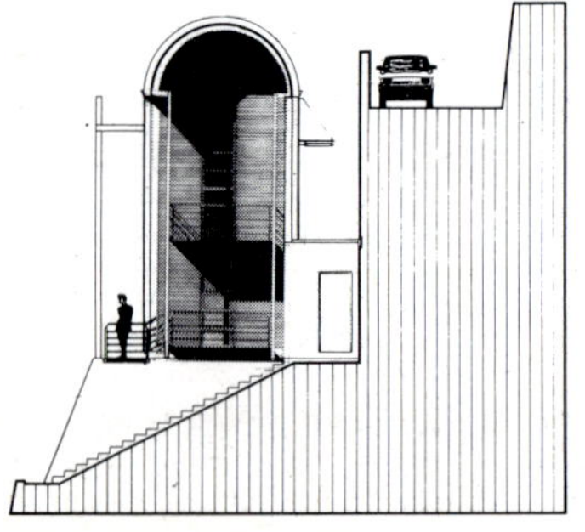

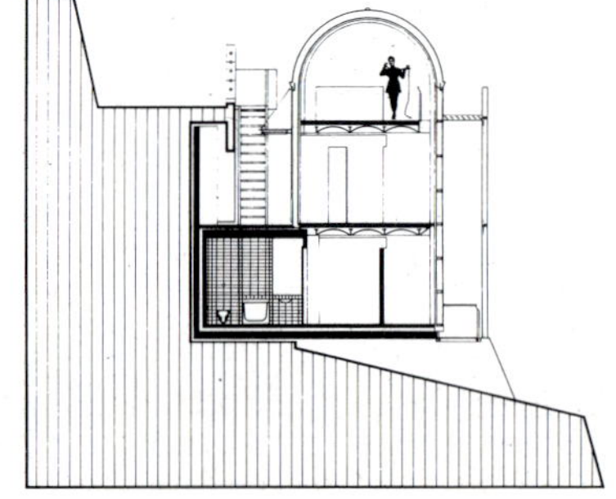

Saillon
Morand-Pasteur House
1934–35
Alberto Sartoris

Designed for a local farmer, the house is situated among the vineyards of the Rhône Valley. The volumes are typical of Sartoris' Mediterranean-style architecture with a flat roof, loggia and pergola. The semi-basement level contains the service premises; the living room, kitchen and garage are on the ground floor, and two bedrooms with fine views on the first floor. The materials are reinforced-concrete vertical structures, steel beams, perforated-brick walls and wooden window frames. The stairs were originally clad in gray rubber. The interior walls were painted in oils, from the same psychodynamic range used for the Cercle de l'Ermitage, while the exterior was rendered in white plaster.

Architectural Review, 80, 1936; P. Angeletti (ed), Alberto Sartoris. Un architetto razionalista, Rome 1979; Alberto Sartoris, Lisbon 1980; Alberto Sartoris et le Valais, Martigny 1983.

Morand-Pasteur House

Sierre

La Terrasse

Avenue Général-Guisan 4

1984–91

Jean Gérard Giorla

with M. Viret, M. Trautmann, A. Rossetti, P. A. Masserey, M. A. Albasini, F. Gatti, A. Mumenthaler, C. Washer, G. Evéquoz, and C. Vannini

Situated at a problematic key point in the town, the complex includes a pedestrian passage joining the station square with the Forum des Alpes, where the housing designed by Michel Zufferey was built in 1985 as part of the redevelopment of the center of Sierre. The building completes the existing block and is aligned with the street as well as linking various street levels through a central plaza. Various facilities are organized round the plaza: shops, offices and dwellings.

Giorla also designed the St Luc Ski Station Restaurant, Tignousa, in 1985–87.

Baumeister, 1, 1990; Archithese, 3, 1991.

Visp

La Poste Cultural Center

1984–92

Napoleonstrasse

Emilio Bernegger, Bruno Keller, Edy Quaglia, Sandro Cabrini, Renato Stauffacher, and Gian Maria Verda

with P. Joliat, R. Studer, G. Beusch, J. Erdin, H. Kurzen, and S. Arnaboldi

Despite the fact that the winning design for the 1984 competition, held by the Visp Town Council, was divided into various stages, the initial architectural idea remained intact. This concept based on the features of the urban layout was pursued by setting a sinuous facade to the road front. The volumes in the complex are organized linearly (tourist office, restaurant, bowling rink) and continue the built-up front, whereas two volumes with the theater and multipurpose room are directly connected through the hall and foyer to a plaza. The massive geometric composition of the west facade gives the building an official public appearance, while the northern facade, restrained by a large black reinforced-concrete cornice, is modeled plastically.

Rivista Tecnica, 9, 1984; 5, 1992; Aktuelle Wettbewerbe, 1, 1985; Architektur + Wettbewerbe, 125, 1986; Archithese, 3, 1991; Schweizer Journal, 1, 1992; Schweizer Holzzeitung, 18, 1992; Guide to Swiss Architecture 1920–1995, vol. 3, 546, p. 221.

La Terrasse, view and section

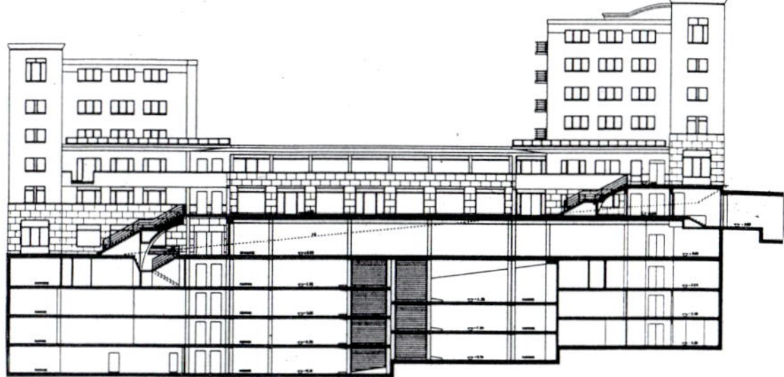

La Poste Cultural Center

Graubünden

Chur

Church of the Holy Cross

Masanserstrasse 161

1963–69

Walter Förderer

with H. Turnherr

As in the parish church of St Nicolas at Hérémence in the canton of Valais, built almost at the same time (1963–71), Förderer again resorted to a Brutalist approach, developed organically from a central plan. In addition to being a place of worship, the church also hosts other community activities. The principal materials are exposed concrete and wood.

Werk, 12, 1971; R. Gieselmann, Neue Kirchen, Stuttgart 1972; L. Dosch, Die Heiligkreuz-Kirche in Chur, Schweiz, Berne 1989; Guide to Swiss Architecture 1920–1990, vol. 1, 306, p. 75.

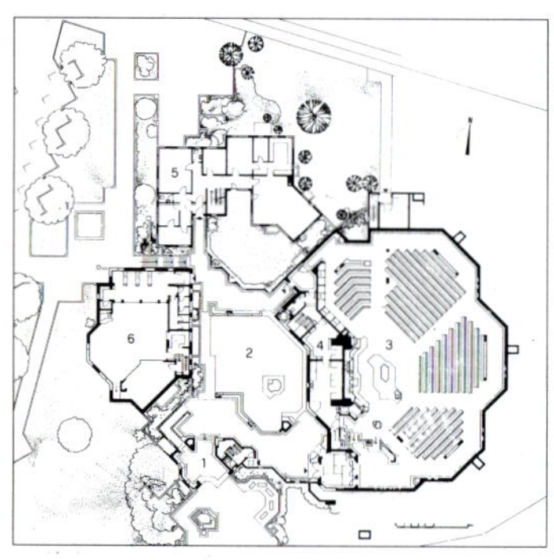

Church of the Holy Cross

Chur

Womens' School

Scalärastrasse 17

1977–83

Robert Obrist and Associates

Adapting to the topographic features of the sloping site, the project responded to the requirements for a school complex by diversifying the parts in various volumes: a wing contains the dormitories, refectory and café; the administrative block also houses the library, conference hall and classrooms; and a third volume contains the gymnasium.

The same architects, in collaboration with Richard Brosi, designed the recently completed layout for the PTT Bus Station in the center of Chur.

Werk, Bauen und Wohnen, 3, 1984; 4, 1992; Architettura Svizzera, 63, 1984; P. Disch (ed), L'architettura recente nella Svizzera tedesca 1980–1990, Lugano 1991, p. 259; Guide to Swiss Architecture 1920–1990, vol. 1, 308, p. 76.

Womens' School

Chur

Protective Structures for Roman Ruins

Seilerbahnweg 17, Welschdörfli
1986
Peter Zumthor
with R. Schaufelbühl

Renovation and Extension of the Fine Arts Museum

Postplatz, Bahnhofstrasse 35
1982–90
Peter Calonder, Hans Jörg Ruch, and Peter Zumthor
with D. Jüngling

Home for the Elderly

Cadonaustrasse 69–73, Masans
1990–93
Peter Zumthor
with T. Durisch, B. Haefeli, M. Gautschi, and I. Molne

Three translucent cubes with trellis walls protect the Roman ruins and enable visitors to explore a fascinating archaeological itinerary along metal footbridges in an atmosphere characterized by soft filtered light.

The restoration of Villa Planta – home of the important Kunstmuseum collection – was the outcome of a competition, whose brief also required the integration of the neighboring Museum of Natural History. The architects met this requirement with a project connecting the two buildings by a glazed bridge. The new extension consists of a side verandah to be used as foyer and bar, inserted into the external spaces inspired by the architecture of the Japanese garden. The recent Home for the Elderly is characterized by the clearly legible structural ele-

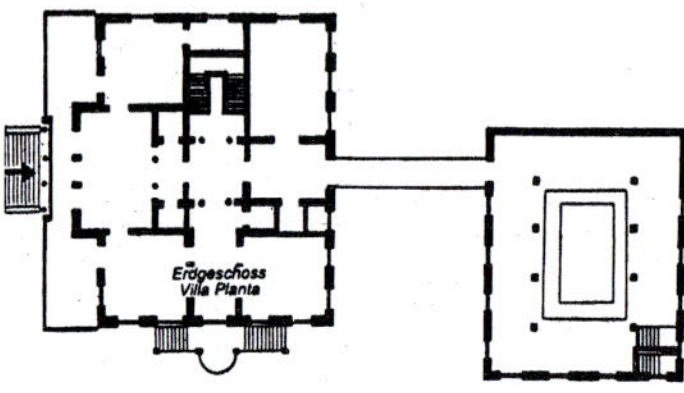

Protective Structures for Roman Ruins

Museum of Fine Arts Extension, view and floor plan

Home for the Elderly

ments and the craft handling of the materials – exposed concrete, tufa, and larch wood. See also Zumthor's extension to the Churwalden Schools (1979–83).

Archithese, 2, 1984; 2, 1985; Werk, Bauen und Wohnen, 10, 1987; 11, 1993; Detail, 5, 1988; P. Disch (ed), L'architettura recente nella Svizzera tedesca 1980–1990, Lugano 1991, p. 262 f.; du, 5, 1992; Construction, Intention, Detail. Five Projects from Five Swiss Architects, London-Zurich 1994; Domus, 760, 1994; Guide to Swiss Architecture 1920–1990, vol. 1, 309, p. 77; K. Gantenbein and J. Lienhart, 30 Bauten in Graubünden, Zurich 1996, p. 30 f. and 36 f.

Davos

Former Regina Alessandra Sanatorium (now Thurgau-Schaffhausen Sanatorium)

Grüenistrasse 18–20, Davos-Platz
1906–09 and 1925–49
Otto Pfleghard, Max Haefeli, and Robert Maillart
Rudolf Gaberel

Celebrated by Thomas Mann's novel for its "magic-mountain" atmosphere, the sanatorium for tuberculosis patients underwent various extensions and renovations. The original design was by Pfleghard & Haefeli, with Robert Maillart as technical consultant. In 1911 a symmetric wing was added to give the building a tripartite structure, recommended by the latest therapeutic prescriptions at the time. Rudolf Gaberel was responsible for various conversion and extension works, and in 1934 he designed the doctors' residences.

S. Giedion, Space, Time and Architecture, the Development of a New Tradition, Cambridge Mass. 1941; INSA. Inventario Svizzero di Architettura 1850–1920, vol. III, Berne 1982; S. von Moos, Estetica industriale, Disentis 1992.

Queen Alexandra Sanatorium

Doctors' Residences

Davos-Clavadel

Zürcher Heilstätte Alpine Sanatorium

Clavadelstrasse 681

1930–32

Rudolf Gaberel

Gaberel's successful experience in designing clinics led him in this case to an emblematic definition of the relations between architecture and therapeutic requirements. Responding to fashionable medical-sanitary theories, whereby hygiene and discipline are the basic parameters for building morphology, Gaberel designed south-facing terraces to obtain optimal sunlight for each room, as recommended for efficient tuberculosis therapy. Designed to respect the sanitary rules, the interiors are built with rounded corners, smooth surfaces, washable materials, and simple furniture. Nonetheless the most striking feature in this new sanitary-based architecture is the adoption of a flat roof (which had began to spread in Graubünden in the late nineteenth century) with a snow-removal system. This technological innovation had been promoted after 1926 by the pioneers of the Neues Bauen in their war against the pitched roof.

INSA. Inventario Svizzero di Architettura 1850–1920, vol. III, Berne 1982; Docu Bulletin, 12, 1985; Hochparterre, 4, 1990; S. von Moos, Estetica industriale, Disentis 1992; K. Gantenbein and J. Lienhart, 30 Bauten in Graubünden, Zurich 1996, p. 18 f.; Guide to Swiss Architecture 1920–1990, vol. 1, 311, p. 78.

Davos

Service Station

Bahnhofstrasse 11, Davos-Dorf

1927–28

Railway Station

Talstrasse 4, Davos-Platz

1949

Rudolf Gaberel

Having arrived in Davos as early as 1904 for health reasons, Rudolf Gaberel lived there and pursued an intense design career until 1952. Among his most interesting works are Burckhardt House (1926–27), demolished in 1978, a manifesto for his almost ascetic language with cubic forms, flat roof and austere detailing, and the service station Dorf-Garage of the same years. Other noteworthy works are his Davos-Frauenkirch School (1936), with a pitched roof, and the Davos Central Station built using the same vocabulary as the health facilities.

Also by Gaberel is the Chur Cantonal Hospital, Loestrasse 170 (1938–41), built in collaboration with Fred G. Brun.

Werk, 1, 1936; 2, 1938; INSA. Inventario Svizzero di Architettura 1850–1920, vol. III, Berne 1982; Docu Bulletin, 12, 1985; Guide to Swiss Architecture 1920–1990, vol. 1, 311, p. 78 f.

Zürcher Heilstätte
Alpine Sanatorium

Dorf-Garage

Davos Railway
Station

Davos
Conference Hall and Sports Center
Promenade 92
1959–90
Ernst Gisel
with C. Zweifel

Opened to the landscape, the sports center, with an indoor swimming pool, outdoor baths, and restaurant, was designed following an organic approach. The various pavilions are linked by a helicoid path to the large conference hall, characterized by skylights creating an undulating ceiling. Outside, the reinforced-concrete structure is partially clad in wood.

Werk, 7, 1962; 9, 1966; 1, 1971; J. Bachmann and S. von Moos, New Directions in Swiss Architecture, New York 1969; Guide to Swiss Architecture 1920–1990, vol. 1, 312, p. 80.

Davos
Kirchner Museum
Ernst-Kirchner Platz 1
1989–92
Annette Gigon and Mike Guyer
with U. Schneider, J. Brändle

In their first major work, the Kirchner Museum, the two young Zurich architects, explored new directions in the relation between the architectural container and the works of art. The guiding principle was restraint, as is revealed by the exhibition rooms with white walls, oak flooring and glass roofing, careful filtering natural light. The four high translucent cubes – the surfaces are handled with various

Conference Hall and Sports Center

kinds of glass – are a deliberate break with the nineteenth century type of large exhibition halls.

Other works by the same architects are the Vinikus Restaurant, Promenade 119, and the Davos Sports Center.

Faces, 19, 1991; 26, 1992–93; Bauwelt, 12, 1992; Hochparterre, 12, 1992; Werk, Bauen und Wohnen, 12, 1992; 1–2, 1993; AMC. Architecture-Mouvement-Continuité, 38, 1993; Domus, 748, 1993; Rivista Tecnica, 5, 1993; Skala, 29, 1993; Techniques & Architecture, 408, 1993; I. Flagge (ed), Kirchner Museum Davos, Berlin 1994; K. Gantenbein and J. Lienhart, 30 Bauten in Graubünden, Zurich 1996, p. 68–71.

Giova

Chapel of Our Lady of Fatima

San Vittore

1986–88

Mario Campi and Franco Pessina

The central plan and vertical development of the building symbolize the universal nature of the church but also correspond to the central physical position of the building on the site. The main volumes – dome and tower – are variations on the lighthouse theme. The synthesis of references and analogies appears to be a symbol of the *turris eburnea.*

Domus, 703, 1989; Rivista Tecnica, 3, 1989; 10, 1992; Kunst und Kirche, 1, 1990; Baumeister, 12, 1991; Häuser, 4, 1993; K. Gantenbein and J. Lienhart, 30 Bauten in Graubünden, Zurich 1996, p. 92 f.

Kirchner Museum, view and interior

Chapel of Our Lady of Fatima

Haldenstein

Semidetached Houses

Pälu 18

1982–83

Peter Zumthor

Atelier Zumthor

Süsswinkel 20

1985–86

Peter Zumthor

with J. Conzett

While the plan for these two semidetached houses reveals the use of traditional design features, such as symmetry and courtyard, the architect's atelier, despite its similarities with rural architecture of the village, appears like a refined *objet trouvé* in wood: a perfectly finished volume with no sign whatsoever of elements to denote its function. Other interesting works by Zumthor include the Malix Multipurpose Center, Pazonia (1981–86) and the much noted Vals Spa (1994–96).

Archithese, 5, 1985; 6, 1986; Detail, 5, 1988; Docu Bulletin, 1, 1988; P. Disch (ed), L'Architettura recente nella Svizzera tedesca 1980–1990, Lugano 1991, p. 261; du, 5, 1992; Guide to Swiss Architecture 1920–1990, vol. 1, 316, p. 81.

Küblis

Power Station

Büdemji

1921–22

Nicolaus Hartmann

The competition-winning design for the first major hydroelectric power station in the canton was by Nicolaus Hartmann, a disciple of the great reformer

Semidetached Houses

Atelier Zumthor

of traditional architecture, Theodor Fischer. The building reconciles the functionalism required by the innovative technology of a power station with suitable forms for a picturesque, seemingly local architecture. Borrowing from the typology and tradition of ecclesiastic architecture proved to be an ideal solution for this task.

This same style was to reappear in the Poschiavo Station built by Hartmann in 1923.

Werk, 6, 1925; Schweizerische Bauzeitung, 92, 1928; 94, 1929; C. Clavout and J. Ragettli, Die Kraftwerkbauten im Kanton Graubünden, Chur 1991; Guide to Swiss Architecture 1920–1990, vol. 1, 318, p. 84.

Pontresina

Coaz Alpine Refuge

Las Plattas

1964 and 1982

Jakob Eschenmoser

Situated at an altitude of 2,610 meters to offer hospitality for mountaineers crossing the Bernina Pass, the refuge (extended in 1982) consists of a massive polygonal-plan central volume and an additional volume, also in stone, with a strip of colored Eternit containing the windows.

Eschenmoser also built the Mount Bertol Refuge above Arolla in the canton of Valais.

R. Obrist, S. Semadeni and D. Giovanoli (eds), Construir-Bauen-Costruire, 1830–1980, Zurich-Berne 1986; Guide to Swiss Architecture 1920–1990, vol. 1, 323, p. 87.

Power Station

Coaz Alpine Refuge

Saint Moritz

Housing and Studio

Via Aruons 10

1970–72

Robert Obrist and Associates

In stark contrast with the traditional "Kurort" (spa) style of the surrounding architecture, the reinforced-concrete building contains the architect's studio-house and ten rented dwellings. Contextual references, however, are present in the plastic terraced shape of the building which refers to the sloping site.

The same spare, well-proportioned language reappears in the Untervaz School Complex, Schulweg 240, built by Obrist and Associates in 1983–85.

R. Obrist, S. Semadeni and D. Giovanoli (ed), Construir-Bauen-Costruire, 1830–1980, Zurich-Berne 1986; Guide to Swiss Architecture 1920–1990, vol. 1, 326, p. 87.

Schiers

Salginatobel Bridge

30 km north of Davos on Route 28, Schiers – Schuders

1929–30

Robert Maillart

Sagastäg Bridge

over the River Landquart

1991–92

Walter Bieler

with R. Zindel

Scuol

Langlau Bridge

on the Pradella-Scuol road

1990

Walter Bieler

Twentieth-century Swiss engineering has been characterized by a consolidated bridge-building tradition exploring new structural possibilities without neglecting the dynamics or form as the

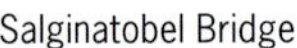

Salginatobel Bridge

Housing and Studio

Sagastäg Bridge

essential element in the static conception.
Of the works left by Robert Maillart, the Salginatobel Bridge is one of his finest, with its typical hollow-box arch spanning ninety meters in a most pure, clear and elegant way. A forerunner in Maillart's own output was the Valtschiel Bridge at Donath (1925) near the San-Bernardino pass.
Walter Bieler has skillfully interpreted Maillart's legacy, building slender new structures and extending research to the structural use of wood.
Bieler also designed the Drostobel Bridge at Klosters (1992).

Sumvitg/Somvix
Chapel of San Benedetg
San Benedetg
1987–88

Peter and Annalisa Zumthor
with R. Schaufelbühl
Tucked away in the Surselva mountains, this small wooden church with a slender silhouette is constructed from a leaf-shaped plan. The plan design is conceived on a lemniscate, an algebraic curve to the fourth power forming the figure of "8", which proportionally shortened also determines the sections. The walls enclose a dynamic interior space converging on a central point of gravity. An extreme synthesis of poetry and rationality, there are also refined allusions to images and memories from the local historic tradition, making this church a gem of twentieth-century Swiss architecture.
Domus, 710, 1989; Werk, Bauen und Wohnen, 4, 1989; Archithese, 6, 1990; du, 5, 1992; P. Disch, L'Architettura recente nella Svizzera tedesca, Lugano 1991, p. 265; Guide to Swiss Architecture 1920–1990, vol. 1, 330, p. 91; K. Gantenbein and J. Lienhart, 30 Bauten in Graubünden, Zurich 1996, p. 110 f.

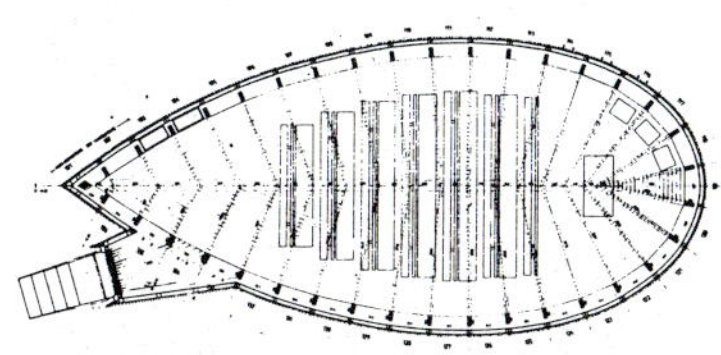

Drostobel Bridge

Chapel of San Benedetg, view and floor plan

Ticino

Airolo

Highway Tunnels from Airolo to Chiasso

San Gottardo Sud, Melide-Grancia, and Bissone-Maroggia Tunnels

1965–80

Rino Tami

The architectural consultant for the Ticino Canton public works department, Rino Tami, proposed a series of guidelines for structures on the highways: uniform treatment, same material (reinforced concrete), and the design of tunnel entrances that reflect the specific features of the sites. Given that the natural inclination of the mountain foothills crossed by the highway were around thirty degrees, this measurement was used for the support walls and bridge shoulders, whereas the projecting canopies of the tunnels at sixty degrees to the road surface set the visual rhythm for the roadscape.

Werk, 1 and 9 1969; Rivista Tecnica, 6, 1982; Werk, Bauen und Wohnen, 12, 1983; 4, 1986; D. Bachmann and G. Zanetti, Architektur des Aufbegehrens. Bauen im Tessin, Basel 1985; Guide to Swiss Architecture 1920–1995, vol. 3, 601, p. 230–232; 759, p. 305.

Highway Tunnels:
Melide-Grancia,
San Gottardo Sud,
Bissone-Maroggia

Ambri

Juri House

Airport area

1990–92

Raffaele Cavadini

with F. Trisconi and S. Marzari

Situated on the edge of the built-up area, the house was designed taking into account both by the harsh winter conditions and the context, character-

ized by the scattered buildings of the adjacent airfield. The result is a compact inward-looking volume with a number of features from traditional middle-class architecture in the region. The one-floor base – containing services and guest bedroom – clearly separates the inhabited section of the house from the ground. On the first floor is a studio and double-height living-room giving onto a spacious open-air balcony, while the upper floor accommodates the night zone.
Ticino hoy, exhibition catalogue, Madrid 1993; Rivista Tecnica, 1–2, 1993; P. Disch, Architettura recente nel Ticino 1980–1995, Lugano 1996, p. 152.

Arcegno
House
Via Frigera 8
1966
Mart Stam
Mart Stam was in close contact with the Swiss avant-garde in the inter-war period and constantly engaged in the debate on Modern architecture, both through his involvement in the review *ABC* and his participation in several major competitions. Nonetheless he only built a few late works in Switzerland, including this house and the Hilterfingen House (1969–70), in the canton of Berne.
Rassegna, 47, 1991.

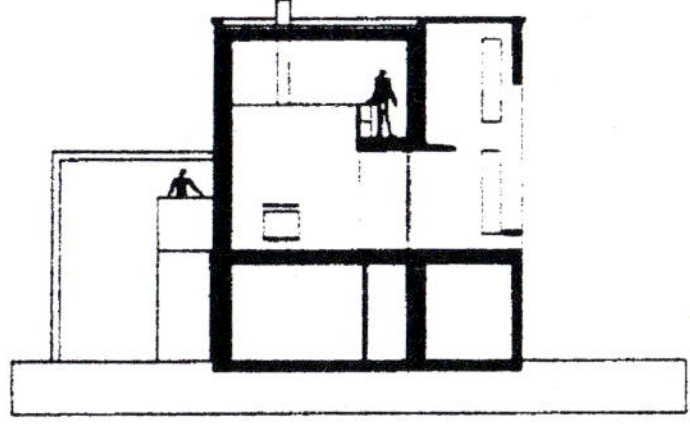

Juri House

House at Arcegno, section and view

Arcegno

Righetti House

Via Loco

1990–91

Michele Arnaboldi
with N. Romerio

Located on a site overlooking Lake Maggiore and the Magadino Plain on the western edge of the town, this two-family house was designed by following one simple gesture: a longitudinal building set perpendicular to the slope is articulated in two staggered volumes. In addition to separating the two residences, this also creates direct access through a series of terraces to the various levels. The restrained formal solution is due to the choice of structure: prestressed reinforced concrete freeing large surfaces areas and enhancing the rooms with a striking spatiality.

Ticino hoy, exhibition catalogue, Madrid 1993; Architettura Svizzera, 10, 1993; Rivista Tecnica, 1–2, 1993; Guide to Swiss Architecture 1920–1995, vol. 3, 604, p. 235; P. Disch, Architettura recente nel Ticino 1980–1995, Lugano 1996, p. 148.

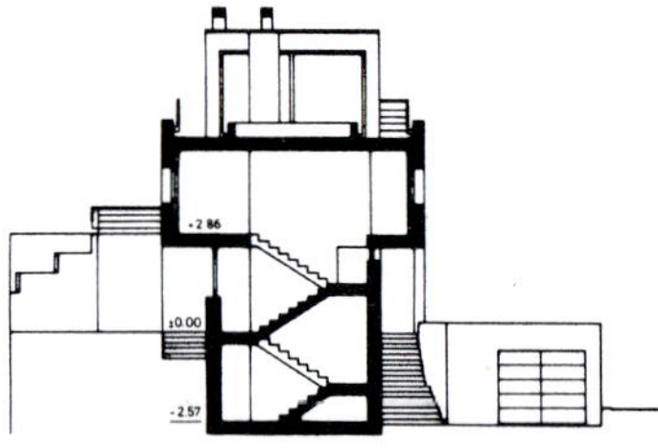

Arosio

Maggi House

1980–82

Mario Campi and Franco Pessina

The long prismatic volume overlooking the village is set against a mountain slope. The house dialogues with the old village church through its massive mask, making it a genuine "domestic temple". The physical and conceptual break between the stone facade and the rendered-wall of the rest of house to the rear – with the rooms arranged

Righetti House, view and section

Maggi House

on two floors and a longitudinal circulation – is highlighted by the sudden interruption to the cornice.

a + u, architecture and urbanism, 11, 1982; Progressive Architecture, 7, 1982; Rivista Tecnica, 2, 1982; Werk, 12, 1982; du, 8, 1986; Werk, Bauen und Wohnen, 6, 1986; Lotus international, 63, 1989.

Arzo

Studio House

Ai Ronchi

1987–89

Roni Roduner

Roduner's career began in 1978 with the Strahm House at Chemin des Fenetta, Villars-sur-Glane, in the canton of Fribourg, and developed coherently for over a decade before he tackled his own studio-house – a manifesto for his design principles. The clear and resolute layout highlighting the contrast between architecture and nature guided the main choices: the volume with the studio protects the rear of the dwelling from the untidy urban sprawl, and makes the roof-garden a transitional element. The living spaces of the house face south towards the Varesotto Hills, while a completely closed parabolic wall delimits the northern edge. Inside, the double-height living-room is the focal point for all activities. See also Roduner's Multipurpose Complex, Place du Manoir, Martigny, canton of Valais, completed in 1993.

Rivista Tecnica, 5, 1991; Abitare, 313, 1992; Architettura Svizzera, 102, 1992; Ticino hoy, exhibition catalogue, Madrid 1993; P. Disch, Architettura recente nel Ticino 1980–1995, Lugano 1996, p. 102.

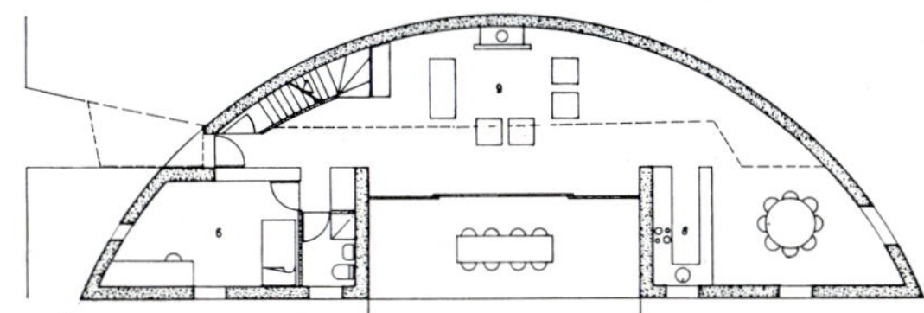

Studio House

Ascona

Albergo Monte Verità

Monte Verità

1927–28

Emil Fahrenkamp

Restoration and Extension

1970 and 1992

Livio Vacchini

with M. Vanetti and M. Giacomazzi

A favorite retreat for the European intelligentsia at the turn of the century, Monte Verità has witnessed many aspects of twentieth-century culture. Anarchists, theosophers, life reformers, social-democrats, trade-unionists, artists and psychoanalysts have all turned to the mountain at Ascona as a place to work out their own particular utopias, or have even viewed it as an earthly paradise in which to try out alternative ways of life. This enigmatic and evocative place is the antithesis of the city, and symbol of a mythical "return to nature" to exorcise the conflicts generated by industrialization. And here the hotel commissioned by Baron von der Heydt testifies to the advent of Rationalism in the Ticino canton. A visit is also recommended to the museum itinerary, which includes Anatta House, Selma House and Chiaro Mondo dei Beati.

E. Keller (ed), Ascona Bau-Buch, Zürich 1934; Rivista Tecnica, 12, 1972; 10, 1988; Monte Verità, Milan 1978; Guide to Swiss Architecture 1920–1995, vol. 3, 605, p. 236.

Ascona

San Materno Theater

Via San Materno 3

1928

Carl Weidemeyer

Situated in the Monte Verità area, the theater was designed for the Charlotte Bara School of Dance and reveals the interest in the principles of new architecture shown by the German architects in the Ascona colony. The building is conceived as a series of gradually declining cubic volumes connected by a semi-circular apse, which has a terrace roof suitable for outdoor exercise. Its curved lines are echoed by the design of the balconies, while the floor above the theater auditorium accommodates a dwelling. The 180–seat auditorium is structured in three parts and can easily be adapted to various kinds of shows. In a poor state of conservation, the building is in urgent need of restoration.

Moderne Bauformen, 1930, 7; E. Keller (ed), Ascona Bau-Buch, Zürich 1934; Rivista Tecnica, 12, 1972; 10, 1988; Monte Verità, Milan 1978; Werk, Bauen und Wohnen, 5, 1984; Guide to Swiss Architecture 1920–1995, vol. 3, 606, p. 236.

Albergo Monte Verità, views

San Materno Theater, views

Ascona
Tutsch House
Strada Cantonale, Ronco
1931
Oppenheimer House
Via Collinetta 73
1934–36
Carl Weidemeyer

Erected on a steep slope, the Tutsch House looks out to the lake from a dynamic series terraces and balconies. A natural stone base joins the house up with the neighboring Hahn House (1929–31), also built by Weidemeyer, but now completely remodeled. The Oppenheimer House, characterized by a flat roof and rounded volumes, is still in its original condition. Nearby is the Koerfer House, Via Emilio Ludwig, built by Marcel Breuer in collaboration with H. Beckhardt, R. Frank, and R. Meyer.

Moderne Bauformen, 7, 1930; E. Keller (ed), Ascona Bau-Buch, Zürich 1934; B. Moretti, Ville, Milan 1934; Rivista Tecnica, 12, 1972; 10, 1988; P. Disch (ed), 50 anni di architettura in Ticino 1930–1980, Bellinzona-Lugano 1983; Guide to Swiss Architecture 1920–1995, vol. 3, 608, p. 237.

Ascona
Villa Tuia
Sentiero Roccolo 11
1961
Richard Neutra
with C. Trippel and B. Honegger

Situated in a magnificent park, the villa is organized on two levels: in the basement is the entrance with a picture gallery, guest rooms, garage, and service premises; on the main floor the day areas have large windows facing onto Lake Maggiore.
A few years later, in 1963, Neutra also

Tutsch House

Oppenheimer House

built the Rentsch House at Wengen in the Berne Oberland, while the Bucerius House at Brione sopra Minusio was designed in 1964–66.

W. Boesiger (ed), Richard Neutra 1961–66. Buildings and Projects, Zurich 1966; P. Disch (ed), 50 anni di architettura in Ticino 1930–1980, Lugano 1983; Manfred Sack, Richard Neutra, Zurich 1992; Guide to Swiss Architecture 1920–1995, vol. 3, 609, p. 238.

Ascona

Lido of Ascona

Via Lido

1981–87

Livio Vacchini

with M. Vanetti, M. Tognola, M. Andreetti, and L. Andina

Two walls perforated by seven circular apertures characterize this container for services at the swimming establishment. Conceived as a filter between city and beach, the building (constructed in reinforced concrete and clad with silicon-limestone bricks) is a space to cross but also a powerful architectural element in the landscape distinguished by the technical boldness of the projecting elements and gestures of the geometry.

Werk, Bauen und Wohnen, 10, 1985; AMC. Architecture-Mouvement-Continuité, 12, 1986; a + u, architecture and urbanism, 191, 1986; Rivista Tecnica, 3, 1986; 7–8, 1988; Casabella, 544, 1988; F. Werner and S. Schneider, La nuova architettura ticinese: Mario Botta, Aurelio Galfetti, Ivano Gianola, Luigi Snozzi, Livio Vacchini, Milan 1990; Guide to Swiss Architecture 1920–1995, vol. 3, 612, p. 239; P. Disch, Architettura recente nel Ticino 1980–1995, Lugano 1996, p. 101.

Villa Tuia

Lido Patriziale

Ascona
Fumagalli House
Via delle Querce
1983–84
Livio Vacchini
with M. Vanetti, L. Andina, and G. Parboni

In this design the response to an untidy periphery is paradoxically an outward-looking house. The free plan and fluid spaces mediated by perimeter porticos and terraces – assumed as typological elements – mean that the villa is both isolated and open. The asymmetric composition of the volumes and dynamic projecting elements create a dialectical relation with the static nature of the whole.

Casabella, 517, 1985; a + u, architecture and urbanism, 191, 1986; du, 8, 1986; Rivista Tecnica, 4, 1986; Werk, Bauen und Wohnen, 6, 1986; F. Werner and S. Schneider, La nuova architettura ticinese: Mario Botta, Aurelio Galfetti, Ivano Gianola, Luigi Snozzi, Livio Vacchini, Milan 1990; Guide to Swiss Architecture 1920–1995, vol. 3, 611, p. 239; P. Disch, Architettura recente nel Ticino 1980–1995, Lugano 1996, p. 73.

Ascona
Diener House
Ronco
1989–91
Luigi Snozzi
with M. Vicedomini

Situated on steep ground overlooking Lake Maggiore, the house may be reached by two routes. A public path on the western side leads to the living-room floor, while a second path from the covered parking uses the pergola stairs to reach the terracing of the

swimming pool and an open area with the guest rooms. The second itinerary then continues under the house before rising back up through the portico to the external space of the living room. The house has an interesting system of windows, designed as a function of their views.
du, 11, 1989; Abitare, 293, 1990; Architektur Aktuell, 137, 1990; Casabella, 567, 1990; Rivista Tecnica, 3, 1990; Häuser, 4, 1991; Möbel Interior Design, 11, 1991; Raum und Wohnen, 2, 1991; P. Disch, Architettura recente nel Ticino 1980–1995, Lugano 1996, p. 115.

Balerna
Craft Center
Via Passeggiata
1977–79
Mario Botta
with R. Leuzinger
Situated in a peripheral area run down by indiscriminate urbanization, the Craft Center attempts to upgrade the context by its own presence. Four massive blocks are connected by a glazed metal roof covering the central plaza – the focus for the workspaces. The first floor accommodates administrative offices, while the residential sector – suitably isolated by broad terraces – is on the top floor. The design is thus an attempt to give new meaning to the daily functions of living by combining dwelling and workplace in one building.
Another Balerna work by Botta is the Municipal Gymnasium, Via San Gottardo (1976–78).
Abitare, 184, 1980; Archithese, 1, 1980; GA Document, 2, 1980; Lotus international, 25, 1980; Baumeister, 2, 1982; GA Architect, 3, 1984; Ville and Giardini, 205, 1986; G. Brown-Manrique, The Ticino Guide, New York 1988; Guide to Swiss Architecture 1920–1995, vol. 3, 706, p. 277.

Craft Center

Opposite page:
Fumagalli House
Diener House, views

Balerna
Arnaboldi House
Strada Regina 14
1988–91
Ivano Gianola
with C. Frisone and R. Genazzi
Starting from the same compact building type chosen for the Bernasconi House, Via Prada 20a (1978), at Balerna, which mediates the relation with the context through a single facade, in this work the architect designed a court shaped by the long building of the residence and the wing containing the swimming pool. The compositional and constructive logic of the design is determined by the wall in which the solids are emphasized over the voids, accentuating the inward-looking nature of the building and stressing the outward tectonic nature. While the shade gives plasticity to the volumes, light filtered through the windows defines the colors and textures of the materials. See also Gianola's Municipal Nursery School, Via Silva 1 (1971–74), at Balerna.
P. Disch (ed), 50 anni di architettura in Ticino 1930–1980, Lugano 1983; a + u, architecture and urbanism, 175, 1985; Ticino hoy, exhibition catalogue, Madrid 1993; Ivano Gianola Architetto. Quattro case e un palazzo, exhibition catalogue, Viggiù 1993; Guide to Swiss Architecture 1920–1995, vol. 3, 709, p. 279; P. Disch, Architettura recente nel Ticino 1980–1995, Lugano 1996, p. 140.

Bedigliora
Secondary School
Strada Cantonale
1979–81
Peter Disch and Angelo Bianchi
The school building consists of a single two-story block situated alongside an existing primary school and gymnasium. The whole constitutes a new school complex for the middle and upper Malcantone. Arranged along a longitudinal axis, underscored by the pattern of skylights, the volume is modulated by an exposed reinforced-concrete load-bearing structure setting the rhythm for the facade with balconies, which protect the continuous glass panels of the classrooms.
P. Disch (ed), 50 anni di architettura in Ticino 1930–1980, Bellinzona-Lugano 1983.

Bellinzona
House
Via Motto d'Arbino 9
1953
Franco Ponti and Peppo Brivio
This single-family house reveals just how far these two Ticino architects were influenced by Wright. Moreover, the compositional principles, the use of natural materials and the organic relation established with the setting also reveal borrowings from the local building tradition. Another emblematic example of the architectural climate of the 1950s in Ticino is the Orselina-Cardada Cableway (1952), built at Locarno by Peppo Brivio and René Pedrazzini.
P. Disch (ed), 50 anni di architettura in Ticino 1930–1980, Bellinzona-Lugano 1983; Guide to Swiss Architecture 1920–1995, vol. 3, 615, p. 241.

Arnaboldi House

Secondary School

House at Bellinzona

Bellinzona

Secondary School

Via Lavizzari 7

1955–58

Alberto Camenzind
with Bruno Brocchi

The planning approach to this school was to set it as an island into the surrounding natural environment. The longitudinal development of the building – organized on a single level with various spaces to create open, closed and partially covered zones – is broken up by the projecting volumes of special teaching rooms. In addition to the administrative sector and the janitor's quarters, the complex includes a gymnasium with sports field.

For another work by Camenzind, see the Swiss-Italian Radio Studios, Via Canevascini, Lugano-Besso (1958–64), designed in collaboration with Rino Tami and Augusto Jäggli.

Werk, 1959, 4; P. Disch (ed), 50 anni di architettura in Ticino 1930–1980, Bellinzona-Lugano 1983; Guide to Swiss Architecture 1920–1995, vol. 3, 616, p. 241.

Bellinzona

Rotalinti House

Via Sasso Corbaro

1960–61

Aurelio Galfetti

One of the most successful re-workings of Le Corbusier's poetics, this house, situated on a slope reached from an avenue, marked a turning point for Ticino architecture in the 1960s. The emptying out and articulation of the volumes highlight the essential exposed reinforced-concrete structure, while, inside, the circulation accessed from above serves four stories through a series of platforms creating a clever spatial play enhanced by the light sources.

Secondary School

Architecture, formes + fonction, 9, 1962–63; L'Architecture d'aujourd'hui, 121, 1965; M. Steinmann and T. Boga, Tendenzen. Neuere Architektur im Tessin, Zürich 1975; a + u, architecture and urbanism, 9, 1976; Quaderns d'Arquitectura i Urbanisme, 155, 1982; P. Disch (ed), 50 anni di architettura in Ticino 1930–1980, Bellinzona-Lugano 1983; Guide to Swiss Architecture 1920–1995, vol. 3, 618, p. 242.

Bellinzona

Fabrizia Offices

Via Vela 6

1963–65

Luigi Snozzi and Livio Vacchini

Situated in a residential quarter near the town center, the building is organized round the services core. The ground floor is thus conceived as a free and transparent space, while the offices are arranged on the upper floors with galleries lit from the glazed vault ceiling. The exterior is characterized by the rhythm of the steel structure, the iron frames and the projecting sun screens protecting the workspaces.

Werk, 9, 1967; Architectural Design, 38, 1968; Detail, 1, 1968; J. Bachmann and S. von Moos, New Directions in Swiss Architecture, New York 1969; D. Bachmann and G. Zanetti, Architektur des Aufbegehrens, Bauen im Tessin, Basel 1985; Rivista Tecnica, 1–2, 1985; T. Boga, Tessiner Architekten, Zürich 1986; Häuser, 3, 1987; Guide to Swiss Architecture 1920–1995, vol. 3, 619, p. 243.

Rotalinti House, view and elevation

Fabrizia Offices

Bellinzona

Public Swimming Pool

Via Mirasole

1967–70

Aurelio Galfetti, Flora Ruchat and Ivo Trümpy

with C. Göckel, A. Bianchini, and J. Armazabal

Public Tennis Courts

Via Brunari

1983–86

Aurelio Galfetti, Walter Büchler and Piero Ceresa

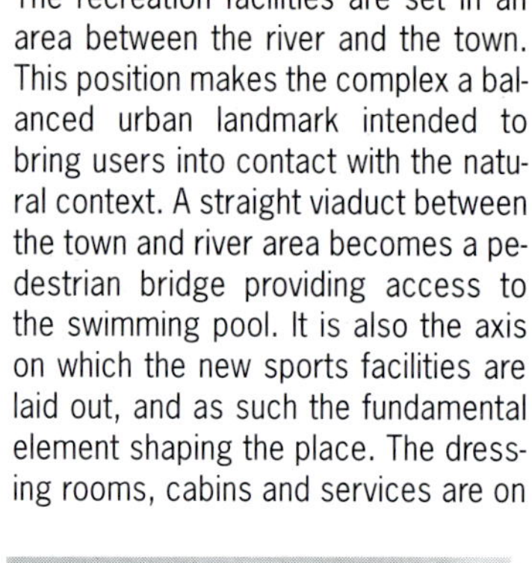

The recreation facilities are set in an area between the river and the town. This position makes the complex a balanced urban landmark intended to bring users into contact with the natural context. A straight viaduct between the town and river area becomes a pedestrian bridge providing access to the swimming pool. It is also the axis on which the new sports facilities are laid out, and as such the fundamental element shaping the place. The dressing rooms, cabins and services are on

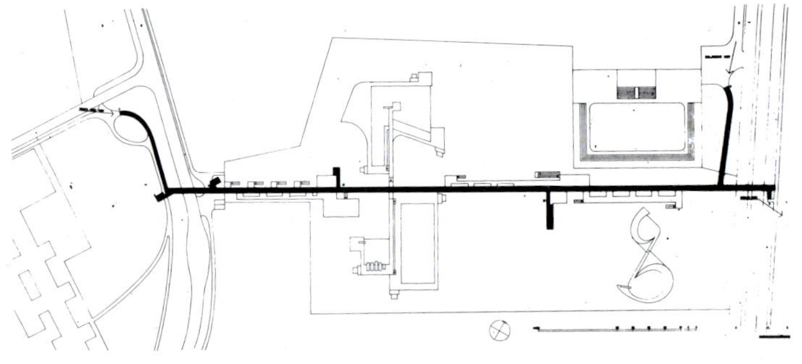

Public Swimming Pool

an intermediate level, while the swimming pool and lawns are reached by various ramps and stairs along the itinerary. The nearby Public Tennis Courts built by Galfetti in collaboration with Piero Ceresa and Walter Büchler in the early 1980s further highlights the basic principles established by the swimming-pool design.

Werk, 2, 1971; 10, 1987; L'Architecture d'aujourd'hui, 190, 1977; Lotus international, 15, 1977; W. Blaser, Architecture 70/80 in Switzerland, Basel 1981; Quaderns d'Arquitectura i Urbanisme, 155, 1982; Rivista Tecnica, 5, 1983; 3, 1986; D. Bachmann and G. Zanetti, Architektur des Aufbegehrens, Bauen im Tessin, Basel 1985; Casabella, 418, 1985; AMC. Architecture-Mouvement-Continuité, 12, 1986; Archithese, 2, 1986; T. Boga, Tessiner Architekten, Zürich 1986; Architectural Record, 4, 1987; G. Brown-Manrique, The Ticino Guide, New York 1989; Abitare, 290, 1990; Guide to Swiss Architecture 1920–1995, vol. 3, 620, p. 243; 626, p. 247; P. Disch, Architettura recente nel Ticino 1980–1995, Lugano 1996, p. 70.

Public Tennis Courts

Bellinzona

Central Post Office

Viale Stazione 18

1977–85

Aurelio Galfetti, Angelo Bianchi and Renzo Molina

with L. Pellegrini, T. Germann, R. Regazzoni, and S. Calori

The design for the Bellinzona Postal Center is in line with the late-1970s trend to protect city centers by sewing up the urban fabric, but at the same time highlighting the contrasts between old and new. The street frontage is reconstructed by a single public *palazzo* articulated in three volumes with different functions: administration, sorting office and rail department. The constituent elements of the facade are defined by a kind of Classical tripartite structure with base, shaft and capital, distinguished by the use of materials. These elements are designed both in function of their urban effect and as forms shaped by light and in response to the dimension of the avenue.

Galfetti has designed other *palazzo* type residences. See, for example, at Bellinzona, the houses Al Portone (1984–85) and Bianco e Nero, Via Vincenzo d'Alberti (1986–87). At Lugano, in collaboration with Antonio Antorini, he designed the Leonardo Housing, Via Maggio (1985–86).

Quaderns d'arquitectura y Urbanisme, 155, 1982; Werk, Bauen und Wohnen, 12, 1982; 10, 1985; Casabella, 518, 1985; Rivista Tecnica, 12, 1985; AMC. Architecture-

Postal Center

Mouvement-Continuité, 12, 1986; du, 8, 1986; Lotus international, 48–49, 1986; a + u, architecture and urbanism, 215, 1988; Detail, 2, 1989; Abitare, 290, 1990; G. Brown-Manrique, The Ticino Guide, New York 1989; Guide to Swiss Architecture 1920–1995, vol. 3, 624, p. 245.

Bellinzona
Mixed-Use Building
Via Nizzola 1
1988–91
Mario Botta
with C. Heras and T. Bamberg

The interpretation of the building regulations governing the urban fabric led to this building being organized along Via Nizzola, in the western sector of the lot, thus distancing it from the disordered urbanization along Via Cantonale. The functional differentiation into offices and dwellings is established by the articulation of the volumes in a single building rising up like a kind of bulwark, patterned by the tight rhythm of the slit windows (an allusion to the mediaeval character of the city). The compact structure is also like a gateway to the city, to be entered by the footbridge across the lawn.
At Bellinzona, see also Botta's Telecommunications Business Center, Via Gaggini (1989–97).

F. Roth (ed), Mario Botta. Schizzi di studio per l'edificio in Via Nizzola a Bellinzona, exhibition catalogue, Bellinzona 1991; Casabella, 592, 1992; GA Document, 35, 1992; a + u, architecture and urbanism, 279, 1993.

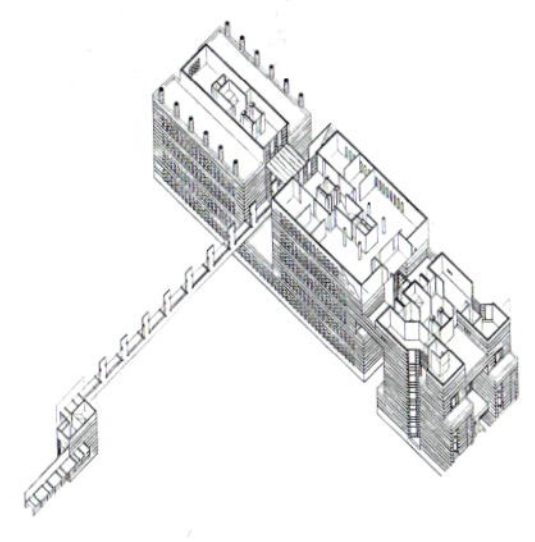

Mixed-Use Building

Bellinzona
Castelgrande Extension
Piazza del Sole
1981–91
Aurelio Galfetti
with T. Bolliger, R. Läuppi, J. Ormazabal, and V. Mazza

The project to convert the *rocca* (top fort) of the castle meets the requirement to redevelop the monument for new functions (exhibitions, shows and restaurant). The non-original superficial elements were demolished and the restoration of a number of buildings completed. The vegetation "imprisoning" the castle was also cleaned up. In this way the "ruin" was uncovered and once more showed its face to the city. Access is from Piazza del Sole by a long tunnel through the mountain taking the visitor to a space covered with a dome. From here an elevator constructed in the rock completes the itinerary up to the castle battlements. The work offers an example of restoration seen as an architectural event able to meet the needs of the present through its evocative power.

See also the restoration of the nearby Castle of Montebello to house a Civic Museum, Salita ai Castelli 4, carried out by Mario Campi and Franco Pessina from 1969 to 1974.

Casabella, 518, 1985; AMC. Architecture-Mouvement-Continuité, 12, 1986; Detail, 2, 1986; du, 8, 1986; Lotus international, 48–49, 1986; Rivista Tecnica, 12, 1986; 12, 1991; Abitare, 252, 1987; F. Werner and S. Schneider, La nuova architettura ticinese: Mario Botta, Aurelio Galfetti, Ivano Gianola, Luigi Snozzi, Livio Vacchini, Milan 1990; G. Brown-Manrique, The Ticino Guide, New York 1989; F. Werner, Aurelio Galfetti: Castelgrande, Bellinzona, Berlin 1992; L. Cavadini, Castelgrande a Bellinzona, Lugano 1993; Domus, 750, 1993; Guide to Swiss Architecture 1920–1995, vol. 3, 625, p. 246; P. Disch, Architettura recente nel Ticino 1980–1995, Lugano 1996, p. 182.

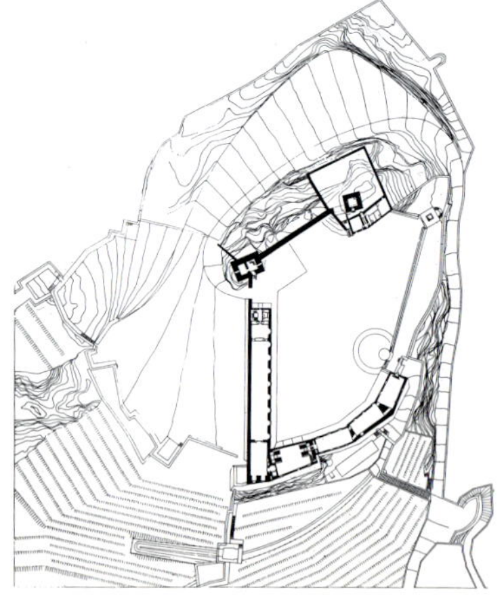

Castelgrande

Bellinzona

Albergo Mövenpick

Bellinzona Sud highway service station
1989

Bruno Reichlin and Fabio Reinhart with A. Lurati, S. Milan, and R. Bagutti

In this roadside hotel the designers have created a striking architectural image with a highly rational approach to the organization of functions. The rusticated front of the man facade alludes to the local castle tradition, but also erects a deliberate mask towards the highway publicity world. This front is in stark contrast with the rear of the building, where the quiet hotel rooms overlook a river. The careful, often playful detailing highlights a decorative logic eschewing constructional realism or the bare presentation of structure. This anti-naturalistic approach and erudite references are also found in some restorations and redevelopment projects by Reichlin & Reinhart at Sopraceneri, such as the Justice of Peace's House at Sornico (1975–77) and the Pellanda House at Biasca (1987).

Werk, 12, 1970; Lotus international, 31, 1981; 58, 1988; Domus, 721, 1990.

Bellinzona
Cantonal Archives
Viale Stefano Franscini
1988–97
Luca Ortelli
with S. Milan, G. Rossi, E. Saurwein, S. Martinelli, N. Braghieri, M. Erba, and P. Giuliani

The building comprises three volumes, each with a different character and use. The largest volume houses the spaces open to the public (consultation, study, and reading rooms), while the adjacent block accommodates the administrative offices for the archives and library. The third volume, made up of two long blocks, contains the institutional offices and the main entrance to the complex.

Hochparterre, 8–9, 1989; Lotus international, 61, 1989; Rivista Tecnica, 4, 1990; 7–8, 1992; L. Sacchetti, Architetti italiani, Milan 1992.

Breganzona
House
Via dei Panora 2
1984–88
Mario Botta
with G. Calderari, R. Blumer, and M. Beretta

The dis-articulation of the parts in the composition for a single-family house, already tried out in the Origlio House (1981–82), is here taken to its logical conclusion. The virtual cube containing the house is plastically shaped by the voids, the intermediate spaces between exterior and interior: entrance courtyard, living-room, the atrium of the night floor overlooking an empty space, and the upper belvedere facing out over the valley. The diagonal emphasis of the volume gives the whole an unusual, dynamic character.

GA Architect, 3, 1984; GA Document, 4, 1987; GA Houses, 24, 1988; Periferia, 8–9, 1988; Rivista Tecnica, 11, 1988; Techniques & Architecture, 377, 1988; a + u, architecture and urbanism, 220, 1989; F. Dal Co and V. Fagone, Mario Botta. Una casa, Milan 1989; Detail, 2, 1989; Guide to Swiss Architecture 1920–1995, vol. 3, 715, p. 282; P. Disch, Architettura recente nel Ticino 1980–1995, Lugano 1996, p. 110.

Breganzona
Kress House
Via Lucino 82
1985–87
Mario Campi and Franco Pessina

The court-type plan of the house, open towards the valley and laid out symmetrically on an axis, connects the main dwelling spaces to the wings containing stairs and terraces. In this way the house is closed into itself and shuns any contact with the anonymous immediate surroundings.

Rivista Tecnica, 11, 1987; Werk, Bauen und Wohnen, 7–8, 1987; Ideales Heim, 4, 1989; G. Brown-Manrique, The Ticino Guide, New York 1989; Architectural Digest, 8–9, 11, 1990; P. Disch, Architettura recente nel Ticino 1980–1995, Lugano 1996, p. 93.

Cantonal Archives, model view

House at Breganzona

Kress House

Brione sopra Minusio
Kalmann House
Via Panoramica 66
1974–76
Luigi Snozzi

The basic guiding principles in the project aim to highlight the morphological features of the site. The entrance itinerary takes into account the rough terrain and generates situations in contrast with the rigorous geometry of the two parts making up the house – the actual dwelling and the terrace projected forwards with the pergola overlooking the landscape.

a + u, architecture and urbanism, 69, 1976; Rivista Tecnica, 12, 1977; 1–2, 1985; Werk-archithese, 9, 1977; AMC. Architecture-Mouvement-Continuité, 45, 1978; Techniques & Architecture, 339, 1981; 364, 1986; Abitare, 206, 1982; Archithese, 3, 1984; L'Architecture d'aujourd'hui, 236, 1984; D. Bachmann and G. Zanetti, Architektur des Aufbegehrens, Bauen im Tessin, Basel 1985; T. Boga, Tessiner Architekten, Zürich 1986; The Architectural Review, 1095, 1988; Guide to Swiss Architecture 1920–1995, vol. 3, 629, p. 248.

Kalmann House

Brissago
Bianchini Apartments
Via Leoncavallo
1987–89
Luigi Snozzi
with M. Vicedomini

The apartment block is in a town-center area altered by the widening of the main road. The lot borders on the recently restored eighteenth-century Bianchini house. Part of the latter structure is incorporated in the project which thus sews up the historic urban fabric and creates a dialectical relation between the new exposed reinforced-concrete volume and the neighboring small tower-house. The architectural contrast is further heightened by the transparent first floor, while the main stairs join up the two buildings.

Abitare, 263, 1988; Werk, Bauen und Wohnen, 9, 1988; Casabella, 567, 1990; Rivista Tecnica, (monographic issue) 1990; F. Werner and S. Schneider, La nuova architettura ticinese: Mario Botta, Aurelio Galfetti, Ivano Gianola, Luigi Snozzi, Livio Vacchini, Milan 1990; Architettura Svizzera, 96, 1991; P. Disch, Architettura recente nel Ticino 1980–1995, Lugano 1996, p. 100.

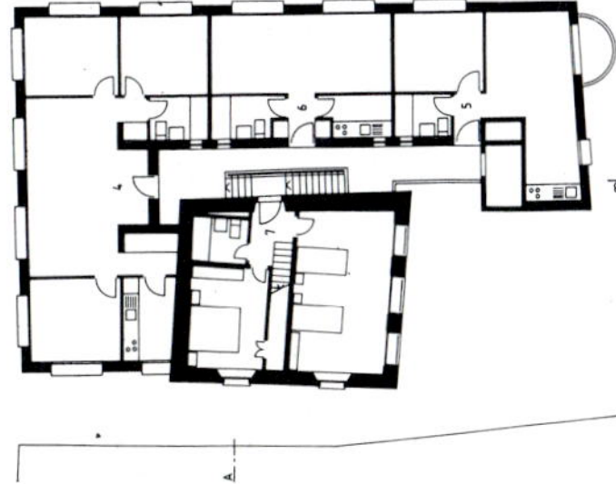

Bianchini
Apartments

Cadenazzo

House

East of the Municipal Car Park
1970–71
Mario Botta

A homage to the language of Kahn, albeit with independent and original aspects, the design for this single-family house highlights architecture's ability to dialogue with the context through precise visual options. The large circular apertures perforating the parallelepiped bring the internal space of the dwelling into relation with the surrounding countryside through a systems of loggias designed as a protective screen. The completely blind eastern front is contrasted by the glass-brick western wall which filters the afternoon light to the three floors containing the services. Botta built another two houses in Sopraceneri: the House at Cavigliano (1986–89) and the House in Via Ubrio at Losone (1987–91).

Werk, Bauen und Wohnen, 9, 1971; L'Architecture d'aujourd'hui, 163, 1972; L'Architettura cronache and storia, 199, 1972; Toshi-Jutaku, 6, 1972; Rivista Tecnica, 2, 1973; a + u, architecture and urbanism, 69, 1976; 105, 1979; GA Houses, 3, 1977; GA Architect, 3, 1984; Guide to Swiss Architecture 1920–1995, vol. 3, 631, p. 249..

Carabbia

House

1989–91
Sandro Cabrini and Gianmaria Verda

Situated on a terraced slope just outside the village, the house is organized round a south-facing central court with a pergola above. The three floors containing the various rooms give directly onto the various levels of the grounds, while the handling of the concrete – either smooth or rough finished – enhances and varies the surface textures.

Rivista Tecnica, 1–2, 1993; P. Disch, Architettura recente nel Ticino 1980–1995, Lugano 1996, p. 144.

Carasso

Casa Patriziale

Via Galbisio 23

1967–70

Luigi Snozzi and Livio Vacchini

Not far from the village, this subsidized housing block has twelve apartments on three floors served by two stairs. Built to a free plan, the domestic space is organized round the service core, while metal mobile partitions provide flexible subdivisions for the rooms. A spacious multipurpose room lit from above by continuous apertures is partly underground and does not interfere with the transparency of the entrance portico.

Werk, 4, 1970; Rivista Tecnica, 2, 1973; T. Boga, Tessiner Architekten, Zürich 1986; Guide to Swiss Architecture 1920–1995, vol. 3, 632, p. 250.

Opposite page:
House at Cadenazzo, exterior view and detail
House at Carabbia

Housing, view and floor plan

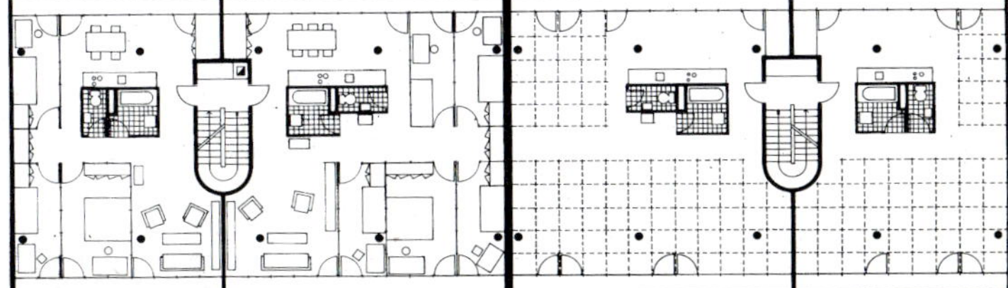

Carona
Citron House
1961–64
Atelier 5

The guiding principle in the design for this holiday house was the integration in an exceptional natural site of a construction built according to modern criteria. The main idea for the day area is a belvedere on pilotis, characterized by the rhythm of the vaults, while the compact volume of the night zone is set directly on the ground. The morphological contrast between solids and voids, together with the highly eloquent use of materials, should be read with reference to the local architectural tradition; this approach is further elaborated in the terraced housing at Caviano, also in the Ticino (1968–73).

Architectural Design, 4, 1965; L'Architecture d'aujourd'hui, 121, 1965; Werk, 9, 1965.

Carona
Bernasconi House
1989–90
Luigi Snozzi
with G. Groisman

The parallel position of the dwelling to the contours of the site establishes a problematic relation between the two sectors of the lot, characterized by a steep slope and a flatish lower area. The situation is solved by creating access from an external open area down a slanting stairway into the void inside the volume. The itinerary continues inside the dwelling with visual, spatial and tactile features which gradually reveal the rooms, enhanced by a skillful control of the light sources.

du, (monographic issue) 1989; Casabella, 567, 1990; Rivista Tecnica, 3/ 1990; Abitare, 316, 1993; Guide to Swiss Architecture 1920–1995, vol. 3, 717, p. 283; P. Disch, Architettura recente nel Ticino 1980–1995, Lugano 1996, p. 117.

Caslano
San Michele Quarter
Via San Michele 3–19 / ViaTorrazza 4
1963–66
Franco Ponti

Franco Ponti's organic style of architecture, strongly influenced by Wright, developed in a number of single-family houses: see, for example, the House at Vezia (1957) and the House at Biogno (1958). This language is further elaborated in the project for a whole village of single-family dwellings for artists of various nationalities. The stimulating idea of a community harmoniously integrated with nature – typical of a number of architectural tends in the 1950s – is also tangible in this design. Situated in a previously marshy terrain, the project also includes a canal for boats to enter the quarter.

B. De Sivo, L'architettura in Svizzera oggi, Naples 1968; P. Disch (ed), 50 anni di architettura in Ticino 1930–1980, Bellinzona-Lugano 1983; Guide to Swiss Architecture 1920–1995, vol. 3, 718, p. 283.

Citron House

Bernasconi House, view and floor plan

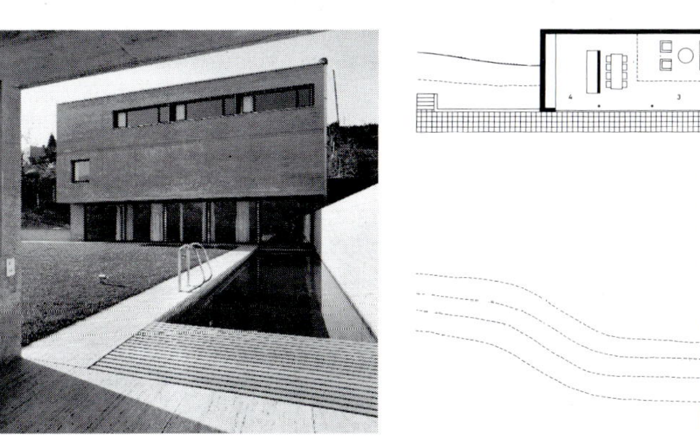

San Michele Quarter

Caslano

Schools

Via Baragia

1972–75

Mario Campi and Franco Pessina

The building reflects an attempt to impose order and rhythm on the surrounding area through the geometry, repetition and formal simplicity of the structures. In the effort to expand into the surroundings, the externally compact volume has a free interior layout, based on the alternation of closed spaces and areas with patios. The functional organization gives the teaching spaces considerable flexibility.

Rivista Tecnica, 12, 1974; P. Disch (ed), 50 anni di architettura in Ticino 1930–1980, Bellinzona-Lugano 1983.

Castel San Pietro

Rusconi House

Via Obino

1983–84

Ivano Gianola

Situated between the village of Obine and a recently developed peripheral area, this heavy massive stone box attempts to incorporate the features of the site. The large central fenestration, overscored by the horizontal emphasis of the balcony, opens up towards the historic village, while the off-center entrance upsets the rhythmic symmetry of the composition, and is thus the exception confirming the rule.

Archithese, 5, 1984; Daidalos, 13, 1984; Rivista Tecnica, 5 1984; a + u, architecture and urbanism, 4, 1985; Parametro, 141,

Schools

Rusconi House

1985; Bauwelt, 41–42 1986; G. Brown-Manrique, The Ticino Guide, New York 1989; P. Disch, Architettura recente nel Ticino 1980–1995, Lugano 1996, p. 79.

Cavigliano
Terraced Houses
1988–90
Franco and Paolo Moro

The contrast between the interiors and exteriors is the distinguishing feature of this design: the house and garden occupy the same-size surface area with perimeter walls whose heights vary according to function. The light two-level pergola structure, covered by a translucent semi-cylinder joins house and court, while the presence of deciduous vegetation ensures the homes are in touch with the rhythm of the seasons.
Other Moro brothers' works are the single-family houses at Coldrerio, Via Ronco (1988–89), and Gordola, Via Carcale 17 (1989–90) as well as the Russo Home for the Elderly, Valle Onsernone (1992–93).

Abitare, 313, 1992; 327, 1994; Ticino hoy, exhibition catalogue, Madrid 1993; Rivista Tecnica, 1–2, 1993; P. Disch, Architettura recente nel Ticino 1980–1995, Lugano 1996, p. 163.

Chiasso

Customs Warehouse

Swiss-Italian Customs Post at Chiasso station

1924–25

Robert Maillart

This large storage space at the border town of Chiasso has an unusual feature in the interior: the ceilings are not supported by beams but by mushroom-shaped pillars. The main attraction of the complex, however, is the roof of the one-story shed in front of the higher building, today unfortunately partly hidden from sight by an addition. It is an unusual structure with a downward-curving lower edge and inward curving columns. This structural configuration endows the whole building with an organic character. Here architectural beauty is coherently developed from constructional requirements. Destruction of several elements has altered the building's exterior.

Werk, 1, 1968; Rivista Tecnica, 1, 1983; Werk, Bauen und Wohnen, 12, 1983; D. P. Billington, Robert Maillart and the Art of Reinforced Concrete, Cambridge, Mass. 1990; Guide to Swiss Architecture 1920–1995, vol. 3, 719, p. 284.

Chiasso

Kindergarten

Via Valdani / Via Simen

1962–64

Flora Ruchat

with A. Antorini, F. Pozzi

Customs Warehouse

Kindergarten

Closed to the major thoroughfare and open on the south towards a large green area, the prismatic volume contains three school units arranged on two floors and characterized by a continuous interior space. The exposed reinforced-concrete structure generates the main facade, patterned by the rhythm of solids – rendered brick infill – and voids – large windows with iron frames.

Werk, 8, 1966; P. Disch (ed), 50 anni di architettura in Ticino 1930–1980, Bellinzona-Lugano 1983; T. Boga, Tessiner Architekten, Zürich 1986.

Coldrerio

Redevelopment of the Tognano Center

Via Tognano

1985, 1987

Ivano Gianola

with C. Rapelli, S. Rizzi, and K. Goris

This project involved converting an old farm building – organized round a courtyard in the tradition of Lombard farmhouses – into a textiles center equipped to hold periodic workshops or short courses. In addition to the owner's living quarters and the guest rooms, there are also common rooms and an atelier for educational activities. Of Gianola's most recent works see also the Orsoline Housing at Mendrisio, Via Municipio 8 (1986) and the Pregassona Housing Complex, Via del Sole 9 (1988–90).

Bauwelt, 41–42, 1986; Abitare, 263, 1988; Rivista Tecnica, 5, 1988; Ivano Gianola. Casa alle Orsoline, Mendrisio 1989; Habitat, 7–8, 1990; Ivano Gianola Architetto. Quattro case e un palazzo, exhibition catalogue, Viggiù 1993.

Redevelopment of the Tognano Center

Comano
Sculptor's Atelier
Via Bellavista
1985–87
Mischa Groh
This project had to deal with a number of themes all contained in the single building: the atelier of sculptor Nag Arnoldi. The design was arrived at by balancing out the various functions – studio, laboratory and gallery – in the whole process, from the approach to the site to the last building detail.
Rivista Tecnica, 6, 1988.

Contra
House
Costa
1992–93
Livio Vacchini
with M. Vanetti, W. Schmidt, M. Andreetti, S. Micheli, and A. Morisoli
As in his own house at Ascona, Via Aerodromo 2, designed in the late 1960s, in this little holiday home, again for himself, Vacchini was free to continue his architectural research in the most coherent way possible. A concise summary of the principles typical of the architect, the work is an exploration of the scope for a new building type, beginning from two illustrious models: Le Corbusier's "cell" and the vault used as a beam by Kahn in the Kimbell Museum. The roof is in fact a large beam, resting on three points at each end, completely independent of the plan. But although the walls dematerialize, the plan never loses its orientation. Another interesting design exercise by Vacchini is the Holiday Home at Vogorno (1984–85) in Val Verzasca.

Sculptor's Atelier

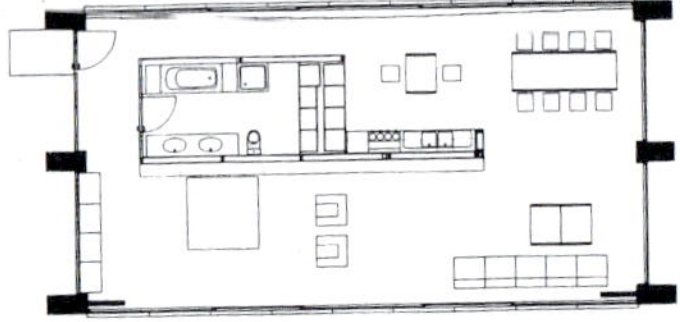

House at Contra, floor plan and view

Ticino hoy, exhibition catalogue, Madrid 1993; Domus, 752, 1993; Faces, 30, 1993–94.

Daro
House
Via Piumerino
1989–92
Mario Botta
with E. Maggetti (site management)

The result of research testing out the limits of the principles underlying his building practice, the single-family house at Daro illustrates the now classic features of Botta's architecture. The north-south stair is established as a compositional constant, while the rooms are organized round a central space, indicated in the main facade by the loggia with glass roofing. The careful "embroidery" in the facade is accompanied by the sinuous movement of the side walls forming a cuneiform volume solidly anchored to the sloping site.

GA Houses, 34 and 36, 1992; Ticino hoy, exhibition catalogue, Madrid 1993; a + u, architecture and urbanism, 279, 1993; P. Disch, Architettura recente nel Ticino 1980–1995, Lugano 1996, p. 160.

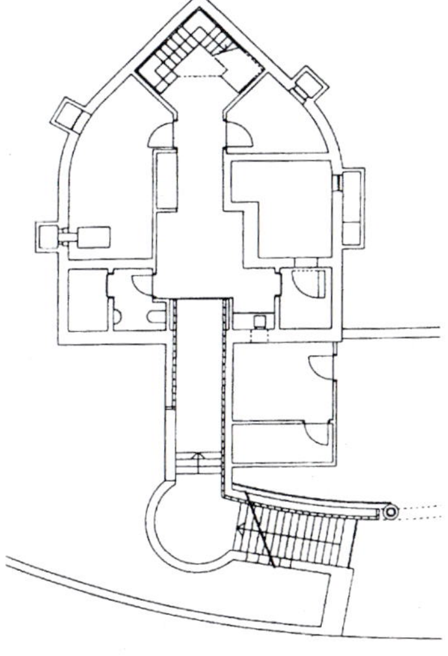

House at Daro

Davesco
Baudino House
1987–89
Mario Campi and Franco Pessina
The project starts from the idea of setting a linear building – closed on the uphill side and completely open on the valley side – parallel to the contours of the hill. The internal sequence is organized on two floors: in addition to the entrance and garage, the first floor contains the night area. The ground floor with the day area is connected to the garden by a portico – a representative element marking the transition from the man-made to the natural.
Rivista Tecnica, 10, 1992; Baumeister, 4, 1993; P. Disch, Architettura recente nel Ticino 1980–1995, Lugano 1996, p. 115.

Giornico
La Congiunta Foundation
Right bank of the River Ticino, 300 meters to the north of the station
1993
Peter Märkli
Designed to house the work of Zurich sculptor Hans Josephsohn, the building is far from museum-like in appearance. It is rather an exhibition place open to the public in the Ticino landscape in the form of an enigmatic cement shell. The silent architecture deliberately seeks to stimulate an active attitude in the visitor, who discovers the museum through its evocative interior. See also Märkli's works in collaboration with Gody Kühnis, such as the House at Sargans, Grossfeldstrasse 82 (1985–86) and the Apartaments at Trübbach, Wächtergut, Hauptstrasse (1988–89), both in the canton of Sankt Gallen.
Domus, 753, 1993; Guide to Swiss Architecture 1920–1995, vol. 3, 635, p. 251.

Gnosca
Restoration of the Church of San Giovanni Battista
Old cantonal street
1991–93
Tita Carloni and Angelo Martella
The eleventh-century Romanesque church of San Giovanni Battista was remodeled several times before being deconsecrated in 1783 and then falling into ruin. The architects proposed consolidating and restoring the ruined church to convert it into a public space. Only modern materials were used – concrete panels for the walls and reinforced concrete for the support masonry – thus highlighting the structural nature of the additions; the rainwater drainage system is based on a square grid (2 x 2 meters).
See also Di Carloni's Sorengo Parish House, Sorengo Hill (1968–69).
Ticino hoy, exhibition catalogue, Madrid 1993; Werk, Bauen und Wohnen, 3, 1994; P. Disch, Architettura recente nel Ticino 1980–1995, Lugano 1996, p. 185.

Baudino House

La Congiunta Foundation, exterior and interior views

Church of San Giovanni Battista

Ligornetto
House
Vignaccia
1975–76
Mario Botta
with M. Boesch

Located on the edge of the village, where the built-up area ends towards the plain, the house is developed longitudinally in the form of a compact wall that gradually gets thicker and interacts with the site features. Slender vertical cuts are effected in the front overlooking the countryside, while the facade on the village side is divided into two separate blocks by a large central void with terraces on the various floors. The handling of the exterior reveals knowledgeable references to the local building tradition and at the same time highlights the man-made nature of the house compared to the surrounding nature. The same sensitive handling and juxtapositions of materials may be seen in the nearby Farmhouse at Ligrignano, Via Ligrignano, converted by Botta in 1977–78.

a + u, architecture and urbanism, 69, 1976; 105, 1979; 9, 1986; GA Houses, 3, 1977; Lotus international, 15, 1977; AMC. Architecture-Mouvement-Continuité, 45, 1978; Rivista Tecnica, 9–10, 1978; Gran Bazaar, 3, 1979; Architectural Design, 5–6, 1980; Parametro, 100–101, 1981; Architectural Record, 6, 1982; GA Architect, 3, 1984; Toshi Jutaku, 4, 1985; Guide to Swiss Architecture 1920–1995, vol. 3, 721, p. 285.

House at Ligornetto

Locarno

Cantonal Secondary School

Via Chiesa 15a

1960–64

Dolf Schnebli, Isidor Ryser, Ernst Engeler, and Berhard Meier with K. Vogt

Based on the concept of the school as an "open house", the building is articulated in three sectors (classrooms, collective spaces and gym) enclosing a central piazza in the form of an amphitheater. The square-plan classrooms are grouped round intermediate connecting spaces and are uniformly lit by a central skylight; the small windows contribute to the "concentrated" atmosphere. The walls and ceilings were decorated with paintings by Livio Bernasconi and Flavio Paoluzzi, while the bronze works are by Max Weiss.

Other significant public designs by Schnebli and Associates include: the Bissone Kindergarten, Collina (1968), the Breganzona School Complex, Via Camara 63 (1970–72), and the Saleggi Kindergarten, Via A. Nessi, Locarno (1971–73).

L'Architecture d'aujourd'hui, 121, 1965; Werk, 87, 1966; J. Bachmann and S. von Moos, New Directions in Swiss Architecture, New York 1969; P. Disch (ed), 50 anni di architettura in Ticino 1930–1980, Bellinzona-Lugano 1983; du, 5, 1992; Guide to Swiss Architecture 1920–1995, vol. 3, 638, p. 253.

Cantonal Secondary School

Locarno
Saleggi Primary School
Via delle Scuole
1970–78
Livio Vacchini
with P. Moro and G. Lotterio

The outcome of a public competition, the school was built in three stages over a ten-year period. The project thus became a kind of ongoing experimental workshop in which the architect could explore the main themes of interest in his design research. The low-slung structure incorporates the features of the site by proposing spatial and volumetric relations between the buildings which set the proportions for the porticos and internal passages as well as defining the architectural elements.

Rivista Tecnica, 12, 1974; 11, 1981; L'Architecture d'aujourd'hui, 188, 1976; 216, 1981; Werk, 7–8, 1976; a + u, architecture and urbanism, 6, 1980; Werk, Bauen und Wohnen, 4 and 9, 1981; W. Blaser, Architecture 70/80 in Switzerland, Basel 1981; Guide to Swiss Architecture 1920–1995, vol. 3, 640, p. 254.

Locarno
Architect's Studio
Via Bramantino 33
1984–85
Livio Vacchini
with M. Vanetti and L. Andina
Post Office
Piazza Grande
1988–1996
Livio Vacchini
with M. Vanetti, L. Andina, and A. Morisoli

The design for an architect's atelier brings together in a single volume three functional zones (parking, workspace and archives) only legible in the spatial configuration. The overall building structure establishes the relation between the parts and the exterior: the ground floor is interrupted by pillars and the end walls; the first floor is free

Saleggi Primary School

Architect's Studio

of any structural constraints; and the top floor is contained inside the two high long beams supporting the roof. This same kind of essential approach is also to be found in the new Post Office in Piazza Grande, where concrete, granite and glass are the main materials.

Casabella, 528, 1986; du, 8, 1986; Rivista Tecnica, 6, 1986; 4, 1990; Werk, Bauen und Wohnen, 6, 1986; F. Werner and S. Schneider, La nuova architettura ticinese: Mario Botta, Aurelio Galfetti, Ivano Gianola, Luigi Snozzi, Livio Vacchini, Milan 1990; G. Brown-Manrique, The Ticino Guide, New York 1990; Guide to Swiss Architecture 1920–1995, vol. 3, 641, p. 254; P. Disch, Architettura recente nel Ticino 1980–1995, Lugano 1996, p. 87 und 241.

Locarno-Monti
Bianchetti House
Via Zoppi 10
1972–77
Luigi Snozzi
with W. von Euw

Situated in the hilly area above the town, the house is defined by the sequences in a guided access itinerary: from the front square to the wall inviting the visitor into the dwelling, the double-height living room overlooking the landscape through large windows, and the bedroom in the floor below. This use of the approach itinerary as a compositional tool is a constant feature in the work of Snozzi, also to be found in the Heschl Houses at Agarone (1983–84) and the Walser House at Loco (1988–89).

Tendenzen. Neuere Architektur im Tessin, Zürich 1975; a + u, architecture and urbanism, 69, 1976; Rivista Tecnica, 12, 1977; Werk-archithese, 9, 1977; AMC. Architecture-Mouvement-Continuité, 45, 1978; Architettura Svizzera, 69, 1985; Häuser, 3, 1987; The Architectural Review, 1095, 1988; Guide to Swiss Architecture 1920–1995, vol. 3, 643, p. 255.

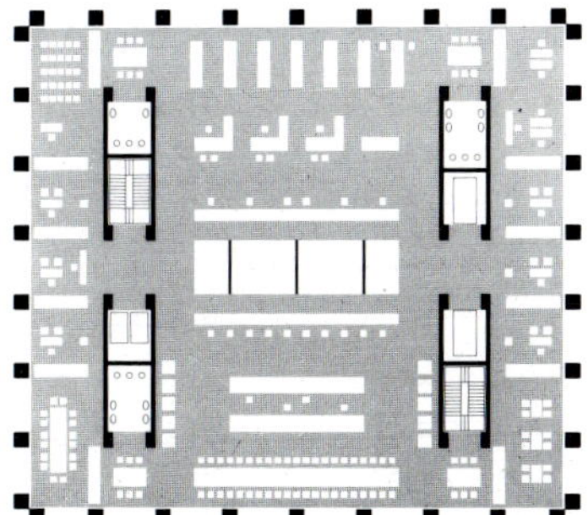

 Post Office   Bianchetti House

Locarno-Monti
Apartments
Via Zoppi
1985
Dolf Schnebli, Tobias Ammann, and Isidor Ryser
with D. Müller

The features of this very steep narrow lot led to the adoption of a block building type. The access from above enjoys sweeping views while the ground-floor apartments are left with private gardens. The upper-floor *maisonette* apartments, on the other hand, have roof terraces. The proportions between whole and parts are carefully balanced in the overall design. The slabs in the walls and the thin round concrete pillars establish the rhythm of the facades, characterized by discrete hues and the play of light and shade.

Rivista Tecnica, 5, 1985; P. Disch, Architettura recente nel Ticino 1980–1995, Lugano 1996, p. 82.

Locarno-Monti
Kalt House
Via del Tiglio 12
1989–91
Raffaele Cavadini
with F. Trisconi and S. Marzari

Resting on an existing stone base, the white reinforced-concrete volume is articulated round a patio, the true hub of the dwelling, which is open towards a garden and the panorama. Beyond the entrance courtyard, closed to the north, an atrium divides the rooms into two sectors: on one side is the double-height living room, and, on the other, a study and double bedroom. The other

bedrooms are on the upper floor. An open-air roof area may be reached from the rooms by an outdoor footbridge.
See also Cavadini's Calzascia House at Gerra Piano (1991–92).
Ticino hoy, exhibition catalogue, Madrid 1993; Rivista Tecnica, 1–2, 1993; P. Disch, Architettura recente nel Ticino 1980–1995, Lugano 1996, p. 130.

Losone
Cantonal Secondary School
Via dei Pioppi
1972–78
Livio Vacchini and Aurelio Galfetti with M. Vanetti and P. Moro
The design for the Losone school center is organized on an orthogonal grid. The original project was in three successive building stages for classrooms, gym and refectory, but the last stage was never built. The classroom building consists of four independent elements, structured on three levels and connected by an arcade round a square. The axial basis of this building determined the position of the gymnasium and was further emphasized by the technical and stylistic choices. The steel load-bearing structure is clearly distinguished from the enameled infill panels.
Vacchini also designed a multipurpose hall for the Losone Barracks (1990–91).
Rivista Tecnica, 4, 1973; 10, 1975; 10, 1990; Tendenzen. Neuere Architektur im Tessin, Zürich 1975; Werk-archithese, 13–14, 1978; a + u, architecture and urbanism, 6, 1980; Lotus international, 33, 1981; Architettura Svizzera, 54, 1982; W. Blaser, Architecture 70/80 in Switzerland, Basel 1981; Werk, Bauen und Wohnen, 3, 1994; Guide to Swiss Architecture 1920–1995, vol. 3, 645, p. 256.

Cantonal Secondary School

Opposite page:
Zoppi Apartments
Kalt House, view and roof detail

Losone
House
Via Reslina 50
1990–91
Giorgio and Michele Tognola
Built on a rectangular base in contrast with the irregular site bounded by a fence near the banks of the River Maggia, the one-story house of the two architects is organized round the circulation axis, its rhythm being defined by the visible concrete structure. The symmetric composition is divided into two functional areas: a day zone facing west to the courtyard, and a night zone overlooking the garden and river.
Ticino hoy, exhibition catalogue, Madrid 1993; Rivista Tecnica, 12, 1993; Guide to Swiss Architecture 1920–1995, vol. 3, 646, p. 257; P. Disch, Architettura recente nel Ticino 1980–1995, Lugano 1996, p. 146.

Lugano
Palazzo Bianchi
Lungolago
1927
Mario Chiattone
This *palazzo* is emblematic of Mario Chiattone's career, who after belonging to the Futurist movement retired to

Tognola House

the Ticino canton, where he continued to pursue his architectural research. Showing a keen interest in sixteenth-century Italian models, Romanesque architecture and traditional rural designs, from 1922 on, he played a leading role in stimulating the local architectural debate, which at the time was very provincial compared to the other more important Swiss cultural centers.

P. Disch (ed), 50 anni di architettura in Ticino 1930–1980, Bellinzona-Lugano 1983.

Lugano

San Rocco Clinic

Via Soldino 30

1934–35

Eugenio and Agostino Cavadini

Situated in the Besso quarter, the clinic still has the features of 1930s architecture which brought it celebrity as one of the first Modern buildings in the canton. At around the same time the Cavadini designed the Carmelo Santa Teresa Clinic at Brione sopra Minusio (1935) and the Carità Hospital at Locarno (1936–37), both altered by various interventions to meet new sanitary requirements.

 Palazzo Bianchi

San Rocco Clinic

Lugano
Cantonal Library
Parco Ciani
1936–40
Carlo and Rino Tami
Mixed-Use Building and Cinema Corso
Via Pioda
1954–57
Apartment Tower
Viale Castagnola
1957
Rino Tami

Throughout his over fifty years of design career Rino Tami explored various themes, at times producing highly significant works. Built following a 1936 competition, the Cantonal Library was a key building in the development of Ticino architecture. The synthesis of his previous pioneering work, it also marked the beginning of a new phase, consolidated after the war. The influence of Salvisberg comes through in the albeit independent use of reinforced concrete, the volumetric arrangement centered on the functions, and the authenticity of the materials.

The 1950s design for the Cinema Corso adopts a dynamic figurative approach to solving the problem of a fragmentary space, while in the Torre Apartments, a building with urban quality is set in a lake environment.

Of Tami's many works see also the Convent Church of Sacro Cuore at Bellinzona, Via Varrone 12, built in collaboration with his brother Carlo Tami in 1936; the Apartments, Via Motta 28 (1952), the now altered Nadig House at Maroggia (1957), and the Indoor Municipal Swimming Pool, Viale Castagnola (1976–78).

Rivista Tecnica, 9, 1938; 12, 1983; 10, 1988; 10, 1992; L'Architettura cronache and storia, 3, 1968; P. Disch (ed), 50 anni di architettura in Ticino 1930–1980, Bellinzona-Lugano 1983; Werk, Bauen und Wohnen, 12, 1983; 4, 1986; D. Bachmann and G. Zanetti, Architektur des Aufbegehrens. Bauen im Tessin, Basel 1985; Guide to Swiss Architecture 1920–1995, vol. 3, 726, p. 288; 729, p. 290; 730, p. 290.

Cantonal Library

Lugano

Workers' Union Headquarters and Casa del Popolo

Via Balestra 19
1968–71
Tita Carloni
with L. Denti and H. Jenni

Situated in a quarter characterized by its twentieth-century development, the building is articulated on various differentiated functional levels – canteen, restaurant, union offices and hotel. The rigorously arranged volumes and the sober handling of the apertures allude to the local building tradition, chosen as the appropriate reference style for the theme.

For other works by Carloni from around the same time, see also the Stabio School, Via Pozzetto (1970–72), Molino Nuovo Subsidized Housing, Via Trevano, Via Beltramina (1965–66) and the low-cost Cereda Housing at Balerna, Via Cereda, Sant'Antonio (1972–74), built in collaboration with the Carloni-Denti-Moretti design cooperative – evidence of the architect's commitment to popular housing.

P. Disch (ed), 50 anni di architettura in Ticino 1930–1980, Bellinzona-Lugano 1983; D. Bachmann and G. Zanetti, Architektur des Aufbegehrens. Bauen im Tessin, Basel 1985; Werk, Bauen und Wohnen, 1–2, 1985; Guide to Swiss Architecture 1920–1995, vol. 3, 735, p. 293.

Cinema Corso, interior

Torre Apartments

Workers' Union Headquarters

Lugano
La Serena Housing for the Elderly
Via Ciani / Via Ferri
1971–77
Giancarlo Durisch
The complex is a good example of the contemporary radical architectural approach to brief requirements. Situated in a residential quarter along the Cassarate, the Home for the Elderly is divided into four vertically developed buildings. They contain self-contained and assisted apartments, staff lodgings, and the chapel. The community spaces on the ground floor open up towards the grounds.
Rivista Tecnica, 20, 1971; P. Disch (ed), 50 anni di architettura in Ticino 1930–1980, Bellinzona-Lugano 1983; T. Boga (ed), Tessiner Architekten, Zürich 1986; Guide to Swiss Architecture 1920–1995, vol. 3, 737, p. 294.

Lugano
Macconi Center
Via Pretorio
1974–75
Livio Vacchini and Alberto Tibiletti with M. Vanetti, and R. Ratti
Designed for administrative and commercial uses, the building stands on a narrow lot in the city center, flanked by a low building completing the street front. The compositional features of the project – rhythm, relation between solids and voids, and building details – are defined by the adoption of a steel structure with Andeer granite infill. The

La Serena Housing for the Elderly

mastery of the design tools and the refined expressiveness revealed in the use of the materials make this center one of Vacchini's most significant works.

Rivista Tecnica, 18, 1973; P. Disch (ed), 50 anni di architettura in Ticino 1930–1980, Bellinzona-Lugano 1983; a + u, architecture and urbanism, 176, 1985; G. Brown-Manrique, The Ticino Guide, New York 1990; T. Boga (ed), Tessiner Architekten, Zürich 1986; Guide to Swiss Architecture 1920–1995, vol. 3, 736, p. 293.

Lugano
Mixed-Use Building
Via Pretorio
1990
Giancarlo Durisch
with F. Colombo

This building for offices and shops in Via Pretorio fits harmoniously into the historic urban fabric through a morphology created by the contrast between a load-bearing services core and a light external casing. The sheet-steel skin with a network of stiffening elements includes various elements (base, canopy and drainpipes) with self-evident functions.

Of the architect's other works, see the Telecom Technical Center at Giubiasco, Viale 1814 / Via Ferriere (1988–1997), and the restoration of the Bellinzona Social Theater, Via Bonzanigo/ Via Dogana (1991–96).

Rivista Tecnica, 6, 1991; P. Disch, Architettura recente nel Ticino 1980–1995, Lugano 1996, p. 126.

Macconi Center

Mixed-Use Building

Lugano

Felder House

Via Riva 9

1977–79

Mario Campi and Franco Pessina

Set beside a seventeenth-century villa on the top of a hill, the new house follows its axial organization and orientation. The virtual square-plan parallelepiped – emptied of the central court onto which the rooms face – is recomposed by the entrance columns.

Rivista Tecnica, 11–12, 1980; Werk, 1, 1980; Gran Bazaar, 7–8, 1981; Werk, Bauen und Wohnen, 4, 1981; 6, 1986; a + u, architecture and urbanism, 11, 1982; Progressive Architecture, 7, 1982; Casabella, 534, 1987; G. Brown-Manrique, The Ticino Guide, New York 1990; L'Habitat, 11, 1991; Guide to Swiss Architecture 1920–1995, vol. 3, 739, p. 295.

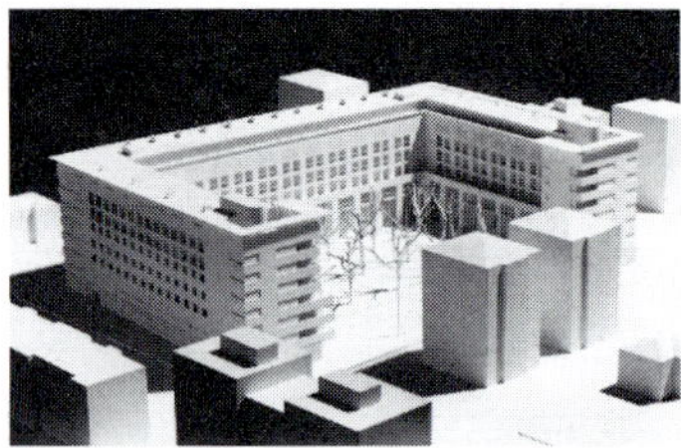

Lugano

Residential Quarter

Via Beltramina

1992–95

Mario Campi and Franco Pessina

The winning design in a 1986 competition proposed the urban and architectural redevelopment of the quarter with the aim of halting and reversing the amorphous untidy urban growth in the area. This was the theoretical starting point for the choice of building heights in keeping with the context and the restoration of two existing buildings to form part of a uniform U-shaped structure. The courtyard of the main building containing 120 subsidized apartments becomes the public space for the renewed quarter.

Rivista Tecnica, 1–2, 1987; 1–2, 1990; 10, 1992; Costruire, 114, 1992; P. Disch,

Architettura recente nel Ticino 1980–1995, Lugano 1996, p. 232.

Lugano
Capuchin Library
Salita dei Frati
1976–79
Mario Botta
with R. Hunziker and F. Robbiani
Ransila I Offices
Via Pretorio
1981–85
Mario Botta
with F. Robbiani, M. Pelli, and M. Groh
Banca del Gottardo
Viale Stefano Franscini
1982–88
Mario Botta
with M. Pelli, P. Merzaghi, D. Eisenhut, M. Moreni, R. Blumer, M. D'Azzo, C. Heras, and C. Lo Riso.

Dug into the terrain to the south of a quadrilateral cloister, the Capuchin Library lends its silhouette to the grounds of the seventeenth-century monastery, while the projecting skylight announces its formal independence from the rest of the complex. Botta uses light – an essential element in his work – to generate the reading room space, while a typical slash in the wall defines the compositional axis. A sculptural cutting away of the volume characterizes the Ransila I building, a corner structure exploring the relation between architectural type and building fabric, while large vertical cuts – another common feature in his vocabulary – give an urban feel to the Banca del Gottardo.

Casabella, 414, 1976; Lotus international, 22, 1979; 28, 1981; 48–49 1987; GA Document, 2, 1980; 6, 1983; 14, 1986; Parametro, 99, 1981; 141, 1985; Rivista Tecnica, 5, 1981; 12, 1982; 7–8, 1984; 12, 1988; GA Architect, 3, 1984; Techniques et Architecture, 377, 1988; a + u, architecture and urbanism, 220, 1989; Domus 704, 1989; Guide to Swiss Architecture 1920–1995, vol. 3, 740, p. 295; 742, p. 296; 743, p. 297; P. Disch, Architettura recente nel Ticino 1980–1995, p. 89 and 106.

Banca del Gottardo

Opposite page:
Felder House Residential Quarter, model view
Capuchin Library, interior view
Ransila I Offices

Lugano
Mixed-Use Building
Via Ciani 16, Molino Nuovo
1986–90
Mario Botta
Cinque Continenti
Via Guisan, Paradiso
1986–91
Mario Botta
with G. Agazzi (site management)
Caimato Offices
Via Maggio, Cassarate
1986–93
Mario Botta

A design logic based on the idea of the project as exercising a purifying effect on the urban context is at the heart of these three Lugano works by Botta. Derived from given urban situations, the designs provide consistent architectural responses with a special emphasis on the image as a determining factor. In all three of these works, including the great cylinder at Molino Nuovo containing the architect's own studio, the volumetric tension is reflected in the inner spatial organization, while the handling of the external surfaces alludes to traditional building practice.

Abitare, 290, 1990; Hochparterre, 11, 1990; a + u, architecture and urbanism, 251, 1991; 279, 1993; Bauwelt, 13, 1991; GA Document, 30, 1991; 11, 1992; Domus, 737, 1992; Interior Design, 3, 1992; Ticino hoy, exhibition catalogue, Madrid 1993; P. Disch, Architettura recente nel Ticino 1980–1995, Lugano 1996, p. 122.

Lugano
Apartments
Via Domenico Fontana 10
1988–91
Marco d'Azzo
with G. Pellegatta

Situated on a wedge-shaped lot, this building echoes the features of the adjacent early twentieth-century villas. Surrounded by a garden, the building consists of two structures: a brick volume with a semicircular end creating the corner and accentuating the perspectives; and a rendered building set to the curving street as the final element in a row of detached houses. The horizontal rhythm of the facades reveals the internal organization (one apartment per floor), whereas the composition of the volumes influenced the choice of materials and the functional distribution. The layout of the complex is reminiscent of Erich Mendelsohn's designs. It mediates between the refined eclecticism of the neighboring villas and the 1970s building speculation which has characterized the context with an inappropriate use of modern architecture.

P. Disch, Architettura recente nel Ticino 1980–1995, Lugano 1996, p. 133.

Cinque Continenti, view and axonometric

Opposite page:

Caimato Offices

Mixed-Use Building, view and floor plan

Apartments

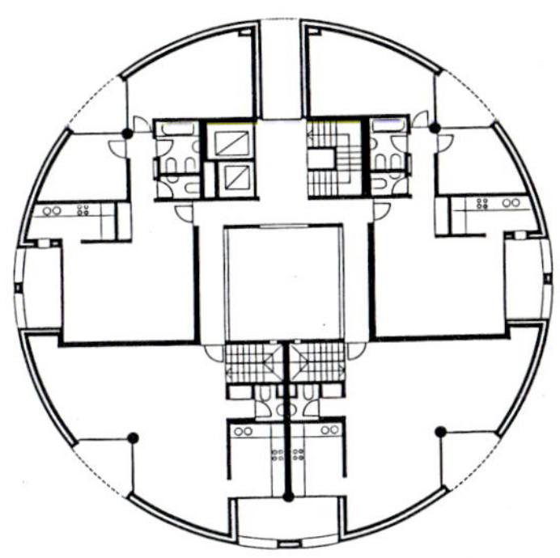

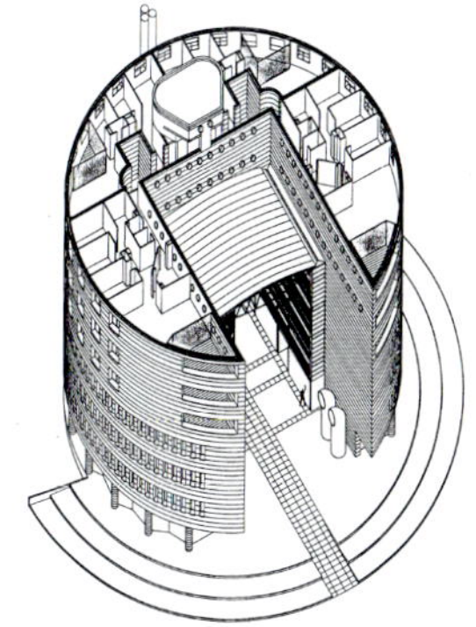

Manno

Barchi House

Strada Regina

1975–89

Mario Botta

This house is the outcome of a long design process, having been begun in 1975, then further developed in 1987. Situated on the top of a slight slope, the building is characterized by a long brick wall standing separately in front of the building. It features a large archway leading into a central courtyard with the rooms organized around it. An explicit reference to the local tradition of farm courtyards, the opening of the arch acts as a counterpoint to the massive walls at the back, characterized by vertical slits, closed to the valley.

Lotus international, 15, 1977; GA Document, 30, 1990; A. Acocella, L'architettura dei luoghi, Rome 1992; a + u, architecture and urbanism, 279, 1993; P. Disch, Architettura recente nel Ticino 1980–1995, Lugano 1996, p. 123.

Manno

Suglio UBS Offices

Via Cantonale, Suglio

1990–97

Dolf Schnebli, Tobias Ammann, Flora Ruchat, Ernst Engeler and Claudio Schmidt

with S. Menz

The winning design in a 1990 competition proposed a pilot project intended to make energy savings, minimize the environmental impact, guarantee flexible uses and improve the quality of working conditions. The careful ecological approach is reflected in the development of the facade (with more ventilation than the other fronts and natural lighting), while the choice of materials was mainly determined by questions of production, use and disposal. Large sections of the roof and the southern front of the building are equipped with solar-energy and photovoltaic panels.

P. Disch, Architettura recente nel Ticino 1980–1995, Lugano 1996, p. 230 f.

Massagno

La Panoramica

Via San Gottardo

1955–57

Alberto Camenzind

with B. Brocchi

Situated on very rough ground, this building meets the requirements of the brief for parking lots (linked by a helicoid ramp) and apartments with corridor on the upper floor, revealing a skillful use of the design tools. The well-proportioned volumes produce an overall effect of great elegance.

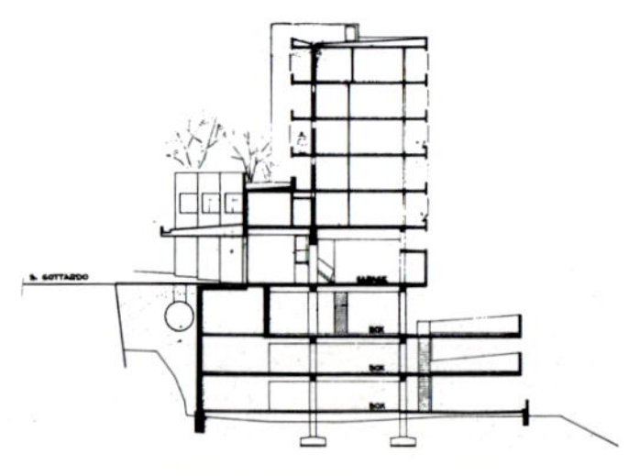

Barchi House

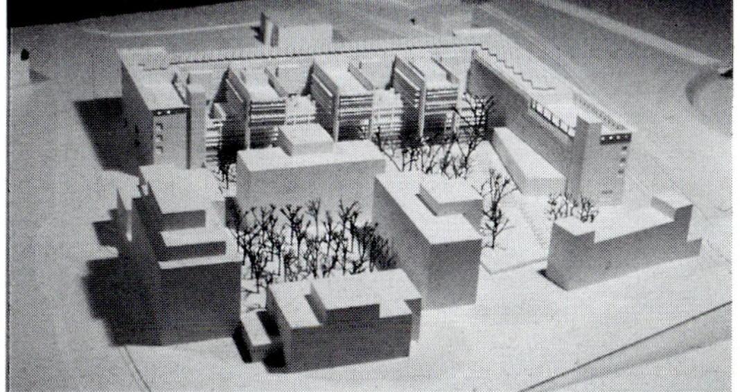

Suglio UBS Offices, model view

La Panoramica, view and, opposite page, section

Massagno

Boni House

Via al Roccolo 3

1980–82

Mario Campi and Franco Pessina

The house is built on a serpentine stone base, aligned with the road, containing the entrance, garage, service premises and custodian's lodge. After entering through an elaborate portal, the visitor is guided to the interior: an open staircase is the compositional fulcrum of the house, and organizes the visual sequence of the main rooms.

Another notable work from the same period by these two architects is the Polloni House at Origlio.

a + u, architecture and urbanism, 11, 1982; Progressive Architecture, 7, 1982; Werk, 12, 1982; Rivista Tecnica, 2, 1983; Häuser, 1, 1985; Bauwelt, 41–42, 1986; Werk, Bauen und Wohnen, 6, 1986; Casabella, 534, 1987; L'Habitat, 11, 1991; Architektur und Technik, 7, 1992.

Massagno

Terraced Housing

Via Praccio

1990–92

Mario Campi and Franco Pessina

This scheme consists of five single-family terraced houses in a sharply sloping triangular-shaped lot. The northern front giving onto the road has considerable urban qualities. The first-floor house entrances are also on this

Boni House

Housing in Massagno

side of the building. On the southern side, on the other hand, the relation between interior and exterior is mediated by the presence of a portico, the main element characterizing the houses.

In the same area, see also the terraced Housing on Viale Foletti, built by Campi and Pessina in 1985–86.

Domus, 728, 1991; Werk, Bauen und Wohnen, 12, 1991; Rivista Tecnica, 10, 1992; P. Disch, Architettura recente nel Ticino 1980–1995, Lugano 1996, p. 151.

Minusio
Quattrini House
Via Borenco 16
1989–91

Michele Arnaboldi with N. Romerio

The entrance and stairway to the apartments and the access avenue to the building are on the same axis ordering the design, characterized by the varied handling of each facade. The main front is an exposed reinforced-concrete wall, patterned by cuts and the stairs. The western facade has large balconies intended as the ideal continuation of the interior spaces. From the top terrace there are fine views of the Maggia delta and Lake Maggiore.

Ticino hoy, exhibition catalogue, Madrid 1993; Architettura Svizzera, 11, 1993; P. Disch, Architettura recente nel Ticino 1980–1995, Lugano 1996, p. 147.

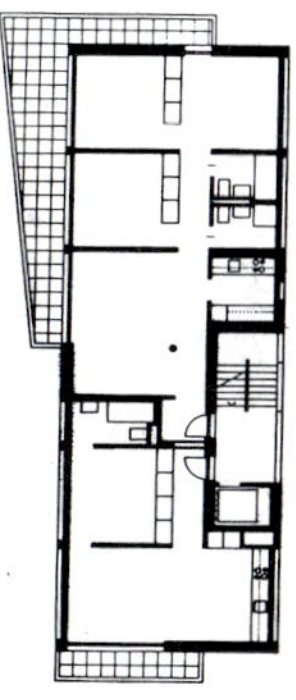

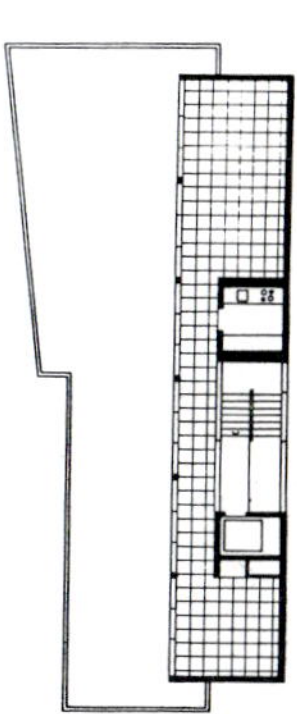

Quattrini House

Mogno
Church of San Giovanni Battista
Comune di Fusio, Vallemaggia
1986–96
Mario Botta
with G. Dazio (site management)

Until destroyed in spring 1986 by an avalanche, like parts of the village, the small Mogno church in the upper Maggia valley had been a popular landmark for the community in the seventeenth-century settlement. After long discussion a massive local-stone volume was erected from the ruins. The elliptical-plan interior converges upwards. Sharp cuts in the perimeter walls and a slanting steel and glass roof thrusting skywards give the building a strong sculptural presence.

Archithese, 4, 1987; Rivista Tecnica, 9, 1987; Werk, Bauen und Wohnen, 7–8, 1987; Casabella, 546, 1988; Domus, 694, 1988; L'Arca, 14, 1988; Perspecta, 24, 1988; Techniques et Architecture, 377, 1988; GA Document, 22, 1989; 36, 1993; J. Petit (ed), Mario Botta progetto per una chiesa a Mogno, Lugano 1992; Habitation, 1, 1993; Languages of Design, 8, vol. I, 1993; P. Disch, Architettura recente nel Ticino 1980–1995, Lugano 1996, p. 224.

Montagnola
Collina d'Oro Primary School
1978–82
Livio Vacchini
with M. Vanetti, C. Bodmer, T. Pfister

In this school for 300 children Vacchini further elaborates his "experimental classicism" as regards the order of relations established between the elements of the building. Based on a courtyard building type, the complex reshapes the center of the town to become the principal public space. Community rooms are on the ground floor, the classrooms on the first floor. Glass, metal and marble provide the

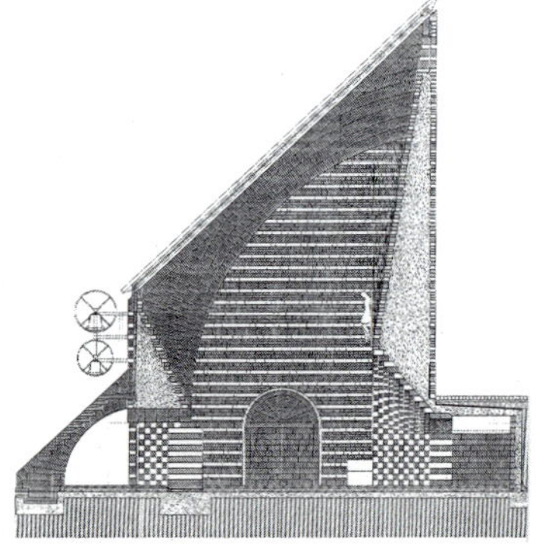

Church of San Giovanni Battista

cladding for the structural skeleton of reinforced concrete.

Rivista Tecnica, 3–4, 1978; 9, 1984; Werk, Bauen und Wohnen, 10, 1983; Archithese, 6, 1984; Casabella, 503, 1984; Quaderns d'Arquitectura i Urbanisme, 160, 1984; a + u, architecture and urbanism, 176, 1985; Lotus international, 44, 1985; Parametro, 141, 1985; AMC. Architecture-Mouvement-Continuité, 6, 1986; G. Brown-Manrique, The Ticino Guide, New York 1989; F. Werner and S. Schneider, La nuova architettura ticinese, Milan 1990; Guide to Swiss Architecture 1920–1995, vol. 3, 765, p. 308; P. Disch, Architettura recente nel Ticino 1980–1995, Lugano 1996, p. 69.

Montagnola
Corecco Houses
Via Matorell 7
1987–89
Mario Campi and Franco Pessina

The complex was created by superimposing layers of individual residences in a terraced block, divided into three volumes, stepping down into the valley. The long stairway flanking the whole building defines the entrances. Each residence is a duplex organized round the double-height space of the living room. Through a series of mediating elements (paving, balconies and pergolas) the building establishes a direct relation with the surrounding landscape, and provides a fine view towards the lake.

Domus, 715, 1990; Faces, 17, 1990; Rivista Tecnica, 5, 1990; 10, 1992; Atrium, 4, 1991; Ideales Heim, 10, 1991; Guide to Swiss Architecture 1920–1995, vol. 3, 766, p. 308; P. Disch, Architettura recente nel Ticino 1980–1995, Lugano 1996, p. 121.

Collina d'Oro Primary Schools, views

Corecco Houses, view and section

Montagnola
House
Via Arasio
1989–93
Mario Botta

The semicircular volume of this single-family house is located on a slope, with the convex living room side facing downhill. A low, partially underground, volume contains a gymnasium with sauna and swimming pool as well as the garage for the client's car collection. The intermediate level, reached by a broad terrace, is characterized by the deep cut into the stone facade of the central glazed living spaces, the compositional pivot in the organization of the house.

P. Disch, Architettura recente nel Ticino 1980–1995, Lugano 1996, p. 221.

Monte Carasso
Village Redevelopment
1979–90
Luigi Snozzi
with W. von Euw, C. Buetti, G. Groisman, G. Mazzi, M. Arnaboldi, M. Bähler, and R. Cavadini

Begun in 1977 as a project to restore the former monastery in the village center as a primary school, this commission was extended two years later to the revision of the village's detailed master plan. As an alternative to decentralizing towards the periphery, Snozzi proposed redeveloping the central area in several stages for use by religious and civil institutions. Various works were gradually completed: a gymnasium (1984), the conversion of the convent into a grammar school (1993), the Raiffeisen Bank Building (1984), a multi-family housing block near the highway (1996), and several single-family homes; Snozzi also redeveloped the cemetery. This unique development scheme clearly emerged as an exemplary project in which each new individual work tested out the efficacy of the rules in the planning process.

Casabella, 506, 1984; 542–543, 1988; 567, 1990; Rivista Tecnica, 12, 1984; 3, 1990; 12, 1991; D. Bachmann and G. Zanetti, Architektur des Aufbegehrens, Bauen im Tessin, Basel 1985; Werk, Bauen und Wohnen, 4, 1985; AMC. Architecture-Mouvement-Continuité, 12, 1986; Archithese, 2, 1986; 4, 1989; Bauwelt, 41–42, 1986; T. Boga, Tessiner Architekten, Zürich 1986; Architectural Record, 4, 1987; The Architectural Review, 1095, 1988; du 11, 1989; Abitare, 290, 1990; F. Werner and S. Schneider, La nuova architettura ticinese, Milan 1990; Guide to Swiss Architecture 1920–1995, vol. 3, 648, p. 258; Luigi Snozzi, Monte Carasso, La reinvenzione del sito, Basel 1995; C. Lichtenstein, Luigi Snozzi, Basel 1997; P. Disch, Architettura recente nel Ticino 1980–1995, Lugano 1996, p. 74 ff., 176 ff., 234.

House at
Montagnola

Monte Carcasso
Village
Redevelopment:
Monastery
Bank
Gymnasium

Morbio Inferiore

Secondary School

Via Franscini

1972–77

Mario Botta

with E. Bernegger, R. Hunziker, and L. Tami

This school is seen as a climax and a major statement of Mario Botta's design principles. At the same time it is representative of a decade of architecture in the region.The project aimed to enhance the overall context which had been degraded due to indiscriminate urbanization. Botta redesigned the urban edge bordering with the countryside by setting in a north-south direction the school block generated by a standard cell type – the constructional and organizing unit – consisting of four classrooms. The central gallery gives spatial order to the internal passages through the use of overhead lighting. The end building contains the main lecture hall and the library, while the amphitheater acts as a compositional pivot between school building and the gymnasium, set slightly off the main axis.

Rivista Tecnica, 4, 1973; 11, 1975; 9, 1979; Werk, 1, 1975; Lotus international, 11, 1976; 15, 1977; Archives d'Architecture Moderne, 12, 1977; L'Architecture

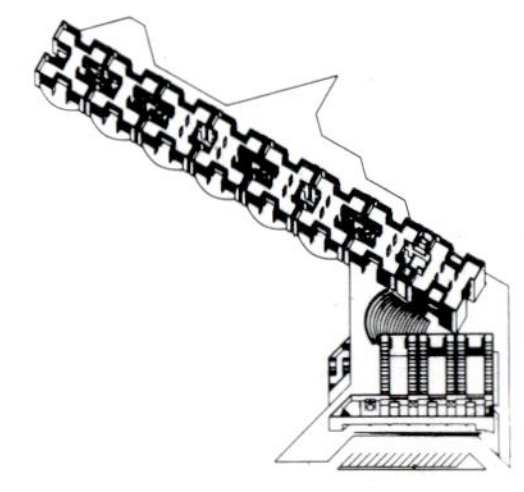

Secondary School

d'aujourd'hui, 190, 1977; AMC. Architecture-Mouvement-Continuité, 45, 1978; Werk-archithese, 13–14, 1978; a + u, architecture and urbanism, 105, 1979; 9, 1986; Architettura Svizzera, 46, 1981; Architectural Record, 6, 1982; GA Architect, 3, 1984; Domus, 579, 1988; G. Brown-Manrique, The Ticino Guide, New York 1990; Guide to Swiss Architecture 1920–1995, vol. 3, 767, p. 309.

Morbio Inferiore
House
Via Vacallo
1986–89
Mario Botta

Botta has often explored the compositional potential of a triangular plan. Here his research is applied to a single-family house built on a hill with a view towards the Chiasso plain, between the towns of Morbio Inferiore and Vacallo. The prominent entrance portico is shaped by two large crossed arches, and the main rooms in the house give onto this area. The facade is richly decorated by exploiting the textural qualities of the brickwork, whose carefully arranged string courses accentuate the luminosity of the surfaces.

GA Global Architecture, 30, 1990; A. Acocella, L'architettura dei luoghi, Rome 1992; Mario Botta, The Complete Works, vol. 2, 1985–1990, Zurich 1994.

House at Morbo Inferiore

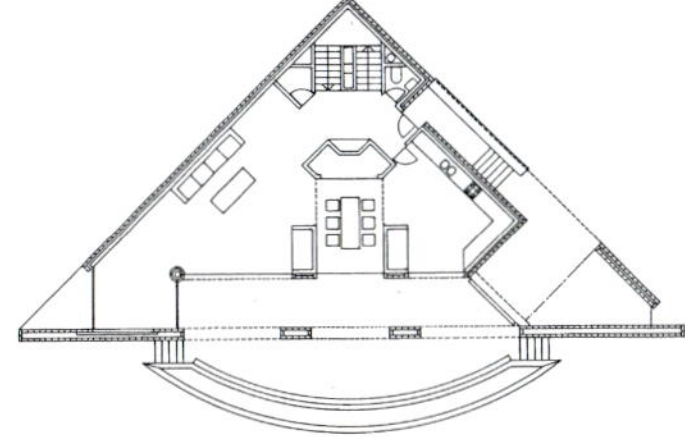

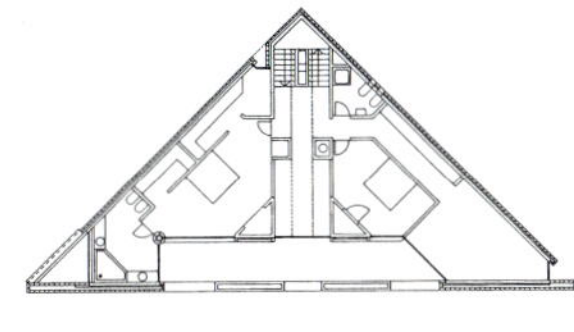

Morbio Superiore
Corinna House
Via Vacallo
1962–63
Peppo Brivio

Situated in a rural farming area, the house is based on a 90 x 90 centimeter module. The morphology is generated by a neoplastic matrix uncompromisingly using carefully chosen materials: exposed brick walls, reinforced-concrete ceilings and natural wooden window and door frames.
Of Brivio's other works in the 1950s, see the Albairone Apartments, Via Ceresio 5, and the Cate Apartments, Via Tesserete 3, both at Massagno.
J. Bachmann and S. von Moos, New Directions in Swiss Architecture, New York 1969; P. Disch (ed), 50 anni di architettura in Ticino 1930–1980, Bellinzona-Lugano 1983; Guide to Swiss Architecture 1920–1995, vol. 3, 768, p. 310.

Morbio Superiore
House
1983–84
Mario Botta
with G. Calderari, F. Robbiani

Nestling on the top of a hill, the single-family house opens up towards the valley with a silvery concave facade, patterned by the alternating brick string courses set at forty-five degrees, and characterized by a central slit ending in a skylight. Sensitive to variations in daylight, this glass screen reveals Botta's interest in harmonizing the architecture with the landscape, but also his skill in trying out new building types with a special focus on the facade and the use of materials.
Architectural Design, 11–12, 1984; GA Architect, 3, 1984; GA Houses, 15, 1984; Rivista Tecnica, 7–8, 1984; Architectural Record, 4, 1986; a + u, architecture and urbanism, 184, 1986; Häuser, 4, 1986; Techniques & Architecture, 377, 1988; P. Disch, Architettura recente nel Ticino 1980–1995, Lugano 1996, p. 72.

Muzzano
Filippini House and Studio
Via al Teglio 7
1968–70
Mario Campi and Franco Pessina

Designed for an artist, this studio-house stands on a narrow deep lot, squeezed between the rock wall of an antique ruin and a road. This unusual location led to a linear solution being adopted for the interiors. The project explores the potential interaction between building type and place – a constant feature in the design research of Campi and Pessina. At Muzzano, see also the Vanini House (1962–65) built by the same architects.
a + u, architecture and urbanism, 9, 1976; Rivista Tecnica, 2, 1973; M. Steinmann and T. Boga, Tendenzen. Neuere Architektur im Tessin, Zürich 1975; T. Boga, Tessiner Architekten 1960–1985, Zürich 1986; Guide to Swiss Architecture 1920–1995, vol. 3, 770, p. 311.

Corinna House

House at Morbio Superiore

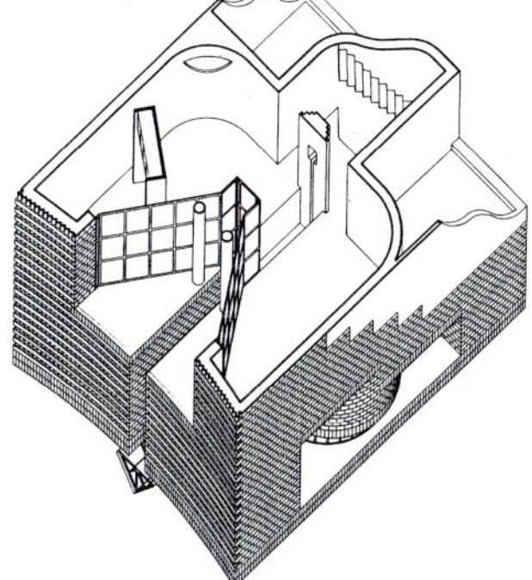

Filippini House and Studio

Muzzano
Platis House
Via Ciusaretta
1979–82
Emilio Bernegger, Bruno Keller and Edy Quaglia

A representative work of Ticino architecture in the late 1970s, this house, situated at the edge of the town, has a triangular plan, while the circulation spine organizes the various rooms on two floors facing the back. The exact geometry of the design contrasts with the ill-defined setting, highlighting the capacity of a project to built its own site. Of the many subsequent single-family residences by the same architects, see Hochstrasser House, Via ai Ronchi (1990), at Muzzano, and the more recent Bick Atelier (1992–93) at Sant'Abbondio.

Rivista Tecnica, 2, 1983; Archithese, 3, 1984; Parametro, 141, 1985; Werk, Bauen und Wohnen, 9, 1986; 3, 1994; G. Brown-Manrique, The Ticino Guide, New York 1989; P. Disch, Architettura recente nel Ticino 1980–1995, Lugano 1996, p. 135.

Novazzano
Residential Quarter
Via Ronco, Quartiere Casate
1988–92
Mario Botta
with F. Robbiani (site management)

The theme of typological repetition – previously explored by Botta in earlier housing-scheme designs – is further developed in this complex. The collective spaces (porticoes, plaza, and a lawn on the valley side) function as structuring elements, although an alternative order is also introduced

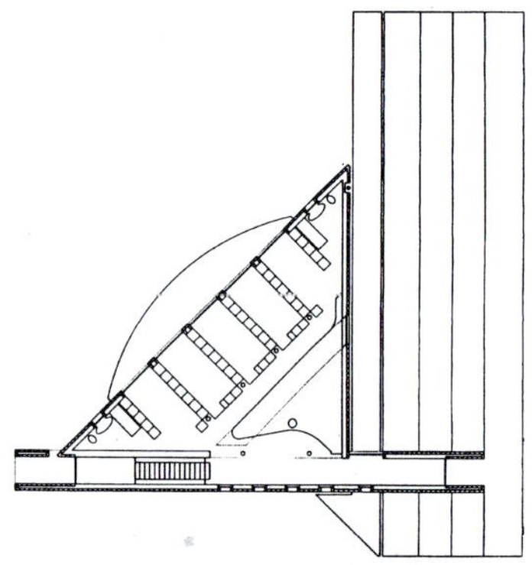

Platis House, view and floor plan

Residential Quarter in Novazzano

through the relation the residential cells establish with the overall scheme. The use of color to highlight the various floors in the facades contributes to controlling the environmental scale and alludes to the modern tradition of making essential design resources an effective instrument for assuring the living quality in housing estates.

a + u, architecture and urbanism, 279, 1993; Abitare, 327, 1994; Guide to Swiss Architecture 1920–1995, vol. 3, 774, p. 313; P. Disch, Architettura recente nel Ticino 1980–1995, Lugano 1996, p. 158.

Pregassona
Housing
Via delle Scuole 21a
1985–87
Antonio Bassi, Giovanni Gherra and Dario Galimberti

Situated in the jumbled Lugano periphery, this building has a balcony-type circulation system. The architecture re-interprets a number of elements from the traditional vocabulary of collective housing, such as the base, echoing the rustication of the nineteenth-century *palazzo*, the Rationalist-type block with railings and no roof cornice, and the more recent features of loggias and tympanums. The result is a kind of collage creating, however, a building in its own right.

Premio internazionale di architettura Andrea Palladio, Milan 1991; L'Habitat, 22, 1991.

Residential Quarter in Novazzano

Housing in Pregassona, views

Riva San Vitale
Municipal School Center
Via Settala
1962–73
Aurelio Galfetti, Flora Ruchat, and Ivo Trümpy

The overall complex for schools, nursery school and gymnasium was built in three stages. The main porticoed block with stairs, services and special teaching rooms is joined to the comb-like structure of the classrooms, articulated as self-contained educational units. The gymnasium building, shaped by two continuous walls marks the end of the open area. The L-shaped nursery school, organized round an open court, is isolated from the rest of the complex.

See also the Viganello Municipal Kindergarten, Via Guisan 10 (1968–70), designed by the same architects.

Werk, 1, 1968; 11, 1969; M. Steinmann and T. Boga, Tendenzen. Neuere Architektur im Tessin, Zürich 1975; Rivista Tecnica, 1981, 11; P. Disch (ed), 50 anni di architettura in Ticino 1930–1980, Bellinzona-Lugano 1983; T. Boga, Tessiner Architekten 1960–1985, Zürich 1986; G. Brown-Manrique, The Ticino Guide, New York 1989; Guide to Swiss Architecture 1920–1995, vol. 3, 776, p. 314.

Riva San Vitale
House
Via della Battuta
1971–73
Mario Botta
with S. Cantoni

An emblematic example of how Botta's architecture dialogues with the landscape, this single-family house resolutely takes possession of the site. A slender metal footbridge provides upper level access. The voids in the volume, providing carefully selected vistas and creating a filter of transition spaces, eschew any references to traditional apertures. The resultant scale is suitable for the relationship with the surroundings and underscores the deliberate diversity of the building.

L'architettura cronache and storia, 223, 1974; Rivista Tecnica, 8, 1974; Domus, 44, 1975; The Architectural Review, 941, 1975; Werk, Bauen und Wohnen, 2, 1975; a + u, architecture and urbanism, 69, 1976; 9, 1986; Casabella, 414, 1976; Lotus international, 11, 1976; Archives d'Architecture Moderne, 12, 1977; GA Document, 1, 1980; Architectural Design, 5, 1981; GA Architect, 3, 1984; G. Brown-Manrique, The Ticino Guide, New York 1989; Guide to Swiss Architecture 1920–1995, vol. 3, 779, p. 316.

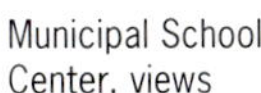
Municipal School Center, views

House at Riva San Vitale

Riva San Vitale
Studio-House
Via dell'Inglese 3a
1973–74
Giancarlo Durisch
Secondary School
Via Vela
1980–82
Giancarlo Durisch and Giorgio Giudici

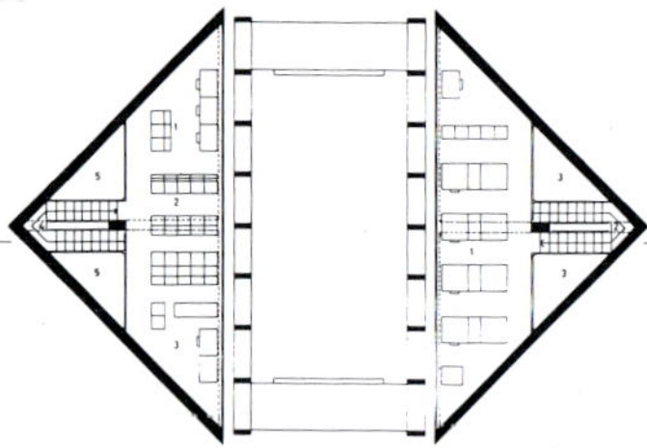

These two works are representative of the themes often explored by Durisch, especially the use of geometry to generate architecture. The designer's own studio-house is divided into two triangular elements, separated by an internal courtyard, the focal point for the various rooms. The school, on the other hand, consists of four volumes forming a square. Access galleries are organized round this atrium space. The boldness of the overall composition is confirmed by a number of transgressions, such as placing the accesses on the diagonals and rotating the roof structure for the central space. The order and proportions highlight the rationality of the building process, while the refined use of light and materials evoke the poetics of silence, so typical of the architect.

M. Steinmann and T. Boga, Tendenzen. Neuere Architektur im Tessin, Zürich 1975; a + u, architecture and urbanism, 69, 1976; L'Architecture d'aujourd'hui, 190, 1977; Lotus international, 15, 1977; 63, 1989; P. Disch (ed), 50 anni di architettura in Ticino 1930–1980, Bellinzona-Lugano 1983; Rivista Tecnica 1984, 9; T. Boga, Tessiner Architekten 1960–1985, Zürich 1986; Guide to Swiss Architecture 1920–1995, vol. 3, 778, p. 315; 780, p. 316; P. Disch, Architettura recente nel Ticino 1980–1995, Lugano 1996, p. 66.

Rivera
Chapel
Monte Tamaro
1990–97
Mario Botta

Built on a hill sloping down to the Magadino plain as part of the local tourist infrastructure, the church establishes a dialogue with the alpine landscape through a series of evocative itineraries: a slender suspended footbridge on a large stone arch and a system of ramps and walkways on the hill ending in the square in front of the church. The meditative atmosphere in the interior, created by light filtering through small circular windows, is further enhanced by the graphic works of Enzo Cucchi.

Guide to Swiss Architecture 1920–1995, vol. 3, 781, p. 317; P. Disch, Architettura recente nell Ticino 1980–1995, p. 225.

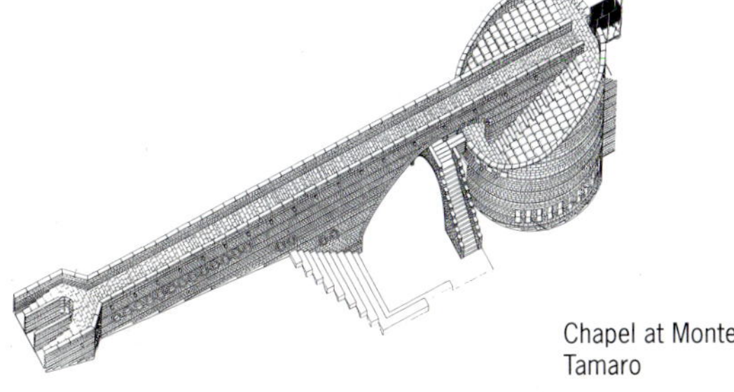

Chapel at Monte Tamaro

Opposite page:
Studio-House, view and plan
Secondary School, view and interior

Rovio
Balmelli House
San Vigilio
1955–57
Tita Carloni and Luigi Camenisch

This house reveals the architects' skill in adapting Wright's language to a building tradition that respects the context and is sensitive to the use of local techniques and materials. Situated at the top of the hill of San Vigilio, the house follows the contours of the terrain. Structured on three levels, the formal play of acute angles shapes the roof profile. Inside, the principal materials are rubble masonry and wood.

The architects further explored the potential for these materials in subsequent works in the next decade, such as the single-family residence in Rovio (1968). For the results of a very different design approach, but still carefully camouflaged in the context, see the architects home at Rovio (1985–86) and the Cereghetti House at Salorino, Via Croù (1992–93), designed jointly with Roberto Nicoli.

Werk, 1, 1968; P. Disch (ed), 50 anni di architettura in Ticino 1930–1980, Bellinzona-Lugano 1983; D. Bachmann and G. Zanetti, Architektur des Aufbegehrens. Bauen im Tessin, Basel 1985; T. Boga, Tessiner Architekten 1960–1985, Zürich 1986; Ticino hoy, exhibition catalogue, Madrid 1993; Guide to Swiss Architecture 1920–1995, vol. 3, 782, p. 317.

San Nazzaro
Town Hall and Schools
1973–79
Luigi Snozzi
with W. von Euw

The complex was designed to be a new civic center, embracing the church and village cemetery. The various architectural events are connected by a walkway along the extension of the existing support wall. The school and town hall are contained in a single building articulated in two wings round a raised court facing out towards the lake. Also intended for cultural activities, the town hall assembly room on the first floor has a broad projecting terrace – a kind of open-air foyer. Unfortunately, a corner tower, completing the court and acting as a counterpoint to the church bell-tower opposite, was never built.

Rivista Tecnica, 4, 1974; 10, 1982; (monographic issue) 1990; P. Disch (ed), 50 anni di architettura in Ticino 1930–1980, Bellinzona-Lugano 1983; Ingegneri and Architetti Svizzeri, 10, 1983; T. Boga, Tessiner Architekten 1960–1985, Zürich 1986; Häuser, 3, 1987; G. Brown-Manrique, The Ticino Guide, New York 1989.

Balmelli House

Town Hall and School

Sorengo
Housing
Via Lugano
1987–89
Elio Ostinelli and Fabio Muttoni with N. Melchiorre, N. Ktenas, F. Ottardi, and A. Scala

Arranged parallel to a central public space, the thirty-two three-story single-family houses have been built using a reinforced-concrete prefabrication system (the assembly time was a week per unit). The tree-lined avenue past the housing blocks ends in the area for collective facilities.

This kind of structure and typology were further explored by the same architects in the Massagno Housing, Via Privata Campagna, (1988–90).

Rivista Tecnica, 5, 1990; Ticino hoy, exhibition catalogue, Madrid 1993.

Stabio
Medici House (Casa Rotonda)
Via Pietane 12
1980–82
Mario Botta with M. Pelli

The rotunda house, one of Botta's most famous buildings, is inserted in the Mendrisiotto countryside as an object which in form refuses to dialogue with the surrounding buildings. The typical features of Botta's language – central slit, rooflighting, and terraces mediating between exterior and interior – are very plastically adapted to the circular-plan building. The volumetry and use of "poor" materials, such as concrete blocks, evoke the rudimentary forms of the local rural tradition.

In the same area, see also the single-family residence, Via Platani 1 (1965–67) built by Botta as a deliberate hom-

Sorengo Housing

age to Le Corbusier. At Genestrerio, on the other hand, is an early Botta work, the Parish House (1961–63) designed under the guidance of Tita Carloni, and already showing the Ticino architect's interest in the tectonic effects of materials.

Architectural Journal, 5, 1982; Architectural Record, 7, 1982; Architettura Svizzera, 50, 1982; Casabella, 482, 1982; Domus, 626, 1982; GA Houses, 10, 1982; Interni, 323, 1982; Rivista Tecnica, 2, 1982; Häuser, 1, 1983; GA Architect, 3, 1984; Architectural Design, 3–4, 1985; a + u, architectura and urbanism, 9, 1986; Techniques et Architecture, 377, 1988; G. Brown-Manrique, The Ticino Guide, New York 1989; Guide to Swiss Architecture 1920–1995, vol. 3, 788, p. 320; P. Disch, Architettura recente nel Ticino 1980–1995, Lugano 1996, p. 67.

Torricella

Tonini House

1972–74

Bruno Reichlin and Fabio Reinhart
with A. Mercolli

An explicit reference to the scheme for Palladian villas according to Wittkower's interpretation of the original villa, the project is a refined exercise in abstraction. The typology leads to the creation of an Alberti-like "heart of the house", lit by the lantern windows and light from the bedrooms.

M. Steinmann and T. Boga, Tendenzen. Neuere Architektur im Tessin, Zürich 1975; Rivista Tecnica, 8, 1975; a + u, architecture and urbanism, 69, 1976; L'Architecture d'aujourd'hui, 190, 1977; Lotus international, 22, 1979; Bauwelt, 39, 1980; Werk, Bauen und Wohnen, 1–2, 1980; Archithese, 1, 1982; P. Disch (ed), 50 anni di architettura in Ticino 1930–1980, Bellinzona-Lugano 1983; T. Boga, Tessiner Architekten 1960–1985, Zürich 1986; Guide to Swiss Architecture 1920–1995, vol. 3, 790, p. 321.

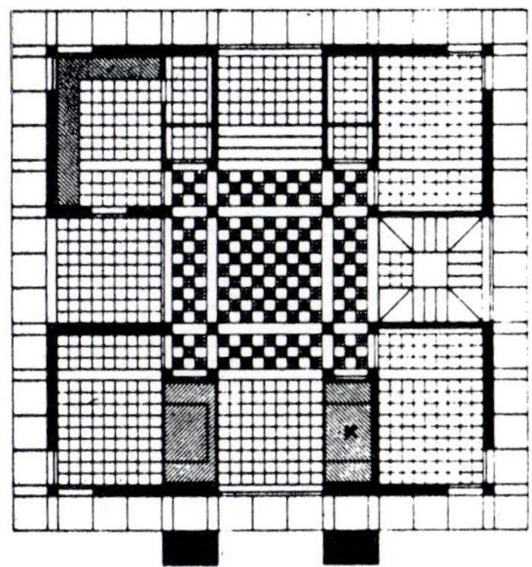

Medici House (Casa Rotonda)

Tonini House, view and plan

Verscio
Snider House
Road to Cavigliano
1965–66
Luigi Snozzi and Livio Vacchini
Cavalli House
Road to Cavigliano
1976–78
Luigi Snozzi

Situated in a small Centovalli foothill village, these two single-family residences are interesting examples of Snozzi's design approach to existing historic buildings. The Snider House is brought into relation with the existing houses through a court. The typology reflects the local architecture but has its own particular volumetric character, in clear contrast with the old buildings in the village. Similarly, the Cavalli House cites the orthogonal grid underlying the village center, in sharp opposition to the recent peripheral sprawl, and establishing the position of the access path – a significant element in the close relations with the context.

Werk, 12, 1967; J. Bachmann and S. von Moos, New Directions in Swiss Architecture, New York 1969; M. Steinmann and T. Boga, Tendenzen. Neuere Architektur im Tessin, Zürich 1975; a + u, architecture and urbanism, 69, 1976; Techniques & Architecture, 339, 1981; Abitare, 206, 1982; D. Bachmann and G. Zanetti, Architektur des Aufbegehrens. Bauen im Tessin, Basel 1985; T. Boga, Tessiner Architekten 1960–1985, Zurich 1986; Häuser, 3, 1987; G. Brown-Manrique, The Ticino Guide, New York 1989; Architektur und Technik, 9, 1991; Rivista Tecnica, 3, 1990; 4, 1992; Guide to Swiss Architecture 1920–1995, vol. 3, 656, S. 262.

Snider House

Cavalli House

Viganello
House
Via Albonago
1980–81
Mario Botta
with C. Lo Riso, F. Robbiani
An emblematic work in Botta's design career, the Viganello House – like the earlier Pregassona House, Via Albostra 27, and Massagno House, Via Praccio – is a typological variation on the theme of the single-family residence. Almost wholly underground on three sides, the triangular-shaped entrance – accessed by a garden promenade and leading into the top-lit interiors – is dark and empty. The facade appears monumental in effect and is patterned by the play of light and shadow generated by the various surface textures.
Architectural Record, 7, 1982; GA Houses, 13, 1983; Lotus international, 37, 1983; The Architectural Review, 1034, 1983; GA Architect, 3, 1984; Rivista Tecnica, 7–8, 1984; a + u, architecture and urbanism, 9, 1986; P. Disch, Architettura recente nel Ticino 1980–1995, Lugano 1996, p. 68.

Vira Gambarogno
House
Corognola
1984
Orlando Pampuri
Based on the reinterpretation of Classical principles, the design sets the house on a massive reinforced-concrete base, which not only emphasizes the distance from the steeply sloping ground, but contains the entrance, bedrooms and service premises. Four iron pillars rise up from this horizontal plane to support the aluminum roof, creating a continuous loggia round the day zone.
Ticino hoy, exhibition catalogue, Madrid 1993; P. Disch, Architettura recente nel Ticino 1980–1995, Lugano 1996, p. 81.

79 Viganello House

House at Vira Gambarogno

Swiss Architecture Today

An Overview

by Roman Hollenstein

The heroic phase of Swiss architecture is over. The fundamental theoretical points have been made, positions have been taken up. Work by Botta, Snozzi, Herzog & de Meuron, Diener & Diener, Gigon & Guyer and Zumthor is familiar to specialists well beyond the borders of Switzerland. The current Swiss architectural scene is interested in refining the vocabulary developed since the 1970s. At the same time – despite the building crisis – there is a rich output of contemporary architecture to be admired. Undoubtedly there have never been so many major buildings by notable architects completed between Basel and Chiasso than in recent years. But more and more critical voices are being raised in the country. People have been saying for a long time now that Ticino architecture, for example, which has been recognized internationally since the *Tendenzen* (Tendencies) exhibition at the ETH Zurich in 1975, has run out of steam in terms of individual interpretations of Modernism, which have become exaggerated to the point of mannerism. Botta is cited as an example. But in fact his most recent works on Swiss soil, the mountain chapel on Monte Tamaro, consecrated in summer 1996, and the Tinguely Museum in Basel, which opened only a few weeks later, show that it is entirely possible to innovate within a specific formal vocabulary.

A few years after the first Ticino successes, it was noticed that a new German-Swiss architecture was starting to emerge. The theoretical foundations were laid at the ETH in Zurich by the circle around Aldo Rossi and Dolf Schnebli, and based on historical and critical analysis of austere Swiss Modernism. This new architecture, committed to a Protestant and puritanical objectivity, first flowered in Basel, where suddenly everyone was talking about the rigid but pictorially rich buildings of Herzog & de Meuron and Diener & Diener. Diener & Diener dared to look at the heritage of Modernism in a new way, from a reduced and minimalist point of view, but Herzog & de Meuron fought for an architecture that was inspired by art. There were already signs of something that was not just pictorial art, but sculptural as well, related to Arte Povera and Minimal Art, in work as early as their plywood house in Bottmingen (1985) and the Ricola warehouse in Laufen (1987).

These two Basel offices, working with theoretician Martin Steinmann, formed the core – long after the Solothurn school, early concrete architecture by Gisel, Förderer and Paillard and the early estate building by Atelier 5 – around which the new German-Swiss architecture started to crystallize. However, this did not prevent the young Zurich scene that had formed around Marcel Meili and Markus

Peter, Peter Zumthor, working in Haldenstein near Chur, but also Patrick Devanthéry and Inès Lamunière in Geneva, from taking up positions that were very much their own. But the northern Alpine discourse increasingly excluded the Ticino architects. They did not impinge on the Swiss consciousness again until Raffaele Cavadini's new buildings and town planning for Iragna.

Swiss architecture has become more differentiated and has further consolidated its position since the early nineties. This process went hand in hand with a refinement of architectural expression. Buildings with ethical and social aspirations – for example in the work of Metron or Michael Alder – and also buildings paying homage to technology like those by Theo Hotz or Rodolphe Luscher, are found alongside architecture committed to art and aesthetics by Jacques Herzog or Peter Zumthor, for example. But what they all have in common is that they come to terms with the modern tradition and reject the fashionable games of post-Modernism or superficially understood Deconstructivism.

As well as Basel and Ticino, the principal centers of architectural activity could now be said to be Zurich, Graubünden and the *métropole lémanique* between Montreux and Geneva. But a creative scene has also grown up in Berne – which was for a long time synonymous with Atelier 5. I need mention only Gartenmann, Werren and Jöhri, who won third prize in the Berlin Spree Bend competition from a field of 835 entries. There are also lively sub-centers like eastern Switzerland, Lucerne, Fribourg and Valais. Although influences overlap a great deal in multicultural Switzerland with its four languages. I shall follow a geographical thread through the regional colors of Swiss architecture in this essay.

Diversity in Basel

Basel is still the creative stronghold of German-Swiss architectural activity. It is not just the place where innovative architects are thickest on the ground. This city-canton, which forms the centre of a conurbation including three countries, is also open to international architects today – unlike many areas in the rest of Switzerland. Basel entrepreneur Rolf Fehlbaum set things in motion when he commissioned buildings from Grimshaw, Gehry, Hadid, Ando and Siza for the Vitra production site in Weil am Rhein in south Baden, just over the border. Fehlbaum also commissioned Frank Gehry to build the company headquarters in Birsfelden in Basel-Land. At the moment Richard Meier is building the large perimeter development Euregio at the Schweizer Bahnhof, and Spaniards Cruz and Ortiz are involved in a nearby commercial development along the tracks. Mario Botta from Ticino created a monumental new Basel headquarters, reminiscent of a bastion, for the Union Bank of Switzerland (UBS). Botta was also responsible for the Tinguely Museum, directly on the Rhine, for chemical giant Hoffmann-La Roche. This opened in 1996, and is convincing both in terms of the museum space it offers and the way in which it fits into the cityscape by the river.

Another important museum building, for the treasures of Basel art dealer Ert Beyeler, one of the most important private 20th century art collections in the world,opened 1997 in Riehen. The elegant hall structure in red stone, steel and glass was very skilfully integrated into the Berower estate landscape park by Renzo Piano. It may be difficult for many people to understand that two important museum commissions went to foreigners, even though Diener & Diener and Herzog & de Meuron have made names for themselves with museum buildings and projects in Berlin, Cologne, Munich, London and New York. However, success on the international stage is doubtless more important to these two leading Basel offices than "missed" opportunities at home; especially as they and their internationally less well-known colleagues have recently had so many attractive commissions in Basel – schools, homes, offices – that only the most important can be named here.

For example, Herzog & de Meuron built a sports hall in St. Louis; this is on French soil, but right on the border, and – typically for Basel's tri-national situation – it is run and used extra-territorially by the Swiss. They also provided two pioneering

Mario Botta, Tinguely Museum, Basel, 1996

Renzo Piano, Beyeler Collection, Riehen, Canton of Basel-Stadt, 1997

buildings for Swiss railways (SBB), at present one of Switzerland's most committed building patrons: one is the Auf dem Wolf locomotive depot – a minimalist structure with a high degree of artistic presence, lit by box-like skylights – and a signal-box, also in the Auf dem Wolf district. The latter is a concrete cube with copper bands wrapped round it, and convinces because of its almost sculptural appearance, which seems both technological and archaic. These buildings by Herzog & de Meuron prove that it is possible to create great architecture outside the cultural building sphere that is so popular with architects at present.

The architectural duo of Meinrad Morger and Heinrich Degelo have also been involved with railway architecture recently: they designed a cubic and precise prototype for a new generation of signal boxes, which was built in Murgenthal, canton of Aargau in 1996. But they were also responsible for a highly-praised intervention in the field of town planning, in the grounds of the Dreirosen school in Basel, which they had to extend by adding a triple gymnasium. The conditions were difficult: fragmented development around the playground and high emission levels in the surrounding area. They came to terms with this by sinking the required gym under the playground and building a residential block in Klybeckstrasse that brought together ideas from classical Modernism and the 1960s. The school building is set at right angles to it, and together they almost completely close the block and at the same time frame the old school building.

Jacques Herzog and Pierre de Meuron, Railway Engine Depot Auf dem Wolf, Basel, 1995

Jacques Herzog and Pierre de Meuron, Signal Box Auf dem Wolf, Basel, 1994

Matthias Ackermann and Markus Friedl have also come to the fore in the field of school building, by converting the changing-rooms of the Bachgraben garden swimming pool into a pavilion-like school building, and with their new building for the Ackermättli school in the Basel district of Kleinhüningen. But the most architecturally consistent contribution in this field must be Diener & Diener's extension to the Vogesenschule. This office's architecture tends to be austere and simple, and this was perhaps most rigorously expressed in an office building in Barfüsserplatz, which subtly alienated the trivial architecture of the 1960s, while their residential and commercial development at the former Warteck brewery in Kleinbasel, with its carefully proportioned exterior spaces, is convincing in urban development terms, but may also be seen as an example of how historically valuable building stock could be handled in the future. Diener & Diener are building on the experience they gained in residential projects in Kleinbasel in the 1980s, and thus enriching a genre of building that is particularly successful in Basel; Michael Adler in particular has shown his mastery of it in recent times.

Peter Zumthor's Spittelhof estate of terraced houses in Biel-Benken, with its dark facades and planted roof, was controversial with residents because it was so bold. It caused more of a stir than Alder's discreet architecture, which adapted itself to the residents' needs. Zumthor's eccentric and amusing development for discerning buyers

Meinrad Morger and Heinrich Degelo, Dreirosen School Complex, Basel, 1996

Diener & Diener, Warteckhof Building, Basel, 1996

Diener & Diener, Vogesen School Extension, Basel, 1994/96

met with a response in Gigon & Guyer's projected Broelberg development and Calatrava's estate of terraced houses in Würenlingen. These artistically ambitious projects are juxtaposed with work by offices like Metron in Brugg or Kuhn Fischer Partner in Zurich, which try to set new standards in reasonably priced and ecological residential building, using the simplest possible solutions.

But the young Basel architect Jakob Steib, who works in Zurich, was more concerned with formal and typological innovation. He built a timber-clad detached block containing fifteen residential units in Zwingen in Basel-Land, in which elements of terraced housing, housing with external corridors, and housing with terraces interact in a sophisticated fashion. But Basel's openness to innovative ideas has also helped other young architects. For example, Peter Steinmann and Herbert Schmid built a temporary service center for the Basel trade fair, which with its framed blue main facade with windows floating in it dominates the site like a great picture. But the fair's directors have turned elsewhere for a permanent building. They have commissioned the Zurich architect Theo Holz, who won the European prize known as the Constructed Prize for his technically mature glass and steel architecture in Baden, Sankt Gallen and Winterthur 1996.

Theo Hotz, Empa Building (Eidgenössische Materialprüfungs- und Forschungsanstalt), Sankt Gallen, 1996

Theo Hotz, Konnex ABB Research Building, Baden, Canton of Aargau, 1995

The Rise of Zurich

Zurich, whose conurbation now has over a million inhabitants, is Switzerland's economic driving force and also the seat of the country's most important school of architecture. Nevertheless, it was for a long time considered to be stony ground for architecture. There are many reasons for this: until the recent economic slump the property market was overheated by inflation, and the middle classes and the left wing have for a long time now been in conflict about building policy.

Polarization was helped on its way by projects like the main station development, which was transformed into a gigantic amorphous structure by architect Ralph Baenziger, working on an idea submitted by Snozzi and Botta in 1978. But cooperation between the building department and potential builders has produced some exemplary development plans, like the Gauss-Stierli grounds, designed by Kreis, Schaad & Schaad. This project, which makes listed industrial buildings, new residential developments and a round office tower into an attractive whole does not seem to be surviving the recession. But there is apparently more optimism about the new suburb of Oerlikon-Nord, planned on a former industrial site, although in mid 1997 this cheerful project has not gone beyond two filigree glass buildings, Toro I and II, by Theo Hotz.

Despite all the economic problems, young Zurich artists have made a breakthrough in the 1990s. Today the city has what is probably the most varied scene in Switzerland: as well as long-serving masters like Ernst Gisel and Theo Hotz there are a lot of young architects: Marie-Claude Bétrix and Eraldo Consolascio have made their name chiefly with their work in Salzburg. The first residential and commercial building by Jean-Pierre Dürig and Philippe Rämi is also in Salzburg. They established themselves by winning international competitions – for a new university in Nicosia in 1992, for example. Marcel Meili and Markus Peter made their first major appearance in Austria, in Steiermark, even though their training college for the timber industry in Biel has been much talked of here for years. In Austria they built a box-shaped timber bridge over the Mur, working with Chur engineer Jürg Conzett, who was responsible for the project and is well known for his unconventional timber structures.

Annette Gigon and Mike Guyer, Broelberg Housing, Kilchberg, Canton of Zurich, 1996

Finally, Annette Gigon and Mike Guyer launched their career with the Kirchner Museum in Davos. But they soon astonished their colleagues with a design for the Hyatt Hotel on the Escherwiese in Zurich. Their project was conceived as a perimeter development with two conceptually different inner courtyards, but it was thrown out after arguments with the client, who could not respond to the duo's highly individual and artistic approach. But they did build an estate on the Broelberg in the elegant Zurich suburb of Kilchberg. This U-shaped complex, facing an inner courtyard, added an enriching urban element to the suburban estate structure. The main source of argument here was the facade coloring, developed with artist Harald Müller – the buildings are red on the courtyard side but dark brown where they face the country – and the apparently random arrangement of the windows in the facades. The interplay of form and colour is also the chief characteristic of a residential development, built above and linking courtyard housing and housing with terraces on the opposite side of the lake in Erlenbach. This was realized by Lorenzo Giuliani and Christian Hönger; they recently made an intellectual statement about Swiss architecture with an unusually abstract concept for a residential building in Unterägeri, in Zug.

Architect Tilla Theus, who specializes in the conscientious renovation of historical buildings, had more success in the field of hotel architecture than Gigon and Guyer. She combined several medieval buildings on Rennweg to make a hotel, and converted the interior using a fluent and sophisticated approach somewhere between Scarpa and High-Tech. But the project for refurbishing and extending the Hotel Zürichberg by Marianne Burkhalter and Christian Sumi attracted attention

Marianne Burkhalter and Christian Sumi, Hotel Zürichberg, Zurich, 1995

Lorenzo Giuliani and Christian Hönger, Multi-Family Housing, Unterägeri, Canton of Zug, 1996

well beyond the Swiss border. The new section, connected to the old building by an underground corridor, is as fascinating as it is disturbing. The timber-clad, oval building, rising among trees like a pavilion, has a surprising top-lit hall inside, from which a spiral ramp leads to the rooms. Burkhalter and Sumi found their way to the veil-like transparency and colour quality of timber structures by studying modern Swiss timber architecture. The forestry workshops they realized in Türbenthal and Rheinau – with a glance back at the primeval hut – are examples of the kind of independent solution these studies have produced.

The innovative use of timber plays a crucial role in the work of Meili and Peter as well, even though the only work they have so far completed in Greater Zurich is a detached house in Wallisellen, which consists of a concrete box floating on seven massive quartzite piers, and their Zurich Park-Hyatt project. This passed to them from Gigon and Guyer, and is animated by transparent, translucent and opaque concrete and glass surfaces. The four-story extension for the training college for the timber industry in Biel, the result of a competition success, was seen as a milestone in timber technology even before it was completed. This box-like structure with a concrete access tower can be seen as combining traditional timber building with high-tech achievements. But timber as a building material is also much in evidence in the two side platform roofs for the main station in Zurich, which they designed with Axel Pickert and Kaschka Knapkiewicz. The buildings are 200 meters long, and seem astonishingly light, thanks to the diagonal concrete supports placed forty meters apart and the daylight-filled roof structure, clad with a timber grid.

Only a few hundred meters further west – and also for Swiss Railways – is an office building by Isa Stürm and Urs Wolf that is growing up like lightning along the railway lines. It is part of a larger development project on a piece of railway land that has become available. But Ueli Zbinden's signal box cube near Tiefbrunnen station is also a recent and above-average new building. While events of architectural interest are taking place on peripheral railway property, in the city center – after Calatrava's extension of Stadelhofen station and Martin Spühler's residential

Marcel Meili und Markus Peter, House, Wallisellen, Canton of Zurich, 1995

and commercial development above the former station at Selnau – it has become increasingly difficult for architects to erect large buildings. But one project that is worth mentioning is the conversion, planned by Franz Romero and Markus Schaefle, of two 1920s residential buildings in Stadelhofen into a commercial building, with a street facade enlivened by a formal front garden designed by landscape architect Dieter Kienast, and a new foyer. But the courtyard facade and the courtyard pavilion also show the young Zurich architects' material sensuality and love of detail.

Only one architect of stature has been able to build on any scale in the city center recently: Theo Hotz. After the Apollo-Haus and the glazed corner building in Löwenplatz he produced two surprising buildings, the glass cube of the Union Bank of Switzerland's Grünenhof conference center, fitted into a cramped inner courtyard in Nüschelerstrasse, and the Feldpausch fashion house, which translates Mendelsohn's streamlined architecture into the language of High Tech. But he celebrated his greatest triumphs outside Zurich. On the other hand, Marcel Ferrier, a Sankt Gallen architect committed to the Parisian Beaux-Arts tradition and Latin rationalism, was given a chance in the form of the Greek Orthodox church. His Modernist cube with a monumental white cylinder towering over it is not just an antithesis to contemporary Zurich architecture, shimmering as it does between timber structures and High Tech, but also a counterpart to Miroslav Šik's

Marcel Ferrier, Greek Orthodox Church, Zurich, 1995

Miroslav Šik, St Antonius Catholic Parish Center, Egg, Canton of Zurich, 1995

new building for the St Antonius Catholic parish center in Egg.

Šik became known as the guiding intellectual force behind so-called Analogous Architecture. He has just successfully completed a municipal musicians' building in Zurich, but his project for the church community center, originally characterized by several pyramid roofs, had to be much revised in the course of the planning and building period, from 1987 to 1995, and ended up as a building of almost barn-like simplicity. Only two kilometers away from Šik's church community center, Marc Angélil (who, with Martin Spühler, will build the fifth extension of Kloten airport) is building residential and commercial premises at the Forchbahn railway terminus in Esslingen, with Graham, Pfenninger and Scholl. The first office building to be realized, which was identified as pointing the way to the future both ecologically and aesthetically by the American Institute of Architects even in the planning phase, is difficult to classify. At first the building, with its sharp bend and gable roof, seems related to Šik's church community center. And yet its glass and steel facade, committed to

Angélil, Graham, Pfenniger, Scholl, Esslingen Station, Canton of Zurich, 1997

Oliver Schwarz, Factory Building, Ebikon, Canton of Lucerne, 1996

Annette Gigon und Mike Guyer, Provisional Extension to Winterthur Art Museum, Canton of Zurich, 1995

the latest eco-technical discoveries, very definitely distances it from melancholy Analogous Architecture.

Angélil's green-field urban development strategy produced an organic conglomeration, but when designing for the Sulzer site in Winterthur Jean Nouvel had to include the industrial complex, some of which was listed, in his architectural and town-planning project. The very name Nouvel makes it clear that there is a sense of new architectural beginnings – different from Zurich – in this industrial town on the eastern periphery of the conurbation. It is signalled, for instance, by the temporary art museum built by Gigon & Guyer, by a tower building designed by Burkard, Meyer, Steiger of Baden or Oliver Schwarz's plan to extend the station building with transparent architecture whose glass roof extends well over the square in front of the station.

Aargau's Intermediate Position

The spa and industrial town of Baden, on the western periphery of the Greater Zurich area, is in many ways comparable with Winterthur, except that Baden has been actively promoting contemporary architecture for a good twenty years. Today it is considered to be the canton of Aargau's main architectural showcase. The canton is to a large extent under the influence of the Zurich and Basel conurbations, and can thus take only tentative steps towards architecture of its own elsewhere. Although architecture in Baden reached its peak in the 1980s, interesting buildings are still appearing here, primarily on the ABB industrial site, which as Baden-Nord is intended some day to be a forward-looking counterpart to the picturesque old town. Some remarkable architecture is likely to emerge in this new district in the next few years. Theo Hotz's glass shrine for the new Konnex engineering building (Ill. p. 385) has already been built, and a start was made on realizing the Citypark development by Matti, Bürgi and Ragaz of Berne early in 1997.

Theo Hotz not only works in Baden. He is also going to build on the station site in Aarau. But younger architects are also increasingly making their presence felt here. Mathis Müller and Ueli Müller built a workshop complex in 1995, and Quintus Miller and Paola Maranta, a duo who made their name with a motorway pedestrian bridge in Sevelen (canton of Sankt Gallen), won the competition for the market hall in the city center on Färberplatz with a building that is responds precisely to urban requirements.

The Metron office in Brugg, which has devoted itself to reasonably-priced residential building, can be seen as typical of this densely populated area. Originally the principle of joint decision-making was a central concern, but the apartment block that

Metron, Multi-Family House, Lenzburg, Canton of Aargau, 1996

Santiago Calatrava, Terraced Housing, Würenlingen, Canton of Aargau, 1997

Metron has just built in Lenzburg shows that the office is coming out increasingly strongly in favor of ecological concerns, and not just a socially tolerable aesthetic of necessity. Compared with Metron's buildings, which take an emphatically ethical stand, Burkhalter and Sumi's most recent work, an apartment block in Laufenberg, seems to be a formally demanding building, although it does not offer forward-looking innovations in the field of residential building. The same could be said of Santiago Calatrava's estate of terraced houses in Würenlingen: concrete architecture in which he combines cubist-style elements with quotations from Antoni Gaudí.

Outsiders in Eastern Switzerland

Architecture in eastern Switzerland is still rarely acknowledged in the rest of the country. This is partly because very little happened here for a long time in terms of architecture, and partly because eastern Swiss architects like Marcel Ferrier and Jörg Quarella can hardly be placed in the mainstream of Swiss building. Since

Peter and Jörg Quarella, Secondary School Center, Jonschwil, Canton of Sankt Gallen, 1995

the 1960s, when Claude Paillard's municipal theatre in Sankt Gallen and Förderer, Otto and Zwimpfer's Economic University appeared as two of the most beautiful pieces of concrete architecture in the country, the city was unable to offer any other comparable buildings, even if Calatrava's bus station in Bohlplatz in the city center excited a lot of discussion locally, and the glass architecture of Theo Hotz's Empa building (Ill. p. 385) is undoubtedly extraordinarily fine.

In the early 1980s, Peter and Jörg Quarella built a residential development influenced by Rossi in Sonnmattstrasse, and they subsequently refined its formal language for the Seehotel in Steckborn in Thurgau. Since then, the two architects have moved towards a fashionably elegant neo-Modernism, which can occasionally summon up the enthusiasm for a deconstructive quotation, as can be seen from the Jonschwil (canton of Sankt Gallen) secondary school center and the double gymnasium in Bühler (canton of Appenzell Ausser-Rhoden). Architectural expression is more consistent in the work of Marcel Ferrier, who showed himself to be a modernist of French provenance in his refurbishment of the Kunstmuseum in Sankt Gallen and the new Greek Orthodox church in Zurich (Ill. p. 389). In recent years he has built a housing estate in the Sankt Gallen city district of Stephansborn and a clearly structured works building in Bischofszell (canton of Thurgau), in which architectural elements have been used deliberately to create an abstract ornamental effect.

Hubert Bischoff has also made a name for himself in recent years with sports halls and school buildings, but above all with the simple concrete shingle building for the Wies primary school in Heiden (canton of Appenzell). Perhaps the finest recent residential development in eastern Switzerland was built by Kaderli and Wehrli of Sankt Gallen in the form of six pavilion-like semidetached houses in Amriswil (canton of Thurgau). Even more purist, abstract and sculptural in its minimalism is a dwelling in concrete, glass and steel built by Beat Consoni in 1995 in the

Beat Consoni, House, Horn, Canton of Thurgau, 1995

form of a floating box in Horn (canton of Thurgau) on Lake Constance. Despite such promising buildings Sankt Gallen and the rest of eastern Switzerland – Appenzell, Thurgau and Schaffhausen – cannot offer such a committed architectural scene as neighboring Vorarlberg. The counterpart to this is more easily found in the canton of Graubünden, higher up the valley.

Graubünden Finds Itself

But while the single-family house was just about to take off architecturally in the Austrian Vorarlberg, Graubünden was finding itself architecturally as a result of public contracts. Peter Zumthor, who had moved in from Basel, catapulted Graubünden architecture into the limelight in the second half of the 1980s with his minimalist protective structures for Roman finds in Chur and the Sogn Benedetg mountain chapel in Sumvitg. He created a climate that led to the founding of several creative offices with structures that are up to date without betraying the spirit of the place. At the time of writing his most recent work is enjoying international acclaim: the baths in Vals, which opened in 1996. This is a rock bath imbued with mysterious magical light; despite all its archaic frugality it offers a large number of evocative spaces.

Today other mountain communities that used to be anxiously conservative are turning out to be surprisingly open to contemporary building. A number of competitions inspired younger people: thus Valentin Bearth and Andrea Deplazes built a school in Malix that thrusts into the slope but is completely glazed on the valley side, and with Zumthor's multi-purpose hall creates a little square within the urban

Peter Zumthor, Baths in Vals, Canton of Graubünden, 1996

Valentin Bearth and Andrea Deplazes, School Extension, Malix, Canton of Graubünden, 1994

Dieter Jüngling und Andreas Hagmann, HTL School Building, Chur, Canton of

texture of this densely built-up village. They were also responsible for a remarkable residential development in Masans, a town house in Chur, a three-story timber-frame building in Scharans, a wooden house in the wine-growing village of Malans and a multi-purpose hall, which is carefully fitted into the mountain village of Tschlin. At the time of writing they are working on a bridge with Jürg Conzett, who has already proved his worth in Murau. He was also responsible, working with Andrea Branger, for the filigree Traversine wooden bridge that has spanned the Via Mala gorge since 1996.

The principal characteristic of the new Graubünden architecture are formal simplicity and primary materials. Thus Conradin Clavuot's concrete transformer station in Seewis stands in a loop of the road like an angular erratic rock, while the Castrisch forestry station, built by Rolf Gerstlauer and Inger Molne in 1996, is presented as two solid bodies in larch wood, one light and upright and one dark and horizontal. Then on the other hand a scaly facade cladding of thin copper sheets gives a hint of architectural poetry to Dieter Jüngling and Andreas Hagmann's HTL school building in Chur, in which three apparently modernistic cubes are drawn into a sculptural unit. They were also responsible for the school in Mastrils, which is terraced like steps in the steep sides of the Rhine valley above Chur. Other interesting features are the school in Duvin by Gion A. Caminada, built as a three-story knitting pattern complex, which is reminiscent of a child's drawing in its simple realism and – as an exotic example – the church in Cazis, built by Werner Schmidt from ovoid concrete shells.

Finally I must mention the special case of Davos, where Rudolf Gaberel once made Modernism socially acceptable, and where in the last few years Gigon and Guyer have introduced a breath of fresh air with the Kirchner Museum, the Vinikus restaurant and the ice-rink, inaugurated 1996. The ice-rink opens to the southwest with a double-layered timbered façade, which was designed in glowing yellow on the basis of a colour plan by Zurich architect Adrian Schiess. Like its predecessor, Gaberel's 1934 sports centre, which burned down in 1991, it fits in with the tradition of Davos sanatorium architecture.

Central Swiss Uncertainty

Unlike Graubünden, central Switzerland was unable to develop an independent vocabulary. It is true that Hans-Peter Amman and Peter Baumann built the new station in Lucerne, to which Calatrava contributed an impressive entrance hall, and this prestigious architecture is continued by Jean Nouvel's immediately adjacent Culture and Congress Center, which is to come into operation stage by stage until it is completed in 2001. But younger architects are also being given a chance on building sites around the gates of Lucerne: for instance, Andi Scheitlin and Marc Syfrig, working with Hans Steiner, converted the former arsenal into the Museum Forum Schweizer Geschichte in Schwyz in 1995, using a three-storey structure that was placed inside like a piece of furniture; they have since built a control center in the form of a partly mirror-surfaced box in black anodized aluminium, set on a concrete base. Oliver Schwarz from Zurich built a Miesian minimalist glass cube in Ebikon near Lucerne (Ill. p. 390).

Scheitlin and Syfrig have also recently offered a detached house in Meggen and a school extension in Nottwil. Even before them, Daniele Marques and Bruno Zurkirchen made a name for themselves as the star architects of central Switzerland with their highly esteemed villas and schools. In 1996 the successful team parted company, but not before producing school extensions in Greppen and Ruswil that were convincing in their formal consistency and analysis of the context.

Daniele Marques and Bruno Zurkirchen, Ruswil School, Canton of Lucerne, 1996

Andi Scheitlin and Marc Syfrig with Hans Steiner, "Museum Forum Schweizer Geschichte", Schwyz, 1995

Rolf Mühlethaler, House, Berne, 1994

Bauart Architekten, Morillon Kindergarten, Wabern-Köniz, Canton of Bern, 1995

The Scene in Berne

The situation in Berne is vaguely comparable with that in central Switzerland. Decades ago it was dominated by Atelier 5, constantly producing new housing estates. Although they no longer showed the consistent attitude of the legendary Halen estate, they are still outstanding examples of contemporary residential building, as is shown by the Fischergarten residential and commercial development in Solothurn or the Boll-Sinneringen estate. But the younger generation is interested in urban development as well. Matti, Bürgi and Ragaz are building the Citypark development in Baden-Nord, and as I have already mentioned, Nick Gartenmann, Mark Werren and Andreas Jöhri managed to win third prize in the Berlin Spree Bend competition. Early in 1997 this trio was able to complete an important commission in their home town of Berne: the new Japanese Embassy, a forty meter long building in exposed concrete and granite, with a discreet air of the Far East about it.

There are other examples of architecture directed at the carefully devised individual property. Thus for example Rolf Mühletaler has built a detached house in the form of a plain wooden cube in an 1870s suburb. The Morillon kindergarten in Wabern is also a wooden building. It was built by Bauart Architekten, who are also putting up an elegantly curved building 240 meters long on station land in the western Swiss university town of Neuenburg, for the Federal Statistics Office.

Western Swiss Latin Trends

The contemporary architectural scene in French-speaking Switzerland has tended to be on the quiet side so far. Only Patrick Devanthéry and Inès Lamunière in Geneva and the Lausanne ETH professor Martin Steinmann have been involved in a pan-Swiss discussion of architecture. They are also influential contributors to the magazine *Faces* which is published by the Geneva School of Architecture, which attempts to focus the innovative forces in French-speaking Switzerland. The architectural situation now seems to be improving, and public commissions – especially in Geneva, which for all too long was characterized by a somewhat feeble post-Modernism – have started to call for high-quality building. This was recently shown in a project for a bridge across the bay in Lake Geneva – finally rejected by the inhabitants – but above all by the Place des Nations competition, won by Massimiliano Fuksas; Peter Eisenman, Dominique Perrault, Rem Koolhaas and Coop Himmelblau are also to be involved.

There have been some interesting solutions in the field of school building. This started in 1993 with the Pré-Picot primary school by Laurent Chenu and Pierre

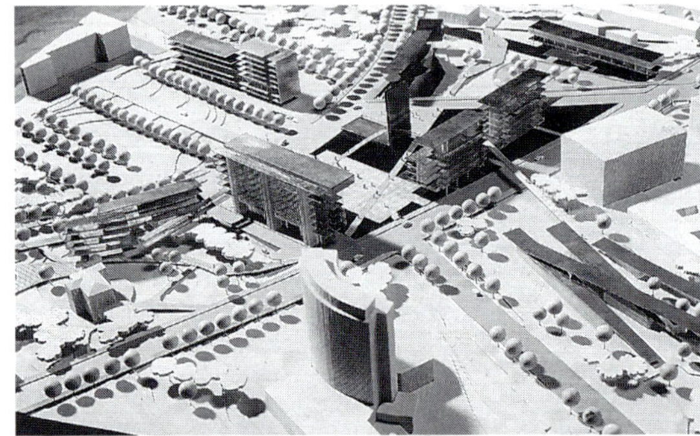

Massimiliano Fuksas, Place des Nations Urban Planning Competition, Genf, 1995

Margrit Althammer and René Hochuli, Corum Watch Factory Extension, La Chaux-de-Fonds, Canton of Neuchâtel, 1995

Jéquier; Patrick Magnin's fashionably elegant extension to the Ecole des Cropettes was completed one year later. But the most important solution is by Devanthéry and Lamunière, who built the students' hall of residence in the Boulevard de la Tour in 1993. This was the new school and leisure center at Le Grand-Saconnex, which is sited in the field of tension between the intricate network of the village center, the tree-covered town hall bastion and stolid residential blocks. Analysis of this urban tissue produced a bipolar composition combining functionality with a poetic overall effect developed from the interplay of form and material.

A unique panorama and nautical links were the starting-point for another school, built by Devanthéry and Lamunière on the lakeside in Pully near Lausanne. Not far from the school there is a little industrial building converted six years ago in an exemplary fashion by Jacques Richter and Ignacio Dahl Rocha for use as a private museum, which unfortunately no longer exists. In 1995, for an apartment block in Prilly, the two architects successfully reinterpreted a moderately modern 1930s Lausanne residential block with characteristically curved bands of balconies, and in 1997 they brought ideas from the 1930s and '60s together under a mantle of Latin elegance for the Eos building in Lausanne. Richter and Dahl Rocha have made a name for themselves outside French-speaking Switzerland with their round tower building in the Boulevard Léopold Robert in Le Corbusier's birthplace, La Chaux-de-Fonds. Moreover, as a result of a competition they won in 1992, the two young Zurich architects Margrit Althammer and René Hochuli built an extension for the Corum watch factory in the watch metropolis in the Neuenburg Jura. The building is in exposed concrete, and its glazed entrance facade makes it look completely transparent; the two architects' intention is that it should illustrate the "precision and aesthetics of the machine".

At the time of writing, Greater Lausanne, where there are remarkable architects other than Richter and Dahl Rocha, has the greatest variety of new buildings and

Patrick Devanthéry and Inès Lamunière, School and Leisure Center, Le Grand-Saconnex, Canton of Geneva, 1996

projects in French-speaking Switzerland. The Paris architect Patrick Berger, who is at present teaching at the ETH in Lausanne, is building his winning competition entry for the new UEFA headquarters in a park landscape by Lake Geneva near Nyon. Bernard Tschumi, probably the most famous Lausanne architect today, now working in New York, was a little less fortunate in his home town with the new design for the central Vallée du Flon he prepared for a competition in 1988. His idea was to build four bridge-like structures across the valley. Unlike the Flon valley, which is still a sleepy place today, the suburb of Dorigny-Ecublens has recently undergone major changes. Here architects Guy and Marc Collomb, and Patrick Vogel from the Lausanne Atelier Cube, completed the university's new chemistry faculty in 1991, and two years later the Tokamak research center for ETH Lausanne.

The early work of Atelier Cube, which was one of the few western Swiss architects' offices to take the step across the language border with its new building for an art postcard press in Schönbühl near Berne, involved mainly residential buildings committed to a relatively poor language, but their most recent work – entirely comprehensibly in terms of the commission – is closer to High-Tech aesthetics. Rodolphe Luscher, who comes from Zurich but has worked in Lausanne for a long time, also feels committed to this, and not only for technical buildings like the Lausanne-Ecublens telecommunications center, which is going up near to Atelier Cube's two large buildings. Luscher was also responsible for the 1996 extension to the Théâtre de Vidy, built by Max Bill for the 1964 Expo, in the form of a largely transparent glass shrine with a Japanese air about it.

Atelier Cube,
Tokamak ETH
Research Center,
Ecublens/Lausanne,
1996

Rodolphe Luscher, Théâtre de Vidy Extension, Lausanne, Canton of Vaud, 1996

Jean-Luc Grobéty used a similar solution for the Cantonal Nursing School in Fribourg in 1994. He fitted a building with glazed facades, bands of windows and striking cornices on to the garden side of an old building, together they made a charming, double-layered building. Another Fribourg architect, Manfred Schafer, created one of the formally most interesting residential developments of recent years in Switzerland with the Cité du Grand Torry in 1995. It had four fortress-like concrete towers on its western side. Docked on to these are residential blocks reached by an internal access route, offering different types of accommodation.

Jean-Luc Grobéty, Cantonal Nursing School Extension, Fribourg, 1994

Manfred Schafer, Cité du Grand Torry, Fribourg, 1995

Self-confidence in Valais

There has been more evidence of an attempt to come to terms with Aldo Rossi and Ticino architecture in Valais than in the rest of French-speaking Switzerland, where it has happened only to a certain extent in the work of Fonso Boschetti or

Jean-Gérard Giorla and Mona Trautmann, Ecole de Goubing, Sierre, Canton of Valais, 1992

Vincent Mangeat, for example. In Valais we have Christian Beck's extension for the parish church in Mase, John Chabbey's motorway workshop in Charrat or Jean-Luc Grobéty's Crochetan theatre in Monthey. Certainly it is now possible to discuss the most recent trends in German Swiss architecture in the presence of originals on the Rhone such as Peter Märklis's ascetic residential block on Kapuzinerweg in Brig, and Peter Steinmann and Herbert Schmid's concrete building springing cubically out of the rock on the sunny slope in Naters. But even in 1994, before these buildings were there, it was possible to discern that Jean-Gérard Giorla and Mona Trautmann were addressing Roger Diener's handwriting in their new school in Zermatt, while two years earlier the Latin element had still been very marked in their Ecole de Goubing in Sierre. Finally, the sunshades in Peter Schweizer's timber-clad detached house in Sion illustrate a combination of Vincent Mangeat's High-Tech residential building in Monthey with hints of the new Graubünden timber architecture.

Ticino Tendencies

Although certain critics now treat Ticino architecture as history, there is still a lively scene south of St Gotthard which has felt a new impetus ever since the Accademia di architettura opened in Mendrisio. Mario Botta's chapels in Mogno and at Monte Tamaro, consecrated in 1996, have attracted a great deal of attention. Several new kinds of architecture have appeared in Greater Lugano: large offices by Botta in Cassarate and Paradiso, a small office building on a granite plinth by Viero Balmelli and Ivano Ghirlanda in Massagno, oscillating between deconstructivism and High Tech, but above all residential buildings. Antonio Bassi, Giovanni Gherra and Dario Galimberti were responsible for a seven-story residential block with maisonettes on the Cassarate river, Mario Campi and Franco Pessina built apartments in Via Beltramina in a U-shape around a central courtyard – an up-to-date response to the classical residential *palazzo* in Italian towns.

Livio Vacchini built a town house that fits precisely into the park-like structure of the estate below the station in Lugano. The three-dimensional grid structure that can be detected on the facade creates an exciting juxtaposition of internal and external spaces. This solitaire embedded in verdant greenery is certainly convincing, but Vacchini's post-office building in Locarno, which opened in 1996, is rather more problematical. A monolith at the entrance to the Piazza Grande, it seems like a foreign body, apparently dematerialized by its horizontally arranged bands of granite and reflecting glass. Vacchini is not interested in coming to terms with a naturally matured context. However, his colleague Luigi Snozzi used his surgically precise interventions into the urban fabric of Monte Carasso to show that it is possible to build in historical contexts without rejecting the existing situation. Snozzi's most recent and largest work in Monte Carasso is the Moreno residential development. He pushes the complex, which consists of two buildings, towards the motorway like a castle. Its long, five-story "wall", given rhythm by narrow apertures, and a nine-story band behind it presents a striking picture to motorists approaching from the south.

Roberto Briccola managed to simplify Snozzi's austere language even further in a residential tower intended as the starting-point for a highly individual estate of terraced housing in Monte Carasso. Raffaele Cavadini used an angular residential block in exposed whole concrete to transform the heart of the old village of Gerra Piano into a convincing whole with an austere beauty of its own. Then in Iragna, a village that lives on quarrying granite, Cavadini managed to fuse contemporary Modernism and centuries of tradition, white concrete and grey stone, bands of windows and heavy masonry into a new unity with three precise interventions – a

Mario Botta, Chapel at Mount Tamaro, Canton of Ticino, 1996

Livio Vacchini, Post Office, Locarno, Canton of Ticino, 1996 town hall, a funeral chapel and a design for a square. This major work of 1990s Ticino architecture, which is crucially different from other architects' often uninhibited interventions, may be seen as a significant contribution in the field of responsibly continuing to build old village structures without being unduly ingratiating. Something similar, albeit in a more modest context and with a concrete, steel and glass structure was tried by Franco and Paolo Moro in Avegno for a kindergarten with a multipurpose hall, which they fitted in between the old stone buildings in such a way that it formed a little piazza. The design, published in 1997, for the new town hall in Cevio, by Michele Arnaboldi and Gian Piero Respini, promises a similarly subtle solution: a plain cube, which reinterprets the simple building forms of the country town in the Maggia valley.

Alongside such context-related solutions individualistic work on single buildings continues. Thus in Castione, at the northern entrance to the town of Bellinzona, Renato Magginetti has taken up the theme of the *murata*, the fortifying wall that closes off the valley, with an industrial building placed at right angles to the railway line and the main road. The building contains workshops, offices and dwellings, and indicates its various functions externally by the alternation of exposed concrete and wood. Castle, wall and tower, Bellinzona's old solitaire architecture,

Mario Campi and Franco Pessina, Multi-Family Housing, Lugano, Canton of Ticino, 1996

Raffaele Cavadini, Town Hall, Iragna, Canton of Ticino, 1996

Renato Magginetti, Industrial Building with Apartments, Castione, Canton of Ticino, 1993

also inspired Botta, who staged a Telecom administrative building as a brick castle with a circular courtyard towering monumentally out of a suburban estate. From a far Pietro Boscetti's radar station on Monte Lema looks like a castle or a mountain chapel. However, the UBS Suglio office building in the industrial district of Manno, north of Lugano airport, can only be called a castle in the figurative sense of a castle of banking. It is by Dolf Schnebli, Tobias Ammann and Flora Ruchat, the largest building in Ticino to date, and built on the basis of the most recent ecological research. Only when it is completed at the end of 1997 will it be possible to see whether the architectural quality does justice to the dimensions of the complex.

Concluding Remarks

Current building in Switzerland reveals a great variety of architectural expression within a small area – both formally and typologically, but also in terms of aesthetics. This diversity can be explained by the cultural zones in the country, which overlap in a number of ways. At the same time it is striking that rather than simple, neutral designs, buildings with greater artistic ambition are often produced, in which architectural art for art's sake is often pursued at the expense of the user. Here developments are pointing towards increasing abstraction. This is shown by a preference for monolithic buildings or for an architectural language that is conspicuous by silence at times, and at times by a new rhetoric. This approach gives a boost to a tendencies to break up urban structures: instead of reinforcing the urban tissue, many new kinds of architecture threaten to break it up. This is true not only of inner cities, but also of the ever-extending mish-mash of settlement between Lake Constance and Geneva, which is growing into one of Europe's largest conurbations. Today what this amorphous agglomeration needs – more urgently than beautiful buildings – is consolidation of the existing stock combined with repair of the worst damage.

Bibliography

The bibliography lists general books on 20th century architecture in Switzerland. Monographs devoted to an individual work have been published on many of the architects mentioned in this guide. These books are easy to locate and become outdated relatively quickly by new publications. They are therefore not included in the following bibliographic information.

Alfred Altherr, New Swiss Architecture. Neue Schweizer Architektur, Teufen 1965

Architecture de la raison. La Suisse des années vingt et trente, Lausanne 1991

Architettura contemporanea alpina. Neues Bauen in den Alpen. Premio d'architettura 1995. Ed. Christoph Mayr Fingerle. Basel/Boston/Berlin 1996

L'Architecture Moderne en Suisse. Neues Bauen in der Schweiz. Führer zur Architektur der 20er und 30er Jahre, Ed. Documentation Suisse du bâtiment, Blauen 1993

Dieter Bachmann, Gerardo Zanetti, Architektur des Aufbegehrens. Bauen im Tessin, Basel/Berlin/Boston 1985

Max Bill u.a., Moderne Schweizer Architektur 1925–1945, Basel 1947

David P. Billington, Robert Maillart and the art of reinforced concrete. Robert Maillart und die Kunst des Stahlbetonbaus. Zurich and Munich 1990

Werner Blaser, Architecture 70/80 in Switzerland, Basel 1981

Thomas Boga, Tessiner Architekten 1960–1985, Zurich 1986

Gerardo Brown-Manrique, The Ticino Guide, New York 1989

J. Christoph Bürkle and Architektur Forum Zürich (Eds.), Young Swiss Architects, 1997

Lucius Burckhardt, Moderne Architektur in der Schweiz seit 1900, Winterthur 1969

Construction, Intention, Detail. Five Projects of Five Swiss Architects. Fünf Projekte von fünf Schweizer Architekten, London/Zurich 1994.

Peter Disch, Architettura recente nel Ticino. 1980–1995. Con un reassunto degli anni 1930–1980. Neuere Architektur im Tessin. Mit einer Zusammenfassung der Jahr 1930–1980, Lugano 1996

Peter Disch (Ed.), L'Architecture récente en Suisse alémanique. L'Architettura recente nella Svizzera tedesca. Architektur in der deutschen Schweiz 1980–1990, Lugano, 2nd edition 1991

Peter Disch (Ed.), 50 anni di architettura in Ticino 1930–1980, Bellinzona and Lugano 1983

Docu Bulletin, périodique officielle de la Documentation Suisse du bâtiment, Blauen

Bibliography

Köbi Gantenbein and Jann Lienhart, 30 Bauten in Graubünden, Zurich 1996

Jacques Gubler, Nationalisme et internationa lisme dans l'architecture moderne de la Suisse, Lausanne 1975

Guide to Swiss Architecture. Schweizer Architekturführer. Guide d'Architecture Suisse. 1920–1990. Vol. 1, Northeast and Central Switzerland. Redaction Christa Zeller, Ed. Willi E. Christen, Publisher Werk AG, Zurich, Verlagsgesellschaft des BSA, Société d'éditions de la FAS, 1992, 2nd edition 1996

Guide to Swiss Architecture. Schweizer Architekturführer. Guide d'Architecture Suisse. 1920–1990. Vol. 2, Northwest Switzerland, Jura, Central Plateau. Redaction Christa Zeller, Ed. Willi E. Christen, Publisher Werk AG, Verlagsgesellschaft des BSA, Société d'éditions de la FAS, 1994

Guide to Swiss Architecture. Schweizer Architekturführer. Guide d'Architecture Suisse. Guida dell'Architettura Svizzera. 1920–1995. Vol. 3, Western Switzerland, Valais, Ticino. Redaction Christa Zeller, Ed. Willi E. Christen, Publisher Werk AG/OEuvre SA, Verlagsgesellschaft des BSA, Société d'éditions de la FAS, 1996

Dorothee Huber, Architekturführer Basel, edited and published by Architekturmuseum Basel, Basel 1993

Carmen Humbel, Young Swiss Architects, Zurich 1995

Hannes Ineichen, Tomaso Zanoni (Eds.), Luzerner Architekten 1920–1960, Zurich and Berne 1985

INSA. Inventario Svizzero di Architettura 1850–1920. Inventar der neueren Schweizer Architektur 1850–1920, Zurich and Berne 1982–, 10 vols. to be published

Ulrike Jehle-Schulte Strathaus, Bauten im 20. Jahrhundert, Basel 1977

Stanislaus von Moos, Julius Bachmann, New Directions in Swiss Architecture, New York 1969

Stanislaus von Moos et al., Neues Bauen in der Ostschweiz. Ein Inventar, Sankt Gallen 1989

Neues Bauen im Kanton Aargau 1920–1940, Ed. SIA Sektion Aargau et al., Baden 1986

Robert Obrist, S. Semadeni, D. Giovanoli (Eds.), Construir – Bauen – Costruire, 1830–1980, Zurich and Berne 1986

B. de Sivo, L'architettura in Svizzera, Naples 1968

G. E. Kidder Smith, Switzerland Builds, New York/Stockholm 1950

Martin Steinmann, Irma Noseda, Zeitzeichen. Schweizer Baukultur im 19. und 20. Jahrhundert, Zurich 1988

Ticino hoy, Exhibition Catalogue, Madrid 1993

Hans Volkart, Schweizer Architektur, Ravensburg 1951

F. Werner and S. Schneider, Neue Tessiner Architektur. Perspektiven einer Utopie. Italian edition: La nuova architettura ticinese. Mario Botta, Aurelio Galfetti, Ivano Gianola, Luigi Snozzi, Livio Vacchini, Milan 1990

Index of Architects

Page numbers in roman type refer to main entries, those in italics to passing references in the text.

A

B

C

N

T

Index of Places

Acknowledgements

Iconographic material courtesy of:
Acau-G. Châtelaine-G. Tournier, A.D.P., AG Bündner Kraftwerke Klosters, Michael Alder, Belen Alves Ferreira and Nicola Pfister, Architekturmuseum of Basel, Asea Brown Boveri Archives, Michele Arnaboldi, Atelier 5, Atelier Cube, Banca Cantonale di Herisau, Christian Beck, Walter Bieler, Peter Böcklin, Jacques Bolliger, Jean Marie Bondallaz, Mario Borges, Mario Botta, Ugo Brunoni, Marianne Burkhalter and Christian Sumi, Santiago Calatrava, Alberto Camenzind, Tita Carloni, Raffaele Cavadini, Cartier Archives, Laurent Chenu, Willi Christen, Collectif d'architectes (Barthassat, Brunn, Butty, Menoud), Marco d'Azzo, Georges Descombes, Patrick Devanthéry and Inès Lamunière, Markus Ducommun, Giancarlo Durisch, Jakob Eschenmoser, Eternit Archives, Federal Archives of Historical Monuments, Feller Archives, Marcel Ferrier, Georg Fischer Archives, Walter Förderer, Aurelio Galfetti, General Motors Suisse Archives, Ivano Gianola, Jean Gérard Giorla, Ernst Gisel, Goetheanum Archives, Regina and Alain Gonthier, Hans Grelling, Mischa Groh, GTA-ETH Archives, Esther and Rudolf Guyer, Fritz Haller, Heberlein Archives, Hoffmann-La Roche Archives, Theo Hotz, Laurie Hunziker, Hürlimann Archives, Ulrike Jehle-Schulte Strathaus, Beat Jordi, Winfried Kleine-Möllhoff, Eduard Ladner, Jean Marc Lamunière, Rodolphe Luscher, Davide Macullo, Magazzini Generali Punto Franco Archives, Maillart Library ETH, Vincent Mangeat, François Maurice, Marcel Meili and Markus Peter, Patrick Mestelan and Bernard Gachet, Robert Monnier, Franco and Paolo Moro, Monte Verità Foundation, Erwin Müller, Eduard Neuenschwander, Office Ammann and Baumann, Office Archambault, Barthassat and Prati, Office Barth and Zaugg, Office Bassi, Gherra and Galimberti, Office Bernegger and Quaglia, Office Bétrix, Consolascio, Office Burkard, Meyer, Steiger, Office Campi and Pessina, Office Catella, Brugger and Associates, Office Chabbey and Voillat, Office Clemençon, Herren, Roost, Office Diener & Diener, Office Disch and Bianchi, Office Eggstein and Rüssli, Office Egli and Rohr, Office Fosco, Oppenheim, Vogt, Office Germann and Achermann, Office Gigon and Guyer, Office Guhl, Lechner and Associates, Office Hochstrasser and Bleiker, Office Hubacher and Maurer, Office Keller, Cabrini, Verda, Office Kössler, Kössler and Morel, Office Kuhn, Fischer and Hungerbühler, Office Edi and Ruth Lanners, Office Marques and Zurkirchen, Office Metron, Office Miller and Maranta, Office Morger and Degelo, Office Naef, Studer, and Studer, Office Nouvel, Cattani and Associates, Office Obrist and Associates, Office Paillard and Leemann, Office Wilfrid and Katharina Steib, Office Suter & Suter, Office du patrimoine historique de la République et Canton du Jura Archives, Luca Ortelli, Elio Ostinelli, Rainer and Leonhard Ott, Orlando Pampuri, Fabio Reinhart, Jacques Richter and Ignacio Dahl Rocha, Roni Roduner, Alfred Roth, Arthur Rüegg, Alberto Sartoris, Chantal Scaler, Walter Schindler, Max Schlup, Dolf Schnebli, Schule und Museum für Gestaltung Archives, Luigi Snozzi, Marina Sommella Grossi, Martin Spühler, Stadtbibliothek Winterthur, Carlo Steffen, Albert Heinrich Steiner, Rino Tami, Giorgio and Michele Tognola, Livio Vacchini, Vitra Archives, Paul Waltenspühl, Peter Zumthor, Jakob Zweifel.
A special thanks to Peter Disch, Max Graf, Urs Graf, Jacques Gubler, and Ruggero Tropeano, for making available their personal archives.

Acknowledgements

We should also like to thank the following photographers: Sergio Anelli, Andenmatten and Schwendimann, Forti Anhorn, Yves André, Ruedi Bass, Willi Baus, Wolf Bender, Stefania Beretta, Natale Bernasconi, Reto Bernhardt, Jacques Berthet, F. Bertin, Therese Beyeler, Leonardo Bezzola, Walter Binder, Monica Bischof, Kurt Blum, Nadine Bolle, Philippe Bonhôte, Pierre Boss, Christian Brand, Roland Brändli, Lilian Brosi, Balthasar Burkhard, Enrico Cano, Marco D'Anna, Jean Philippe Daulte, Max Doerfliger, Bernard Dubuis, Marius Durand, Alberto Flammer, Terence du Fresne, Hans Finsler, Foto Alrège, Foto L. Bacchetta, Foto Battaglia, Foto Brunel, Foto Comet, Foto O. Darbellay, Foto G. Klemm, Foto-Studio Lucas, Foto-Studio Lutry, Foto Swissair, Foto Vicari, Foto Zimmermann, Tanja Fritschi, Reto Führer, Paolo Fumagalli, Martin Gasser and Christoph Eckert, Hans Eggermann, Guillaume Estoppey, Jean Pierre Flury, Henri Germond, Emile Gos, A. Grandchamp, Peter Grünert, Grundriss + Schnitt, H. Hänggi, Walter Hauser, Adriano Heitmann, Heinrich Helfenstein, Hannes Henz, Lucien Hervé, Eduard Hueber, Ralph Hut, Hansruedi Jutzi, Roger Kaisel, Atelier Kinold, Klaus Kinold, Peter Kopp, Toni Küng, Ferit Kuyas, Franco Lafranca, Hermann Linck, Patrik Marcet, Franco Mattei, Fritz Maurer, J. Meier, André Melchior, Daniel Meyer, Jean Mohr, N. Monkewitz, Harry Moor, Christian Moser, Bernhard Moosbrugger, André Muelhaupt-Buehler, Irma Müller-Eschmann, Pino Musi, Gino Pedroli, Paolo Pedroli, Otto Pfeifer, Marco Pfister, Fausto Pluchinotta, Jean-Blaide Pont, Pius Rast, Hans Rath, Roy Robel, Viktor Rödelberg, Paolo Rosselli, O. Ruppen, F. Schenk, Rudolf Schmutz, Daniel Schönbächler, Hans Schönwetter, Wolf Schuoeter, Hans Peter Siffert, Filippo Simonetti, Wolfgang Siol, Philippe Spahni, Michael Speich, Rudolf Steiner, Matthias Thomann, Deidi von Schaewen, Ruedi Walti, Charles Weber, Michael Wolgensinger, Alo Zanetta, and Reinhard Zimmermann.

All illustrations of the essay on "Swiss Architecture Today", unless otherwise noted, are courtesy of the architects' offices, except for the photographs on pp. 386, 387 left, 388, 390 bottom, 392 top and 397 top which are courtesy of Heinrich Helfenstein. Photographers: Pino Musil, Como (382 top), Michel Demance (382 bottom), Margherita Spiluttini (383, from "Herzog & de Meuron 1989–1991", Basel 1996), Ruedi Walti, Basel (384 top), Disch Photograph, Basel (384 middle and bottom), Markus Fischer, Zurich (385 right), Marcel Ferrier (389 top), Erich Schär, St. Gallen (393), Henry Pierre Schultz (395 top) Christian Kerez (395 bottom), Daphné Iseli (397 middle), Reto Baer, bauart Architekten, Bern (397 bottom), Olivier Currat (398 top, from "Place des Nations, Genève", Basel 1996), F. Bertin (400), Mario del Curto, Lausanne (401 top), Yves Eigenmann, Fribourg (401 bottom right), J.-B. Pont (402), Enrico Cano (403 left), Guido Baselgia, Baar (404 bottom), Pier Brioschi, Bellinzona (405 bottom).

Lastly, a collective thanks – since it would be impossible to do otherwise – to all those people and institutions that contributed to the photographic campaign with material, advice, and assistance in the field.